# APPRAISING STRICT LIABILITY

# Appraising Strict Liability

Edited by

## A. P. SIMESTER

*The Centre for Penal Theory and Penal Ethics*
*Institute of Criminology, University of Cambridge*

OXFORD
UNIVERSITY PRESS

# OXFORD
UNIVERSITY PRESS

Great Clarendon Street, Oxford OX2 6DP

Oxford University Press is a department of the University of Oxford.
It furthers the University's objective of excellence in research, scholarship,
and education by publishing worldwide in

Oxford  New York

Auckland  Cape Town  Dar es Salaam  Hong Kong  Karachi
Kuala Lumpur  Madrid  Melbourne  Mexico City  Nairobi
New Delhi  Shanghai  Taipei  Toronto

With offices in

Argentina  Austria  Brazil  Chile  Czech Republic  France  Greece
Guatemala  Hungary  Italy  Japan  South Korea  Poland  Portugal
Singapore  Switzerland  Thailand  Turkey  Ukraine  Vietnam

Published in the United States
by Oxford University Press Inc., New York

British Library Cataloguing in Publication Data

Data available

Library of Congress Cataloging in Publication Data

Appraising strict liability / edited by A. P. Simester.
    p. cm.
  ISBN 0–19–927851–2
1. Criminal liability. 2. Strict liability. I. Simester, A. P.
  K5064. A967 2005
  345'.04—dc22                                    2004027965

        ISBN 0–19–927851–2(Hbk)
        EAN 978–0–19–927851–0

    1 3 5 7 9 10 8 6 4 2

Typeset by Newgen Imaging Systems (P) Ltd., Chennai, India
Printed in Great Britain
on acid-free paper by
Biddles Ltd., King's Lynn

# General Editor's Preface

English criminal law uses forms of liability that may fairly be termed 'strict' in large numbers: quite possibly there are more offences imposing strict liability than requiring fault, and more offences of this kind than in most other European countries. Yet the moral objections to holding people liable to conviction of a criminal offence when fault has not been proved against them run deep and are well known. Can the approach of English criminal law be justified? In this volume the complexity of that question is laid bare. There are questions of definition, of fundamental moral and political principle, of human rights, of the implications of the presumption of innocence, of the need for this kind of offence (as compared with neighbouring countries), and many others. Some of the authors are persuaded of the justification for certain forms of strict liability in particular types of situation, but most of them argue against. This is a volume that is rich in the texture of its reasoning, and draws together an array of leading scholars, mostly in the Anglo-American tradition, to light up this rather neglected but nonetheless hugely significant area of contemporary criminal law. If there is cause for pessimism about the prospects for a major change in the direction of English law in this respect, that would take nothing away from the searching examination of the issues in these ten scholarly essays.

*Andrew Ashworth*

# *Preface*

By April 1949, the Nationalists were losing. Mao's forces had reached the Yangtze River and were advancing upon Nanking. Their successes meant that the movement of neutral shipping was now under threat. In order to protect British interests, including the embassy at Nanking, the Royal Navy frigate Amethyst was ordered to sail for the Nationalist capital.

The Amethyst proceeded up the Yangtze on 19 April, navigated by Peter Berger (as he was then). But on 20 April, sixty miles from Nanking, she was crippled in a devastating attack. Shells hit gunnery control, the wheelhouse, and—twice—the bridge. Many, including the captain, were killed. The steering jammed and the ship ran aground. Berger himself suffered severe wounds to the chest, arm, and leg. But, in what became known as 'the Yangtze Incident', Berger organized sailors to defend the ship while he destroyed its cipher machine and code books. Dosing himself on morphine, he and the First Lieutenant managed to get the Amethyst refloated and away from the Communist batteries. The Amethyst was saved: and Berger had a DSC.

One may safely conclude that Vice-Admiral Sir Peter Berger, KCB, LVO, DSC was a man of considerable courage, with no pressing desire for the life of the armchair. After retiring from the Royal Navy in 1981, Berger was appointed Bursar of Selwyn College in Cambridge, an office he held with distinction for a further ten years. Yet his retirement, when it came, was two years early.

Why? Sir Peter had discovered that, as the law stands concerning food hygiene and health and safety, the College (and possibly its officers) were almost certain to be convicted if anything went wrong in the College or its kitchens, and this was so irrespective whether anyone was actually at fault: it all turned, in effect, on whether the inspectors would exercise their discretion to prosecute. He said to his friends that, as an honourable man, he viewed being prosecuted and convicted for a criminal offence as something serious—and did not wish to be in the position where he might incur a conviction in respect of something for which he was not at fault.

The moral resonance of a criminal conviction is often underestimated.[1] We may think of health and safety offences, and other regulatory violations, as being in some sense not 'truly' criminal. But, as the retirement of Sir Peter illustrates, that distinction has yet conclusively to grip the Anglo-American mind. Unlike many European nations, the common law knows no systematic and clear distinction between 'true' crimes and regulatory or administrative violations. We

---

[1] One glaring example of this is Robert Schopp's discussion of duress in *Justification Defences and Just Convictions* (Cambridge 1998) Ch. 5, where he argues that a defendant blamelessly acting under duress should receive a 'vindicating' conviction but no (further) punishment.

lack formal categories such as the German *Ordnungswidrigkeiten* or the French *contraventions*.[2]

Part of the reason is historical. During the nineteenth century,[3] the UK Parliament came increasingly to regulate trade, manufacturing, and other commercial activities directly by legislation; enacting statutes to regulate and license processes and actions that were otherwise valuable, and not to be prohibited outright, but which were potentially dangerous or harmful. These measures were generally policed by administrative inspectors and other civil servants, and depended for their force upon embedded criminal offences which were typically summary in nature. For pragmatic reasons of enforcement,[4] many such offences imposed strict and sometimes vicarious liability—as when an owner, licensee, or proprietor was held liable for regulatory breaches occurring on his premises.[5] The statutes themselves, however, tended to be haphazard in their imposition of *mens rea* requirements; reflecting the fact that the drafting of each set of regulations was often influenced by the particular bureaucrats responsible for their administration, as well as by the group being regulated.[6] Sometimes, offences might allow a defence of due diligence,[7] or more serious offences might specify a requirement for proof of some form of *mens rea*; but the omission of such provisions for other offences (especially in the same statute) came to be an *indicium* of legislative intent to impose strict liability.[8] Although, formally, the maxim *actus non facit reum nisi mens sit rea* applies even to summary offences,[9] for summary offences of a regulatory nature 'it became the usual implication that unless a mental state was specified . . . the offence would be strict.'[10]

With the rise of regulation, and its dramatic increase in the range and number of statutory offences, criminal law thus came, indirectly, to be used as a device of administration,[11] no longer—even primarily—the preserve of the *mala in se*. In

---

[2] Cf. the contribution to this volume by John Spencer and Antje Pedain, Ch. 10. Indeed, one of the most powerful reasons for introducing a criminal code in England and Wales is the opportunity it may create to decriminalize many regulatory wrongs, by formally redesignating them as administrative violations.

[3] Perhaps the most notable early measure was the Factories Act 1833: 3 & 4 Will. IV, c. 103 (although factories legislation dates back to 1802).

[4] Compare, too, the suggestion in this volume by Spencer and Pedain (Ch. 10, § 2) that, even in serious offences, 'A major reason why the French and German criminal laws have been able to dispense with strict liability, either partially or wholly, is almost certainly the fact that the rules of criminal procedure and evidence in those countries make it relatively easy for the defendant's fault to be established.'

[5] Although the defendant may be able to escape liability by nominating the individual who was actually responsible for the breach: see, e.g., the Factories Act 1833, ss. 30, 31.

[6] The latter frequently exercised considerable political influence: see, e.g., I. Paulus, *In Search of Pure Food* (London 1974) Ch. 1.

[7] e.g. Sale of Food and Drugs Act 1875, s. 5; compare now the Food Safety Act 1990, s. 21.

[8] See e.g. *Fitzpatrick* v. *Kelly* (1873) LR 8 QB 337; *Roberts* v. *Egerton* (1874) LR 9 QB 494; *Cundy* v. *Le Cocq* (1884) 13 QBD 207.

[9] e.g. *Fowler* v. *Padget* (1798) 7 Term Rep 509 at 514, 101 ER 1103 at 1106; *Hearne* v. *Garton* (1859) 2 El & El 66 at 74, 121 ER 26 at 29; *Sleep* (1861) L & C 44 at 54, 169 ER 1296 at 1301; *Sherras* v. *de Rutzen* [1895] 1 QB 918 at 921; *Paul* v. *Hargreaves* [1908] 2 KB 289 at 291.

[10] W. R. Cornish and G. Clark, *Law and Society in England 1750–1950* (London 1989) 606.

[11] Cf. Lindsay Farmer, *Criminal Law, Tradition and Legal Order* (Cambridge 1997) 122.

the absence of a distinctive, clearly delineated, criminal code to prohibit and label the core criminal wrongs, these administrative or regulatory statutory offences were, in effect, bolted on to the existing criminal law. The result was that we acquired two paradigms of criminal law: the serious, stigmatic, crime and the minor, largely technical, offence governing otherwise acceptable activities for the sake of the public welfare. But there is no clear boundary. Each was, and is, a crime. Each was, and still is, followed by criminal rather than civil proceedings, resulting in a conviction rather than a civil verdict.[12] Inevitably, there has been cross-fertilization. Virtually unknown at common law,[13] strict liability came to be imposed for indictable offences, most famously in *Prince*,[14] and indeed was the norm for under-age sexual offences throughout the twentieth century.[15] Conversely, the borderline is also permeable with respect to censure and stigma. The association, at least in the public mind, of the criminal law with prohibited wrongdoing, and of convictions with the condemnation of blameworthy wrong-doers, can carry over into the realm of 'largely technical'[16] offences. If regulatory offences are no more than 'quasi-criminal', they retain by that very token something of the criminal character—which is, no doubt, why their prosecution is generally regarded by inspectors and monitoring agencies as the most punitive response available to regulatory breaches; something normally to be undertaken only when the defendant's conduct was in fact culpable.[17] As things stand, the symbolic social meaning of a quasi-criminal conviction may be diluted, but it is not vacated: this is why Sir Peter Berger's decision was rational and not simply a mistake.

We learned the tale of Sir Peter's retirement from John Spencer, a Fellow of Selwyn College, at a workshop on strict liability held in Cambridge on 25 May 2002. In the course of a wide-ranging debate, I had hypothesized that one might distinguish the objections to strict liability in serious crimes from those applicable to regulatory offences. John quite rightly countered that, at least as things stand, the distinction was not at all clear-cut. But many other things were gained on that fascinating Saturday. At the invitation of Andrew von Hirsch, we had gathered under the auspices of the Centre for Penal Theory and Penal Ethics to discuss the moral and legal legitimacy of strict liability in the criminal law. I suspect that many of us were wondering how much there really was to say; more particularly, whether we would be able to sustain a largely unstructured conversation all the way to dinner. Andrew had prepared a preliminary note summarizing some of the standard criticisms of strict liability—its unpredictability; the sheer unfairness of

---

[12] Compare the definition espoused by Glanville Williams, 'The Definition of Crime' (1955) *Current Legal Problems* 107, 123.

[13] Sullivan notes some exceptions: this volume, Ch. 8, § 1 n. 2.

[14] (1875) 2 CCR 154; cf. *Bishop* (1880) 5 QBD 259.

[15] *Prince* came, at last, to be rejected by the House of Lords in *B (a minor)* v. *DPP* [2000] 2 AC 428 and *K* [2002] 1 AC 462.   [16] The phrase is Farmer's: *Criminal Law, Tradition and Legal Order*, 123.

[17] For an excellent discussion, see K. Hawkins, *Law as Last Resort* (Oxford 2002) especially Ch. 11; also K. Hawkins, *Environment and Enforcement: Regulation and the Social Definition of Pollution* (Oxford 1984).

convicting a person who is blameless—and they seemed persuasive criticisms. Strict liability seemed obviously wrong, and perhaps there was little more to say.

We need not have worried. It quickly became apparent that 'strict liability' did not describe a unitary phenomenon.[18] Moreover, at least in some guises, it could not always be dismissed as morally, let alone legally, illegitimate. There was a collective sense of unravelling: as the day progressed, our sense grew that what had seemed a straightforward problem for criminal-law theory comprised, instead, a variety of tangled and difficult issues, which needed careful separation and a great deal of further reflection. In legal systems where regulatory sanctions are (or might be made) explicitly non-criminal, many of the objections to imposing those sanctions on a strict liability basis become less persuasive or even inapplicable.[19] Rather more surprisingly, even in serious criminal offences we realized that, arguably, strict liability need not lead to convictions of persons who are blameless for committing the crime of which they are convicted.

Moreover, there are different ways of making this argument. One may argue simply that, on occasion, certain *mens rea* elements are redundant: proof of the remaining elements suffices to establish that D is at fault for the entire *actus reus*.[20] Alternatively, Antony Duff draws upon analysis of criminal-law presumptions to support his case for limited strict liability provisions. If, as Duff argues, legal presumptions do not always violate the presumption of innocence but, sometimes, operate instead as specifications of what is to count as proof of *guilt* (here, as proof beyond reasonable doubt of D's culpability for the entire crime), strict liability can be understood and occasionally justified as a kind of irrebuttable legal presumption.

Paul Roberts firmly rejects Duff's reasoning.[21] The analogy between strict liability and legal presumptions is, he maintains, false. Substantive *mens rea* and strict liability doctrines are not interchangeable with procedural doctrines of proof, because the institutional distinction between procedural and substantive doctrines has a public, communicative, salience that is itself morally significant. The presumption of innocence—which in the context of the European Convention on Human Rights (ECHR) is, for Roberts, a procedural and not substantive matter—therefore has no implications for strict liability.

Yet, while also taking a contextual approach, Bob Sullivan reaches a very different conclusion. According to Sullivan, Article 6 (amongst others) of the ECHR offers resources with which to attack the imposition of strict liability in serious offences.[22] Article 6(1), which guarantees the right to a fair trial, can be interpreted so as to mandate proof of a voluntary act or omission on the part of the defendant; it is open to read into Article 6(2), the presumption of innocence, a requirement to prove some element that is capable of being the gravamen of an offence. In each of these arguments, Sullivan relies on provisions that are essentially procedural to establish a right with substantive implications for the law

---

[18] Hence the importance of clear definitions, as Stuart Green points out: this volume, Ch. 1.
[19] Cf. Simester in this volume, Ch. 2, § 3.     [20] Simester, ibid. § 4.
[21] Roberts, this volume, Ch. 7.     [22] Sullivan, this volume, Ch. 8, § 5.

of strict liability. Strict liability may not be ruled out by human rights jurisprudence,[23] but—*pace* Roberts—it may be subject to limitations.

Again, however, there is more than one way of integrating strict liability with the law of human rights. Whereas Sullivan proposes general restrictions to strict liability, Alan Michaels offers an activity-specific, selective, account. Suppose that a statute criminalizes selling any book that contains descriptions of some specified unlawful activity, where the sale of the book must be intentional but there is no *mens rea* requirement going to the content of the book. A crime of this sort acts as a fetter on the activity of selling books. One may sell books, but only at the risk of randomly becoming a criminal. The sole way to guarantee that one avoids conviction is, as with Sir Peter, to retire. This is, of course, what strict liability effects in regulatory offences: one may sell milk, but only at the risk of committing an offence should the milk become adulterated.[24] Now selling milk is not a human right; but selling books may implicate the right of freedom of expression under Article 10 of the ECHR. Similarly, suggests Michaels, a strict-liability crime of sexual intercourse with an under-age person may be a fetter on activity protected by Article 8, which guarantees the right to respect for private and family life. This analysis attacks strict liability only incidentally; it is driven, rather, by the need to protect defined substantive rights. If certain activities are to be protected by means of fundamental rights, then those—particular—activities should not be restricted by offences that permit them only at the risk of uncontrollable criminal liability. Strict liability is diminished here neither directly nor generally, but by the occasional gusts of side-winds.

The technique works because strict liability has implications not merely for the possibility of punishment without fault but also for the scope of criminalization. Suppose that the distribution of cocaine per se is decriminalized and, in its stead, an offence is enacted of 'distributing cocaine intentionally, where the cocaine causes the death of the recipient' (the latter element being one of strict liability). An offence of this sort, Doug Husak observes,[25] offers middle ground: it allows for the prohibition of dangerous conduct only when its risks materialize. Indirectly, it restricts the underlying activity (hence, when the underlying activity is constitutionally protected, it may be unconstitutional), while at the same time cutting back the reach of the criminal law. One may readily steer clear of potential criminal liability in this case, but only by refraining from distributing cocaine. And that, let me assume, is not too much to ask.

The problem arises when the key structural features of this hypothetical offence are missing. Refraining from selling books or milk, or from acting as Bursar of a Cambridge college, *is* too much to ask. In these cases, the risk of something going wrong[26] does not supply a reason why one's underlying conduct

---

[23] Sullivan, ibid. §§ 3, 5.
[24] Even if the milk became adulterated only by the malicious intervention of a third party: *Parker v. Alder* [1899] 1 QB 20.  [25] This volume, Ch. 4, § 4 (scenario five).
[26] Or, as Gardner would put it, of one's doing something wrongful, i.e. in breach of duty: this volume, Ch. 3, § 2.

is wrong.[27] Conversely, we cannot say that, in virtue of performing the underlying conduct, one is at fault for the thing that goes wrong. At this point, what John Gardner calls 'the fault principle' is in play: criminal liability should be imposed only for wrongs that are culpably committed.[28] Criminal liability is a liability to be punished and, without fault, punishment is not deserved.[29] By contrast with the cocaine distribution example, the fault principle would be violated by a criminal offence of intentionally selling milk *simpliciter* as well as by an offence of intentionally selling milk that is, as it turns out, adulterated. The addition of a strict liability element can do no work in ensuring that a defendant, when convicted of an offence, was in fact at fault.

Sometimes, there may be institutional factors that, outwith the formal terms of the statute, increase our degree of assurance that the fault principle is being observed: as when the enforcement procedures adopted by a regulatory agency are designed to ensure that prosecutions are undertaken only where the defendant is at fault.[30] We have noted, too, that the discretion to prosecute strict liability offences is normally exercised with an eye to the defendant's culpability. But, to the extent that these are not guarantees, one cannot be certain that the fault principle is being observed. And wherever it is not, there is cause for concern—in both 'serious' and 'regulatory' offences. Lindsay Farmer has observed of quasi-criminal regulations that 'the means adopted—the downgrading of seriousness, the penalizing of conduct rather than intent, and the facilitation of prosecution—were entirely consistent with the spirit of the modern criminal law.'[31] As interpretation, this is surely true. But it is a grievous truth. Even quasi-criminal offences are, in practice, to some extent punitive. To the extent that they, and more serious crimes, permit conviction and punishment without fault, the spirit of the modern criminal law is morally impoverished. And, ethically speaking, its content is in need of reform.

*Michaelmas 2004*
A. P. S.

---

[27] i.e. unjustified: ibid.       [28] Ibid. §§ 4–5.
[29] Husak would say that it is *disproportionate*: this volume, Ch. 4, § 3.
[30] Jeremy Horder discusses this possibility in the context of regulating truancy: this volume, Ch. 5.
[31] *Criminal Law, Tradition and Legal Order*, 125.

# Contents

# List of Contributors

**R. A. Duff**, Professor of Philosophy, University of Stirling.

**John Gardner**, Professor of Jurisprudence, University of Oxford.

**Stuart P. Green**, Professor of Law, Louisiana State University.

**Jeremy Horder**, Porjes Foundation Fellow and Tutor in Law, Worcester College, and Reader in Criminal Law, University of Oxford.

**Douglas Husak**, Professor of Philosophy, Rutgers University.

**Alan C. Michaels**, Edwin M. Cooperman Designated Professor of Law, Moritz College of Law, Ohio State University.

**Antje Pedain**, University Lecturer in Law, University of Cambridge, and Fellow of Magdalene College.

**Paul Roberts**, Professor of Criminal Jurisprudence, University of Nottingham.

**A. P. Simester**, Professor of Legal Philosophy, University of Nottingham.

**John R. Spencer**, Professor of Law, University of Cambridge, and Fellow of Selwyn College.

**G. R. Sullivan**, Professor of Criminal Law, University of Durham.

# 1

# Six Senses of Strict Liability: A Plea for Formalism

*Stuart P. Green*

In recent years, criminal law theorists have made considerable progress in developing a vocabulary for describing the moral content of criminal offences. We now have a framework not only for distinguishing among different kinds of harms (e.g. against persons, against property, and against public order), but also for talking about the probability and magnitude of harm, the aggregation of harms, the relative importance of harms, and the difference between harm and offence.[1] The way in which we speak about culpability has also been refined: the vast collection of overlapping and obscure *mens rea* terms that once characterized the common law has, under the influence of the Model Penal Code, been distilled into a concise and reasonably well-defined list of terms, including purposely, knowingly, recklessly, and negligently.[2] And criminal law theory has begun to recognize as well that the moral content of criminal offences is not exhausted by harmfulness and culpability, but also reflects a third component, usually dubbed 'wrongfulness', which involves the violation of one or more of a wide range of moral norms.[3]

I am grateful to Antony Duff, Douglas Husak, and Andrew Simester for their insightful comments on an earlier draft.

[1] See e.g. Joel Feinberg, *The Moral Limits of the Criminal Law* (4 vols., Oxford 1984, 1985, 1986, 1988). See especially *Harm to Others*, at 187–217 (assessing and comparing harms).

[2] See Model Penal Code § 2.02(2). See also e.g. Stephen Shute, 'Knowledge and Belief in the Criminal Law', in Stephen Shute and A. P. Simester (eds.), *Criminal Law Theory: Doctrines of the General Part* (Oxford 2002), 171.

[3] See e.g. John Gardner, 'Rationality and the Rule of Law in Offences Against the Person' (1994) 53 *Cambridge LJ* 502, at 511; John Gardner and Stephen Shute, 'The Wrongness of Rape', in Jeremy Horder (ed.), *Oxford Essays in Jurisprudence* (Oxford 2000), 193; Stephen Shute and Jeremy Horder, 'Thieving and Deceiving: What is the Difference?' (1993) 56 *Modern LR* 548, at 553; A. P. Simester and Andrew von Hirsch, 'Rethinking the Offense Principle' (2002) 8 *Legal Theory* 269, at 270–2. My own work on the concept of moral wrongfulness includes the following: 'Why It's a Crime to Tear the Tag Off a Mattress: Overcriminalization and the Moral Content of Regulatory Offenses' (1997) 46 *Emory LJ* 1533, at 1547–52; 'Lying, Misleading, and Falsely Denying: How Moral Concepts Inform the Law of Perjury, Fraud, and False Statements' (2001) 53 *Hastings LJ* 157; 'Cheating' (2004) 23 *Law and Philosophy* 137; 'What's Wrong With Bribery', in R. A. Duff and Stuart P. Green (eds.), *Defining Crimes: Essays on the Criminal Law's Special Part* (Oxford, forthcoming).

But analysis of the moral content of criminal offences is not limited to a consideration of what elements of harmfulness, culpability, and wrongfulness such offences *include*; it also needs to take account of the kinds of moral content in which criminal offences are *deficient*. Often, we will want to consider the elements of moral content that have traditionally been included in such an offence, but which, in one way or another, have been reduced or omitted.

The problem is that the vocabulary we have for speaking about the *absence* of moral content in criminal offences is much more limited and imprecise than the vocabulary we have for speaking about its *presence*. We have few ready-made terms for describing offences that require *less* culpability, harmfulness, or wrongfulness than the criminal law has traditionally required. Instead, there is a tendency to use the same overburdened term—'strict liability'—to refer to a broad range of divergent ways in which a criminal offence might be deficient in moral content.

My goals in this essay are threefold: first, to survey the various meanings that have been ascribed to the term 'strict liability'; secondly, to show why such proliferation of meanings leads to conceptual confusion; and thirdly, to recommend a particular, 'formal' sense of strict liability as the meaning that should be preferred. What is ultimately at stake here is more than just a point about terminological clarity. By exposing the inadequacy of the language we use to describe the problem of moral deficiency in criminal law, I hope to show not only the complexity of the problem but also, ultimately, to point the way to its possible solution.

## 1. Six Senses of Strict Criminal Liability

In this section, I consider the various ways in which the term 'strict liability' has been used in the criminal law literature. Six different senses of the term will be identified: (1) offences that contain at least one material element for which there is no corresponding *mens rea* element; (2) statutory schemes that bar the use of one or more *mens-rea*-negating defences; (3) procedural devices that require a defendant's intent to be presumed from other facts; (4) offences that require a less serious form of *mens rea* than has traditionally been required by the criminal law; (5) offences that require a less serious form of harmfulness than has traditionally been required by the criminal law; and (6) offences that require a less serious form of wrongfulness than has traditionally been required by the criminal law.

### Offences Omitting Requirement of *Mens Rea*

The most common use of the term 'strict liability' in the criminal law—and the only one, ultimately, that I can recommend—is to refer to offences that contain at least one material element for which there is no corresponding *mens rea* requirement.[4]

---

[4] See e.g. Andrew Ashworth, *Principles of Criminal Law* (1st edn., Oxford 1991), at 135–6; Wayne R. LaFave, *Criminal Law* 272–3 (4th edn., St Paul, Minn. 2003).

By *mens rea*, I mean the requirement that a defendant perform a voluntary physical act with intent, purpose, knowledge, belief, recklessness, negligence, or some other prescribed mental state. Thus, strict liability in this first sense is simply criminal liability in the absence of intent, purpose, knowledge, and the like.

I will have more to say later about what, if anything, is so significant about strict liability of this sort, but for now several clarifications are in order. First, we can distinguish between offences for which no *mens rea* is required with respect to any material element (referred to here as 'pure' strict liability), and offences for which no *mens rea* is required with respect to at least one element but is required with respect to at least one other element (referred to as 'impure' strict liability).[5]

It may not be possible to find any real world example of pure strict liability, since virtually all criminal acts will require (if only implicitly) at least some underlying mental element. But the ordinance at issue in *Lambert* v. *California* surely comes close. That ordinance made it unlawful for 'any convicted person' to remain in the City of Los Angeles for more than five days without registering as a convicted person.[6] The ordinance required nothing more than that the offender commit the *actus reus* of living in Los Angeles and failing to register. It did not require that she have the intent not to register or be aware that such registration was required. If the ordinance entailed any implicit mental element at all, it required at most that the defendant simply know that she was remaining in the City of Los Angeles.[7]

A good example of impure strict liability is found in felony murder and statutory rape statutes. Felony murder is properly viewed as a strict liability offence because, although the prosecution must typically prove the defendant's intent to commit the underlying felony,[8] the more serious offence does not require that the defendant intend, or, typically, even be aware, that his conduct will cause death.[9] Similarly, statutory rape is properly viewed as a strict liability offence because, although the defendant must be shown to have engaged intentionally in sexual intercourse with an under-age person, the offence does not require that the defendant know that the victim was under age.[10] That is, a defendant may be convicted of statutory

---

[5] See e.g. Michael Moore, *Placing Blame: A General Theory of the Criminal Law* (Oxford 1997), at 246; A. P. Simester and G. R. Sullivan, *Criminal Law: Theory and Doctrine* (2nd edn., Oxford 2003), 167–8, 186–9.

[6] 355 US 225 (1957) (holding the ordinance unconstitutional on the grounds that it violated the defendant's right to due process).

[7] Perhaps, if the defendant had been reasonably mistaken about whether she was in Los Angeles, she would have had a defence.

[8] An exception would be where the underlying felony is itself a strict liability offence.

[9] e.g. La. Rev. Stat. 14:30.1(2)(a). (Second degree murder is the killing of a human being '[w]hen the offender is engaged in [one of a number of enumerated felonies] even though he has no intent to kill or to inflict great bodily harm.')

[10] e.g. La. Rev. Stat. 14:80. (Felony carnal knowledge of a juvenile is committed when a 'person who is nineteen years of age or older has sexual intercourse, with consent, with a person who is twelve years of age or older but less than seventeen years of age'; 'lack of knowledge of the juvenile's age shall not be a defence'.)

rape even though he reasonably but mistakenly believed that the victim was old enough to consent to intercourse.

Secondly, within the category of impure strict liability, we can distinguish between 'constructive' and 'non-constructive' strict liability.[11] Felony murder involves constructive strict liability in that what must usually be proved is *mens rea* as to some crime—i.e. the underlying felony. But the *mens rea* required for non-constructive forms of strict liability (such as statutory rape) is not *mens rea* as to a crime. Indeed, it is not *mens rea* as to any form of wrongdoing. Rather, it is simply *mens rea* as to some defining element, such as, in the case of selling adulterated food or drugs, knowledge that one has sold food or drugs. Thus, once we consider non-constructive forms of strict liability, we can see how much broader the class of impure strict liability is than the class of pure strict liability.

Thirdly, there are some offences that, while they do not require proof of *mens rea*, do allow the defendant to offer a defence of 'due diligence'.[12] Because such offences omit the requirement of *mens rea*, they should be regarded as imposing strict liability in this first sense identified;[13] although, as we shall see below, they might not satisfy the requirements of so-called 'substantive' strict liability.

Fourthly, we can distinguish between offences that do not require a showing of *mens rea*, but do allow the assertion of affirmative defences such as mistake of fact; and offences that not only do not require a showing of *mens rea* but also prohibit the assertion of affirmative defences (this latter kind of strict liability is usually referred to as 'absolute liability'[14]).

In addition, following the Model Penal Code's culpability scheme, we can distinguish among strict liability with respect to a (1) conduct element, (2) result element, and (3) attendant circumstance element.[15] Driving an automobile above the speed limit is an example of an offence that typically imposes strict liability with respect to the defendant's conduct. The prosecution need not prove that the defendant intended to drive above the speed limit, or even that he believed that he was driving in such a manner, in order for liability to be imposed. Felony murder is an example of an offence that imposes strict liability with respect to a result element. The defendant need not intend, or even believe, that his conduct might result in death in order for liability to be imposed. Statutory rape imposes strict liability with respect to an attendant circumstance—namely, the circumstance of whether the female victim is below the statutory age. Once again, the defendant need not be aware that the attendant circumstance existed.

---

[11] Thanks to Antony Duff for bringing this distinction, and its implications, to my attention.

[12] See e.g. *R. v. City of Sault Ste Marie* (1978) 85 DLR 3d 161 (SCC) (discussing one such offence).

[13] The same conclusion is reached by Andrew Ashworth and Meredith Blake, 'The Presumption of Innocence in English Criminal Law' (1996) *Criminal LR* 306, at 313.

[14] See e.g. Hyman Gross, *A Theory of Criminal Justice* (Oxford 1979), 343.

[15] For a similar analysis on this point, see Kenneth W. Simons, 'When Is Strict Criminal Liability Just?' (1997) *Journal of Criminal Law and Criminology* 1075, at 1079–81.

## Statutory Schemes Barring Use of One or More *Mens-Rea*-Negating Defences

A second context in which strict liability is sometimes said to occur is statutory schemes that deny the defendant the opportunity to offer evidence relevant to a *mens-rea*-negating defence. Ordinarily, one would have a defence if she could show that her intent to commit a particular crime (e.g. theft) was 'negated' by, say, intoxication or reasonable mistake of fact (regarding, for example, whether the property was abandoned).[16] Certain forms of *mens rea* can also be negated by mistake or ignorance of the law.[17] Under some statutory schemes, however, the defendant is effectively denied the opportunity to offer such a *mens-rea*-negating defence.

Consider the homicide scheme applicable in Montana. In order to prove that a defendant committed murder, the state must prove that the defendant has caused a death 'purposely' or 'knowingly'.[18] In *Montana* v. *Egelhoff*, the defendant sought to argue that his state of intoxication negated whatever purpose or knowledge he might otherwise have had.[19] But he was precluded from doing so by a separate provision of Montana law providing that 'an intoxicated condition . . . may not be taken into consideration in determining the existence of a mental state which is an element of the offense unless [the intoxication was involuntary]'.[20] Some commentators have referred to statutory schemes of this sort, which effectively bar a defendant from arguing that his *mens rea* was negated by intoxication (or by mistake of law), as entailing a form of 'strict liability', despite the fact that such schemes clearly do require a showing of *mens rea*.[21]

## Procedural Devices Requiring Presumption of Defendant's Intent

A third context in which strict liability has been said to occur is that in which a statute requires the fact-finder to presume the existence of a defendant's intent from the existence of other facts. Of course, in a certain sense, a defendant's intent must always be presumed from the existence of other facts: because we

---

[16] On mistake of fact negating *mens rea*, see generally Richard Singer, 'The Resurgence of *Mens Rea*: II—Honest but Unreasonable Mistake of Fact in Self-Defence' (1987) 28 *Boston College LR* 459. On intoxication negating intent, see e.g. *State* v. *Stasio*, 396 A. 2d 1129 (NJ 1979).

[17] See Sharon L. Davies, 'The Jurisprudence of Willfulness: An Evolving Theory of Excusable Ignorance' (1995) 48 *Duke LJ* 341. 　　　　　　[18] Mont. Code Ann. § 45-5-102 (1995).

[19] 518 US 37 (1996). 　　　[20] Mont. Code Ann. § 45-2-203 (1995).

[21] See e.g. Stephen J. Morse, 'Fear of Danger, Flight from Culpability' (1998) 4 *Psychology, Public Policy and Law* 250, at 254–5; Ronald J. Allen, 'Foreward [*sic*]: *Montana v. Egelhoff*—Reflections on the Limits of Legislative Imagination and Judicial Authority' (1997) 87 *Journal of Criminal Law and Criminology* 633, at 640 (reading Montana statute as imposing strict liability). See also Joshua Dressler, *Understanding Criminal Law* 143 (3rd edn., New York 2001) (referring to the 'rule that a person who is ignorant of, or who misunderstands the meaning of, a criminal law may be punished for violating it, even if her ignorance or mistake was reasonable', as a 'strict liability doctrine').

cannot read the defendant's mind, it is—absent a full confession—invariably necessary to infer his intentions from his actions. But the kind of inference that is said to entail strict liability is different. Strict liability is said to occur when a statute or jury instruction creates an irrebuttable presumption to the effect that the jury 'shall' or 'must' infer the defendant's intent from the existence of certain facts. For example, there are statutes that provide, or have been interpreted to provide, that: (1) anyone who possesses illegal drugs within 1,000 feet of a schoolyard shall be presumed to have the intent to distribute such drugs;[22] and (2) anyone who possesses US Treasury cheques stolen from the mails shall be presumed to have knowledge that such cheques were stolen.[23]

By definition, procedural devices that relieve the prosecution of its burden of proving the defendant's *mens rea* do not impose strict liability in the first sense identified above. Nevertheless, the term 'strict liability' has been used in connection with such devices.[24] The tendency is strongest among British scholars. For example, in this volume, in the course of showing why such an approach ultimately fails, Paul Roberts develops an elaborate argument positing a 'functional equivalence' between strict liability and procedural devices such as reverse onus clauses that shift the burden of proof.[25] Similarly, according to Antony Duff, speaking about the offence of statutory rape:

[T]he effect of . . . irrebuttable presumptions and of strict liability is the same: in neither case can any evidence concerning the defendant's beliefs about or attempts to determine the other person's age secure him an acquittal. . . . This raises the question of whether the way in which that effect is achieved matters: what, if anything (other than procedural convenience) hangs on whether the defendant is convicted via the procedural route of an irrebuttable presumption, or the substantive route of a strict liability provision?[26]

In the discussion below,[27] I will attempt to explain why I think there is a significant difference between such presumptions and strict liability.

## Offences Requiring a Less Serious Form of *Mens Rea* than is Traditionally Required

A fourth context in which strict criminal liability has been said to occur is that in which an offence or offence element, rather than omitting the requirement of

---

[22] 21 USC §§ 841(a)(1) and 845(a) (interpreted in *United States* v. *Crews*, 916 F 2d 980 (5th Cir. 1990)).

[23] 18 USC § 1708 (interpreted in *Barnes* v. *United States*, 412 US 837, 845–6 (1973)).

[24] e.g. Andrew Little, Comment, 'Caught Red-Handed: The Peculiarities of the Federal Schoolyard Statute and Its Interpretation in the Fifth Circuit' (2000) 31 *Texas Tech LR* 245, at 257. (Under Schoolyard drug law, 'if police apprehended a defendant in possession of drugs in a school zone, they did not need to prove his intent to distribute the drugs within the 1000 foot zone. In essence, this holding created a strict liability possession crime as to location' (footnote omitted).)

[25] Paul Roberts, 'Strict Liability and the Presumption of Innocence: An Exposé of Functionalist Assumptions', this volume, Ch. 7. See also Ashworth and Blake, 'Presumption of Innocence' (considering presumptions as one form of strict liability).

[26] R. A. Duff, 'Strict Liability, Legal Presumptions, and the Presumption of Innocence', this volume, Ch. 6.　　[27] See below, discussion accompanying nn. 59–60.

*mens rea* entirely, instead requires a showing of some lesser form of *mens rea* than has traditionally been required in the criminal law—typically, negligence.[28]

Conventionally, the paradigm of criminality entailed a subjective *mens rea* element of intent or, at least, knowledge of wrongdoing. As more criminal offences began to be enacted in statutory form, the importance of *mens rea* was de-emphasized. While some offences eliminated *mens rea* entirely, others merely reduced the required level of culpability to negligence. Although simple tort-like negligence is relatively rare (though not unknown[29]) in criminal law, statutes requiring a showing of 'criminal', 'culpable', or 'gross' negligence are now quite common, particularly in offences such as involuntary manslaughter, negligent homicide, and battery.

There is, however, a controversy about whether negligence should even be regarded as a form of *mens rea* to which criminal liability properly attaches. In contrast to recklessness, which involves an awareness of risk disregarded, negligence involves a lack of awareness of a risk of which one should have been aware.[30] Thus, some commentators have suggested that because the negligent actor is unaware of the circumstances that make her conduct criminal, she cannot properly be said to be blameworthy.[31] Moreover, they argue, offenders who are unaware that their conduct is wrong are not susceptible to being deterred. Apparently as a result of such reasoning, some commentators have referred to criminal negligence as entailing a form of strict liability.[32] As such, offence elements requiring a showing of negligence constitute another focus of the analysis here.

## Offences Requiring Less Serious Forms of Harmfulness than Traditionally Required

Just as the criminal law is believed to have suffered an erosion in the seriousness of *mens rea* with which an offence must be committed, it is also thought to have

[28] Regarding the controversy over whether negligence should properly be considered a form of *mens rea*, see below, n. 31 and accompanying text.

[29] See e.g. *State* v. *Williams*, 484 P 2d 1167 (1971) (mental element required for manslaughter was ordinary negligence); *Yogasakaran* (1990) 1 NZLR 399 (CA) (similar; now overturned by s. 150A of the Crimes Act 1961 (NZ)); *Meiring*, 1927 App. Div. 41, 46 (S. Africa) (similar).

[30] See e.g. Model Penal Code § 2.02(2)(c), (d).

[31] See e.g. Jerome Hall, 'Negligent Behavior Should be Excused from Penal Liability' (1963) 63 *Columbia LR* 632. Unfortunately, there is not space to consider the issue fully here. For present purposes, I will simply assume that a negligent actor's failure to perceive the riskiness of the conduct in which she is engaged constitutes 'culpable indifference' to the rights and interests of those with whom she interacts, and that she is thereby properly subject to retribution. For a further discussion of the issues, see R. A. Duff, *Intention, Agency and Criminal Liability: Philosophy of Action and the Criminal Law* (Oxford 1990), 156; A. P. Simester, 'Can Negligence be Culpable?' in Jeremy Horder (ed.), *Oxford Essays in Jurisprudence: Fourth Series* (Oxford 2000), 85; Kenneth Simons, 'Culpability and Retributive Theory: The Problem of Criminal Negligence' (1994) 5 *Journal Contemporary Legal Issues* 365; Heidi M. Hurd, 'The Deontology of Negligence' (1996) 76 *Boston University LR* 249; George P. Fletcher, 'The Theory of Criminal Negligence: A Comparative Analysis' (1971) 119 *University of Pennsylvania LR* 401.

[32] See Douglas N. Husak, 'Varieties of Strict Liability' (1995) *Canadian Journal of Law and Jurisprudence* 189, at 204 ('In many cases, liability for negligence is an instance of strict liability, albeit

experienced a diminution in the seriousness of harm that must be caused. Thus, whereas criminal sanctions were once (at least in some idealized vision of criminal law history) applied only to particularly serious kinds of harms (such as killings, stealings, and rapes), such sanctions are increasingly being used for less serious, more disparate, and less well-defined kinds of harms, such as those that occur in the context of regulation.[33]

The association of strict liability with offences that require lesser forms of harm than have traditionally been required by the criminal law is most famously identified with Francis Sayre's work on so-called 'public welfare' offences.[34] But it is important to understand the import of what Sayre actually said, and how his project has been misinterpreted. Sayre was careful to limit his definition of public welfare offences to offences that both (1) involved certain kinds of less serious, regulatory, harms, *and* (2) eliminated the requirement of *mens rea* (such offences were, in Sayre's words, 'punishable irrespective of the actor's state of mind').[35]

Unfortunately, despite Sayre's care in defining 'public welfare' offences, the term is now often used indiscriminately to refer to offences involving less harmfulness than has traditionally been associated with criminal law (usually in the regulatory area), regardless of whether they require a showing of *mens rea*.[36] And by a process that might be thought of as a kind of linguistic osmosis, the term 'public welfare offences' is linked to 'regulatory offences' generally, and the term 'regulatory offences' is in turn linked to 'strict liability', so that 'strict liability' is now sometimes used to refer to low-harm offences regardless of whether they require a showing of *mens rea*.[37]

---

a kind that is less strict than liability that dispenses with *mens rea* altogether'); Alan Brudner, 'Imprisonment and Strict Liability' (1990) 40 *University of Toronto LJ* 738, at 738 n. 5 ('I shall use the terms "strict liability offence" and "negligence offence" interchangeably'); Jerome Hall, *General Principles of Criminal Law* (2nd edn., Indianapolis, Ind. 1960), 133–41.

[33] I say some idealized vision of criminal law history because, in fact, there are many instances prior to our own time in which severe criminal sanctions were applied to conduct that was only trivially harmful. For a particularly notorious example, see E. P. Thompson, *Whigs and Hunters: The Origin of the Black Act* (New York, 1975) (under the Black Act of 1723, the death penalty applied to offences as trivial as deer stalking in disguise at night and cutting down young trees).

[34] Francis Sayre, 'Public Welfare Offenses' (1933) 33 *Columbia LR* 55.       [35] Ibid. at 56 n. 5.

[36] See e.g. John C. Coffee, Jr., 'Does "Unlawful" Mean "Criminal"?: Reflections on the Disappearing Tort/Crime Distinction in American Law' (1991) 71 *Boston University LR* 193, at 198, 216–17 (using the term 'public welfare offense' to refer generally to regulatory violations, including those that require a showing of *mens rea*). Coffee's article is discussed further below, n. 76.

[37] See e.g. Laurie L. Levenson, 'Good Faith Defenses: Reshaping Strict Liability Crimes' (1993) 78 *Cornell LR* 401, at 413–15 and n. 77 (equating strict liability and regulatory offences), discussed below, n. 73. See also Simons, 'When Is Strict Criminal Liability Just?', 1077 (offering the trivially harmful, but *mens-rea*-requiring, hypothetical offence of 'knowingly carrying a match in or near a forest', which, he says, 'imposes strict liability, by failing to require a degree or type of culpability sufficient to justify punishment in a retributive theory'); Douglas Husak, this volume, Ch. 4 (imaging hypothetical strict liability offence of 'knowingly scratching one's head'). On the issue of criminalizing trivial harms generally, see Douglas N. Husak, 'Limitations on Criminalization and the General Part of Criminal Law', in Shute and Simester, *Criminal Law Theory*.

## Offences with Lower Levels of Wrongfulness than Traditionally Required

A final way in which the term 'strict liability' is used is to refer to crimes that require less moral wrongfulness than the criminal law has traditionally required. Morally wrongful conduct is that which violates a moral norm or standard. It is distinguishable from culpability (which refers to a defendant's mental state) and harmfulness (which refers to setbacks against interest caused to a person or group of persons). Once again, there is a perception (whether it is accurate is another matter) that the criminal law is increasingly being used not only to sanction conduct that involves trivial culpability and harmfulness, but also to sanction conduct that is only trivially wrongful.

As before, the association of the term 'strict liability' with conduct that is only trivially wrongful is due to a kind of linguistic osmosis. Criminal conduct that involves trivial wrongfulness is often referred to as *malum prohibitum* (as opposed to *malum in se*). Regardless of whether such usage is correct (and I am inclined to think that it is not[38]), the relevant point here is that the fact that a crime requires little in the way of wrongfulness tells us almost nothing about whether it requires a showing of *mens rea*. In some cases, so-called *malum prohibitum* crimes do not require a showing of *mens rea*; in other cases, they do. For example, it is not at all unusual for statutes and ordinances making it a crime to engage in relatively trivial regulatory offences to require that such acts be done knowingly or intentionally.[39] Nevertheless, despite the fact that an offence's failure to require moral wrongfulness bears no necessary relation to an offence's failure to require *mens rea*, the terms *malum prohibitum* and strict liability have been used interchangeably.[40]

## 2. A Plea for Formalism

The first part of this chapter considered six contexts in which strict criminal liability has been said to occur. I shall now argue that the only context in which the

---

[38] Properly speaking, offences are said to be *malum in se* when they criminalize conduct that would be considered morally wrongful even if not prohibited (examples are murder, rape, and assault). Offences are said to be *malum prohibitum* when they criminalize conduct that is considered morally wrong, if at all, primarily because it is prohibited (examples are cases in which an otherwise competent driver drives without a licence or fails to stop at a stop sign at a deserted intersection). I have discussed the distinction extensively in Green, 'Overcriminalization', 1569–77.

[39] e.g. Endangered Species Act, 16 USC §§ 1538(a)(1)(B); 1532(19) (act must be done 'knowingly').

[40] e.g. *United States* v. *Duncan Ceramics, Inc.* 544 F Supp. 1297, 1300 (ED Cal. 1982) (suggesting equivalence between *mala prohibita* and offences requiring no proof of intent); William L. Clark and William L. Marshall, *A Treatise on the Law of Crimes* (7th edn., Mundelein, Ill., 1967), 310 (using *mala prohibita* as a synonym for strict liability crimes); Mark D. Knoll and Richard G. Singer, 'Searching for the "Tail of the Dog": Finding "Elements" of Crimes in the Wake of *McMillan v. Pennsylvania*' (1999) 22 *Seattle University LR* 1057, at 1059 n. 11 ('The major exception to the mens rea requirement would be those crimes which are malum prohibitum, or strict-liability offenses wherein no mens rea is required').

term is properly used is the first—that is, in connection with offences or offence elements that do not require a showing of *mens rea*. Each of the remaining five contexts involves phenomena that should, I believe, be referred to by labels other than 'strict liability'.

## Formal versus Substantive Strict Liability

A number of commentators have distinguished broadly between two different senses of the term 'strict liability': (1) 'formal' strict liability (also referred to as 'narrow', 'legal', or 'elemental' strict liability); and (2) 'substantive' strict liability (also referred to as 'broad' or 'moral' strict liability).[41] In order to determine whether a statute involves strict liability in the substantive sense, we need to apply a normative test; that is, we need to ask whether, under such a regime, a defendant can be convicted without a showing of moral 'fault'.[42] By contrast, determining whether a criminal statute involves strict liability in the formal sense can supposedly be determined by a 'mechanical' test without consideration of the statute's deeper moral content, simply by asking whether the offence requires a showing of some form of mental element.[43]

Of the six kinds of strict liability identified in the previous section, only the first—omission of the *mens rea* requirement—qualifies as formal. The other five—barring *mens-rea*-negating defences; presuming intent; and reducing the level of required culpability, harmfulness, or wrongfulness—are all substantive. Thus, the position that I am advocating in this chapter can be reframed as follows: the term 'strict liability' should be used solely in its formal or legal sense, and not in its substantive or moral sense.

In this section, I offer five reasons for eschewing the substantive senses of strict liability and adhering strictly to its formal sense. First, moving away from the substantive sense of strict liability and towards a formalistic approach is consistent with an important parallel trend in the criminal law away from the broad, 'blameworthiness' sense of *mens rea* and towards its narrow, 'elemental' sense. Secondly, there are significant, perhaps irresoluble, difficulties in determining whether an offence entails substantive strict liability. Thirdly, talking about strict liability in the substantive sense contributes to a mistaken impression of moral equivalence among different forms of what I shall refer to as 'moral deficiency' in the criminal law. Fourthly, talking about strict liability in the substantive sense creates

---

[41] e.g. Duff, 'Strict Liability'; Husak, 'Varieties of Strict Liability', 7; Simons, 'When Is Strict Criminal Liability Just?'

[42] Husak, 'Strict Liability, Justice, and Proportionality,' this volume, Ch. 4.

[43] Ibid. Here, we should distinguish between determining whether a particular statute requires recklessness or negligence, which would not seem to require any normative judgment; and determining whether a particular defendant acted with recklessness or negligence, which would seem to involve a normative judgment about matters such as whether it was reasonable to take some risk, whether the defendant's conduct fell below some standard of care, and so forth. (Thanks to Antony Duff for bringing this point to my attention.)

confusion in determining whether a statute should be interpreted as omitting *mens rea*. Finally, talk of substantive strict liability leads to a miscalculation of the extent of the overcriminalization problem.

## Consistency with the Modern Conception of *Mens Rea*

The distinction between formal and substantive strict liability corresponds almost perfectly to a familiar distinction between two senses of *mens rea*: the narrow 'elemental' sense and the broad 'blameworthiness' sense. *Mens rea* in the former sense refers directly to the particular mental state either required in the definition of an offence, or with which the defendant actually committed the offence—such as purposely, intentionally, knowingly, and so forth. Used as such, *mens rea* has a fairly straightforward, technical meaning: the presence or absence of such mental states can typically be determined empirically, without the necessity of making a moral judgment about the defendant's conduct or character.[44]

The broader sense of *mens rea* is harder to characterize, in part because there are actually two separate sub-meanings at work here. The term has sometimes been used to refer to those conditions that must be satisfied in order for the criminal law to ascribe 'blameworthiness' to a defendant, including not only the mental elements of a particular offence but also the absence of any potentially applicable defences, such as insanity, duress, intoxication, or choice of evils.[45] There is also a second, vaguer, 'blameworthiness' sense in which the term *mens rea* has been used: it can refer to a 'general immorality of motive' or 'evil will', rather than a specific mental state, with which the offender acted.[46]

Not surprisingly, an offence can require *mens rea* in the elemental sense of the term but not in either of the blameworthiness senses of the term, and vice versa. For example, consider a statute that makes it a crime intentionally to possess a small amount of marijuana for one's personal use. The statute obviously requires *mens rea* in the elemental sense, though it could be argued that it does not require *mens rea* in the culpability sense of the term, since (one might believe) the underlying act of intentionally possessing marijuana in such circumstances is not morally blameworthy. Conversely, think of a statute that makes it a crime to have sexual intercourse with a child under the age of 10 regardless of whether the defendant knows the child's age. The statute would not require *mens rea* in the elemental sense of the term (at least with respect to the attendant circumstance of the child's age) but, one might argue, it would require *mens rea* in the culpability sense of the term because (one might well believe) having sex with a child under the age of 10 invariably involves some form of moral culpability.

---

[44] See e.g. Paul Robinson, '*Mens Rea*', in *Encyclopedia of Crime and Justice* (2nd edn., New York 2002), iii. 995.     [45] Ibid.

[46] See e.g. Hall, *General Principles of Criminal Law*, 72–3 (tracing this approach to St Augustine and Seneca).

By qualifying my discussion with the phrases, 'one might argue' and 'one might believe', my intention is to highlight the difficulties presented by the idea of *mens rea* in the blameworthiness sense. Unlike *mens rea* in the narrow, elemental sense, the presence or absence of which can generally be determined with relatively little debate, determining whether a statute entails *mens rea* in the broader, blameworthiness sense is likely to invite controversy, with judgments varying from observer to observer. For instance, in the example offered above, people are likely to differ over whether intentionally possessing marijuana is a morally blameworthy act (at least in the *malum in se* sense of blameworthiness). Thus, it is not surprising that, at least since the promulgation of the Model Penal Code, there has been a decisive shift in American law towards the elemental, and away from the blameworthiness, understanding of *mens rea*.[47] And, despite a lack of comprehensive criminal law codification in Great Britain, a similar shift in usage can be observed there as well.[48]

This is not to deny, of course, that there is still a great deal of interesting work being done on the question of character and criminal liability.[49] Rather, I am making a much narrower set of points about terminology: namely, that it is confusing to talk about *mens rea* in the broader sense of blameworthiness, that we would do better to apply the term exclusively to the specified mental state with which a defendant must act in order for liability to be imposed, and that we ought to use different terminology to talk about the broader role of character and blameworthiness in the criminal law.

A parallel shift in usage should be effected when we talk about the *omission* of the *mens rea* requirement. Just as it makes sense to avoid the confusion caused by talking about *mens rea* in the broad, blameworthiness sense by adhering strictly to the narrow, elemental sense, so too does it make sense to avoid the confusion caused by talking about strict liability in the 'substantive' sense by adhering strictly to the 'formalistic' approach. It is to the nature of such confusion that we now turn.

## The Difficulty of Determining Whether a Statute Entails Substantive Strict Liability

No scholar has gone further in articulating the substantive conception of strict liability than Douglas Husak. Rather than surveying the contexts in which the term 'strict liability' has actually been used, Husak's interest has been in finding a core, unifying concept that all cases of substantive strict liability should (he believes) reflect.[50] Husak's approach thus provides a useful shorthand for the approach I am

---

[47] Model Penal Code Commentary, § 2.02, at 230 (seeking to 'dispel the obscurity with which the culpability requirement is often treated'); see also Paul H. Robinson and Jane A. Grall, 'Element Analysis in Defining Criminal Liability: The Model Penal Code and Beyond' (1983) 35 *Stanford LR* 681.          [48] See e.g. Ashworth, *Principles of Criminal Law*, 127–8.
[49] See e.g. 'Special Issue—The New Culpability: Motive, Character, and Emotion in Criminal Law' (2000) 6 *Buffalo Criminal LR* 1 *et seq.*          [50] Husak, 'Varieties of Strict Liability'.

critiquing. While recognizing that no one else has used the term quite so expansively, I think it is nevertheless fair to use Husak's work as a paradigm of what is meant by substantive strict liability and, ultimately as a focus of what's wrong with the tendency towards such expansive usage.

For Husak, an offence should be considered as entailing strict liability if and only if it 'allows a defendant to be convicted of an offense even though he is substantially less at fault than the paradigm perpetrator of that offense'.[51] Husak assumes that every offence has a 'stereotypical offender, whose quantum of fault lies within fairly narrow boundaries'.[52] Under this approach, one cannot say whether an offence entails strict liability *simpliciter*; rather, strict liability is thought of as a relative concept, with offences on a sliding scale, more or less strict in their approach to liability.[53] In effect, Husak uses the term 'strict liability' as a kind of shorthand for criminal offences that reflect any form of moral deficiency.

There are, however, at least three major problems with Husak's approach. First, it assumes that there is a paradigm form of culpability for every offence. But the fact is that the elements of many offences are defined disjunctively, so that generalizations about moral character are very perilous. For example, in order for a rape to be committed under the Model Penal Code, a male must have sexual intercourse with a female not his wife, and he must either (*a*) compel the victim to submit by force or threat, (*b*) substantially have impaired the victim's power to appraise or control her conduct through drugs or similar means, (*c*) perpetrate the act on a victim who is unconscious, or (*d*) perpetrate the act on a victim who is less than 10 years old.[54] In determining whether such an offence would allow a defendant to be convicted although his degree of fault was substantially less than the typical perpetrator of that offence, it is unclear exactly which formulation of the offence Husak would want us to consider. Moreover, the problem is compounded by the wide variation, across jurisdictions, in the way in which the elements of a given offence are defined.

Secondly, Husak's account assumes not only that there are paradigm offences, but also that there are paradigm perpetrators (or, perhaps more precisely, paradigm

---

[51] Ibid. 193.    [52] Ibid. 194.

[53] Ibid. ('Whether an offense qualifies as an instance of strict liability must be determined relative to some comparison class that provides a norm or baseline.') There is an interesting parallel here to the controversy over the use of the terms *malum prohibitum* and *malum in se*. Most scholars and courts have spoken as if a crime had to be one or the other, without any middle ground. In opposition, I have suggested that being *malum prohibitum* or *malum in se* should be thought of as paradigmatic qualities, and that every crime, at least in the real world, reflects some of each. See Green, 'Overcriminalization', 1569–80. Thus, I am sympathetic, at least in principle, to the kind of theoretical move that Husak is making here—to take what is frequently spoken of as a yes/no, on/off, binary concept and view it as a relative, continuum-like quality that exists, to one degree or another, in any given offence. Unfortunately, for the reasons offered in the text, I do not think such a move is warranted in this particular context.

[54] Model Penal Code § 213.1. I have previously considered the difficulty of finding paradigmatic descriptions of particular offences in Stuart P. Green, 'Prototype Theory and the Classification of Offenses in a Revised Model Penal Code: A General Approach to the Special Part' (2000) 4 *Buffalo Criminal LR* 301.

perpetrations). But this assumption is problematic as well. For example, is the paradigm perpetrator of murder more like the loving son who intentionally kills his desperately ill father in order to save him from further suffering,[55] or the barbarous stepfather who inflicts unspeakable cruelty on his 6-year-old stepson in the process of killing him?[56] Assuming that the mercy killer really is 'substantially less at fault than the paradigm perpetrator' of murder, then we must wonder whether Husak really wants to say that such a case of intentional killing involves strict liability.

Thirdly, even if it were possible to find a paradigm perpetrator, Husak's approach would still lead to anomalous results. Consider an offence such as that contained in the Federal Food, Drug, and Cosmetic Act, which makes it a crime to transport adulterated food and drugs in interstate commerce.[57] What does a paradigm perpetrator of this offence look like? Given that the offence does not require, and never has required, a showing of *mens rea*, it is quite possible that the 'paradigm' perpetrator of this statute transports adulterated food or drugs unintentionally and unknowingly. Thus, in answer to the question, does the Food and Drug Act 'allow a defendant to be convicted of an offense even though he is substantially less at fault than the paradigm perpetrator of that offense', we would have to answer: no. As such, under Husak's approach, the Food and Drug Act—which would surely rank high on almost anyone else's list of strict liability crimes—would not qualify as such.

## Misleading Impression of Moral Equivalence

The previous section considered the difficulty of determining whether a particular criminal offence should be regarded as entailing substantive strict liability. In this section, I want to show why, even if we could say with certainty which offences entail substantive strict liability, such usage would still be confusing. In particular, I want to show why it is confusing to use the term 'strict liability' to refer to the five sorts of deficiency in moral content referred to above: statutory schemes that bar *mens-rea*-negating defences; offences that employ procedural devices requiring a presumption of a defendant's intent; and offences that require a less serious form of culpability, harmfulness, or moral wrongfulness than has traditionally been required by the criminal law. The confusion arises out of the misleading impression that there is a moral equivalence between such schemes and offences that eliminate the requirement of *mens rea*. Let us consider each of the five kinds of deficiency in turn.

First, it is undoubtedly true that cases like *Montana* v. *Egelhoff* raise substantial constitutional questions about the extent to which a defendant's right to mount a defence has been abridged.[58] But denying a defendant the right to present intoxication evidence that could have been used to negate proof of his *mens rea* is simply

[55] *State* v. *Forrest* 363 SE 2d 252 (NC 1987).
[56] *State* v. *Sepulvado* 655 So. 2d 623 (La. 1995).    [57] 21 USC § 331.
[58] See n. 19 above. See e.g. Allen, '*Montana v. Egelhoff*'; Peter Westen, '*Egelhoff* Again' (1999) 36 *American Criminal LR* 1203.

not equivalent, as a substantive matter, to eliminating the requirement that the government prove that the defendant had *mens rea* in the first place. Even under statutory schemes in which the defendant is barred from introducing certain kinds of exculpatory evidence, the prosecution must still prove that the defendant did in fact have intent; and a defendant who is barred from presenting evidence of his intoxication still has other avenues of showing that he lacked such intent. For example, the defendant might present evidence suggesting that he did not understand the likely consequences of his act. Thus, it is inaccurate to say that barring the defendant from presenting *mens-rea*-negating evidence is substantively equivalent to not requiring the prosecution to show intent at all.

Secondly, I disagree with those scholars (like Duff[59]) who maintain that there is no functional difference between offences that impose formal strict liability and procedural devices that create mandatory, or irrebuttable, presumptions of fact; and I agree with those (like Roberts[60]) who hold the contrary view. For one thing, the message sent by each of the two schemes differs significantly. The first scheme says that *mens rea* is irrelevant to guilt, while the second says that *mens rea* is very much relevant, but acknowledges the difficulty of proving it. In terms of truth-in-labelling, the two kinds of scheme are not at all alike. In addition, it might be argued that mandatory presumptions undermine the role of the jury and denigrate the presumption of innocence in ways that strict liability provisions do not.

Thirdly, there is, by definition, no equivalence between offence elements that require no *mens rea* at all and offence elements that require negligence or some other low-level form of *mens rea*. To equate an offence that requires a showing of negligence with one that requires no *mens rea* at all is rather like equating milk that is 'low fat' with milk that is 'fat free'. On a continuum, negligence is undoubtedly closer to formal strict liability than is intent, just as low-fat milk is closer to fat-free milk than is whole milk. But, as a substantive matter, it is clearly inaccurate to equate the two.

Fourthly, there is also no substantive equivalence between offence elements that eliminate *mens rea* and offence elements that reduce the requirement of harmfulness. For example, felony murder is one of the most harmful offences there is, despite the fact that it does not require a showing that the defendant adverted to the consequences of his action. Conversely, Louisiana's offence of begging or panhandling on an interstate highway, despite the relative triviality of the harm it involves, nevertheless requires the defendant to have acted 'intentionally'.[61]

Finally, there is little correlation between offences that eliminate the requirement of *mens rea* and those that entail low levels of moral wrongfulness. Felony murder is surely a *malum in se* offence despite the fact that at least one of its elements does not require a showing of *mens rea*. On the other hand, the Indiana law that makes it a crime to 'knowingly carry liquor into a restaurant or place of

---

[59] 'Strict Liability, Legal Presumptions, and the Presumption of Innocence'.
[60] 'Strict Liability: An Exposé'.     [61] La. Rev. Stat. 14:97.1.

public entertainment for the purpose of consuming it', is probably as close as one can get to a pure *malum prohibitum* crime notwithstanding the *mens rea* requirement that such an offence obviously includes.[62]

In short, referring indiscriminately to various discrete forms of moral deficiency in criminal offences as a form of 'strict liability' is confusing because it creates the unwarranted impression of moral equivalence between offences that are not in fact morally equivalent.

## Confusion in Determining Whether a Statute Omits *Mens Rea*

Another problem with the notion of substantive strict liability is that it can lead, indirectly, to confusion about whether an offence entails *formal* strict liability. The mere fact that a criminal statute makes no explicit mention of *mens rea* is almost never sufficient to establish that no *mens rea* is required. Indeed, most courts entertain a presumption against formal strict liability.[63] Rare are statutes such as that in Louisiana, which makes it a crime to 'knowingly *or unknowingly*' possess certain listed controlled substances.[64] Far more common are statutes like the National Firearms Act, which makes no mention of *mens rea* one way or another, and that had to be interpreted by a court to determine if *mens rea* was required.[65]

The problem is that courts sometimes determine whether a statute was intended to entail *formal* strict liability by asking whether it entails some form of *substantive* strict liability.[66] Such an approach is highly problematic. As we saw in the previous section, the mere fact that a statute entails one form of strict liability tells us very little, if anything, about whether it entails the other.

Justice Stevens's muddled dissenting opinion in *Staples* v. *United States* provides a good example of the confusion that results from such an approach.[67] The question there was whether a provision of the National Firearms Act, which makes it a crime to fail to register an automatic weapon, should be read to require the

[62] Indiana Code § 7.1-5-8-6.
[63] e.g. *United States* v. *Garrett*, 984 F 2d 1402 (5th Cir. 1993).
[64] La. Rev. Stat. Art. 40:969(C) (emphasis added) (held unconstitutionally overbroad in *State* v. *Brown*, 389 So. 2d 48 (La. 1980)).
[65] The National Firearms Act, 26 USC § 5861(d), provides that 'it shall be unlawful for any person . . . to receive or possess a firearm which is not registered to him in the National Firearms Registration and Transfer Record'. The term 'firearm', in turn, was defined to include 'any weapon which shoots . . . or can be readily restored to shoot, automatically more than one shot, without manual reloading, by a single function of the trigger [i.e. any fully automatic weapon]'. The statute was interpreted in *Staples* v. *United States*, 511 US 600 (1994), discussed below, text accompanying nn. 67–9.
[66] In addition, courts sometimes decide the question whether a statute imposes formal strict liability by looking at the consequences that would follow if it did. In the United States, courts ask whether construing a particular statute as imposing formal strict liability would lead to an unconstitutional infringement of the defendant's right to engage in protected conduct. If it would, the court will often read into the statute a *mens rea* requirement that may or may not have been intended by the enacting legislature. See generally Alan Michaels, 'Constitutional Innocence' (1999) 112 *Harvard LR* 828.     [67] *Staples* v. *United States*, 511 US 600, 624 (1994) (Stevens J dissenting).

government to prove that the defendant knew that the weapon had automatic firing capability. In arguing that such *mens rea* should not be read into the statute, Stevens engages in a *tour de force* of question-begging. He begins by assuming that, because the statute involves the regulation of 'dangerous or deleterious devices or products of obnoxious waste materials', it must be a 'public welfare' statute.[68] And because public welfare statutes, by definition, require no showing of *mens rea*, he concludes that this statute does not require *mens rea* either.[69] The problem, of course, is that whether the statute requires a showing of *mens rea* is precisely the question the court was obliged to decide. Simply because a statute requires a lesser form of harm than criminal statutes have traditionally required is hardly a basis for deciding that it must also require a lesser form of *mens rea*. At best, this is a non sequitur.

This is not to say that, in practice, there will not often be an empirical correlation between lower levels of culpability and lesser harmfulness or wrongfulness. As a matter of policy, there might be good reasons why offences involving relatively trivial regulatory harms are often formulated to require less *mens rea* than offences involving serious harms and serious penalties.[70] The important point here, though, is that, conceptually, low *mens rea* and low harmfulness are distinct variables, and the reduction of one does not necessarily imply the reduction of the other.

## Errors in Assessing the Nature and Extent of the Moral Deficiency Problem

A final problem with the indiscriminate use of the term 'strict liability' is that it is likely to result in errors in assessing the extent and nature of the moral deficiency problem. Determining whether and to what extent the criminal law is morally deficient is a complex task. Let us assume that criminal sanctions are appropriately applied to conduct if and only if such conduct involves a sufficient level of culpability, harmfulness, and wrongfulness; and let us define 'moral deficiency' as anything that departs from that model. Viewed schematically, we can identify seven distinct ways in which such a deficiency might occur. An offence or offence element might have: (1) insufficient *mens rea*; (2) insufficient harmfulness; (3) insufficient wrongfulness; (4) insufficient *mens rea* and insufficient harmfulness; (5) insufficient *mens rea* and insufficient wrongfulness; (6) insufficient harmfulness and insufficient wrongfulness; or (7) insufficient *mens rea*, insufficient harmfulness, and insufficient wrongfulness.

Such deficiencies in moral content can, of course, be achieved in many ways and for many reasons. Consider the crime of tax evasion. Under current US federal law, the government must typically prove that the defendant: (1) did actually underpay taxes; (2) used deception to evade taxes, conceal income, or mislead the authorities; and (3) did so 'willfully'.[71] Defendants in such cases are usually permitted to present a defence that they: (*a*) were mistaken about how much tax was due, (*b*) were mistaken about the meaning of the tax law itself, (*c*) relied on the advice of an accountant in calculating their tax liability, or (*d*) acted in good faith and with due diligence in the payment of their taxes.[72] Now imagine that, in a given jurisdiction, tax revenues are down, many people are failing to pay taxes owed, and the government is having difficulty proving the cases it has brought. As a result, the legislature decides that it wants to reduce the 'moral content' of the offence of tax evasion. How might it proceed?

First, the legislature could decide to reduce the amount of *culpability* required by: (1) lowering the *mens rea* required to, say, 'knowingly' or 'negligently'; (2) eliminating the *mens rea* requirement entirely; or (3) barring the use of (one or more of) mistake of fact, mistake of law, due diligence, good faith, or advice of accountant defences. Secondly, the state could decide to reduce the amount of moral *wrongfulness* required by eliminating the requirement that the defendant use deception in misleading the authorities. Finally, the state could reduce the level of *harmfulness* required by eliminating the requirement that any tax actually be owed. The last approach would allow the prosecution of a defendant who believed he was underpaying taxes, but in fact was not. Such an approach would essentially merge the offences of attempted and completed tax evasion into a single offence of 'tax evasion', just as the offences of attempted bribery, attempted fraud, and various other attempted white-collar offences can be prosecuted, respectively, as the completed offences of 'bribery', 'fraud', and so forth.

From the perspective of the long-standing law of tax evasion, any of these changes might be characterized as involving a moral deficiency, and a law of tax evasion that reflected such deficiency might be said to be overcriminalized. The essential point, however, is that each of these various forms of moral deficiency or overcriminalization has a distinctive character. If we refer to each of these very different ways of reducing moral content with the undifferentiated label of 'strict liability', we are likely to impair our ability to see the differences they entail and to assess how serious the problem of overcriminalization actually is.

Two examples will suffice.[73] First, in order to demonstrate the growth in the frequency of what she refers to as 'strict liability' offences and the consequent problem of 'prosecut[ing] individuals who are not clearly culpable', Laurie Levenson relies on statistics from the Justice Department's Bureau of Justice Statistics showing the increase in the number of defendants prosecuted and

---

[71] 26 USC § 7201. See also *Spies* v. *United States* 317 US 492 (1943).

[72] See generally Sarah N. Welling *et al.*, *Federal Criminal Law and Related Actions: Crimes, Forfeiture, the False Claims Act and RICO* (St Paul, Minn. 1998), ii. 329–35.

[73] The analysis in this paragraph borrows from my article, 'Overcriminalization', 1557–8 nn. 69, 70.

convicted of, and the length of prison sentences imposed for, all 'regulatory offenses'.[74] This is despite the fact that many of the offences referred to—particularly in the antitrust and fair labour standards areas—clearly do require a showing of *mens rea*.[75]

A second example can be found in the work of John Coffee.[76] Immediately after offering a careful explanation of what Francis Sayre meant by the term 'public welfare offence' (which, as we saw above,[77] clearly entailed the omission of the *mens rea* requirement), Coffee uses the term to apply to 'over 300,000 federal regulations that may be enforced criminally'.[78] In the context of his discussion, however, it is clear that many of the federal regulations referred to do require a showing of *mens rea*. Thus, we see once again that the conflation of formal and substantive strict liability, and the confusion such conflation entails, is likely to lead to substantial overcounting of the number of strict liability offences.[79]

## 3. Limiting the Use of 'Strict Liability' to its Formal Sense

Having sought in the previous five sections to show why it is conceptually confusing to use the term 'strict liability' in its various substantive senses, it remains for us to inquire into the significance of the term in its formal sense. Even if one were convinced that it is a mistake to speak of strict liability substantively, one might still wonder if formal strict liability was worth thinking about much at all.

Let me suggest two possible responses to this concern—one quite sceptical, the other less so. The first possibility is that the kind of moral deficiency properly designated by the term 'strict liability' is significant, but in much the same way that other kinds of moral deficiency in the criminal law (such as insufficient harmfulness and insufficient wrongfulness) are significant.[80] Under this approach, we would reach a conclusion that, in the light of the subject matter of

---

[74] Levenson, 'Good Faith Defenses', 413–15 and n. 76.

[75] See e.g. Fair Labor Standards Act, 39 USC § 216(a) (any person who 'willfully' violates various provisions of statute is subject to criminal prosecution); *United States* v. *United States Gypsum Co.*, 438 US 422, 435 (1978) (proof of criminal intent is necessary for criminal antitrust conviction).

[76] See Coffee, 'Does "Unlawful" Mean "Criminal"?', 216–17.

[77] See discussion above, text accompanying n. 35.

[78] Coffee, 'Does "Unlawful" Mean "Criminal"?'

[79] The literature concerning the incidence of strict liability in British criminal law tends to be much more precise in its usage. See e.g. Ashworth and Blake, 'Presumption of Innocence', 307–8.

[80] And why is moral deficiency in the criminal law significant? This is an enormously complicated question that goes well beyond the scope of this chapter, but suffice it to say that convicting offenders of crimes with insufficient moral content would seem to be inconsistent with the basic principle of retributivism—i.e. that it is unfair and unjust to stigmatize a person as a 'criminal' if he is not deserving of condemnation. See generally Moore, *Placing Blame*; David Dolinko, 'Three Mistakes of Retributivism' (1992) 39 *UCLA LR* 1623; Jean Hampton, 'Correcting Harms Versus Righting Wrongs: The Goal of Retribution' (1992) 39 *UCLA LR* 1659; Simester and Sullivan, *Criminal Law*, 25; Duff, 'Strict Liability, Legal Presumptions, and the Presumption of Innocence'; Simester, 'Is Strict Liability Always Wrong?'; Husak, 'Strict Liability and Justice'.

this volume, might seem rather heretical: namely, that there *is* nothing particularly special or unique about strict criminal liability, and that a more appropriate focus of analysis would be on the broader topic of 'moral deficiency in the criminal law'.

Alternatively, we might consider the possibility that the elimination of *mens rea* from criminal statutes *can* be distinguished from other kinds of moral deficiency in the criminal law. The difference, if there is one, is likely to turn on what we mean when we say that an offender was at 'fault' in committing a criminal act. I would argue that strict liability—at least in those cases of 'pure' strict liability, in which *mens rea* is omitted with respect to every material element in a given offence[81]—removes the element of fault that retributive theory would seem to require.

Other kinds of deficiency in moral content do not have such an effect. A person who intentionally or knowingly commits an offence involving a trivial harm may well be less at fault than a person who commits an offence involving a serious harm; but such a person can still fairly be said to be *responsible* for his conduct. The same can be said of defendants who: (1) commit criminal acts negligently, rather than intentionally; (2) are barred from presenting evidence of voluntary intoxication; or (3) have their intent mandatorily presumed. Whatever moral deficiencies such criminal offences or procedural devices reflect, they nevertheless satisfy the threshold retributive requirement of responsibility.

But the total omission of *mens rea* is arguably different. Eliminating the requirement of *mens rea* remains a radical (if now common) departure from the paradigm of criminal responsibility. The idea that we might impose society's most serious sanction on conduct that was performed without any culpable state of mind continues to be a deeply troubling one.

If this, admittedly controversial, claim regarding the distinctiveness of strict liability is correct, then the case for formalism would appear even stronger than it otherwise would be. By using the term 'strict liability' solely in its formal sense, and using different terminology to describe other forms of moral deficiency in criminal law, we not only maintain conceptual clarity, but also confront the serious moral challenge that strict liability poses for the retributive theory of crime.

---

[81] Such a practice is what was referred to above, n. 5 and accompanying text, as 'pure' strict liability. In the case of impure strict liability—when no culpability is required with respect to at least one element, but is required with respect to at least one other element—my claim would not apply: there would be little problem in saying that a defendant who committed an impure strict liability crime, such as statutory rape or felony murder, was 'at fault'. On the other hand, we might still be able to say that the defendant was not 'at fault' with respect to the crime of which he was actually convicted.

# 2

# Is Strict Liability Always Wrong?

*A. P. Simester*

## 1. Three Claims

The imposition of strict liability in the criminal law is widely thought by scholars to be unjustified. There is, moreover, a broad consensus about why it is wrong. Strict liability leads to conviction of persons who are, morally speaking, innocent. Convicting and punishing those who do not deserve it perpetrates a serious wrong. Thus strict liability is a misuse of the criminal law—an institution which, because of its moral significance and grave implications for the lives of convicted defendants, should be reserved only for the regulation of serious wrongs done by culpable wrongdoers.

There is much that is right about this view. In this chapter, I argue that it *is* wrong to convict the blameless of stigmatic crimes. We would be right to object to the enactment of a strict liability homicide offence of, say, causing death by one's action. The mere causing of death does not imply culpability, and such an offence would expose morally innocent persons to criminal liability in a way that is profoundly objectionable. This is the central claim: where strict liability leads to conviction of the blameless, its use in stigmatic crimes is always unjustified.

It does not follow, however, that all types of strict liability offences are wrong. In particular, there are reasons for thinking that strict liability may be legitimate in non-stigmatic offences (what I shall call quasi-criminal regulations). This chapter canvasses a variety of instrumental arguments both for and against using strict liability. Although, in the context of stigmatic crimes, these instrumental arguments are defeated by intrinsic objections to strict liability, they need to be taken more seriously when it comes to quasi-criminal regulations. Even where strict liability leads to conviction of the blameless, its use in non-stigmatic offences on occasion may be justified.

Versions of this chapter were presented as papers at Boston University, the University of Pennsylvania, and the University of Toronto. I am grateful to participants there, and at the Cambridge colloquia, for many insightful comments and criticisms; and to Alon Harel, Paul Roberts, and Ken Simons for detailed written comments.

Additionally, and perhaps more interestingly, there are also cases where the imposition of strict liability regarding some element of the *actus reus* need not lead to systematic conviction of the morally innocent. In these cases, the intrinsic objections to strict liability fall away, so that its use might sometimes be legitimate even in stigmatic offences. Consider the following example:[1]

Deborah is driving through a village at a speed 20 miles per hour in excess of the speed limit. Unexpectedly she loses control of her car, mounts the pavement, and kills Allan, who had been walking quietly toward the corner shop in order to buy a newspaper.

Driving through the village at such excessive speed is, let me stipulate, dangerous driving. Suppose, further, that there is an offence of dangerous driving causing death, which offence requires no *mens rea* element to be proved in respect of the death.[2] A key element in the *actus reus* of that offence therefore involves strict liability. Yet it seems to me there is nothing wrong with convicting Deborah of that offence. Not only is Deborah culpably guilty of 'dangerous driving', she is also culpably guilty of 'dangerous driving causing death'—because (as I will argue) she is also culpable with respect to the death.

Of course, one example of a legitimate conviction does not a legitimate offence make. The offence may still be objectionable because of its application to some class of cases within which Deborah does not fall. None the less, the example usefully suggests the possibility that offences with substantial strict liability elements may be enacted without their being objectionable in the straightforward manner that strict liability offences so often are. That possibility will be explored in this chapter.

## Two Definitions

For present purposes, I take an offence *formally* to impose 'strict liability' if it contains at least one material[3] element of the *actus reus* without a corresponding *mens rea* element (where negligence counts as a *mens rea* element[4]). This definition accommodates the fact that most strict liability offences contain *mens rea* elements. They are strict because of what they lack: a *mens rea* requirement in respect of one or more elements of the *actus reus*. A good example of this is the notorious case of *Prince*,[5] in which D was convicted of an offence under the

---

[1] Taken from A. P. Simester and G. R. Sullivan, *Criminal Law: Theory and Doctrine* (2nd edn., Oxford 2003), 188.                    [2] See e.g. s. 1 of the Road Traffic Act 1988 (UK).

[3] Following the definition stated in § 1.13(10) of the Model Penal Code (1985), an element is material where it 'does not relate exclusively to the statute of limitations, jurisdiction, venue, or to any other matter similarly unconnected with (i) the harm or evil, incident to conduct, sought to be prevented by the law defining the offense, or (ii) the existence of a justification or excuse for such conduct.'

[4] I argue that negligence is capable of tracking culpability in 'Can Negligence be Culpable?' in J. Horder (ed.), *Oxford Essays in Jurisprudence: Fourth Series* (Oxford 2000), 85.

[5] (1875) 2 CCR 154.

Offences Against the Person Act 1861. Section 55 provided that 'whosoever shall unlawfully take . . . any unmarried girl, being under the age of sixteen years, out of the possession and against the will of her father or mother . . . shall be guilty of a misdemeanour'. D did as proscribed, whereupon he was convicted notwithstanding that he reasonably believed the girl's age was 18. The prohibition was, in that respect, absolute. Yet it is clear that the offence involved *mens rea* regarding other elements of the *actus reus*. Had D thought that the girl was in no one's possession or that he was authorized by her father to accompany her, D could not have been convicted.

Several chapters in this volume distinguish between *formal* and *substantive* strict liability.[6] According to this distinction, an offence imposes substantive strict liability when it contemplates the conviction of persons who are blameless for committing that particular offence.[7] For the sake of clarity, I will confine my usage of 'strict liability' *simpliciter* to the formal sense. But one way of reading §§ 2 and 4 of this chapter is to see them as a two-part investigation: into the possibility that substantive strict liability may sometimes be justified in the context of non-stigmatic offences; and into the possibility that formal strict liability does not always impose liability that is substantively strict.

## Stigmatic Crimes and Quasi-Criminal Regulations

A distinction can also be drawn between non-stigmatic offences and 'serious', stigmatic, crimes.[8] It is generally thought to be a defining marque of the criminal law that its verdict, the conviction, operates as a condemnatory statement on behalf of society. By labelling the defendant a 'criminal', the conviction asserts publicly that she is a reprehensible wrongdoer. Hence it is intelligible to speak of 'the disgrace of criminality',[9] something reinforced—not constituted—by the censorious nature of any punishment that may additionally be imposed.

Yet not every offence against the criminal law involves the sort of public condemnation that is implicit in convictions for a serious crime. A parking offence, for instance, involves little or no stigma. There is a large number of offences prohibiting 'acts not criminal in any real sense, but . . . which in the public interest are prohibited under a penalty'.[10] These, too, are 'criminal' offences, in so far as their commission may be followed by prosecutions that are criminal in nature and subject to rules of criminal (not civil) evidence and procedure. But in substance, it would be more accurate to describe such offences as 'quasi-criminal'.[11] They fall within the rubric

---

[6] See e.g. the contributions to this volume by Stuart Green (Ch. 1) and Doug Husak (Ch. 4).

[7] That is, blameless in respect of the offence for which they are convicted, as opposed to being culpable for some other wrong or offence.

[8] *Sweet* v. *Parsley* [1970] AC 132, 149 (Lord Reid), 163 (Lord Diplock); *Alphacell Ltd.* v. *Woodward* [1972] AC 824, 839 (Viscount Dilhorne), 848 (Lord Salmon); *Gammon (Hong Kong) Ltd.* v. *A-G for Hong Kong* [1985] AC 1, 12–14.

[9] *Warner* v. *Metropolitan Police Comr.* [1969] 2 AC 256, 272 (Lord Reid).

[10] *Sherras* v. *De Rutzen* [1895] 1 QB 918, 922 (Wright J).

[11] Cf. *Pearks, Gunston & Tee Ltd.* v. *Ward* [1902] 2 KB 1, 11.

and forms of the criminal law, but they lack a key underlying feature that sets the criminal law apart from the civil: the declaration of reprehensible wrongdoing that is implicit in the verdict against, and punishment of, the accused. Hence it was intelligible in *Wings Ltd.* v. *Ellis* for Lord Scarman to say that the Trade Descriptions Act 1968 'operates by prohibiting false descriptions under the pain of penalties enforced through the criminal courts. But it is not a truly criminal statute. Its purpose is not the enforcement of the criminal law but the maintenance of trading standards. Trading standards, not criminal behaviour, are its concern.'[12]

Accepting that it may be appropriate to describe such crimes, in a familiar judicial idiom, as 'not truly criminal in character',[13] I shall use the phrase 'quasi-criminal regulations' to refer to crimes that do not import any significant element of stigma, in contradistinction to what I shall call 'stigmatic crimes'. Notwithstanding its blurred boundary, the dichotomy strikes me as meaningful—most parking offenders worry about the cost of the fine rather than about any element of censure. None the less, in § 3 I shall revisit the question whether such a boundary really can be drawn *within* the criminal law.

The category of quasi-criminal regulations need not be identical to what are sometimes termed 'regulatory' or 'public welfare' offences in criminal law texts, although there will no doubt be a considerable overlap.[14] Still less do I have in mind the distinction between crimes *mala in se* and those *mala prohibita*. Some crimes *mala prohibita*, such as those regulating trades in financial markets, can import a significant element of censure.[15] Wherever they do so, they count for present purposes as stigmatic crimes rather than quasi-criminal regulations.

## Three Propositions

With these definitions in mind, we can formulate the main claims made in this essay as three propositions:

    (i) Substantive strict liability is always wrong in stigmatic crimes.
    (ii) Substantive strict liability may not be wrong in quasi-criminal regulations.
    (iii) In some circumstances, formal strict liability may not be wrong in stigmatic crimes.

The following discussion begins with proposition (ii), by elaborating the instrumental arguments for and against using strict liability in quasi-criminal regulations. In § 3, the core moral objections to strict liability are considered. It will be argued that those objections defeat any instrumental reasons in favour of strict liability

---

[12] [1985] AC 272, 293.

[13] *London Borough of Harrow* v. *Shah* [2000] 1 WLR 83, 88 (Mitchell J).

[14] The latter designation is often used to refer to offences that regulate and control excesses in an otherwise acceptable trade or practice; some such offences may be stigmatic.

[15] Cf. A. P. Simester and Stephen Shute, 'On the General Part in Criminal Law', in Stephen Shute and A. P. Simester (eds.), *Criminal Law Theory: Doctrines of the General Part* (Oxford 2002), 11.

for stigmatic offences: this is proposition (i). However, provided a clear distinction can be maintained between stigmatic crimes and quasi-criminal regulations, the same objections do not necessarily defeat the instrumental considerations, set out in § 2, favouring quasi-criminal regulations. Finally, § 4 considers—*per* proposition (iii)—whether there are any types of offences where formal strict liability does not generate substantive strict liability. The possibility and justification of such offences will be identified, and the boundaries of their legitimate deployment explored.

## 2. Instrumental Arguments Concerning Strict Liability in Non-Stigmatic Offences

This section canvasses some of the instrumental reasons for and against using strict liability in quasi-criminal regulations. Prima facie, many of these considerations apply to the use of strict liability more generally, including in serious crimes; however, as we shall see in § 3, there are decisive reasons why strict liability should be restricted, if at all, to non-stigmatic offences. We begin here with the arguments in favour, before turning to the counterarguments.

### Instrumental Arguments for Strict Liability

Let us suppose that the state has good reason for wanting to reduce the incidence of øing by citizens, and that its prohibiting øing would be consistent with the harm principle, in virtue of reducing either direct or remote harm to others. Suppose, too, that øing is the type of activity that can be defined without reference to a mental element.[16] Prima facie, there are instrumental reasons to frame the prohibition as a strict liability offence. It is arguable that the use of strict liability increases the efficiency and the effectiveness of law enforcement administration, especially in respect of corporate defendants. Strict liability may also increase the deterrent effect of the prohibition, leading to fewer instances of øing because (it may be contended) the use of strict liability tends to encourage potential defendants to take greater precautions. Alternatively, strict liability may be an efficient mechanism for allocating the costs of risk-creating activities.

These claims, which are both contingent and vulnerable to countervailing arguments, require closer examination.

---

[16] Some activities cannot be specified in this way. Any definition of 'theft', for example, would fail adequately to define theft unless it contained reference to the actor's mental state, e.g. her intention to deprive. There is nothing wrong at all, no hint of criminality, in picking something up: it is only D's accompanying intention that gives such an otherwise innocent act its criminal character. In the criminal law, this point is more likely to affect the criminalization and labelling of certain stigmatic crimes than it is quasi-criminal regulations.

## Cost

From an administrative perspective, the costs involved before and during trial are likely to be considerably decreased if øing is made a strict liability offence, since the number of elements required to be proved at trial, and thus the number of potential issues, is reduced.[17] This consideration matters because criminal justice is very expensive. It is plausible that, if every one of a nation's offences required proof of *mens rea* with respect to all elements of the *actus reus*, administration of the criminal law would be not merely cumbersome but unaffordable. As such, the state essentially has two options: first, to reduce the number of criminal offences by eliminating or not enforcing some proscriptions; secondly, to simplify some of the remaining proscriptions by dispensing with some of their elements (especially, some of their *mens rea* elements). It may, of course, do both. But if we assume that all the existing offences are consonant with the harm principle, the second option presents a *via media* by which harms may feasibly be proscribed. If it is impossible fully to protect victims from harm while maintaining a Rolls-Royce system of criminal justice, the conflicting interests of defendants and victims may be mediated, in part, by simplifying the *mens rea* elements of certain offences.

Once this possibility is accepted, the use of strict liability becomes an issue of priorities. The range of harms that call for prevention exceeds the range of offences for which the state can, in practice, administer a criminal justice system where every offence contains *mens rea* requirements corresponding to every element of the *actus reus*. Thus, it may be concluded, the state should consider *which* offences to 'skimp' on. If the choice is either cutting corners or abandoning the prohibition altogether, a pared-down regulation (say, with reduced sanctions attached) may well be preferable. Grave instances of øing might, at the same time, be addressed by enacting a supplementary, more serious, version of the crime, one that involves proof of *mens rea* and greater penalties.

## Accuracy

Reducing the number of potential issues, by removing one or more *mens rea* elements from the definition of an offence, is also likely to promote accuracy in criminal adjudication (i.e. the reliability of the court's verdict that the elements of the offence did, or did not, occur). Reducing the number of substantive issues at trial decreases the points at which the court's finding may err; and, moreover, decreases them by removing elements of a type—*mens rea*—that is characteristically more difficult to ascertain. To prove and know the content of a person's mind is typically harder, because more a matter of inference, than to prove and know the occurrence of physical events.

Admittedly, forensic accuracy is not the exclusive aim of the trial process. It is constrained by rights that bias that process in favour of the defendant, notably including

---

[17] Against this would need to be weighed any increased costs (after deducting additional revenue from fines) that may be incurred should strict liability lead to a greater number of trials.

the right to be acquitted unless each element of the offence is proved beyond reasonable doubt: we prefer that inaccurate verdicts favour the defendant and not the prosecution. But a right of this sort takes forensic error as a given; it is not compromised by measures that increase the accuracy of verdicts. Neither does it suppose that inaccuracy per se is desirable, even where that error falls to benefit the defendant.[18]

For all that, fault elements normally can be excised from the offence definition only if they are reintroduced at the sentencing stage. The judge cannot pass sentence without considering whether the offence was committed knowingly, negligently, or blamelessly[19] and, if such matters are disputed, a further hearing may be required to determine them.[20] In the light of this, one might suppose that the evidence may as well be heard straightforwardly before conviction.[21]

However, that conclusion is too hasty. Error at the point of sentence is different from, and less important than, error at the point of conviction. The court's principal options at trial are stark: to convict or acquit. By contrast, the sentencing decision involves selection from a continuum of options, ranging upwards from an absolute discharge.[22] Unlike the (binomial) conviction decision, imprecision is thus relatively tolerable within a sentencing decision, and there is less reason to protect the defendant against error.[23] Hence, *overall* accuracy of disposition may be improved by incorporating questions of culpability into the sentencing decision.[24]

## Regulating Corporate Activity

Both efficiency and accuracy seem especially in point for corporate defendants.[25] The proof of *mens rea* presents especial difficulty in prosecutions of corporate

---

[18] The same is true of other types of rights, such as constraints on methods of gathering evidence, which are not motivated by the need to protect against the costs of inaccuracy but, rather, by concerns for human dignity, the need to fetter state power, and the like.

[19] See e.g. *Smedleys Ltd.* v. *Breed* [1974] AC 839, 857 (Viscount Dilhorne); *Lester* (1975) 63 Cr. App. R. 144. This is now, it seems, a requirement of Article 6 of the European Convention on Human Rights: *International Transport Roth GMBH & ors* v. *Secretary of State for Home Department* [2003] QB 728 (CA).

[20] *Newton* (1983) 77 Cr. App. R. 13. Until recently, the position was different in the US; however, in *Blakely* v. *Washington* 124 S. Ct. 2531 (2004), the Supreme Court ruled that where a finding of fact is required in order to increase a criminal sentence, the fact must be proved before a jury beyond a reasonable doubt.

[21] As was suggested by the Canadian Supreme Court in *R* v. *City of Sault Ste Marie* (1978) 85 DLR (3d) 161, 172.

[22] Within the terms of this argument, the power to discharge absolutely supplies an important safeguard against inaccuracy (and injustice), since it provides the means by which blameless defendants can be absolved altogether from punishment.

[23] e.g. where a hearing is required to decide contested facts that were not settled by conviction and which are relevant to sentence, it is arguable that proof should be required only to the balance of probabilities. Indeed, to require the higher standard may result in worse rather than better justice, since it is likely to lead to defendants consistently being punished less than they deserve. In England, none the less, it appears that the normal burden of proof beyond reasonable doubt applies: *R.* v. *Ahmed* (1984) 80 Cr. App. R. 295 (CA).

[24] Notice that this argument is undermined if the conviction decision is not, in itself, neutral, which is one reason why the argument loses its force in the context of stigmatic crimes.

[25] The argument here is adopted from Simester and Sullivan, *Criminal Law*, § 6.3(i).

bodies, since there may be no one person whose conduct can be attributed to the corporation and with whom the corporate mind can be identified. Strict liability, by contrast, is much more easily applied to corporations since it can be administered without reference to the defendant's mental state. The significance of this consideration is all the greater to the extent that corporate activity frequently occurs on a larger scale than that by individuals, and correspondingly creates more widespread risks of harm. Further, where offences regulate the specialist commercial behaviour of corporations the prosecutor is likely to be poorly placed to understand the nature of the defendant's own specialist activity. This forensic disadvantage compounds the challenge of proving the conduct of particular individuals within large and complex organizations.

Commercial activity needs to be regulated in a cost-efficient manner, especially where the offences involved are minor and, taken individually, pose no risk of serious harm. Moreover, effective regulation of trivial infractions can protect against cumulative harms that may be very substantial indeed. As we shall consider below, from an economic perspective the costs of regulating a commercial activity are part of the costs of carrying on that activity. It is therefore arguable that the burden of criminal penalties should be borne as a form of production expense by those who voluntarily undertake risk-creating activities.[26]

## Deterrence

It is also arguable that strict liability increases the deterrent effect of a prohibition. That is to say, there are likely to be fewer instances of the *actus reus* when øing is prohibited on a strict-liability basis, because (it may be thought) the use of strict liability tends to encourage a higher level of precautions by potential defendants.[27]

The proposition that strict liability increases deterrence is implicit in one of the most common arguments given for abandoning a full *mens rea* requirement, i.e. that protection of the public sometimes requires a high standard of care on the part of those who undertake risk-creating activities. This rationale is consistent with the fact that strict liability offences are often enacted in order to protect the public from risks created by industrial and other specialist activities. Extra care, the argument goes, needs to be taken by such persons, and without liability for inadvertence the careless will have insufficient incentive to reduce or eliminate those risks. The threat of strict criminal liability supplies a motive for persons in risk-generating activities to adopt precautions that might not otherwise be taken, in order to guard against unforeseen mishaps and errors.[28] Particularly where the

---

[26] See the discussion of cost allocation below, p. 29.

[27] Cf. Lord Salmon: strict liability 'encourages riparian factory owners not only to take reasonable steps to prevent pollution but to do everything possible to ensure that they do not cause it'. *Alphacell Ltd.* v. *Woodward* [1972] AC 824, 848–9. See also Donovan J, in *St Margaret's Trust Ltd.* [1958] 2 All ER 289, 293: 'There would be little point in enacting that no one should breach the defences against a flood, and at the same time excusing any one who did it innocently.'

[28] *R.* v. *City of Sault Ste Marie* (1978) 85 DLR (3d) 161, 171. For an extreme version of this type of argument, see B. Wootton, *Crime and the Criminal Law* (2nd edn., London 1981), 47 ff.

harmful impact of the *actus reus* is severe and widespread, the law has pressing reason to provide incentives through criminalization for persons not only to refrain from advertent wrongdoing, but also to take care against inadvertent harms.

## Cost Allocation

Alternatively, strict liability need not be justified in terms of deterrence but could instead be analogized to a statutory tort. Normally, the legal implications of risk without fault lie within the realms of insurance and tort liability, but there is no reason why, at least in quasi-criminal regulations, they could not also be a concern of the criminal law. This is the force of the proposition that the burden of criminal penalties may be analysed as an element of the production costs incurred by those who initiate risk-creating activities. As Lord Salmon observed, in *Alphacell Ltd.* v. *Woodward*,[29] 'In the case of a minor pollution . . . a comparatively nominal fine will no doubt be imposed. This may be regarded as a not unfair hazard of carrying on a business which may cause pollution on the banks of a river.' On a cost-allocation model, one may expect the regime of fines to be calibrated according to the harmful costs imposed by the regulated activity. A system of strict liability offences serving this function could, moreover, systematically be complemented by a regimen of more serious crimes requiring proof of *mens rea* and carrying more severe, punitive, sanctions.

The rejoinder is obvious: no doubt harmful activities *could* be criminalized on this basis, but why should they be? Why not control them with other legal mechanisms? The answer is that there are certain advantages to using the criminal law. One is the symbolic significance of declaring that øing is prohibited. The creation of a quasi-criminal regulation may be a tool for communicating to the public that the prohibited activity is a legal wrong that *must* not be done—rather than signalling that it must be paid for if done (for example through a licensing system). Where the imperative voice is desirable, there is reason to favour a criminalization response.

When contrasted with tort law, there are also practical benefits. First, tort law requires a victim. But certain activities, e.g. forms of environmental pollution, may wrong no identifiable victim with standing to sue. Alternatively, even where there are particular victims, the aggregate harm to individually wronged plaintiffs may be less than the overall cost to society that the activity imposes. Relying exclusively on tort law is likely, in these cases, to result in under-enforcement.

Secondly, given that the state pays the costs of detecting, prosecuting, and punishing offences, it may be better placed to regulate øing than private individuals through the law of tort. Suppose that my next-door neighbour throws a stone through one of the panes in my greenhouse, which it will cost £20 to replace. It is likely to be impractical for me to pursue her through the law of tort. But a criminal prosecution requires only my time. In this sense, criminal regulation by the state

[29]  [1972] AC 824, 848.

may augment the rule of law, through increasing the consistency with which legal rights are enforced in like cases, rather than leaving the matter to irregular enforcement by individual claimants.

## Weaknesses in the Instrumental Case for Strict Liability

The force of prima facie arguments favouring strict liability may be disputed. Absent empirical evidence, it is not clear that the criminal justice process will operate more efficiently if fault must still be established prior to the imposition of an appropriate sanction. There is also little evidence that strict liability is an effective deterrent spurring potential defendants to increased precautions.[30]

### Deterrence

Indeed, it is conceivable that strict liability will lead to *reduced* precautions being taken, by comparison with a negligence-based standard of liability. A negligence standard has the virtue of signalling to actors, *ex ante*, what level of precautions will, if taken, secure immunity from conviction. By guaranteeing non-conviction in this way, the criminal law creates a powerful incentive for actors to take reasonable precautions. Where that guarantee is removed, however, actors are left with no guidance from the criminal law about what level of *ex ante* precaution is optimal. In such a case, the rational actor will commit herself to taking the equilibrium level of precaution; i.e. the level of precaution at which the marginal cost of taking additional precautions exceeds the reduction in expected liability costs. This equilibrium could occur at any point on the continuum from zero to the maximum-possible precautions. As such, and depending on how the scale of sanctions is structured, strict liability is just as likely to result in fewer than reasonable, rather than enhanced, precautions being taken by the actor. (This possibility becomes all the more likely where actors have idiosyncratic risk preferences.)

In order to avoid underdeterrence, one way of manipulating the incentives created by strict liability would be to introduce a finer-tuned, more differentially geared, structure of sanctions. However, that approach may be expected to sacrifice any advantages in efficiency that strict liability might otherwise offer. Alternatively, the sanctions could simply be increased to the point where no rational actor would contemplate taking fewer than reasonable precautions. Yet that, too, seems undesirable, since it runs the risk of deterring the underlying activity altogether.

Of course, this is an inherent feature of strict liability: the actor must either desist from the risk-creating activity *tout court*, or persist and accept that he must

---

[30] See B. S. Jackson, '*Storkwain*: A Case Study in Strict Liability and Self-Regulation' [1991] *Criminal LR* 892; G. Richardson, 'Strict Liability for Regulatory Crime: The Empirical Research' [1987] *Criminal LR* 295; R. Baldwin, 'Why Rules Don't Work' (1990) 53 *Modern LR* 321; Jerome Hall, *General Principles of Criminal Law* (2nd edn., Indianapolis 1960), 344–6.

run all remaining risks, however esoteric and unlikely, of the prohibited harm occurring. Assuming that the first option is not intended, the deterrent function of regulatory laws is intelligible only as an attempt to discourage people from entering into an activity (or from executing it in a manner) which creates *unreasonable* risks of the unwanted harm occurring. But *that* aim can be achieved by negligence liability. Moreover, imposing a negligence standard does not lead to underdeterrence. What suffices as reasonable care depends, in part, on the seriousness of the harm involved. Thus, where the risks created by D's activity are of, say, a severe and widespread harm, a correspondingly higher standard of precautions will be demanded from D. Strict liability lacks this element of tailoring. Instead, it forces the blameless defendant to become an unrewarded risk-taker in respect of non-negligent misfortunes, subject to a criminal legal lottery over which he has no reasonable control.

## Regulating Corporate Activity

The need for effective regulation and prosecution of corporate defendants could also be met by a negligence-based standard. Proof of negligence can be established without reference to the company's mental state (i.e. without proving the state of mind of a controlling officer), since negligence is measured in terms of conduct. It is, of course, true that negligence obliges the prosecution to establish relevant conduct that is attributable to the company—but the same constraint applies to strict liability.

Alternatively, proof difficulties in respect of specialist commercial activities might be met by reversing the burden of proof. This step has been taken successfully in a number of Commonwealth jurisdictions,[31] where 'strict liability' offences require the prosecution to prove only the *actus reus* beyond reasonable doubt—whereupon the defendant may exculpate himself by proving absence of fault (i.e. a 'no-negligence' defence) on the balance of probabilities. In essence, these approximate fault-based offences of negligence where, however, the burden of proving a lack of negligence rests on the defendant.[32]

This raises a question. Compared to the normal requirements for proving *mens rea*, which burden the prosecution to establish guilt 'beyond reasonable doubt', is it wrongful for the state to lower the standard of proof demanded and therefore to take an increased risk of wrongly convicting D? As will be noted in § 3, we already accept a certain level of systemic risk in criminal trials, by demanding only proof beyond reasonable doubt. Is there a peremptory argument against reducing that demand to e.g. a 'balance of probabilities' standard?

Arguably, allocating the burden of proof is part of balancing the costs and risks of an activity between actors and potential victims. At least in quasi-criminal

---

[31] e.g. *R.* v. *City of Sault Ste Marie* (1978) 85 DLR (3d) 161; *Millar* v. *MOT* [1986] 1 NZLR 660. Similarly, due diligence defences are commonly found in consumer protection statutes.

[32] Without their being equivalent, according to Paul Roberts: 'Strict Liability and the Presumption of Innocence: An Exposé of Functionalist Assumptions', this volume, Ch. 7.

regulations, it is not clear that D has a right that trumps this balancing process. Indeed, where D's activity is a specialist one that imposes risks upon others, the state has a right, when licensing that activity, to specify how that activity is to be done;[33] arguably, this right embraces a requirement both that D conduct the activity in a prescribed manner and that she be able to prove that she has done so. Hence D's being able to document her conduct may be a legitimate condition of the overall regime by which that conduct is permitted and facilitated.[34] Moreover, given the advantage the defendant may have of familiarity with a specialist activity, it is arguable that the shift in evidential burdens can result in more efficient and better justice. Very often, it may be more difficult for the prosecution to prove *mens rea* where the defendant's activity is a specialist one, not readily understood by others, than it is for the defendant to prove lack of fault.

### Discretionary Enforcement

A further concern is that regimes of strict liability offences are administered by enforcement agencies, which, in practice, tend to use the prospect of strict liability as a discretionary bargaining tool in securing compliance by potential defendants.[35] Typically, prosecutions are brought only in cases where the accused was actually at fault.[36] Indeed, they should be brought only where doing so is in the public interest;[37] it may frequently be difficult to see how prosecution of blameless offending satisfies that criterion.[38] As Parker J observed, in *James & Son* v. *Smee*, 'Where legislation, as here, throws a wide net it is important that only those should be charged who either deserve punishment or in whose case it can be said that punishment would tend to induce them to keep themselves and their organization up to the mark . . .'.[39]

Unfortunately, the lack of public interest in a prosecution is not, as such, a defence. Consequently, defendants are on occasion found guilty of offences even though, in the view of the court, a prosecution should not have been brought.[40] Given that strict liability offences are characteristically used as an ad hoc negotiating tool, this reliance on dispensations by the enforcement agency

---

[33] For example, it is clearly appropriate for the state to permit driving but demand that it be done in accordance with prevailing traffic regulations—on a particular side of the road, subject to certain maximum speeds, etc.

[34] Cf. the contribution by Antony Duff in this volume, Ch. 6, § 5; *Oliver* [1944] KB 68; *John* v. *Humphreys* [1955] 1 WLR 325.

[35] See e.g. K. Hawkins, *Environment and Enforcement* (Oxford 1984); B. Hutter, *The Reasonable Arm of the Law* (Oxford 1988). Prosecution is, it seems, a last resort: K. Hawkins, *Law as Last Resort* (Oxford 2002).

[36] G. Richardson, A. Ogus, and P. Burrows, *Policing Prosecution* (Oxford 1982).

[37] *Code for Crown Prosecutors* (<www.cps.gov.uk>, accessed 25 Sept. 2004), § 6; *Smedleys Ltd.* v. *Breed* [1974] AC 839, 856 (Viscount Dilhorne).

[38] That is, unless there are general deterrence-based reasons for prosecuting. Alternatively, on a cost-allocation model of non-stigmatic offences, prosecutions may be driven by cost-recovery considerations.                                              [39] [1955] 1 QB 78, 93.

[40] e.g. *Smedleys Ltd.* v. *Breed* [1974] AC 839; *Hart* v. *Bex* [1957] Crim. LR 622; cf. *James & Son* v. *Smee* [1955] 1 QB 78.

puts at risk the rule of law, in so far as it leaves the prospect of criminal conviction to the discretion of enforcement officers.

## A Case for Strict Liability?

Despite these powerful counterarguments, the instrumental case for strict liability is not entirely defeated. Strict liability might be more efficient. Depending on the nature and structure of each particular offence, it might lead rational actors to take more than reasonable precautions. It may also be justified as an instrumental tool for allocating the costs of specialist, risk-creating, activities. In this latter role, its advantage over taxing such activities is that it allocates the cost to the harmful *outcome* of the activity, not to the risk-creating activity more generally. Hence, the criminal mechanism offers incentives to take precautions which a generic tax would not. In doing so, moreover, it identifies and communicates more clearly the precise harm at which the prohibition is directed.

## 3. Intrinsic Objections to Strict Liability

It is, in short, arguable that there are instrumental benefits to be gained from the device of strict liability, although their scope and extent is uncertain. However, assuming they exist, those benefits must be weighed against the intrinsic moral objections to strict liability set out below. In the context of stigmatic crimes, it seems to me that these objections are decisive.

### Objections Specific to Paradigm (Stigmatic) Crimes

Suppose that the state were to create a crime of 'homicide', defined as a strict liability offence of causing death. Objections to crimes of this type depend, in turn, on the nature of the criminal law. Without dwelling on the familiar analysis,[41] there seem to me to be certain paradigm features associated with the criminalization of $\mu$ing. *Ex ante*, $\mu$ing is prohibited and declared to be wrong: citizens are not merely requested but instructed not to $\mu$. *Ex post*, where D is found to have transgressed, he is convicted of $\mu$ing and liable to punishment which may be substantial, perhaps including imprisonment. The conviction and the punishment also express censure,[42] to D, V, and the public at large. As well as suffering hard treatment, D is labelled as a particular sort of criminal (a '$\mu$er'), a labelling that conveys a public implication of culpable wrongdoing.

These paradigm features of the criminal law imply certain objections to making $\mu$ing a strict liability crime, at least where strict liability leads to conviction of

---

[41]  See e.g. Simester and Sullivan, *Criminal Law*, 1–5.
[42]  In the context of punishment, see e.g. J. Feinberg, 'The Expressive Function of Punishment' (1965) 49 *Monist* 397; A. von Hirsch, *Censure and Sanctions* (Oxford 1993).

blameless defendants. (The subset of cases where strict liability does not lead to conviction of blameless defendants is considered in § 4.)

## Wrongful Censure

The main objection to strict liability in stigmatic crimes law is that it involves the conviction and punishment of persons who are not at fault. Morally speaking, it is wrong to convict the innocent. If a person does not deserve to be convicted then he has a right not to be; and his conviction cannot be justified by such consequential considerations as deterrence.[43]

Since both are censorious, this objection applies to both conviction and punishment. The imposition of punishment is, *qua* punishment, justified only when D deserves it, in virtue of culpably having done wrong. Indeed, the imposition of hard treatment cannot count as punishment unless it conveys this message. But in the context of strict liability, the state does not rely on the proposition that D is culpable as a precondition of imposing punishment. So the state cannot claim to be punishing D in accordance with D's desert; it is simply imposing hard treatment in virtue of the fact that μing (an *actus reus*) has occurred.

This criticism may be evaded, in part. Even if μing is a strict liability offence, the quantum of punishment imposed for transgressions might still be related to desert in a criminal legal system that required *sentences* to take account of D's level of culpability, with fault being a post-conviction matter for consideration during sentencing.

However, the same get-out is not available with regard to the conviction itself.[44] Independently of the sanction imposed, the conviction also conveys censure. A conviction for μing has the effect of naming D a criminal (in respect of that particular offence), a branding which is communicated to society as well as to D. Assuming that, if imposed on a strict liability basis, the label 'criminal-μ' continues to retain its stigmatic quality, this amounts to systematic moral defamation by the state.[45] Given the public understanding of that designation, when it labels him a criminal the state is no longer telling the public the truth about D. People have a right not to be censured falsely as criminals, a right that is violated when one is convicted and punished for a stigmatic crime without proof of culpable wrongdoing.

That falsehood is no ordinary lie. There is something especially troubling when wrongful censure is imposed by the state. In ordinary defamation cases, the attack

---

[43] Cf. H. Mannheim, 'Mens Rea in German and English Criminal Law' (1936) 18 *Journal of Comparative Legislation* 78, at 90: 'the number of larcenies committed, *e.g.*, is also very great; nevertheless, nobody would suggest that acts of larceny should be punished when committed without *mens rea*'.

[44] An exception may be if the sentencing options include an absolute discharge (i.e. without conviction) and the courts were willing to treat this form of disposal as commonplace.

[45] 'Morally defamed', as opposed to defamed in law, since the state is a privileged wrongdoer in such cases. The phrase is used here to convey the sense of an untrue and adverse labelling by the state, in that the defendant is labelled with a stigmatic criminal conviction where the implicit social meaning of that label is unjustified.

is characteristically private; it may affect D, and even harm D's interests, but it lacks the authoritative voice of the state and normally does not undermine his membership of the community. An act of defamation may bring D into conflict with P, but it normally does not alienate D from society.[46] By contrast, convictions are official. They condemn D on behalf of society as a whole. To say that D has a criminal record is to say that he has been labelled as a reprehensible wrongdoer; that the state has made a formal adverse statement about *him*. Moreover, the statement marks D out in such a way that it becomes appropriate, within the community, for the regard in which he is held to be affected. Certain exclusions, both social and professional, may legitimately follow.[47] As such, the criminal record becomes part of the material that frames D's engagement with his community, with adverse implications for D's ability to live his life—a life that is, in part, defined in terms of D's interactions within, and membership of, his society. The conviction (and indeed the punishment, in its censorious facet) tends not only to censure D for the particular act that is proscribed, but also to undermine D's participation in the society itself.

### Censure and Stigma

We can elaborate this concern by distinguishing between censure, which the state expresses through its *action* of convicting (and punishing) the defendant, and the *effect* of that action, in terms of the stigma that attaches to D and his conduct. Of course, as the foregoing discussion has suggested, one reason why the state ought not falsely to censure D for a serious crime is supplied by the consequences for D's life. But the two do not always go together, and D has a right to be neither falsely censured *nor* falsely stigmatized. Even if D suffers no stigma,[48] the state should not purport to censure him without believing him to be culpable. Telling lies is wrong in itself and not merely because of the consequences.

Consider, on the other hand, an argument that the state is not *really* censuring D, since both the state and D know that fault has not been proved when D is convicted of a strict liability offence. The problem with this 'private colloquy' reasoning is that the state should not ignore the significance of its actions for others. When labelling D guilty of a stigmatic crime, the state is bound by the public meaning of the words it uses. Thus, for example, Parliament cannot legitimately enact an offence of 'paedophilia', defined as 'parking for more than

---

[46] Save in special cases, e.g. where the sentiments are pervasively held, or where P has representative standing in the community.

[47] Depending on the crime for which D is convicted, he may be ostracized by his peers, disenfranchised (for life in some US states), excluded from certain professions (e.g. law), disqualified as a company director, prevented from working with children, refused insurance coverage (if a fraudster), etc.

[48] In some circumstances, particular convictions may even become something of a badge of honour; e.g. for members of some gangs, or more generally—such as a conviction for contempt of Congress following refusal to testify before the House Un-American Activities Committee during the McCarthy era.

36 *A. P. Simester*

one hour on a central London street'.[49] It cannot do so because that is not what paedophilia means.[50] Even if D understands that the label is a technical usage, the state may not disregard the rest of its audience, and the effect that such a label will have on D's life.

Treating a conviction for 'paedophilia' as highly stigmatic is, of course, a reasonable public response. A more difficult case would arise if the reaction of the public, in terms of stigmatizing D, is unreasonable and far exceeds what is deserved in light of the state's censure. Suppose that, in the public mind, parking offenders (labelled as such) came to be regarded like paedophiles. In that event, a strict liability parking conviction, although not intended as censorious, would be highly stigmatic. Even in this sort of case, at least where the stigma is predictable, it seems to me that the state should take account of the consequences of a conviction for defendants. The offence should no longer involve strict liability.[51]

## Rights and Instrumental Reasons

Of course, some error in the criminal justice system is unavoidable. When the state convicts a person of a stigmatic offence, it generally requires that guilt be proved beyond reasonable doubt. Inevitably, this leaves open the possibility that a particular defendant, properly convicted on that standard of proof, is not in fact guilty. The defamation and wrongful punishment of such persons is none the less justified. Moreover, it is justified by consequential reasons: in particular, by the need to set an achievable standard of proof if society is to have a practicable criminal justice system *at all*. It might be thought that an analogy can be drawn between these instrumental considerations, which permit wrongful convictions whenever the criminal proof standard is met, and those set out in § 2, which support convictions on the basis of strict liability.

But the analogy strikes me as false. Where guilt is proved beyond reasonable doubt in stigmatic crimes, the state convicts in good faith—D is believed to be culpable. Further, although error is systemic it remains unsystematic: the distribution of error is unknown, and we cannot predict the likelihood that any particular conviction is a mistake. By contrast, where strict liability is employed in a stigmatic crime, the state consistently labels D as a culpable wrongdoer without believing this to be true. Moreover, defamation is predictable—there are reasons for thinking that the state is particularly likely to censure and punish D wrongly in that class of cases. Hence, while instrumental considerations of an institutional nature may sometimes be relied upon to justify the risk of good-faith erroneous

---

[49] For the sake of illustration, this example is deliberately extreme. But it may be less far-fetched (especially in the current political climate) to imagine anti-terrorism legislation that enacted an offence, so defined, of 'Endangering the Safety of the Realm'.

[50] This constraint binds individuals too: D should not call E a paedophile when he overstays his parking permit.

[51] Notice, however, that this is not a problem specific to strict liability; these sorts of cases also present difficulties for *mens rea* offences.

convictions, arguments of this type seem inadequate to justify strict liability for stigmatic crimes.

## Rights and Quasi-Criminal Regulations

I have argued that the right not to be wrongly censured defeats any instrumental case for strict liability in stigmatic crimes. When it comes to non-stigmatic offences, however, that right is not engaged. For such offences, therefore, the arguments canvassed in § 2 are not ruled out, and remain capable of justifying strict liability. But before we can safely reach that conclusion, we need to consider at least two other intrinsic concerns about the use of strict liability, concerns that do not depend on there being a censorious implication from conviction to censure. These concerns consequently apply to quasi-criminal regulations as well as to stigmatic crimes.

### Undeserved 'Hard Treatment'

Punishment for stigmatic offences involves, in addition to censure, the imposition of hard treatment—that is, onerous deprivations of assets or liberties. This is also a feature of sanctions, characteristically fines, attached to quasi-criminal regulations. The infliction of hard treatment itself stands in need of justification. Ordinarily in the criminal law, the hard treatment is justified in virtue of the fact that D deserves it. But that justification is normally unavailable where the offence is one of strict liability.

How pressing is this concern? Not very. Hard treatment or deprivation may legitimately be imposed for a variety of reasons. Tort law frequently deprives D of assets for reasons grounded in the interests of P. Similarly, deprivations through the taxation system are imposed for all sorts of purposes. Unlike punishment, hard treatment need not be justified in terms of D's desert. Thus fines for strict liability offences, understood as mere hard treatment and not punishment, may in principle be justified by considerations of deterrence or as part of a regime distributing the costs of an activity, voluntarily undertaken, that benefits D and which typically imposes risks on others who, unlike D, have not volunteered for exposure to D's risk-creating activity.

On the other hand, the matter would be very different if parking tickets were to attract a sanction of imprisonment,[52] for at least two reasons. First, if the imposition of a sanction is to be morally legitimate, its level and nature should be warranted *within* the terms of the rationale by which the offence is justified. It seems clear that imprisonment cannot be accommodated, for example, within a cost-allocation model of non-stigmatic offences.

More generally, it is arguable that imprisonment is inherently a punitive sanction; as such, its imposition is always illegitimate unless deserved. Indeed,

---

[52] Note, too, the interesting issue of disqualifications, which can substantially impair a individual's freedom and opportunities.

there may very well be a human right not to be imprisoned save in accordance with justified punishment.[53] Such a right would straightforwardly interdict imprisonment for parking offences.

But one can concede all this without foreclosing the possibility of strict liability offences. No doubt it is wrong to imprison a person without proof of fault. But that is a matter of sentencing rather than offence: as such, it mandates certain limitations upon sentencing rather than a bar to conviction. Thus it appears to be a special case of a different right, namely the right not to suffer grossly disproportionate punishment.[54] The state might avoid abrogating this right, for example, by enacting dual—strict and *mens rea*—regimes of offence, the former incurring fines and the latter imprisonable, where it was thought that certain culpable transgressions should attract prison sentences.

Indeed, strictly speaking, the injunction against grossly disproportionate punishment does not even foreclose the possibility of strict liability offences carrying terms of imprisonment, provided that sentences of imprisonment were not actually imposed without proof of fault. Such offences, however, may be more likely to be regarded by the public as stigmatic crimes rather than quasi-criminal regulations and, as such, risk violating the injunction against undeserved censure.

## A Right to Fair Warning

Prima facie, strict liability also breaches the requirement for fair warning, since citizens may have no way of knowing or predicting when they might be about to incur criminal liability.[55] No doubt the public needs to be protected from the harms that non-stigmatic offences are designed to prevent. But the public also needs to be protected from random liability. It is a rule of law value that D should have fair opportunity to evade criminal labels and sanctions. Arguably, criminal liability without fault breaches rule of law requirements, because it undermines the confidence one can have of staying on the right side of the law.

We need, however, to be careful here. The claim that strict criminal liability violates rule of law requirements is not *unarguably* true. Certainly, the criminal law is there not solely to tell police and judges what to do after someone offends, but also to tell citizens what not to do in advance. As such, the law should offer guidance to citizens. But typically, strict liability rules *do* offer *ex ante* guidance. Provided that strict liability offences are clearly drafted in sufficiently precise terms ('when driving, do not exceed 70 miles per hour on the highway'), they are capable of putting citizens on notice that precautions must be taken to avoid

---

[53] Cf. the right not to suffer inhuman or degrading treatment espoused in Article 3 of the European Convention on Human Rights; discussed in this volume by Sullivan, Ch. 8. Compare, in Canada, *References re Section 94(2) of Motor Vehicle Act (BC)* (1985) 24 DLR (4th) 536.

[54] Cf. D. van Z. Smit and A. Ashworth, 'Disproportionate Sentences as Human Rights Violations' (2004) 67 *Modern LR* 541.

[55] See A. Ashworth, *Principles of Criminal Law* (3rd edn., Oxford 1999), 76–7; Simester and Sullivan, *Criminal Law*, § 2.3.

perpetrating an *actus reus*. Indeed, this potential is implicit in the very use of strict liability offences for deterrent purposes.

Admittedly, there may be strict liability offences, especially situational offences, where the prohibition is action-unspecific and D cannot be said, in virtue of his conduct, to have advance notice that the offence is about to occur. But this is not an inherent feature of strict liability offences; indeed, in practice they tend to regulate voluntary specialist activities. Neither is the objection specific to strict liability offences. Negligence-based offences, especially those involving omissions, present the same difficulty. At root, this objection seems to be no more than a special case of the objections to moral luck and to liability for inadvertent conduct or status more generally.

A distinction can be drawn between fair warning and avoidability. In *Smedleys Ltd.* v. *Breed*,[56] the defendants were convicted of an offence against section 2(1) of the Food and Drugs Act 1955 after supplying to a retail store a tin of peas that was found to contain a caterpillar. The defendants, whose factory canned 3.5 million tins of peas during the picking season, were found to have taken all reasonable precautions during the canning process to prevent the presence of the caterpillar in the tin; its presence was, in practice, unavoidable.[57] Yet there is fair warning in such cases: those who participate in canning peas will, inevitably, commit an offence against the Food and Drugs Act 1955.

The warning is, of course, generic to the underlying activity of canning peas and not to the specific occasion on which the offence is committed. Nevertheless, in the case of non-censorious hard treatment, this level of advance notice seems sufficient. In other areas of law, especially tort, generic warnings are frequently the only form of advance notice available. The facts of *Smedleys Ltd.* v. *Breed*, for example, are analogous to cases of product liability, where remedies are awarded against defendants who have voluntarily assumed the risks that their activities generate without knowing, *ex ante*, when or how those risks may crystallize.[58] Similarly, in *Rylands* v. *Fletcher*,[59] the rule that the defendant should compensate the plaintiff can be justified by reference to the defendant's voluntary creation of a potential hazard, rather than by any finding that the defendant was wrong to create that hazard or that the particular occurrence which caused loss was specifically predictable. Even though the crystallization of risk in these cases is unknown, as in *Smedleys Ltd.* v. *Breed*, it can—and should—be planned for, and the financial costs smoothed, by taking out insurance and making financial provisions through reserves.[60]

---

[56] [1974] AC 839.

[57] The caterpillar was similar in colour, size, density, and weight to the peas in the tin, was sterile and would not have constituted a danger to health if consumed.

[58] Compare, too, the eggshell-skull rule, which holds that defendants are liable for the abnormal and individually unpredictable frailties of plaintiffs, in part on the basis that it is foreseeable that some proportion of plaintiffs in society will have eggshell skulls, albeit the particular distribution to individual plaintiffs is unknowable. [59] (1868) LR 3 HL 330.

[60] Sullivan argues in this volume, Ch. 8, that 'A company like Smedleys can absorb these uncertainties, and the costs of appellate litigation, into its risk assessments and financial contingencies. Yet

## The *Criminal* Institution: Can We Really Separate Stigmatic from Non-Stigmatic Offences?

The case against strict liability in stigmatic crimes assumes that crimes can be stigmatic even though strict. Conversely, the case for strict liability in non-stigmatic offences assumes that the connection, normally found in the criminal law, between hard treatment and punishment can be severed, so that quasi-criminal regulations attract convictions and sanctions that are not perceived as censorious. Each of these assumptions stipulates a category that is conceptually possible. But it is a contingent matter whether those categories are populated.

So far as the first category is concerned, the presumption that, if imposed on a strict liability basis, the label 'criminal-μ' continues to retain its stigmatic quality is plausible but non-trivial, and need not readily be accepted. It is characteristic in many offences for the public to look behind the fact of a conviction where such convictions are routinely imposed on a strict liability basis, although whether this will actually occur may depend on the scale of the associated sanctions and other factors. If, for example, a crime potentially attracts sentences of imprisonment, it may very well be regarded as stigmatic even when liability is strict.[61]

The conceptual category of quasi-criminal regulations is rather more problematic. Using the 'criminal' law in non-stigmatic offences necessarily links such transgressions to the paradigm of censure and sanctions by which crimes are distinguished from other forms of legal wrong. It is no surprise, therefore, that the line between quasi-criminal regulations and 'true' stigmatic crimes is not easy to draw. If a clear distinction between 'quasi-criminal' and 'truly criminal' offences cannot be drawn, or if that distinction fails to secure public recognition, then the present objection to strict liability carries over to quasi-criminal regulations, trumping for both models the instrumental arguments set out in § 2. Strict liability convictions are likely then to generate both over- and understatement: they risk being understood as communications, in some cases, that D is a culpable wrongdoer when she is in truth blameless and, on other occasions, that D may not

---

the proprietor of a small business in similar circumstances might well not be able to sustain such costs and pressures.' But if we disregard the costs of appellate litigation (surely rare in this context), and assuming the offence is committed in the same proportion, it is not clear how a smaller business is in different case. It will commit the offence fewer times, and *ex ante* should make the same proportionate provisions. If it cannot afford to do so then, assuming the hard treatment is justified (e.g. as a form of cost allocation), it should not be in the business.

[61] Another consideration will be whether the same label, μ, is standardly used for different types of offences, in which case the class of strict liability convictions is less likely to be distinguished in the public mind from convictions for μing that rest on proof of culpability. An example of this might be the strict liability offence of homicide reviewed in *New Jersey* v. *Rodriguez* (1994) 645 A 2d 1165, discussed in this volume by Doug Husak, Ch. 4. The serious stigma attached to other forms of culpable homicide may be expected to inform, rather than be undermined by, public perceptions of the offence in *Rodriguez*.

be a culpable wrongdoer (since convicted only of a strict liability offence) when she is in truth culpable and deserving of public censure.

Moreover, it is not at all obvious that extending criminal liability to non-stigmatic offences is good for the criminal law. To do so risks undermining the moral authority of the criminal law generally, through weakening the paradigm association of criminal laws with culpable wrongdoing. Thor's hammer was not meant for driving nails: as Sayre once observed, 'When it becomes respectable to be convicted, the vitality of the criminal law has been sapped.'[62] Blurring the condemnatory messages that are part of the institution's defining marque leaves the criminal law more closely aligned to civil law. It threatens superfluous duplication and diminishes a distinct, valuable tool for social control and doing justice.

The problem is exacerbated when strict liability is deployed in stigmatic crimes. In addition to the intrinsic wrongness of convicting the blameless of such crimes, there is the instrumental objection that this, too, tends to muffle the distinctive moral voice of the criminal law. If the public begins to discount the importance of criminal prohibitions and convictions, we risk the loss of criminal law not only as a distinctive labelling device but also as a tool of education; a means by which conduct, perhaps not widely recognized as untoward, can be marked out and condemned as a serious wrong.

All this suggests that a clear line between quasi-criminal regulations and stigmatic crimes cannot, and should not, be drawn within the existing system of *criminal* justice. To the extent that quasi-criminal regulations are, or are perceived to be, 'criminal' at all, they invoke the intrinsic objections made earlier in this section, which rule out strict liability. And if they are not stigmatic at all, then they should not even be 'quasi' criminal.

Yet the force of the instrumental justifications for strict liability, set out in § 2, remains. One possible accommodation would be for the state to modify the existing system, entrenching more deeply the distinction between stigmatic crimes and non-stigmatic offences, by instituting a second regime—say of administrative *violations*—covering minor offences, punishable only by small fines, where strict liability might legitimately be deployed.[63] Violations, so labelled, would be 'criminal' in so far as they share some of the features of criminal law and procedure, including rules of evidence, but would be, by their formal categorization, clearly marked off from the criminal law. In what follows, I shall assume for the sake of argument that a perceptible boundary either exists or can be constructed between the two varieties of proscription, such that any given offence falls clearly on one side or the other.

---

[62] 'The Present Significance of *Mens Rea* in the Criminal Law', in R. Pound (ed.), *Harvard Legal Essays* (Cambridge, Mass. 1934), 399 at 409.

[63] Similar, perhaps, to the French system of *contraventions*, described in this volume by John Spencer and Antje Pedain, Ch. 10.

## 4. Defending Strict Liability (Sometimes) in Stigmatic Crimes

Sometimes, formal strict liability is not in substance strict. This occurs where the fault element contained in the rest of the offence, i.e. disregarding the strict liability elements, is sufficient to underpin an attribution of culpability for the offence in its entirety. There are a number of ways in which this can occur, although not all are important or controversial.

### Strict Liability Going to a Non-Material Element

I mention this case only for completeness. Trivially, strict liability is likely to be appropriate when it is imposed with respect to a non-material element, such as a limitation of time or jurisdiction.[64] That death occurs within a year and a day of D's homicidal act was a common-law limitation to the law of murder that D need not contemplate in order to become guilty of that crime.[65] Neither, morally speaking, need he: it is a condition that does not affect D's moral culpability with regard to the homicide as a whole.

### Strict Liability Going to an Evaluative Element of the Offence

Evaluative elements are an important and difficult topic in their own right. However, for present purposes they are a peripheral case, and there is room here only to sketch their analysis. An illustration is the New Zealand case of *Police* v. *Starkey*,[66] which involved an offence against section 55 of the Local Elections and Polls Act 1976 (NZ). The section prohibits (*a*) publication of a document containing (*b*) an untrue, (*c*) and defamatory, statement (*d*) which was calculated to influence the vote of any elector. In respect of element (*c*), the court held that no *mens rea* element was required.

Formally speaking, section 55 therefore imposes strict liability. None the less, the decision seems unobjectionable. The question whether the statement was defamatory is for the court to decide, since it involves the application of an evaluative standard, the setting of which falls within the *demesne* of law. Hence it is no answer for D to say, 'I did not think it was defamatory,' or, 'in my view this was fair comment'. D must know the facts of the matter—thus D must know the content of the statement he publishes—but he need neither know nor concur with the normative evaluation of those facts that the law makes.[67]

[64]  See above, n. 3. Strictly speaking, the possibility of this case was foreclosed by the definition of 'strict liability' I adopted in § 1.

[65]  Now repealed in Britain: Law Reform (Year and a Day Rule) Act 1996 (UK).

[66]  [1989] 2 NZLR 373.

[67]  As it happens, s. 55 requires that D intend to publish the statement. In principle, a negligence standard, such that D ought to have known the content of the statement that he published, would suffice to avoid the offence's being one of substantive strict liability.

Similarly, whether conduct is 'dangerous', 'indecent', or, say, 'obscene' is a matter for the jury, something to be measured by a standard independent of the defendant: D's deliberate conduct either is or is not dangerous (obscene, etc.), irrespective of D's own view of the matter.[68] If D puts his hand up V's skirt while dancing in a nightclub, the assault (if it be one) is indecent[69] regardless whether D thinks it is appropriate behaviour in that context. Such *actus reus* elements mix fact and law. They operate as normative standards, requiring an objective assessment which may well be at variance with D's evaluation of his conduct.[70]

One rationale for imposing formal strict liability in respect of evaluative elements is authoritarian. The rule of law requires not only that criminal laws be not discretionary in the hands of individual officials, but also that they be fixed in the hands of citizens. The very point of a law prohibiting, say, obscene conduct is to co-ordinate social interaction by imposing a common standard of acceptable behaviour, displacing the potentially divergent standards that persons have for themselves. Such co-ordination would be unachievable if people were exempted from the scope of that law simply because they had different personal values. Even in stigmatic crimes, what counts as wrongful behaviour must be determined by a standard independent of the particular defendant.

Suppose, then, that for a valuable purpose the legislature enacts a stigmatic crime imposing some common evaluative standard, in respect of which liability is formally strict. Does the crime thereby impose substantive strict liability? Sometimes it will, as English law often does when it disallows any claim of reasonable mistake of law as a defence. In such cases, the rule of law justification results in a crime that is objectionable for the reasons given in § 3. But in other cases, formal strict liability need not result in conviction of the blameless.

In these latter cases, D's very mis-assessment of the situation can be constitutive of his culpability. That D thinks his conduct is not dangerous may be unproblematic because D is simply wrong, and culpably so. The adjudication whether, say, a particular instance of D's driving is dangerous is not arbitrary: the considerations affecting that judgment are, in turn, considerations that we can expect individuals such as D to take account of, and we can blame D for failing sufficiently to acknowledge them when acting. If D knowingly takes a blind corner at 80 miles per hour, he not only drives dangerously; we can reprove him for thinking it an acceptable manœuvre. Moreover, evaluative terms, at least those in common

---

[68] Again, D would have to be at least negligent regarding the facts of the matter. If for instance D had no reason to know that he was in fact driving well in excess of the speed limit (perhaps because the speedometer was malfunctioning), his driving might therefore not be accounted dangerous. The evaluative *actus reus* standard is applied to the facts that, as the case may be, D knew or ought to have known.          [69] Or now, in the UK, 'sexual': Sexual Offences Act 2003, s. 3.

[70] The same holds when evaluative elements occur in defences, as when D uses unreasonable force in self-defence. It is for the court to determine whether the force used was reasonable (taking account of the circumstances that D believed to exist); and it is no defence that D herself thought her response proportionate. See *Owino* [1996] 2 Cr. App. R. 128, contradicting *Scarlett* [1993] 4 All ER 629; Simester and Sullivan, *Criminal Law*, § 17.1(v).

parlance, need not make liability unpredictable or unavoidable. We understand them and know how to apply the implicit judgments they import; especially where there is a high degree of social consensus about what counts as appropriate behaviour in the relevant context. In matters of road safety, for instance, a proscription of 'careless' or 'dangerous' driving may tell drivers all they really need to know.

## Constructive Liability

Suppose that a stigmatic crime is enacted of the form, it is an offence to do X in circumstance Y or with consequence Y. Further, suppose that the *actus reus* elements of X all have corresponding *mens rea* elements, that Y is a matter of strict liability, and that Y is a material element. (Let us call this type of crime an 'X + Y' crime.)

Provided certain conditions are met, strict liability crimes of this type need not involve the conviction of persons who are blameless in respect of the occurrence of Y. Consider the example set out at the beginning of this chapter:

Deborah is driving through a village at a speed 20 miles per hour in excess of the speed limit. Unexpectedly she loses control of her car, mounts the pavement, and kills Allan, who had been walking quietly toward the corner shop in order to buy a newspaper.

This scenario may be proscribed by an X + Y offence, where X specifies dangerous driving and Y specifies the causing of death. Such an offence is one that, formally, imposes strict liability. Yet it does not invoke the objections raised in § 3. (Although it does raise the question, to be taken up later, whether it is fair to punish Deborah *more* because Allan is killed.) Certainly it is, in one sense, unchosen and outwith Deborah's control that Allan is killed. But the possibility of that outcome is not random or unrelated to the wrong that Deborah does in driving dangerously. Here, the risk of causing death forms part of the very reason why dangerous driving is wrongful and, indeed, is typically criminalized in its own right.[71]

What sorts of constraints apply to legitimate constructive liability? The most important constraint concerns the relationship between X and Y. To illustrate, consider an alternative scenario:

Jane bears a grudge against Daniel. She throws a stone at him while in an open field, intending to injure him. Daniel ducks and she misses. The stone damages Daniel's binoculars, which were lying concealed in the long grass.

An X + Y offence covering this case, of assault causing property damage, would not be appropriate. To impose strict liability here would be wrong because there is no connection between Jane's culpability and the harm she has done. Vandalism is

---

[71] Cf. s. 1 of the Road Traffic Act 1988 (UK).

a very different type of offence from assault, and the prospect of property damage does not supply reasons why, *ex ante*, Jane's assault was a wrong. Strict liability is objectionable in this case because it makes a stigmatic conviction turn on luck rather than desert.

The distinction at work here is between two types of risk: intrinsic and extrinsic.[72] Jane should not be held criminally liable for damaging Daniel's property because that risk was extrinsic to her culpability. Such risks affect the outcome, and perhaps affect our retrospective judgments about what D did, but they are not factors to take into account when deciding, in advance, what D should do. By contrast, in the dangerous driving case the risk of death was intrinsic to Deborah's culpability: it formed part of the reason why, even *ex ante*, her behaviour was wrong. It is her commission of X that brings the risk of Y into play. Where that risk is intrinsic, there seems no difficulty about holding D responsible and culpable for Y.

Moreover, X + Y crimes are consistent with the rule of law. Where the connection in such offences is predicated on intrinsic risk, they do not defeat the desire to give fair warning in criminal law. D is sufficiently forewarned of her potential criminal liability since she can only be convicted if she has committed the preliminary wrong specified in X (e.g. dangerous driving) with *mens rea*;[73] and the risk of Y forms part of the rationale for blaming D and regarding that preliminary commission of X as wrong.[74] Thus liability for the full constructive crime is both predictable and something she has a fair opportunity to avoid.[75] At the same time, crimes of this form have the advantage of publicly highlighting the seriousness of the wrong (killing) involved in D's conduct, with an emphasis that cannot be achieved by enacting a generic offence of dangerous driving.

X + Y crimes are also capable of advancing the goal of representative labelling in the law.[76] It would be incomplete and therefore inaccurate merely to describe Deborah's conduct as dangerous driving. Even where the *mens rea* for two offences

[72] Cf. B. A. O. Williams, 'Moral Luck', in *Moral Luck* (Cambridge 1981), 25–6.

[73] See J. Gardner, 'Rationality and the Rule of Law in Offences Against the Person' [1994] *Cambridge LJ* 502, at 521–3. I have assumed, but cannot argue here, that dangerous driving is a *mens rea* offence of (gross) negligence. Compare s. 2A(1) of the Road Traffic Act 1988 (UK), which defines a person's driving as dangerous if '(a) the way he drives falls far below what would be expected of a competent and careful driver, and (b) it would be obvious to a competent and careful driver that driving in that way would be dangerous'.

[74] This further point presupposes that the goal of giving potential offenders fair warning of their crimes does not always require advertence by defendants to the *actus reus;* i.e. that crimes of negligence are capable of giving fair warning.

[75] The intrinsic/extrinsic risk distinction supports a better analysis of constructive liability than is offered by Jeremy Horder: 'A Critique of the Correspondence Principle in Criminal Law' [1995] *Criminal LR* 759, at 764. Horder argues that a person who deliberately wrongs another changes his normative position *vis-à-vis* the risk of adverse consequences to that other person, whether or not foreseen or reasonably foreseeable. This is, in effect, an outlaw theory, and should be rejected. Not anything goes: although a person's deliberate wrong does change his normative position, it does not do so with respect to risks extrinsic to that wrong. Horder's account offers only an opportunity to avoid liability and not predictability. [76] See e.g. Simester and Sullivan, *Criminal Law*, § 2.4.

is the same, representative labelling in the criminal law is responsive to harm. Inchoate crimes, such as reckless endangerment by dangerous driving, attempts to kill, and the like, are wrongful not because they involve any direct (e.g. physical) harm to the victim, but because D wrongfully manipulates, subordinates, or attacks V's interests and autonomy. By contrast, when an attempt succeeds, when dangerous driving kills, the harm is rather different. V is dead. Only by acknowledging that fact can the criminal law communicate what D has done.

Not all existing offences meet the constraint set out here. Perhaps the best-known X + Y offence in English criminal law is manslaughter by an unlawful act. If D commits a crime which creates a foreseeable risk of *some* harm to V, D becomes guilty of manslaughter should his preliminary crime in fact cause V's death—there is no *mens rea* requirement concerning the crucial *actus reus* element, death. The problem with this form of manslaughter is that the range of offences capable of constituting the predicate unlawful act is too wide for death to be an intrinsic risk.[77] The offence therefore imposes a form of *substantive* strict liability, since defendants are at risk of being convicted of a homicide offence without proof of sufficient culpability with respect to V's death. The device of constructive liability is misused, evading what should normally be the minimum culpability requirements for a homicide conviction. As such, moreover, defendants have insufficient warning that their conduct might lead to a conviction for manslaughter; neither does that label necessarily reflect the extent of the offender's culpability for homicide. Similar objections may be made to the law of felony-murder in the United States.

Implicit in the discussion so far is a second constraint: that X must be a wrong. Where X is permissible notwithstanding the risk of Y, an attribution of culpability cannot be made out. Blame presupposes a wrong: something for which one can be blamed. Thus one cannot be blameworthy for doing the right thing, although one may not always deserve praise for the action (e.g. when one's motives for giving to charity were selfish). Many legitimate activities create at least remote risks of harm. Turning on a light switch may, if there is miswiring or a short circuit, cause injury. Even careful driving risks death. Yet these activities are not wrong; neither do they become wrongs simply because they lead to injury or death. Imposing constructive liability in such cases would, therefore, be illegitimate since it would lead to conviction and punishment of the blameless.

*Semi-Constructive Liability*

A feature of constructive liability is that, typically, X specifies something that is an offence in its own right. In paradigm constructive liability crimes, the occurrence of Y operates as an aggravating element, constituting a second, more serious, crime. Is this a necessary feature of legitimate X + Y criminalization?

---

[77] See e.g. *Mallet* [1972] Crim. LR 260. D punched V who fell awkwardly, striking his head and sustaining fatal brain injuries. D received only a suspended sentence of imprisonment.

Seemingly not. Perhaps the easiest case is where X is not itself a criminal offence, but where it would be legitimate to make it one. In this case, the strict liability element can operate as a form of dispensation; the gravamen of the crime is X, but there is a fortuitous exemption from criminal liability where Y does not eventuate.[78] If there were no offence of dangerous driving, say, it would still be legitimate to enact an offence of dangerous driving causing death, for the same reasons that justify constructive liability.

A distinction exists between two types of case. The first is where (while X itself may or may not be criminalized) Y operates as an aggravating factor; the second is where Y (or more precisely, the absence of Y) operates purely as a dispensing element. In the first case, the occurrence of Y makes the X + Y crime of which D is convicted more serious than would have been a crime simply of X; it may also— and typically does—lead to the imposition of greater punishments.[79] I have argued that, where the relationship between X and Y is one of intrinsic risk, such crimes do not impose substantive strict liability. The culpability element in X extends also to element Y, so that X + Y is not a crime of substantive strict liability.

In the second case, X is not criminalized (though it might have been); Y need not aggravate the seriousness of the crime and may operate purely as a dispensing condition. If Y does not add to or change the wrong in X, its presence may reflect institutional considerations; there seems no reason why the relationship between X and Y in such cases need be one of intrinsic risk, provided it is not arbitrary.[80]

This form of dispensation has rule of law benefits, since it confines what otherwise might be wide-ranging discretionary powers of arrest and prosecution. Suppose, for example, that the legislature were to contemplate criminalizing a failure to disclose one's HIV-positive status to sexual partners. One way of min-imizing the risk of malicious or discriminatory prosecutions would be to qualify the offence by a strict liability requirement that one's partner consequently becomes infected. This requirement would also have the practical advantages of reducing the costs of policing and the need for invasive methods of surveillance: Y must occur before the criminal justice system, with all its intrusion and expense, is in play.

However, pay-offs of this sort do not warrant adding *any* filtering element to the offence. The element should not be arbitrary. Suppose that there were no offence of dangerous driving, but that the state were to enact an offence of danger-ous driving within one mile of any building painted red (where the latter element were one of strict liability). The strict liability element here has no impact on the proscribed wrong. It is normatively immaterial, so that defendants who are culp-able in respect of driving dangerously cannot claim to lack culpability for the full offence. None the less, arbitrary dispensations of this sort violate constraints of

---

[78] Cf. A. Michaels, 'Constitutional Innocence' (1999) 112 *Harvard LR* 828.

[79] I return to this issue below.

[80] See too the discussion of objective conditions of liability in German law by John Spencer and Antje Pedain in this volume, Ch. 10.

fairness in the distribution of convictions and punishment. It is unfair to single
out one person rather than another for punishment, when both are equally
deserving, unless there are good reasons—which may in part be institutional—for
distributing such burdens unevenly. Arbitrary rules violate this requirement.

### Compounding the Wrong?

A difficult case remains where X is morally dubious but not itself sufficiently
serious to warrant criminalization. The claim that X + Y crimes may be legitimate
in these cases rests on the proposition that the wrong committed if Y occurs is different from, and more serious than, the wrong specified in X alone. Hence
(according to this claim), a case may be made for enacting an offence of 'being
drunk in a public place and causing injury to another' that is stronger than the
case for enacting an offence of 'being drunk in a public place'.[81] Even where
the latter is not thought to warrant criminalization, the former may. Moreover,
the strict liability component of the offence continues to supply a reason why the
commission of X is itself a wrong (albeit not criminalized), something that is
signalled by the state when it enacts the compound form of crime.

The most plausible cases of this variety are where X is a wrong but, for institutional reasons, is insufficiently serious to warrant criminalization *simpliciter*,
e.g. because the enforcement of its proscription would be impractical. Again,
provided that the risk of Y is intrinsic to the reasons for which X is a wrong, these
cases do not seem to impose substantive strict liability. But, like constructive
liability crimes, they raise a related concern: is it right to treat strict liability
elements as aggravating or compounding the seriousness of the wrong done?
*Should* the occurrence of Y escalate the punishment imposed for constructive
liability crimes? It may be appropriate to label Deborah's conduct as dangerous
driving causing death, but should the occurrence of death lead to significantly
increased punishment? Similarly, should the occurrence of Y compound some
lesser wrongs sufficiently to warrant criminalization where, absent Y, they do not?

This is a familiar problem of moral luck, not specific to strict liability.[82]
Notoriously, grossly negligent or reckless endangerment of life is not criminalized
even though, if death occurs, the case becomes one of manslaughter. Attempted
crimes are punished less severely than if the attempt succeeds. Like constructive
liability offences, what makes the difference in each case is an *actus reus* element
for which no additional *mens rea* element is required.

Two types of objection may be levelled at the role of moral luck in criminal law.
First, it may be suggested that the dependence of outcomes on luck means that
we should not be held responsible for such outcomes. Horder, for example, has
suggested that the 'autonomy principle' (requiring that responsibility depend

[81] Compare the offence contained in s. 362 of the Insolvency Act 1986 (UK) of becoming bank-
rupt within two years of losing property by gambling.
[82] But see, in the strict liability context, the discussion by Ken Simons, 'When is Strict Criminal
Liability Just?' (1997) 87 *Journal of Criminal Law and Criminology* 1075, at § V.

upon an exercise of choice or control) rules out moral luck,[83] while Lacey opposes blame for negligent harm with a similar argument.[84] This objection is too strong. Even though many factors affecting an outcome may be beyond an agent's control, it does not follow that the outcome itself is beyond her control. It is only *given* the agent's behaviour that the outcome is (thereafter) beyond her control. Thus an agent exercises control over the outcome *through* her behaviour. It is her negligence, or her pulling the trigger, that brings the uncontrolled factors into play, and makes outcome luck relevant. Where that luck is intrinsic and forms part of the reasons why her antecedent behaviour (negligence, attempt, etc.) is wrong, there seems no difficulty about blaming the agent for the outcome.

A more powerful objection is that, while not defeating the allocation of responsibility altogether, moral luck should make no *difference* to our moral judgments of agents.[85] In turn, the criminal law's response to wrongdoing should be unaffected by the actual outcome to the extent that it depends on luck. Hence, even in legitimate instances of constructive liability, the occurrence of the strict liability element should have no effect on the *quantum* of punishment D receives—since it makes no difference to D's culpability. I can offer no answer to this objection here, since it raises large questions that go beyond the scope of this chapter. In legitimate constructive liability crimes, we may be culpable for the entirety of X + Y, and X + Y may specify a different wrong from X; but are we more culpable than if X alone occurs?

Whatever the answer to that question, notice that, even if we are no more culpable, it does not follow that punishments for X + Y crimes should be reduced to those warranted for X alone. The reverse may apply; lesser punishment for X alone may then be seen as dispensation, an extension of mercy to undeserving offenders who, fortunately, did no harm.

## 5. Conclusion

Nagel once remarked that strict liability 'may have its legal uses, but seems irrational as a moral position'.[86] At the core, Nagel was right. The moral condemnation

[83] Horder, 'Critique of the Correspondence Principle', 760.

[84] *State Punishment* (London 1988), 64: 'In a sense . . . the harm becomes fortuitous: all that the defendant is directly responsible *for* in the capacity sense is her failure to meet a reasonable standard in her actions. For example, the consequences of the actions of a negligent driver will depend on a number of extraneous circumstances, such as traffic conditions and the standard of care and skill exercised by other drivers: once she sets out on her journey in a careless or absent-minded frame of mind, whether or not she commits a serious criminal offence will be largely a matter of luck.' Cf. J. L. Mackie, *Ethics: Inventing Right and Wrong* (New York 1977), 211: 'Morally we do often blame ourselves for what we bring about thoughtlessly. But it would be more rational, more in agreement with the general system of moral thought, only to blame ourselves for the thoughtlessness itself.'

[85] Articulated elegantly by A. Ashworth: 'Taking the Consequences', in S. Shute, J. Gardner, and J. Horder (eds.), *Action and Value in Criminal Law* (Oxford 1993), 107.

[86] 'Moral Luck', in *Mortal Questions* (Cambridge 1979), 31.

and punishment of blameless actions is wrong. Moreover, it is wrong even when a person is in some other way culpable: perhaps Jane may be to blame for throwing a stone at Daniel, but we are not therefore entitled to blame her for damaging Daniel's binoculars.[87] None the less, it should come as no surprise that this core objection to strict liability is surrounded by a complex penumbra. There are instrumental (moral) reasons for deploying strict liability in the criminal law, reasons that may on occasion justify its use in quasi-criminal regulations. Additionally, we have seen that the difference between two wrongs can be a matter of formal strict liability—indeed, of moral luck—without that foreclosing the attribution of blame for the more complex, constructive, wrong. Substantive strict liability may sometimes be justifiable on instrumental grounds but is always irrational as a moral position: formal strict liability need not be.

Once this is seen, imposing legitimate strict liability through constructive stigmatic crimes becomes an issue of criminalization. Strict liability for the consequence (Y) of a particular activity (X) turns the underlying activity, X, into a gateway. Consequential risk is not normally something over which we have full control, so that the prospect of a criminal conviction is avoidable only by sacrificing the underlying activity. It may be that Y is the harm the offence is designed to prevent. But its prevention via constructive liability is permissible only where X is a wrong from which we may legitimately expect citizens to desist.

---

[87] See above, p. 44.

# 3

# Wrongs and Faults

*John Gardner*

## 1. The Elementary Moral Distinction

The ultimate objects of moral assessment are *people* and their *lives*. I will call this 'the elementary moral distinction'. Many today seem to have lost sight of it. How often are we told that we should show respect for other people, only to discover that what we are actually being asked to show respect for is how those other people live?[1] Although these two possible objects of respect are connected, their equation should be resisted. We do not always respect a person by respecting how she lives; sometimes quite the reverse. If someone is wasting her life but still deserves to be respected, the default way to show her the respect that she deserves is to do something that improves the way she is living—shake her out of it, block her path, change her incentives, shield her from further exploitation, etc. Sometimes, of course, there is no action open to us that will yield any improvement in how she lives, while on other occasions the only things we can do are disproportionate. In such cases we have to tolerate her continuing to live as badly as she does. But toleration is one thing and respect is quite another. Toleration is the moral virtue of those who appropriately curb their wish to eliminate what they do not respect. One cannot respect the way someone is living and tolerate it at the same time.[2]

In philosophy, the contemporary neglect of the elementary moral distinction owes much to Kant. I am not thinking here of Kant's much-advertised (and much-misrepresented) doctrine of respect for persons. In so far as Kant said

Some parts of this chapter, in earlier draft, were delivered as a Brendan Francis Brown Lecture at the Catholic University of America in Washington DC on 21 September 2003. Thanks to Bill Wagner for leading the discussion on that occasion, and for various other contributions. Later drafts have profited from the detailed and insightful criticisms of Andrew Simester and John Tasioulas, to whom I am very grateful. I should also mention my gratitude to Doug Husak and Antony Duff, who together talked me out of a bad mistake.

[1] A good example: R. M. Dworkin, *Taking Rights Seriously* (London 1977), 272 ff.

[2] Of course tolerating a person's unrespectable way of living may involve respecting other things of hers, e.g. her rights. This was one of the themes of a paper that I wrote with Stephen Shute, 'The Wrongness of Rape' in Jeremy Horder (ed.), *Oxford Essays in Jurisprudence: Fourth Series* (Oxford 2000).

anything of note about respect for persons, his views were consistent with those I have just sketched.[3] Rather, I am thinking of Kant's more distinctive doctrine that a morally perfect person cannot but lead a morally perfect life. This doctrine is now often remembered, thanks to a famous exchange between Bernard Williams and Thomas Nagel, under the heading of 'moral luck'. Kant is cited by both Williams and Nagel as the philosopher who most sweepingly rejected the possibility of moral luck.[4] But on closer inspection Kant did nothing of the kind. He merely argued that morally perfect people cannot be morally unlucky in their lives.[5] Thanks to the nature of morality, he said, they cannot live lives falling short of the morally perfect lives that they deserve to live. But Kant did not deny (and did not show any reason to doubt) that morally *im*perfect people can live lives that are morally worse, or indeed morally better, than those that they deserve to live. Nor, for that matter, did he deny (or show any reason to doubt) that whether someone is a morally perfect or a morally imperfect person could itself be a matter of luck.

So Kant certainly did not abolish or attempt to abolish the elementary moral distinction. But it is true that a decline of philosophical sensitivity to that distinction has been among Kant's most enduring philosophical legacies. Kantian thinking, philosophical and popular, has simplified and radicalized Kant's own views on the subject of moral luck. So much so that even a retreat to Kant's own more modest views is sometimes perceived as a bold anti-Kantian move. Consider, for example, the group of contemporary moral philosophers who march, albeit not always in an orderly fashion, under the banner of 'virtue-ethics'. Claiming to revive a pre-Kantian tradition of ethics traceable back to Aristotle, many of them favour 'virtuously' as an answer to the question 'How should one live?'[6] Ironically, this was precisely Kant's answer to the same question, and it was one that Aristotle explicitly rejected.[7] One should of course be a morally virtuous person. That much is analytically true and accepted by Aristotle and Kant alike. But no amount of moral virtue, on Aristotle's view, ensures that one leads a morally perfect life. The morally perfect life, rather, is the life that a morally perfect person would *want* to live. Owing to bad luck, even a morally perfect person may live a morally imperfect life. This is the aspect of the human condition known as tragedy. Any large undeserved suffering or loss is nowadays casually

---

[3] Kant reminds us: 'The *object* of reverence is the [moral] law alone. . . . All reverence for a person is properly only reverence for the law (of honesty and so on) of which that person gives us an example.' *Groundwork of the Metaphysic of Morals* (trans. Paton, New York 1964), 69 n.

[4] B. Williams, 'Moral Luck', *Proceedings of the Aristotelian Society*, Suppl. 50 (1976), 115; Thomas Nagel, 'Moral Luck', *Proceedings of the Aristotelian Society*, Suppl. 50 (1976), 137.

[5] *Groundwork*, 62 ff.

[6] See R. Crisp's introduction, 'Modern Moral Philosophy and the Virtues' in Crisp (ed.), *How Should One Live: Essays on the Virtues* (Oxford 1996), 5–6.

[7] Compare Kant, *Groundwork*, 62, with Aristotle, *Nichomachean Ethics* 1153$^b$16–21. Kant holds that perfectly good character is necessary and sufficient for a perfectly good life; Aristotle that it is necessary but insufficient.

referred to as tragic. But tragedy, in the stricter classical sense illuminated by Aristotle himself, is not just any large undeserved suffering or loss. It is undeserved moral downfall. It is moral failure out of proportion to, or in extreme cases without, moral failing. It is the fate of all the great heroes from Oedipus to Othello.[8] Oedipus is an extreme case (ruled out by Kant) of moral failure not owed to moral failing. Othello is a less extreme case (never ruled out by Kant, but implicitly ruled out by many Kantians) of moral failure out of proportion to moral failing. Othello is obnoxiously jealous, but Iago exploits this moral failing to drive Othello to murder, a moral downfall more spectacular than he deserves.

Has modern theatre, like modern moral philosophy, turned its back on tragedy? Some argue that it has.[9] But our primary interest here will not be in how the elementary moral distinction has been interpreted and exposed in the arts. We will be concerned, in the main, with how it has been interpreted and exposed in the law. This may strike you as an improbable and unpromising project. For although legal systems are necessarily in the business of moral assessment, a decent legal system rarely makes moral assessments either of people or of their lives. Instead it mainly makes moral assessments of people's actions taken one at a time. Isn't this a further and different task? Aren't there really three ultimate objects of moral assessment, namely people, their lives, and their actions taken one at a time? For reasons that I hope will become clearer as we go along, this suggestion should be resisted. The elementary moral distinction is the distinction between people and their lives. Actions have moral importance on both sides of this distinction. They matter morally because both people and their lives matter morally, and both people and their lives are partly constituted by their actions. But not always at the same time, by the same actions. The two can come apart. In particular, as the great tragedies teach us, some actions morally blemish a life without morally blemishing, or more than they morally blemish, the person who lives it. And this point, I will argue, is very clearly reflected in the law. The law does not need to make moral assessments of either people or their lives in order to mark the elementary moral distinction between people and their lives as objects of moral assessment. It marks the elementary moral distinction by assessing actions, taken one at a time, in two different dimensions or under two different aspects. It assesses actions, taken one at a time, as life-constituting on the one hand and as person-constituting on the other.

---

[8] *Poetics* 1453ª1–17. For further discussion see M. Nussbaum, *The Fragility of Goodness* (Cambridge 1986), 378 ff.

[9] See Arthur Miller's 1949 *New York Times* essay 'Tragedy and the Common Man', repr. in Robert Martin (ed.), *The Theater Essays of Arthur Miller* (New York 1978), 3–7. Miller diagnosed a loss of interest in tragedy associated with the modern democratization of theatre. In response he argued, and demonstrated in *Death of a Salesman* (1949), that tragedy is not an undemocratic genre. That classical tragedians used grandees as heroes was not essential to their art. Grandees make a bigger splash when they fall, which can be good for dramatic impact, but those whose heroism is the heroism of ordinary life may fall just as far, and just as disproportionately to their failings, and hence conform just as fully to the classical idea of the tragic.

## 2.  Lives and Wrongs

My life may go well or badly because of things that happen to me. I may be injured in a train accident or inherit a fortune from a long-lost aunt. With limited exceptions[10] things that happen to me do not directly affect how well my life goes. They have an indirect effect. They affect how well my life goes by affecting what I do with my life. That I inherit a fortune does not make my life any better unless it means that I *live* better, doing more rewarding things with more interesting people, making better use of my talents, cultivating better tastes, and so forth.

One way to assess how well I live my life is morally. A morally better life is, *ceteris paribus*, a better life. The importance of living a morally better life is typically both exaggerated and underplayed. On the one hand moral success is often portrayed as the highest kind of success. A morally better life is held up as a better life come what may, not merely a better life *ceteris paribus*. On the other hand moral success is often portrayed as a self-contained kind of success, such that one can succeed in more ordinary ways (e.g. in one's marriage or career) without any moral success. In attempting to correct these two complementary errors one may easily be drawn into a tiresome demarcation dispute. Which successes and failures count as moral ones? This question seems more pivotal, the more wedded one is to the two errors just mentioned. As one leaves them behind, the classification of a certain success or failure as moral loses its most dramatic implications. For present purposes we do not, in any case, need to have a complete picture of what the moral assessment of a life includes. We need only agree on this limited, and I hope ecumenical, proposal. Whenever a life is blemished by the *wrongdoing* of the person living it, that blemish is a moral one. Notice that this proposal does not entail that all wrongdoing is moral wrongdoing. It only entails that when wrongdoing is not moral wrongdoing (e.g. it is wrongdoing only according to an immoral law), it leaves no blemish on the life of the wrongdoer.

The proposal may be ecumenical, but it is also ambiguous. For there are two quite different things we might mean by saying that someone acted wrongly. We might mean that he did something unjustified. Or we might mean that he did something in breach of duty (a.k.a. obligation). This is another fundamental distinction that sometimes gets lost in modern thinking. Many modern philosophers, indeed, have tried to establish the co-extensiveness of the two classes of

---

[10] The main exceptions are pleasures and pains. They are capable of having a direct as well as an indirect effect on the quality of my life. Among pleasures and pains there are raw or sensory pleasures and pains, that straightforwardly happen to us. But there are also pleasures and pains reflecting an awareness of value, such as the joy of falling in love and the pain of losing a loved one. Arguably the latter belong (in non-pathological cases) to the active side of our lives, and so are not ideally represented as things that happen to us. On the other hand they are also misrepresented as things that we do. For discussion see Harry Frankfurt, 'Identification and Externality', in his *The Importance of What We Care About* (Cambridge 1985), and Joseph Raz, 'When We Are Ourselves: The Active and the Passive', in his *Engaging Reason* (Oxford 1999).

wrong actions. Utilitarians of Benthamite persuasion have claimed that if an action is unjustified, it must also be in breach of duty. Indeed one's only duty, on a rigidly Benthamite view, is the duty not to perform unjustified actions. Kant and his followers, meanwhile, had the converse idea: if an action is in breach of duty, it must also be unjustified. A duty is a reason that can never be defeated by countervailing reasons; not even countervailing duties. Duties, said Kant, are incapable of conflicting with each other.

Both of these views overgeneralize. There can be actions that are in breach of duty partly because they are unjustified, and actions that are unjustified partly because they are in breach of duty.[11] But breach of duty and absence of justification do not, in general, go hand in hand. Many actions are unjustified even though they are not in breach of duty. (Today I failed to bring my umbrella out with me even though rain was forecast—silly me!) Many other actions are justified even though they are in breach of duty. (Yesterday I was late for work because I stopped to assist someone who had just been mugged.) To put it more paradoxically, there are many actions that are wrong without being wrongful, or wrongful without being wrong. The emphatic word 'wrongful', and similar terms like 'wrongdoing', 'wronged', and 'a wrong', are normally used to denote a breach of duty, whether or not it is unjustified. Whereas if we simply say that someone did the wrong thing, that normally carries the implication of an unjustified action, whether or not it is in breach of duty. At any rate, this is the linguistic convention that I will be adopting when a linguistic convention is needed.

The distinction between doing the wrong thing and doing something wrongful is of pervasive importance in most developed legal systems. The famous tort case of *Vincent* v. *Lake Erie Transportation Co.* illustrates its importance in the common law.[12] When an unexpectedly violent storm made it too perilous to set sail, a captain kept his ship moored to somebody else's pier without permission. By this action he saved his ship and crew, but damaged the pier. The pier owner sued for damages in trespass. The Minnesota Supreme Court ruled that the captain had not done the wrong thing (he had acted with ample justification), but he had acted wrongfully (he had breached a duty owed to the pier-owner not to moor his ship to the pier without permission). Because this ruling sounds paradoxical, many lawyers are reluctant to swallow it whole.[13] A common reaction to *Vincent* is to explain it away as something other than a genuine tort case. Perhaps the

[11] We will return to cases in the former class in § 4 below.    [12] 124 NW 221 (1910).

[13] For different degrees of indigestion see Ernest Weinrib, *The Idea of Private Law* (Cambridge, Mass. 1995), 196 ff., and Arthur Ripstein, *Equality, Responsibility and the Law* (Cambridge 1999), 118–21. The following thought often deepens lawyers' worries about *Vincent*. The captain is justified in keeping his ship trespassorily moored to the pier, but since it remains an actionable trespass the pier-owner is also justified (under the common law's doctrine of self-help) in using the minimum necessary force to cut the trespassory ship adrift. One may therefore imagine a situation in which the pier-owner uses minimum necessary force to cut the ship adrift, but the captain responds in like kind by using minimum necessary force to keep the ship moored. The situation escalates, and third parties join in on each side, all claiming justification. Whose side does the law take? Who is the criminal aggressor and who is the legitimate self-defender? I agree that this is a potential problem for the law.

'damages' awarded by the court for the 'tort' of 'trespass' were really more akin to a reimbursement for services rendered under the law of unjust enrichment? Perhaps the captain wronged nobody in using the pier without permission in an emergency, so long as he paid for any damage he caused in the process? Perhaps the court was merely enforcing this payment condition? It is easy to see what makes this reinterpretation appealing. But it is unnecessary. *Vincent* can be read unproblematically as a tort case. It isolates a general proposition of central importance to the common law: the mere fact that one was justified (= not wrong) in acting wrongfully does not mean that one did not act wrongfully, and does not by itself[14] block one's liability to pay reparative damages to those whom one wronged.

The same proposition is at stake in the long-running debates about 'efficient breach' in the law of contract. Some writers, especially in the Benthamite wing of the 'economic analysis' tradition, say that since damages for breach of contract are awarded in many cases in which the breach was amply justified, we should not persist in thinking of 'breach of contract' as the name of a legal wrong.[15] Any 'damages' awarded by the court for 'breach of contract' should really be evaluated on some other model, e.g. as a reimbursement for services rendered under the law of unjust enrichment. One wrongs nobody by abandoning the contract without the other party's permission so long as one pays for the other party's expenses to date. All the court does in a standard 'breach of contract' case is enforce the payment by which one licenses one's rightful abandonment of the contract. Those who resist this conclusion, especially those with broadly Kantian sympathies, have often answered that the breach only *seems* to be justified in such cases. Really, when the indomitable moral force of the contract is properly acknowledged, the breach was not justified and hence remained wrongful.[16] The two sides here are driven to their polarized conclusions by a shared error: the failure to see that, barring special cases, wrongfulness (= breach of duty) is one thing and wrongness (= absence of justification) quite another. *Pace* the Kantians, one need not deny that the breach was justified in order to insist that it was a breach of duty. Nor,

But it is not a philosophical problem. There is no reason to doubt that the two sides could both be justified simultaneously even though the justified action of one impedes or frustrates the justified action of the other. There is only the practical problem of how we are going to prevent such situations proliferating and escalating to the point at which everybody is acting unjustifiably rather than justifiably. This is an ordinary co-ordination problem to which there are a number of rival solutions, more than one of which is in all probability a justifiable solution. This being so, different legal systems may justifiably choose different solutions. In my view they may also justifiably remain silent on the problem until a relevant case arises and even then only solve it very locally, without anticipating all the possible variations on the scenario.

[14] It may block one's liability when taken in combination with other facts, such as the fact that what justified one in doing as one did was the need to protect or rescue the very person whom one thereby wronged.

[15] For a good sketch see R. Craswell, 'Two Economic Theories of Enforcing Promises', in P. Benson (ed.), *The Theory of Contract Law* (Cambridge 2001).

[16] e.g. D. Friedmann, 'The Efficient Breach Fallacy', *Journal of Legal Studies* 18 (1989), 1.

*pace* the Benthamites, need one deny that it was a breach of duty in order to insist that it was justified. The point recurs throughout the common law of tort and contract. The reason why *Vincent* brings it out more graphically than countless other tort and contract cases, and hence belongs on every student tort syllabus, is that in *Vincent* the captain was not only justified in mooring his ship to the pier, but would also have been unjustified in failing to do so. He was therefore in a strictly tragic position: the only justified action open to him was a wrongful action (one that violated the pier-owner's rights). We may be reminded of one of Aristotle's own most famous examples of tragedy, in which a sea-captain's only justified option is to jettison his cargo.[17]

Why do these cases count as tragic cases? How do wrongful actions that cannot justifiably be avoided contribute to lives that are morally less perfect than the people who live them? In the next section I will explain why justification matters in the assessment of people. But first let me explain why wrongdoing matters in the assessment of lives. Notice that this is not the same as asking why wrongdoing matters *full stop*. Wrongdoing is the breach of a duty, and a duty (or to be more exact, the fact that one has a duty) is a reason with a doubly special *categorical* and *mandatory* force (more on which in a moment). So, for any rational being—any being to whom reasons apply—wrongdoing is something especially to be avoided. That is why it matters. But why wrongdoing matters full stop is not the question. The question is why wrongdoing matters *in the assessment of lives*. Why is it the case that, when wrongdoing is *not* avoided, it leaves an imperfection—what I have been calling a 'blemish'—on the life of the wrongdoer? Why is my life damaged, in extreme cases destroyed, by my breaches of duty?

To get to the answer, one needs to begin by grasping a general truth about reasons. Reasons await full conformity. If one does not fully conform to a reason—if one does not do exactly what it is a reason to do—the reason does not evaporate. It does not evaporate even though one was justified in not conforming to it. It does not evaporate even though it is now too late fully to conform to it. Instead it now counts as a reason for doing the next-best thing. And failing that, the next-best thing again. And so on. Suppose, to borrow an example from Neil MacCormick, I promised to take my children to the beach today, but because of some emergency I have to cancel the trip.[18] Without further ado, the reason I had to take the children to the beach today—namely the fact that I promised—now becomes a reason for me to take them to the beach tomorrow, or failing that the next day, or failing any of this to provide them with some alternative treat or privilege, etc. Of course the details may vary. Perhaps, if it was a birthday treat, a trip to the beach or an alternative treat tomorrow does not really count as second-best. Perhaps it only adds insult to injury. Perhaps the best I can do is apologize. Perhaps not even that.

---

[17] *Nichomachean Ethics* 1110ᵃ8.

[18] MacCormick, 'The Obligation of Reparation', in his *Legal Right and Social Democracy* (Oxford 1982). MacCormick gets into a muddle with efficient breach—he imagines that a justified breach of duty can't be a breach of duty—and so ends up inverting the lesson of the example.

Perhaps there is nothing I can now do by way of even minimal conformity. Even then the reason does not evaporate. It still makes its force felt as a reason for me to *regret* that I did not do as I promised.[19] Regret is the rational response to any measure of non-conformity with any reason, and the reason for the regret is the very same reason that was incompletely conformed to (coupled, of course, with the fact of incomplete conformity to it). So, in MacCormick's case, the difference between what I promised and what I did is cause for regret as soon as I postpone the outing to the beach even by one day. It is then cause for additional regret if I postpone the outing again, and for still more regret if I have to substitute a different treat, until the point of maximal regret at which my non-conformity with the original reason is total.

Here we have another important truth that has largely been expunged from modern moral philosophy. It has become the accepted wisdom, most conspicuous in the Benthamite tradition but equally taken for granted among Kantians, that at every moment we start again from *tabula rasa*, rationally speaking. There must always be a new reason for us to take an interest in an old reason. Regret, apology, reparation, remorse, atonement, punishment: all this retrospectivity is irrational unless it now commends itself afresh, as a way of (say) reducing future suffering, or expressing renewed respect for oneself or others. But retrospectivity is in fact built into the bricks of rationality. True, there are invariably new reasons both for and against dwelling on the past. These should not be dismissed lightly. Yet equally one should avoid the opposite error. One should not dismiss the *old* reasons, the unconformed-to reasons that are still hanging around waiting for conformity. These reasons still have their force and to the extent that they remain unconformed-to their residual force confers prima facie rationality, without further ado, on regretful attitudes towards the path of one's own life.[20]

This view may strike some as having scary implications. After all, whatever we do there is always something else we have some reason, however slight, to be doing instead. Doesn't it follow that over time the old unconformed-to reasons will tend to pile up and overwhelm the new ones, and leave us rationally doomed to a life of

---

[19] In 'Moral Luck', Bernard Williams introduces the label 'agent-regret' to designate regret with (something like) this rational structure. Unlike Williams, I tend to think that all regret is agent-regret, in the sense that it reflects (what the regretter takes to be) incomplete conformity with reason. Some regret is, however, *vicarious* agent-regret. It is regret on behalf of others, reflecting the continuing force of some reason that *they* did not completely conform to. Vicarious regret clearly needs some justification beyond the existence of the unconformed-to reason. We need to know why one should ever respond to another's non-conformity to a reason as if it were one's own. I will not give any attention to this question here, nor indeed to any of the closely associated puzzles of vicarious liability in law.

[20] See J. Gardner and T. Macklem, 'Reasons', in J. Coleman and S. Shapiro (eds.), *The Oxford Handbook of Jurisprudence and Philosophy of Law* (Oxford 2001), 463–4, 467–8. I have benefited from reading two more recent papers, each of which independently defends much the same view in greater detail: M. Henken, 'No Way Out: Conflict, Regret and Compensation' (unpublished, 2002), and J. Raz, 'Personal Practical Conflicts', in P. Baumann and M. Betzler (eds.), *Practical Conflicts: New Philosophical Essays* (Cambridge 2004), 172. The latter volume also contains an interesting critique of the same view, Monica Betzler's 'Sources of Practical Conflict and Reasons for Regret'.

little else but regret? Of course it can be so. We have all read books or seen movies about lives consumed by rational regret. But normally things are not quite so bad. Among the many reasons that we do not conform to, there are many that are *non-categorical*. We have them by virtue of our personal goals and we no longer have them when our goals change. Furthermore, many are *non-mandatory*. They simply weigh in the balance of reasons and do not exclude any countervailing reasons from consideration. When we do not fully conform to a non-categorical and/or non-mandatory reason, the reason that remains to haunt us still is non-categorical and/or non-mandatory. Such a reason is therefore permanently vulnerable to the abandonment of old goals and/or to defeat by the new reasons that militate powerfully in favour of getting on with our lives. When things are not so easy is when we are left with old unconformed-to reasons that are both categorical and mandatory, i.e. when we had duties that we failed to perform, and hence acted wrongfully. In such cases the reason left over and still awaiting conformity does not surrender to a change in our personal goals. And it continues to exert mandatory force such that at least some conflicting reasons (some of the otherwise powerful reasons that we have to get on with our lives) are excluded from consideration and cannot suffice to defeat it. Wrongful action, in short, leaves us with regrets that are hard to expunge and the repression of which is hard to justify. That is how my acting wrongfully may damage, and in extreme cases destroy, my life. Of course I am not thinking here of the mere *experience* of regret, the psychological haunting of the wrongdoer. No doubt one may avoid this by various displacement activities, self-deceptions, etc. Rather I am thinking of the continuing force of the reason which makes the regret rationally appropriate, and which it is now too late completely to eradicate. It is the enduring presence of this reason which, to a greater or lesser extent, constitutes the damage to one's life.

Was the captain in *Vincent* doomed to such a damaged life? In some measure, yes. After he had kept his ship moored to the pier without the owner's permission, albeit with full justification, it was too late for him fully to perform his duty not to do so. The pier-owner's rights were violated; there was no going back. But a partial conformity, a second-best option, was still available. By paying reparative damages for the violation and its consequences the captain could still imperfectly perform his duty and leave himself with a less damaged life. You may have been wondering how all my discussion of regrets and blemishes relates to the law, and now you have your answer. In the law we have two duties, a primary duty that we violate when we commit a tort or breach a contract, and a secondary duty to pay reparative damages that is brought into being by the law when and because we breach the primary duty. But part of the case for bringing the secondary duty into (legal) existence is that (morally) it is already there. It is the same primary duty that one violated when one breached the contract or committed the tort. It continues to bind one and to press for second-best conformity. When one pays reparative damages, one imperfectly performs the same duty that, earlier, one failed perfectly to perform. That is what is captured in the common lawyer's saying that the purpose of reparative damages, in tort as in contract, is to put the plaintiff, so far as money can do it, back in the position that she would have been in had the wrongful action not been committed against her.

This being so, there is no need to seek an independent rationale for the law's secondary duty. We do not need to build it up rationally from *tabula rasa*. There is no need to argue in Benthamite vein that reparative damages are optimally deterrent, or in Kantian vein that they are a way of re-establishing respect for persons. Of course considerations of deterrence and respect for persons may be relevant in assessing whether and when we should go to all the trouble of making the duty to repair enforceable through the law. The point is that they are not needed to explain why we should *want* to do so. We should want to do so because when a primary duty is breached, a next-best performance of the same duty is automatically called for without further ado. Often—often enough to dictate the common law's standard remedies for wrongdoing—the payment of reparative damages counts as such a next-best performance.

In these remarks I have explained why the fact that I acted wrongfully matters in the moral assessment of my life, which also affords an explanation of why the fact that I acted wrongfully often matters in the determination of my legal position. Some have thought that this kind of explanation is back-to-front. Remember the moral philosophers who offer 'virtuously' as an answer to the question 'How should one live?' Why do these writers fondly imagine that they are at odds with Kant? Partly because they think (mistakenly) that Kant gave a different answer to their question. But also partly because they think that Kant asked a different question. Instead of asking 'How should one live?', they think, Kant asked 'Which actions should one perform?' And they want to restore the former question to the primacy which they think it had in Aristotle's work.[21] For some such writers, restoring the former question to primacy means this: that one needs to determine which lives are morally imperfect in order to determine which actions are wrongful.[22] The picture I have just painted reverses this order of determination. According to my picture, one needs to determine which actions are wrongful in order to determine which lives are morally imperfect. My picture was the one endorsed by Aristotle and Kant alike. Neither believed in the primacy of the question 'How should one live?' over the question 'Which actions should one perform?' if by 'primacy' one means that the first question is to be answered first. On the other hand Aristotle did stress, in a way that Kant did not, the primacy of the question 'How should one live?' over the question 'Which actions should one perform?' if we mean something else by 'primacy'. For Aristotle stressed, as I have stressed, that the *moral importance* of wrongful actions, independently identified, lies primarily in how they affect people's lives for the worse. In the examples that matter for the law, there are always at least two

[21] R. Crisp, 'Modern Moral Philosophy and the Virtues', in Crisp (ed.), *How Should One Live*, 1.
[22] This seems to be Alasdair MacIntyre's view in *After Virtue* (London 1985), 204 ff.

affected lives. There is the life of the wrongdoer and the life of the person wronged. Lawyers are used to thinking of the person wronged as the main person whose life was made worse by the wrong. He can't use his pier, for example, or he can't use his legs. Here I have emphasized instead the moral damage to the life of the wrongdoer. Lawyers may find this emphasis counterintuitive. But I have tried to suggest that, even if counterintuitive, the same emphasis is reflected in a great deal of familiar legal doctrine.

## 3. People and Faults

In casual conversation we might say that the damage to the pier in *Vincent* v. *Lake Erie Transportation Co.* was the captain's fault, or that he was to blame for it. We sometimes use these expressions merely to pick out a person who failed in her duty to prevent, or not to bring about, some eventuality (also sometimes known as 'the person responsible'). The captain fits this description. But when we are watching our words more carefully, we should avoid saying that the damage to the pier in *Vincent* was the captain's fault or that he was to blame for it. For the captain was not at fault and should not be blamed. His action, being wrongful, blemished his life. Yet, being justified, it did not reflect badly on *him*. In particular it did not show him up as cowardly, imprudent, lazy, mean-spirited, irresponsible, or otherwise morally at fault. People with different moral faults differ in respect of which reasons they overplay and which reasons they underplay, and hence in respect of which actions they are over- or underdisposed to perform. Cowardly people overplay the importance of their own safety, mean-spirited people underplay the importance of other people's feelings, imprudent people underplay the importance of longer-run consequences, and so on. But what they all have in common, and what constitutes their moral fault, is that they all end up acting for defeated rather than undefeated reasons. A justified action, meanwhile, is one performed for an undefeated reason. It follows that so long as I do not perform any unjustified actions, I remain a person free of all moral faults.

Here I am already challenging a familiar classificatory scheme used by some writers on criminal law as well as some moral philosophers. It is sometimes said that holding an action to be justified or unjustified is an instance of *act*-assessment, whereas holding a person to be of good or bad moral character is an instance of *agent*-assessment.[23] This is misleading. It encourages a distorted view of justification as well as a distorted view of moral character. If we must talk of acts and agents, justification depends on the agent as much as the act, and moral character depends on the act as much as the agent. But for reasons that will emerge I would rather not put the point this way at all.

[23] See e.g. Paul Robinson, *Fundamentals of Criminal Law* (2nd edn., New York 1995), 526; Claire Finkelstein, 'Excuses and Dispositions in Criminal Law' (2003) 6 *Buffalo Criminal LR* 317, at 326.

The most distracting and irrelevant thought that the contrast between act-assessment and agent-assessment brings to mind is the thought that moral character is something that endures in people while their actions are fleeting. This thought encourages us, in Humean vein, to think of someone's moral character as standing in a contingent relation with her actions: character causes action, action evidences character.[24] But this is a blunder. People's moral characters are constituted, and not merely evidenced, by what they do. Someone who has never done anything dishonest in her life is not a dishonest person, even if she is often tempted to act dishonestly. Rather, she would have been a dishonest person if only she had not had so much self-control.[25] Conversely someone who acted dishonestly just once, even though this was the only occasion on which he ever felt tempted, is to that extent a dishonest person. Of course, we might say of such a person that he acted 'out of character'. In this phrase we juxtapose the fact that he is normally honest with the fact that today he was dishonest. But it does not alter the fact that today he—not just his action, but he—was dishonest. This dishonesty constitutes a blemish on his moral character.

So 'out of character' cannot be interpreted to mean 'not constitutive of character'. The thought that it can comes of the running-together of two questions. One is the question: 'What is character?' The other is the question: 'How is character formed?' When we think about the formation of character we cannot but think about the cultivation of lasting dispositions or tendencies. There is no way, even in principle, to cultivate occasional honesty or occasional dishonesty. But it does not follow that there is no such thing as occasional honesty or occasional dishonesty. A discussion of character traits that centres on the question of formation inevitably plays up the idea of character as an enduring condition.[26] This explains why the fact that a certain action was 'out of character' can be a consideration relevant to the aptness of some putatively rehabilitative or reformative reactions to it. But when we are simply interested in assessing people—as opposed to deciding how we might improve them—we should not similarly sideline their occasional abberations.[27] I don't mean, of course, that we should treat an isolated occasion of dishonesty as somehow obliterating a fine record of honesty. Rather we should think of it as blemishing that record. The record now reads: normally very honest, but on one infamous occasion extremely dishonest. This record is a record of

---

[24] Hume, *Enquiries concerning Human Understanding and concerning the Principles of Morals* (3rd edn., ed. Selby-Bigge and Nidditch, Oxford 1975), 98.

[25] Of course this does not make her a positively *honest* person. As Aristotle explained it makes her an *enkratic* (self-controlled) person who is to that extent neither honest nor dishonest: *Nichomachean Ethics* 1145ª15 ff.

[26] This is why Aristotle plays up the 'settled disposition' aspect of moral virtue in his discussion of moral education in book 2 of *Nicomachean Ethics*, but plays it down from book 3 onwards, having turned his mind to moral assessment.

[27] In his proto-utilitarian way, of course, Hume thought that assessing people was mainly a step towards improving them, which helps to explain why he thought that an action being out of character made it irrelevant to assessment. See *Enquiries*, 97–9.

character itself, not a record of conflicting evidence about character, nor (obviously) a record of reformative plans for character.

This is the main way in which it is misleading to think of the assessment of moral character as an agent-assessment as opposed to an act-assessment. But how is it misleading to think of holding a certain action justified as an act-assessment rather than an agent-assessment? It is misleading in that whether one acts with justification depends not only on what one does, but also on why one does it.[28] If there is an undefeated reason to φ, then φing is justifi*able*. But φing is justifi*ed* only if the agent φed *for* that undefeated reason. If one claims that the tyrannical behaviour of Saddam Hussein towards his own people justified one's pre-emptive strike on Iraq, one claims not only that the tyrannical behaviour of Saddam Hussein towards his own people was an undefeated reason for a pre-emptive strike on Iraq, but also that this was the reason why one launched the strike. And if one asks whether the risk of attack from a burglar justified the use of lethal force against the burglar by the householder, one asks not only whether the risk of attack was an undefeated reason for the householder to use lethal force against the burglar, but also whether that was the householder's reason for using such force. In justifying an action, in short, it is not enough that there were undefeated reasons for that action unless that actor also acted for at least one of those reasons. Why is this? Why is it not enough, from the point of view of justification, that someone conforms to an undefeated reason without also acting for it?

To get the answer straight one needs to begin by thinking carefully about what justification is *for*, why justification *matters*, what is the *point* of justification. You may think this a strange question. What justification is for, you may think, is surely to make the world a better place, to fill it with better actions rather than worse ones. But in the only sense in which this proposition is true, it is question-begging. Why are justified actions better actions? Some moral philosophers, mainly in the Benthamite tradition, tried to show that they are better actions quite apart from being justified actions, and that their betterness explains why they are justified actions. They are rationally better because they are better *tout court*. But this project foundered as Bentham's heirs, from J. S. Mill onwards, gradually rediscovered the deontic aspects of practical thought. Some actions are better actions, or not-worse actions, only in virtue of being justified actions. They are better *tout court* only because they are rationally better, not *vice versa*. When we ask 'What is justification for?' we want to know how this can be so. Why, when our independent tests of betterness run out, does making the world a rationally better place still continue to make the world a better place? The answer, in brief, is that people are (*inter alia*) rational agents, and rational agents necessarily aspire to excellence in rationality. Excellence in rationality means excellence in seeing reasons, in using them, and in negotiating conflicts among them. To act for a defeated reason, any defeated

[28] See further my 'Justifications and Reasons' in A. P. Simester and A. T. H. Smith (eds.), *Harm and Culpability* (Oxford 1996).

reason, is to come unstuck as a negotiator of rational conflicts. Subject to an important proviso to be entered in a moment, this reflects badly upon one (constitutes one's fault) as a rational agent. And that is why justification matters. It matters because, as rational agents, people are the worse for acting without it. And a world with worse people in it is, *ceteris paribus*, a worse world.

I have simplified this explanation in various ways. Most significantly, I have bracketed a special class of unjustified actions that do not reflect badly on their agents. Sometimes one lacks an adequate justification for what one does, yet one has an adequate justification for the beliefs or emotions on the strength of which one does it. In such a case one's action is excused. The simplest excuse of all is the *justified mistake* excuse. Suppose that the captain stays moored to the pier, in a case otherwise akin to *Vincent*, only because a malicious hoaxer broadcast a false storm warning as if it came from the coastguard. In such a case the captain lacked an undefeated reason to stay moored. Yet he had an undefeated reason to *think* that he had an undefeated reason to stay moored. (His excuse is 'How was I to know it was a hoax?'[29]) We would not expect this imaginary storm to relieve the captain of tort liability for trespass any more than the real storm did. On the other hand, we would expect both to be equally available as defences to any criminal charge against the captain that might arise from the incident. That is because both the justification and the excuse equally extinguish the captain's fault. In this respect an excuse is every bit as good as a justification. True, any rational agent, given the choice, would rather be justified than excused. It is better to act for an undefeated reason than to be drawn, even for an undefeated reason, into acting for a defeated one. One kicks oneself when one realizes that one acted for a defeated reason. One looks back on it with extra regret. But that is because, like a wrongful action, an action on the strength of a mistaken belief leaves a blemish on one's life. It is not because it reflects badly upon one as a rational agent. It reflects badly on one as a rational agent only if (*a*) the mistaken belief is unjustified or (*b*) the action would not have been justified even if the mistaken belief had been true. Something very similar, albeit a little more complex, is true of actions performed in anger, fear, frustration, desperation, etc. Roughly, they reflect badly upon one as a rational agent only if (*a*) one's anger, fear, frustration, desperation, etc. was itself unjustified or (*b*) one's anger, fear, frustration, desperation etc. was insufficient to explain one's action, assuming an acceptable level of self-control.[30]

The thought that rational agents would rather be justified than excused is not the only possible source of doubts about the fault-negating power of excuses. Another is the thought that at least some excuses are available as 'concessions to human frailty', in the words favoured by some criminal lawyers. The same thought may be conveyed less grandiloquently by saying that people only need

---

[29] In special circumstances this might serve as a justification rather than an excuse (e.g. if the captain undertook in his contract of employment, or as part of his professional accreditation, to heed all credible storm warnings).

[30] See further my 'The Gist of Excuses' (1997) 1 *Buffalo Criminal LR* 575.

excuses because of their limitations. They do not have unlimited reserves of patience, courage, charity, attentiveness, insight, etc. and that is why they did something unjustified and need to fall back on an excuse. Isn't the display of a limitation also the display of a fault? So doesn't it follow that excuses, or some of them, must perform some function in the assessment of people other than the negation of their fault?[31] The mistake here begins with the misleading suggestion that one's limitations explain why one did something unjustified. This is mistaken if it is taken to mean that one displays no limitations in one's justified actions. Even one's justified actions are not always exemplary. They do not always exhibit the highest measure of virtue. Here is one proof of the point. The highest pinnacle of virtue is often exhibited in supererogatory actions. That I do not perform such actions whenever they are there to perform often (not always) displays one or more of my limitations. Yet it does not follow that I am unjustified in failing to perform supererogatory actions. How could it follow? It is part of the very idea of a supererogatory action that one is permitted not to perform it. One is permitted not to perform it not merely in the weak sense of having no duty to perform it, but in the stronger sense that the reasons to perform it (although they may be undefeated) lack the ability to defeat their opponents. So any reason not to perform a supererogatory action remains undefeated. So one is always justified in not performing it.[32] Hence one cannot be at fault in failing to perform it. It follows that the mere fact that one does not exhibit perfect virtue in one's action does not entail that one exhibits a fault.

A fault, in the sense that matters here, is not just any shortfall of virtue. A fault is a shortfall of virtue that consists in the performance of actions that are both unjustified and unexcused. Any other shortfall of virtue is a mere limitation. It does not reflect badly upon one as a rational agent. Rather, it reminds us what life is inevitably like for a rational agent. Even undefeated reasons pervasively conflict among themselves. If one is to have a character at all one cannot but lean towards reasons of some types, at the expense of reasons of other types. It follows that it is impossible to have a character which is such that one excels even-handedly in one's relations with all undefeated reasons. In other words, nobody, not even a saint, can be without her limitations. Every excellence has some limitation as its flip-side. The more perfectly charitable, the less perfectly just; the more perfectly frank, the less perfectly diplomatic; and so on. This is an inevitable feature of the human condition. But all of this is consistent with always acting for an undefeated reason, or at any rate for a reason that one has undefeated reason to treat as undefeated. It

---

[31] A recent reassertion of this view is William Wilson, 'The Filtering Role of Crisis in the Constitution of Criminal Excuses' (2004) 17 *Canadian J Law and Jurisprudence* 387.

[32] I am here borrowing some points from Joseph Raz, 'Permissions and Supererogation', *American Philosophical Quarterly* 12 (1975), 161. A common mistake, pointed out by Raz, is to think that the permissibility of not performing a supererogatory action constitutes an excuse rather than a justification for its non-performance. But even if we were to let this mistake stand, the final conclusion still follows: nobody is at fault in failing to act supererogatorily.

is consistent with always being justified in what one does, or at least excused. So it is one thing to think of an excuse as a 'concession to human frailty' in the sense of a recognition that human beings inevitably have limitations (imperfect virtues) as the price of their excellences (more perfect virtues). It is another thing to think of an excuse as a 'concession to human frailty' in the sense of a recognition that human beings inevitably have their share of *bad* character, i.e. their faults or vices. This is just not true. Perhaps all human beings do have their faults or vices, but there is nothing in the human condition (or at any rate in our predicament as rational beings) that makes this inevitable, and there is no case for 'concessionary' extension of justifications or excuses to fault-constituting actions. How could there be? It is the very fact that actions are unjustified and unexcused that *makes* them fault-constituting.

Here I once again take sides on an issue much discussed by contemporary 'virtue ethicists'. That it is rational to exhibit moral virtue is analytically true and accepted by Aristotle and Kant alike. But are morally virtuous actions rational because morally virtuous, or morally virtuous because rational? Kant famously defended the idea that they are morally virtuous because rational. Some contemporary writers in the 'virtue ethics' school defend the opposite view and claim thereby to be Aristotelian revivalists.[33] But on this point as on so many others Aristotle is widely misunderstood. Aristotle and Kant agreed, rightly, that virtuous actions are virtuous because rational.[34] In the terms I just introduced, it is the fact that actions are justified or excused that entails that they are not fault-constituting, not the other way around. Why is Aristotle mistakenly associated with the opposite view? Perhaps because he repeatedly and rightly emphasized that one's moral virtues—one's qualities as a person—make an intrinsic as well as an instrumental contribution to the quality of one's life.[35] If the morally virtuous person lives *by that token* a rationally better life (a better life for a rational being), surely the moral virtue must be what *makes* it rational? So how can the fact that it is rational also be what makes it morally virtuous? Actually the answer is straightforward. That one is a virtuous person brings *extra* value to one's life above and beyond the ordinary value, the rational pursuit of which constitutes one's virtue. First there is the rationally salient value that one pursues, and successful pursuit of which makes one morally virtuous. And then there is the extra value that lies in one's successfully pursuing the rationally salient value.[36] This extra value is not rationally salient. It is the value of rationality itself. *Pace* Kant, pursuing rationality (or indeed morality) itself, for its own sake, is normally self-defeating. One does

[33] 'A pure virtue ethics . . . will suggest that the only reasons we ever have for acting or living in a certain way are *grounded* in the virtues.' R. Crisp, 'Modern Moral Philosophy and the Virtues' in Crisp (ed.), *How Should One Live*, 7. Crisp rightly points out that a virtue ethics need not be pure, but he wrongly ascribes the pure position to Aristotle.

[34] *Nichomachean Ethics* 1114$^b$28–9; *Groundwork*, 102–3.

[35] e.g. *Nichomachean Ethics* 1098$^a$16–17.

[36] I have defended this explanation in more detail, with the virtue of solidarity as my example, in 'Reasons for Teamwork' (2002) 8 *Legal Theory* 495.

not exhibit moral virtue in acting with the intention of exhibiting moral virtue. One exhibits moral virtue in acting with other aims, themselves rationally defensible (i.e. sufficient to justify or excuse one's action). Thereby one makes one's life better in two ways at once. A life is better for the fact that it was a life of greater conformity with reasons. A person without faults is better equipped, instrumentally, to live this life (even though tragedy may still strike). But being a person without faults also contributes intrinsically to one's quality of life. A life is better for the very fact that it is lived by someone with fewer or lesser faults. Virtue, as they say, is its own reward: one's success in seeing reasons, in using them, and in negotiating conflicts among them is an instrument of better living, but also a constituent of it. When tragedy strikes, one may still console oneself with the second aspect. One may say: a life blemished, but at least not blemished for having been lived by a blemished person.

## 4. Fault-Anticipating Wrongs

Let me mention one particular way in which a life lived by a better person can be, by that token, a better life. The avoidance of fault sometimes entails the avoidance of wrongdoing. Being at fault, to put it the other way round, sometimes contributes constitutively, and not just instrumentally, to the wrongfulness of one's actions. Some wrongs are 'fault-anticipating'. They are wrongs that are committed only in the absence of justification or excuse—in other words, only in the presence of fault.

A common view is that all wrongs are fault-anticipating. If there is no fault, there is no wrong. But on more careful reflection the very opposite conclusion seems more tempting: there can be no such thing as a fault-anticipating wrong.[37] If one committed no wrong, surely one has nothing to justify or excuse? If one has nothing to justify or excuse, then surely one neither has nor lacks a justification or excuse? Doesn't it follow that one must commit a wrong to lack a justification or excuse? That being so, how can it ever be that one must lack a justification or excuse to commit a wrong? How are fault-anticipating wrongs possible? The answer is startlingly simple. Fault-anticipating wrongs are always parasitic or

---

[37] The best and best-known defence of the view that there are no fault-anticipating wrongs is W. D. Ross, *The Right and the Good* (Oxford 1930). The conclusion is stated most starkly at p. 45. Ross's argument for it fails, but in the process he makes light work of demolishing the ultra-Kantian view at the opposite extreme that *all* wrongs are fault-anticipating wrongs. Sadly, Ross's demolition fell mostly on deaf ears. The ultra-Kantian view continues to exert a hold over many non-philosophers, including many legal scholars. I call the view ultra-Kantian because even in his most hardline moments Kant claimed only that breach of duty is never justifiable. He did not suggest that it is never excusable, and therefore always faulty. The idea that he did reflects, like so much else, an exaggeration of his views about moral luck. From the thesis that perfect people cannot but lead perfect lives, it is tempting but fallacious to derive the thesis that an imperfect life can have been led only by someone who is at fault. This line of thought ignores the existence of limitations, i.e. imperfections of character that are not vices. Ross himself tends to paint Kant, mistakenly, in ultra-Kantian colours.

secondary wrongs. One commits them only if one lacks justification or excuse for something *else* one does in committing them. In some cases the 'something else' is not a wrong at all—not a breach of duty—but merely a failure to conform to an ordinary reason for action. One has a weighty reason not to take one's children mountaineering, for instance, but one's only duty is not to do so negligently. What is wrongful, because a breach of duty, is faulty (unjustified and unexcused) non-conformity with the weighty reason. In other cases, however, the 'something else' is the commission of another wrong. One violates a duty whenever one spreads gossip about one's colleagues, for example, but one violates an additional and more stringent duty when one spreads the same gossip maliciously or dishonestly. The fault-anticipating wrong, the more heinous wrong, lies in the faulty commission of another less heinous wrong that is not fault-anticipating.

Elsewhere I have argued, against Kant, that the primary or basic type of moral wrong is one to which the endeavours of the wrongdoer make no constitutive difference.[38] The basic moral question is what you did or didn't do (Did you kill? Did you cause offence? Did you keep your promise?) never mind what you were trying to do or trying not to do. I argued that wrongs that are constitutively sensitive to what the wrongdoer was trying to do or trying not to do (Did you murder? Did you cheat? Did you conspire?) are wrongs of a secondary or parasitic type, relative to those that are constitutively insensitive to what the wrongdoer was trying to do or trying not to do. To defend this strong conclusion I made a long argument. What I offered just now was a much shorter argument for a much more modest conclusion. The more modest conclusion is that wrongs that are constitutively sensitive to the wrongdoer's *fault* are wrongs of a secondary or parasitic type, relative to those that are constitutively insensitive to the wrongdoer's fault. This conclusion is more modest because, while every fault-anticipating wrong is constitutively sensitive to what the wrongdoer was trying to do (in that it is constitutively sensitive to her reasons for doing as she did), many wrongs that are constitutively sensitive to what the wrongdoer was trying to do are not fault-anticipating. Many wrongs can only be committed intentionally, for example, and yet can still be committed without fault. We know that they can be committed without fault because we can conceive of circumstances in which their commission can be justified or excused. Intentional wounding can sometimes be justified as an action in self-defence, or excused as an action under duress. Not so reckless wounding. To conclude that I wounded recklessly (or likewise negligently, stupidly, unjustly, callously, in a cowardly way, etc.) is already to conclude that I had no justification or excuse. If there is a distinct wrong of reckless wounding or cowardly wounding or callous wounding, it is a fault-anticipating wrong. A distinct wrong of intentional wounding, on the other hand, is not.

Writings about the law, especially the criminal law, often get into a muddle on this front. Consider strict liability. Some criminal lawyers think of (and object to)

---

[38] John Gardner, 'Obligations and Outcomes in the Law of Torts', in Peter Cane and John Gardner (eds.), *Relating to Responsibility: Essays for Tony Honoré on his 80th Birthday* (Oxford 2001).

strict liability as liability irrespective of fault. Meanwhile some criminal lawyers think of (and object to) strict liability as liability for wrongs that have no *mens rea* constituent (i.e. wrongs that can be committed without the wrongdoer's intending or being aware of any of the wrong-making features of her action). Some seem to think that these two ideas (and hence the two objections) are interchangeable. But if strict liability is liability irrespective of fault, then there may in principle be strict liability for intentional crimes and other crimes of *mens rea*. A wrong partly constituted by the intention or awareness of the wrongdoer may nevertheless be committed faultlessly, with adequate justification or excuse. If the law does not recognize any such justification or excuse, then it holds the intentional or knowing offender strictly liable, in the sense of liable irrespective of her fault. Conversely, if strict liability is liability for wrongs that have no *mens rea* constituent, then there may in principle be strict liability that is not liability irrespective of fault. For the law may recognize justifications and excuses as *defences* to a wrong, and hence allow some of the wrongdoer's reasoning at the time of the wrong to be relevant to her liability, even though the wrong itself has no *mens rea* constituent (and nor for that matter a fault constituent).

This muddles matters because the success of any objection to strict liability depends on the defensibility of the principle that strict liability is said to contravene. And there are clearly two different principles that are being advanced here. One, which we could call 'the *mens rea* principle', is a principle requiring criminal wrongs to have certain constituents, namely the wrongdoer's intending or being aware of at least some of the (other) wrong-making features of her action. The other, which we could call 'the fault principle', is a principle regulating the conditions for the imposition of criminal liability, rather than the constituents of criminal wrongdoing. Criminal liability should be imposed only for wrongs that are faultily committed, whether or not the fault in question is a constituent of the wrong (i.e. whether or not the wrong in question is fault-anticipating). Sometimes the law may be able to satisfy both principles at once by treating a certain wrong as fault-anticipating—as partly constituted by, say, the dishonesty or the malice of the wrongdoer. But just as often the *mens rea* principle and the fault principle place different demands upon the criminal law and the criminal law needs to satisfy them separately.

Our main interest here will be in the rationale for the fault principle. But for contrastive purchase it is worth saying a few words, first, about the rationale for the *mens rea* principle. There are many wrongs that, even apart from the law, are partly constituted by some intention or awareness on the part of the wrongdoer. When these wrongs are recognized by law the relevant intention or awareness naturally carries over into the legal constituents of the wrong. Cheating, lying, manipulating, coercing, torturing: these are wrongs of *mens rea* even before the law gets its hands on them. But as a general principle extending beyond such wrongs, the *mens rea* principle has a largely institutional rationale. According to the ideal known as the rule of law, those of us about to commit a criminal wrong should be put on stark notice that that is what we are about to do.[39] The criminal law should not ambush us unexpectedly. Of course, to avoid unexpected ambushes we all need to know what the law requires of us. For that reason, criminal laws should be clear, open, consistent, stable, and prospective. They should also forbid specific actions (not courses of action, activities, ways of life, etc.). Even all this, however, is not enough to ensure that those of us about to violate the criminal law are put on stark notice that we are about to violate it. For we may know the law and yet have no grasp that what we are about to do might constitute a violation of it. That is because often we have no idea which actions we are about to perform. I make a light-hearted remark and (surprise!) I offend one of my guests. I turn on my oven and (surprise!) I blow all the fuses. The *mens rea* principle is the principle according to which such actions—the self-surprising ones—should not be criminal wrongs.

More precisely: according to the *mens rea* principle, criminal wrongs should be such that one does not commit them unless one intends or is aware of at least one wrong-making feature of what one is about to do, such that (assuming one knows the law) one is also alerted to the fact that what one is about to do will be of interest to the criminal law. The principle does not extend similarly to wrongs under private law, such as torts and breaches of contract. The main reason is that the *mens rea* principle is a systematically pro-defendant principle. It is one thing for the law to be systematically pro-defendant in the criminal process, and quite another for it to be systematically pro-defendant in a civil dispute. Criminal investigators and prosecutors have much more extensive, and potentially oppressive, power than do private-law plaintiffs. The *mens rea* principle is one of several principles by which, inasmuch as we live under the rule of law, we are protected against the oppressive use of such power.[40]

## 5. Defending the Fault Principle

Like the *mens rea* principle, the fault principle is one that extends to criminal law but not, or not generally, to private law. Fault can certainly be relevant to liability in tort and contract, but that is because some torts and breaches of contract are fault-anticipating wrongs. Private law cares about wrongdoing. It cares about the wrongdoer's fault if and only if his fault is a constituent of his wrong. Criminal law, by contrast, cares about fault even when fault is *not* a constituent of the

[39] But they need not have similarly stark notice of their possible justificatory and excusatory defences. For explanation, see George Fletcher, 'The Nature of Justification', in Stephen Shute, John Gardner, and Jeremy Horder (eds.), *Action and Value in Criminal Law* (Oxford 1993), 175.

[40] It has become fashionable across the political spectrum to attack the pro-defendant principles of criminal law by reconceptualizing the criminal process on the model of a civil dispute, i.e. as wrongdoer v. person wronged rather than wrongdoer v. the law. I criticized this consumerist trend in 'Crime: in Proportion and in Perspective', in A. J. Ashworth and M. Wasik (eds.), *Fundamentals of Sentencing Theory* (Oxford 1998).

wrongdoer's wrong. It gives independent importance to the wrongdoer's fault. It does this by offering her various possible justificatory and excusatory defences to non-fault-anticipating criminal wrongs. At any rate, that is what the fault principle would have it do.

H. L. A. Hart famously assimilated the fault principle to the *mens rea* principle in respect of rationale. He argued that the criminal law should admit justifications and excuses for the same reason that it should require *mens rea*: to ensure that wrongdoers have a fair opportunity deliberately to steer clear of criminal liability, in keeping with the ideal of the rule of law.[41] No doubt the criminal law's adherence to the fault principle, like its adherence to the *mens rea* principle, can help with its adherence to the ideal of the rule of law. But this does not get to the bottom of the fault principle's rationale. The fault principle is not primarily an institutional principle. It does not apply to the criminal law because the criminal law is part of a legal system and legal systems need to regulate the potentially oppressive power of their own officials. Rather it applies to the criminal law because the criminal law exacts punishments. Punishments are subject to the fault principle irrespective of whether they are exacted by a legal system and irrespective of whether there is any potential for abuse of official power. If I punish one of my friends for wrongdoing (e.g. by not sending him an invitation to my party) it is no cause for complaint on his part that he had no idea and indeed no way of knowing that I might take an interest in his actions. As a friend I am not bound by the rule of law, nor (hence) by the *mens rea* principle. It is not my job to put people on notice that they are about to get into trouble with me. But I am bound by the fault principle. My friend does have serious cause for complaint if I punish him for a wrong that he committed faultlessly. This is the same complaint that the captain in *Vincent* v. *Lake Erie* would have had if, in addition to expecting him to pay reparative damages for his violation of the pier-owner's rights, the law went on to punish him for what was, even in the law's eyes, a faultless wrong. Reparation for faultless wrongs is one thing; punishment for them, whether by the criminal law or otherwise, is quite another. The fault principle is a principle governing punishment, and it applies to the criminal law because criminal liability is a liability to be punished.

One should proceed carefully here, because while criminal liability is a liability to be punished, it is normally a liability to be punished only at the court's discretion.[42] The criminal court is normally at liberty (at the 'sentencing stage' of the trial) to attach some non-punitive measure to the wrong, such as probation, hospitalization, or conditional discharge, instead of a punitive one, such as imprisonment, community service, or a fine. Can't the criminal law deal with fault at this sentencing stage, as

---

[41] See 'Legal Responsibility and Excuses', in his collection *Punishment and Responsibility* (Oxford 1968).

[42] In my view, Stephen Shute, Jeremy Horder, and I exaggerated the importance of this distinction in our introduction to *Action and Value in Criminal Law*, and hence went too far in disengaging the principles of criminal law from the principles of punishment.

a matter to be considered in the exercise of judicial discretion? Not with equanimity. When things go well for the law, the determination of criminal liability is a determination that a punishment for the wrong is deserved. And a punishment for the wrong is deserved only if the wrong was faultily committed. Judicial discretion at the sentencing stage exists primarily to enable consideration of factors relevant to the justification of punishment *other than* those that bear on whether the punishment is deserved: whether to make an example of the defendant, whether to give her credit for other respects in which she is of good character, whether to pursue her rehabilitation or reform, and so on. So the question of fault should not, ideally, be left to figure in the judge's exercise of discretion. But things do not always go so well for the law. Even with the best will in the world, the law's determination of criminal liability cannot always be a satisfactory determination of the deservedness of criminal punishment. The rule of law, by insisting on clarity, stability, prospectivity, etc., often prevents the law from showing full sensitivity to the differential moral merits of every wrong that is committed and every credible justification or excuse for its commission. Some questions bearing on fault, normally but not always relating to the fine-tuning of fault, are inevitably left over to be dealt with at the sentencing stage. So the fault principle is a principle to be honoured at the sentencing stage to the extent that, alas, it was not fully honoured in the determination of criminal liability. That is a reason for the law to retain a separate sentencing stage complete with judicial discretion to punish or not to punish. But it is not a reason for the law to disregard the defendant's fault in determining his criminal liability and hence in determining his exposure to that same judicial discretion.[43]

These remarks already lead us a little closer to the rationale for the fault principle. A punishment, I proposed, is *deserved* only if the wrong being punished was faultily committed. The proposition is easy to agree to and yet remarkably difficult to vindicate in a satisfying way. Some ascribe the difficulty to the very idea of desert, which they claim to find mysterious. But it is hard to do without the idea of desert. Replacing 'deserved' with 'justified', for example, falsifies the proposition we are interested in rather than simplifying its vindication. As I just mentioned, various considerations apart from the deservedness of punishment are relevant to the justification of punishment.

In any case, there is nothing remotely mysterious about the idea of desert. I used it unremarkably near the start of this chapter, in elucidating the classical idea of the tragic. Tragedy, I said, is undeserved moral downfall, moral failure out of all proportion to moral failing. The idea of desert that I invoked in saying this is

---

[43] An alternative (more Aristotelian) conceptualization of the main idea in this paragraph: ideally a determination of criminal liability settles that punishment would be just, while questions about whether it would be humane, merciful, efficient, etc. are dealt with at the sentencing stage. Thanks to the demands of the rule of law, however, some considerations of justice (the particularized considerations of justice known by the name of 'equity') are inevitably left over to the sentencing stage. See *Nichomachean Ethics* 1137[b]12–1138[a]2.

straightforward. It is a variant on the idea of aptness or fittingness. What I deserve is simply what is apt or fitting for me because of some excellence or deficiency of mine. As the fastest runner in the race, I deserve to be declared its winner. As the least beautiful contestant, I deserve to come last in the beauty pageant. These latter examples are, of course, examples of non-moral deserts, in the sense that the excellences and deficiencies at stake are not moral excellences and deficiencies. Because of the widespread tendency to think of moral success as the highest kind of success, many people nowadays find such examples disquieting. They tend to think that the non-morally deserving are not really deserving at all.[44] The ones who really deserve to win the race are the most dedicated or the most courageous runners, the ones who show the most moral fibre, never mind their short legs and poor co-ordination. Even the element of skill in athletics makes one a deserving winner, in the view of some, only because and to the extent that the cultivation of skill makes demands on moral character. As for beauty pageants, the thinking continues, they have no plausible connection with desert at all, and should be abolished. But all of this is absurdly moralistic. In tests of speed and beauty, the speediest and the most beautiful respectively are those who deserve to succeed. Whether there should be any tests of speed and beauty is another question altogether. To put it another way: one may readily agree that beauty pageants should be abolished, without agreeing that truly beautiful people do not (in respect of their beauty) deserve our admiration and recognition.[45]

So the problem is not to understand what it is to deserve something. The problem is not even to understand what it is to deserve something morally. (There is no harm in thinking of a human life as, in part, a moral test, and in thinking of the morally virtuous person as the person who deserves to pass the test.) The problem, rather, is to understand how *punishment* can ever be the thing that is deserved, and how *faulty wrongdoing* comes to be the basis for deserving it. An instructive but fallacious attempt at a solution begins with the observation that there is a conceptual connection between punishment and wrongdoing.[46] If suffering or deprivation is deliberately inflicted but not as a response to (supposed) wrongdoing, that is not a case of punishment. And if the wrongdoing is only supposed, and not real, it is a case of mistaken punishment. This is all true, but inconclusive. It does not establish that punishment is ever deserved as a response to wrongdoing, because it does not establish that punishment is ever deserved. It only establishes that punishment can

---

[44] The most influential statement of this view is John Rawls, *A Theory of Justice* (Cambridge, Mass. 1971), 103–4.

[45] The same point is nicely made by Michael Sandel, *Liberalism and the Limits of Justice* (Cambridge 1982), 135–47. Sandel focuses on the advantages enjoyed by the (innately) academically talented in university admissions. As Sandel shows, if these advantages of talent are undeserved it is not because (as Rawls puts it) 'the notion of desert seems not to apply to these cases'. One may clearly deserve the rewards of one's talents, e.g. in winning a talent contest. The only question is whether competition for university admissions should be anything like a talent contest, and that depends on the nature and value of universities, not on anything about the concept of desert.

[46] I am here rehashing Anthony Quinton's 'On Punishment', *Analysis* 14 (1954), 512.

sometimes be mistaken. More importantly, it does not help to explain why, for punishment to be deserved as a response to wrongdoing, the wrongdoer must also be at fault. For there is no relevant conceptual connection between punishment and fault. Punishing a faultless wrongdoer is punishing undeservedly. But it is still punishing. If it were not punishing it would not be regulated by the principles that regulate punishing, such as the fault principle. So we could not condemn it for violation of those principles. Those deliberately inflicting suffering or deprivation on the faultless could always say: 'Since I'm not punishing, why should I care which punishments would be deserved?' The conceptual connection between punishment and wrongdoing is certainly important, but for the opposite reason. It is important because those who respond to (supposed) wrongdoing by deliberately inflicting suffering or deprivation are thereby automatically made answerable to the principles that govern the infliction of punishment, such as the fault principle. They cannot avoid such principles by claiming not to be punishers. But nor can the same principles be vindicated—shown to be sound—merely by pointing out that an infliction of suffering or deprivation without a supposition of wrongdoing is not punishment.

Those looking for a better defence of the fault principle may see some hope in what I called the elementary moral distinction, and in particular in the proposal, implicit in my characterization of tragedy, that better people deserve better lives. We know that there are tragic cases of lives that are badly damaged through no (or disproportionately little) fault of those who live them. Equally, there are converse cases of lucky people whose serious faults inflict disproportionately little damage on their lives. Isn't punishment deserved simply as a way of bringing such people's lives closer to the lives they deserve? There are two related objections to this hypothesis. First, if someone deserves to be punished, he has committed a wrong. Necessarily his life has already been damaged by his having done so. Indeed he may now have, morally speaking, exactly the life that he deserves, or even worse. So why should we want his life to be *further* damaged by the deliberately inflicted[47] suffering or deprivation of a punitive measure? As if it were not bad enough that we deliberately bring additional suffering and deprivation into the world, we seem to be doing it by kicking someone who is already down. Herein

---

[47]  In the sense relevant to an understanding of punishment, suffering or deprivation is not deliberately inflicted unless inflicting it is one of the inflictor's objectives. If no suffering or deprivation materializes, then the punishment fails *qua* punishment. This explains why making a wrongdoer pay reparative damages, however vast, is not normally a punitive act. Normally the deprivation of the wrongdoer who pays reparative damages is a mere side-effect of getting her to do her duty. So the fact that she is insured against the deprivation is a plus from the reparative point of view, even though it would have been a minus from the punitive point of view. The puzzle I am raising in the text is therefore a puzzle about the inflicting of punishment that does not extend to the awarding of reparative damages. It is a heightened version of the more general puzzle: how could the fact that someone escapes suffering and deprivation *ever* count as a minus for a rational agent? How could bringing more suffering or deprivation into the world ever be a worthy objective, as opposed to an unavoidable side-effect of a worthy objective?

lies the first mystery of deserved punishment. Why would we want to inflict yet more damage on what is, *ex hypothesi*, an already damaged life? Secondly, just as there are many wrongful actions that are not faulty, so there are many faulty actions that are not wrongful. If the point of deserved punishment were to give vicious people the lives they deserve, then one would expect punishment to be deserved on the strength of fault alone. One would expect the commission of a wrong to be irrelevant. But it is not. If luckily no wrong was committed in spite of one's fault, then luckily no punishment is deserved. The fault principle captures a necessary but not a sufficient condition for being deserving of punishment. Herein lies the second mystery of deserved punishment. Why isn't fault alone sufficient, never mind wrongdoing?

I believe, although I cannot develop the position in any detail here, that one can tackle both mysteries together by returning to another proposal that I made earlier in this chapter. In § 2 I explained how wrongful action leaves us with regrets that are hard to expunge and the repression of which is hard to justify. As I said there, not everyone actually experiences the relevant regrets. My point was that experiencing them is rationally appropriate. Our lives should be blemished subjectively because and to the extent that they are blemished objectively. More generally, our lives should feel as good, but only as good, as they are.[48] This is not as it stands a doctrine of desert. It is not because of some deficiency on the part of the wrongdoer that she should be burdened with regrets for her wrongs. Many wrongdoers, like the captain in *Vincent* v. *Lake Erie*, emerge without any stain on their characters. But the doctrine that lives should feel as good, but only as good, as they are is nevertheless a doctrine of aptness or fittingness. It is apt or fitting that people, including those with unblemished characters, should suffer for their wrongs. What they should suffer, in the normal case, is regret for the very fact that they committed a wrong, for their incomplete fulfilment of their duty.

But the case of a wrongdoer who was at fault in committing a wrong presents special problems. Such a person has already shown himself insufficiently responsive to the reasons against doing as he did. That he was at fault means that he committed the wrong for defeated reasons. He did not even have undefeated reasons to treat the reasons for which he acted as undefeated. In failing to see that the reasons for which he acted were defeated, he was insufficiently responsive to the force of the reasons on the other side, those that made his action wrongful. This rational underresponsiveness also militates against his experiencing, without intervention, the apt measure of regret. The reasons for his regretting his wrong are, after all, the very same reasons to which he was not, when he committed the wrong, sufficiently responsive. They are reasons the force of which, thanks to his fault, he underestimates. Depending on which fault he exhibits, he either notices the

[48] Of course, how a life feels is itself part of how that life is. A life is damaged by the suffering of regrets, even apt regrets. By my doctrine, such a life is itself apt to be regretted by the person living it. 'I regret that I spent so much time regretting what I did' would be an intelligible, if sad, deathbed utterance.

reasons yet underestimates their force, or underestimates their force such that he fails to notice them. Either way, the faulty wrongdoer is prone to live a life that feels better than it is. In fact, doubly so. His life is blemished by his wrong and (as we saw at the end of § 3) further blemished by his fault in committing it. His fault tends to make him oblivious to both blemishes. Punishment, assuming it is successful, serves to correct this oblivious misalignment of the subjective with the objective. It gives people who do not regret their faulty wrong (or do not regret it enough) something extra about their faulty wrong to regret. To the extent that they do not regret committing their faulty wrong *qua* faulty wrong, they regret it instead *qua* bearer of unwelcome consequences for them. They regret the (other kinds of) suffering and deprivation that constitute their punishment. And here we have, at last, a relevant principle of desert. It is only because of the wrongdoer's deficiency—the fault she displayed in committing the wrong—that the deliberate infliction of such suffering or deprivation upon her in response to the wrong is apt. Had she been free of fault, the apt measure of suffering (the suffering of apt regret for the wrong) would have been self-administering and would not have called for deliberate infliction by anyone. No punishment, in other words, would have been deserved.

This line of thought provides, or at any rate promises upon adequate elaboration to provide, an integrated solution to our twin mysteries about deserved punishment. It indicates why one would want to inflict yet more damage on what is, *ex hypothesi*, a life already damaged by wrongdoing. And it indicates why wrongdoing, and not only fault, figures in the equation of deserved punishment. Yet it also creates new puzzles of its own. In particular, we may worry about faulty wrongdoers who act 'out of character'. I do not mean those who possess many virtues (say, kindness, generosity, courage, loyalty) but one vice (say, dishonesty). There may be a case for punishing such people less when they commit a vicious wrong, but the case for punishing them less is not that they deserve less punishment for the vicious wrong. Rather, I am thinking of those who act 'out of character' in the sense identified in § 3: those who are normally honest, say, but who were on this one occasion dishonest. These people are not normally underresponsive to the reasons to which they were, on the occasion of their wrong, underresponsive. So, depending on how 'out of character' their faulty action was, they may well recognize, in the wake of their wrongs, the full force of the reasons that they underestimated in committing those wrongs. They may well see their wrong and their fault in the sharpest relief. If so, they are not prone to suffer less regret than is apt. Do they or do they not deserve to be punished?

I tend to think that they represent an intriguing borderline case. Here, briefly, is why. The apt response to faulty wrongdoing, thanks to its doubly blemishing impact upon the life of a wrongdoer, is not the ordinary regret of the faultless wrongdoer. It is a special kind of self-critical regret known as *remorse*. The remorseful give themselves a hard time for their wrongs, a hard time which they hold themselves to deserve on the model of punishment. In the wake of their remorse, they deserve to be punished less, or in extreme cases not at all. Suppose, for simplicity's sake, we are looking at a case of remorse in which no punishment is now deserved. How do we explain the fact that no punishment is now deserved? One way to do so is to say that the remorseful person *never* deserved punishment, because without intervention she reacted entirely fittingly to what she did. The alternative way to explain the same result is to say that she *did* deserve to be punished, but that she was punished enough by the hard time she already gave herself. Both explanations are intelligible, and both are sometimes given, because remorse lies at the borderline between regret, suffered spontaneously, and punishment, inflicted deliberately. But whichever explanation we prefer, the consideration of remorse undoubtedly belongs at the sentencing stage of the criminal trial. It is true that being at fault and deserving (further) punishment at the law's hands somewhat come apart in the case of the remorseful wrongdoer. But the quantification of the (further) punishment deserved by such a wrongdoer cannot, consistently with the rule of law, be built into the law's determination of criminal liability. To make a deduction from punishment for remorse (or indeed for punishments exacted extrajudicially, such as being abandoned by one's spouse) the court must first determine that a criminal wrong has been committed without a legally recognized justification or excuse. Only then can the law legitimately authorize a prima facie quantification of the punishment deserved for the offence to which the relevant 'remorse' deduction (and other adjustments) can be applied.

## 6. Beyond Meaning and Consequence

Some say: only those who are at fault (= blameworthy) should be punished for their wrongs, because punishment expresses or communicates blame. I agree. I also agree with those who say, as Kant says, that faulty wrongdoers have an interest in being punished for their wrongs because the punishment expresses or communicates the fact of their being responsible agents, meaning agents who are capable of having and offering justifications and excuses for what they do.[49] But these proposals, sound though they are, leave us hanging in mid-air. We still want to know: *why* does punishment express or communicate these things? Is it an accident of social history? Doffing one's cap, except when done in irony, expresses or communicates deference. But one can readily imagine a culture in which it is a gesture of contempt. Is punishment similar? Could it imaginably, in some place or at some time, be a communication of forgiveness or exoneration rather than blame, or a denial rather than an assertion of responsible agency? I tend to think, and many seem to agree, that the expressive link between punishment and blame (and hence between punishment and responsible agency) is less contingent than that between hat-doffing and deference. It is logically possible to punish those

---

[49] This was the theme of my paper 'The Mark of Responsibility', *Oxford Journal of Legal Studies* 23 (2003), 157.

whom one does not blame—to make a scapegoat of an innocent person—but at the same time the social meaning of a punitive act as an act of blaming is not just an accident of social history, an ethnographical curiosity, a symbolism grafted onto the logic of punishment by local convention. Rather, this social meaning is somehow the proper social meaning for punishment, one that could only awkwardly or perversely be defied by a dissident civilization.

Why? This is where the deservedness of punishment, as I have explained it, enters the story. It is not true, as many claim, that the reason why only the blame-worthy deserve to be punished is that punishment expresses or communicates blame. The truth is the opposite: the reason why punishment expresses or communicates blame is that only the blameworthy deserve to be punished. Admittedly, the fact that punishment expresses or communicates blame is itself a complete reason not to punish the blameless, and a reason with considerable force. Possibly it is this reason that does most of the hard work in making it the law's *duty* not to attach criminal liability to faultless wrongdoing. Nevertheless it is a reason that takes its shape from another, namely the reason we have (quite apart from what punishment expresses or communicates) to punish only those who deserve to be punished. So even if you are not seduced by my sketchy and tentative proposals above in defence of the view that faultless wrongdoers do not deserve to be punished, there is still this message to take away with you: some such proposals are needed. We need some relatively independent explanation of the deservedness of punishment to explain why, from the *Iliad* to the Koran and the French Revolution to the Cultural Revolution, punishment expresses or communicates blame.

At least from Kant and Hume onwards, modern thinkers across many disciplines lost sight of the need for such proposals and lacked the resources to make them. They lacked the resources to make them because they endorsed as an article of faith the *tabula rasa* view of rationality, thought of as progressive and superstition-busting, according to which one always needs some further (new) reason to dwell on (old) reasons that were not perfectly conformed to at the right time. The old reasons are water under the bridge, the thinking goes; the time for conforming to them is over; we are no longer interested in them unless there is something else that can now be achieved, expressively or instrumentally, by attending to them. Without this 'something else' we cannot even get started with an argument for regret, reparation, remorse, punishment, and similar retrospective responses. Thus modern thinkers came to blows, mostly, about what the 'something else' in question might be. Reduction of net suffering? Restoration of respect? Reform of bad character? All of these and many other considerations can, of course, be relevant to the justification of regret, reparation, remorse, punishment, and so on, and especially to the costly and difficult institutionalization of such responses in the law.[50] Nevertheless they are all, in one way or another,

---

[50] Here I have bracketed this question: granted that punishment or some other response to wrongdoing is called for, why is this the business of the law? Elsewhere I placed the need to control the excessive reactions of others, such as victims and their families, at the centre of the answer. See my 'Crime: in Proportion and in Perspective'.

parasitic considerations. One cannot provide adequate foundations for the expressive or the instrumental significance of any of these responses to wrongdoing unless one first understands how and when they are apt responses quite apart from their expressive or instrumental significance.[51] In particular, one cannot make a philosophically satisfying expressive or instrumental case for punishment unless one first makes proposals for explaining how and when punishment is deserved.

As well as lacking the resources to make such proposals, many modern thinkers, taking their cue from Kant and Hume, lost sight of the need to do so. Underestimating or even denying the central place of tragedy in the human condition, they saw little or no space for lives that are morally better or worse than the people who live them. Experientially better, yes. So one may indeed ask whether someone has a better life than she deserves, meaning an experientially better life. But morally better, no. Either lives are not objects of moral assessment at all, but only of experiential assessment (in the Hume–Bentham tradition); or else the moral assessment of lives closely tracks the moral assessment of the people who live them (in the Kantian tradition, to which most contemporary 'virtue-ethicists' belong *malgré eux*). Either way, the elementary moral distinction takes a back seat. The idea that a life is often morally blemished through no fault of the person living it becomes philosophically alien. Alienated in the process is the idea that the primary or basic type of wrongdoing is faultless wrongdoing, and the associated idea that the primary or basic responses to wrongdoing (regret, apology, reparation) are apt responses irrespective of fault. Faultless wrongdoing and the strict liability to repair that is associated with it come to be thought of, mistakenly, as moral oddities in need of special explanation. Meanwhile fault-anticipating wrongs, and liability dependent on fault, come, mistakenly, to be thought of as the normal or default case, in need of no special explanation.[52] Hence the need for a special explanation of the fact that punishment expresses or communicates the blameworthiness of the wrongdoer goes increasingly unnoticed. Since punishment (conceptually) is for wrongdoing, and wrongdoing is by default blameworthy,

---

[51] By 'instrumental' here I mean 'based on the consequences of punishment'. When punishment is successful (i.e. when the person whom we attempt to punish is actually punished) it has a certain *result*, namely that the person punished suffers or is deprived and thereby has something else to regret apart from his wrong. A result of an action is an outcome that is partly constitutive of that action. A consequence is an outcome that is not. An action's results, to the extent that they bear on its value, bear on its intrinsic (non-instrumental) value. That the deservedness of punishment depends on the result of punishment does not show, therefore, that the case for deserved punishment (or for the principle by which it is deserved) is partly instrumental.

[52] Bernard Williams saw the importance of this mistake and made sustained efforts to correct it. See especially his *Ethics and the Limits of Philosophy* (London 1985), 174 ff., and 'Internal Reasons and the Obscurity of Blame' in his *Making Sense of Humanity* (Cambridge 1995). Alas, Williams misdiagnosed the mistake and ended up reinforcing it. He traced the blameaholics' emphasis on blame to an emphasis on wrongdoing (breach of obligation), which in turn he criticized. If he had learnt the lesson of his own paper 'Moral Luck', he would not have made this connection. Not all blameworthy actions are wrongful and not all wrongful actions are blameworthy. An emphasis on wrongdoing does not naturally carry an emphasis upon blame in its wake.

what else would punishment express or communicate but blame? At this point, the main question left over is about the relative importance of expressing or communicating things. Should we deliberately inflict suffering and deprivation merely to express or communicate something? Or should we be prepared to do it only to reduce other suffering and deprivation? In this debate the claim that punishment for faulty wrongdoing is deserved loses its independent role. The deservedness of punishment becomes the output rather than the input of endless arguments about punishment's meanings and consequences and the relative justification importance of the two. Moral philosophy has lost sight of the need to rely on the deservedness of punishment to *explain* punishment's meanings and consequences. In the process it has lost sight of the need to explain, in a way that does not depend on punishment's meanings or consequences, why the only actions that deserve to be punished are *both* wrongful *and* blameworthy (two different and only very obliquely related properties).

# 4

# Strict Liability, Justice, and Proportionality

*Douglas Husak*

I will begin by describing what I hope nearly everyone will agree to be an outrageous case of strict liability in the criminal law. The particular example I will select raises a number of fascinating issues in its own right, but I will use it primarily to illustrate the importance of a distinction between two conceptions of what strict liability *is*. This distinction is crucial in helping to identify what, if anything, is unjust about strict liability. I will introduce *New Jersey* v. *Rodriguez* in § 1.[1] In § 2, I will contrast *substantive* with *formal* conceptions of strict liability. I will apply this distinction in § 3 in an effort to understand better the injustice of strict liability. In § 4, I will speculate about the extent of this injustice by trying to identify whether and to what extent various statutory reforms would count as an improvement upon it. I will conclude that the single difficulty shared by most cases of strict liability is that they infringe principles of proportionality in punishment. Occasionally, however, strict liability may give rise to no injustice at all. Moreover, attempts to rectify the problem may actually be counterproductive, increasing the net injustice of the substantive criminal law.

## 1. Strict Liability Drug Homicide

In May of 1988 in the state of New Jersey, Susan Hendricks and Fred Bennett came to the apartment of Carlos Rodriguez for the purpose of buying cocaine. Immediately after their purchase, Hendricks and Bennett proceeded to weigh and place the cocaine into smaller bags. At that moment, police broke into Rodriguez's apartment. In an attempt to destroy the evidence, Hendricks and Bennett each swallowed several of the bags. Within minutes, Hendricks collapsed in convulsions on the floor. Emergency medical workers were summoned to try to resuscitate her. They asked whether anyone else in the room had

I would like to thank the other contributors to this volume, and Andrew Simester in particular, for very helpful comments on earlier drafts.

[1] 645 A 2d 1165 (1994).

swallowed drugs; Bennett denied having done so. About half an hour later, Bennett also went into convulsions and died at the scene. Hendricks subsequently died in the hospital.

This story could be related to demonstrate the folly of the war on drugs.[2] Official government statistics listed the tragic deaths of Hendricks and Bennett as caused by acute cocaine overdose. These data are cited to indicate the perils of illicit drug use. When the full story is told, however, these statistics reveal little about the dangers of cocaine, and much about the dangers of cocaine prohibitions.[3] But I want to use this story to make a very different point. This case came before the Supreme Court of New Jersey because Rodriguez was prosecuted and convicted not simply for the offences of possession of a controlled substance, possession with intent to distribute, distribution of a controlled substance, and distribution of a controlled substance within 1,000 feet of a school zone—each of which was uncontrovertible. In addition, Rodriguez was prosecuted and convicted of *homicide*—for causing the death of Fred Bennett.[4]

Rodriguez was not convicted of one of the familiar kinds of homicide— murder, manslaughter, or negligent homicide—that have long existed in criminal codes throughout the United States. Instead, Rodriguez was convicted of a wholly new kind of homicide[5] created by the Comprehensive Drug Reform Act of 1986, the relevant portions of which are as follows:

a. Any person who manufactures, distributes or dispenses . . . any . . . controlled dangerous substance classified in Schedules I or II . . . is strictly liable for a death which results from the injection, inhalation or ingestion of that substance, and is guilty of a crime of the first degree.

b. The provisions . . . (governing the causal relationship between conduct and result) shall not apply in a prosecution under this section. For purposes of this offence, the defendant's act of manufacturing, distributing or dispensing a substance is the cause of a death when:

    (1) The injection, inhalation or ingestion of the substance is an antecedent but for which the death would not have occurred; and

---

[2] See Douglas Husak, *Drugs and Rights* (Cambridge 1992); and *Legalize This! The Case for Decriminalizing Drugs* (London 2002).

[3] The National Institute on Drug Abuse lists over 25,000 fatalities from illicit drug use. But a majority of these deaths is more properly attributed to drug prohibition than to drug use. Some 14,300 fatalities are due to hepatitis and AIDS—diseases that are not caused by illicit drugs, but (mostly) by the dirty needles that heroin addicts tend to share. Needle exchange programmes could prevent many of these fatalities. There may be no single innovation that could result in greater improvements in the health of illicit drug users.

[4] The opinion does not indicate why the defendant was not also charged with a second count of homicide—for causing the death of Susan Hendricks.

[5] 'What is created is an additional species of homicide, akin to felony-murder.' *New Jersey Statutes Annotated*: Official Comment to 2C:35-9 (2004). This new kind of homicide is not peculiar to New Jersey. At least thirteen other states impose strict criminal liability for a death resulting from the distribution or manufacture of drugs. Two states subject defendants to capital punishment when convicted under their drug death statutes, and two others impose life imprisonment. See the references in *Rodriguez*, at 1175.

(2) The death was not:
    (a) too remote in its occurrence as to have a just bearing on the defendant's liability; or
    (b) too dependent upon conduct of another person which was unrelated to the injection, inhalation or ingestion of the substance or its effect as to have a just bearing on the defendant's liability.

c. It shall not be a defence to a prosecution under this section that the decedent contributed to his own death by his purposeful, knowing, reckless or negligent injection, inhalation or ingestion of the substance, or by his consenting to the administration of the substance by another.

d. Nothing in this section shall be construed to preclude or limit any prosecution for homicide . . . [6]

In *New Jersey* v. *Rodriguez*, the Supreme Court of New Jersey unanimously upheld the constitutionality of this statute and affirmed Rodriguez's conviction.[7] The court noted that the statute imposed *strict liability*, which it characterized as 'criminal liability regardless of a defendant's state of mind, or put differently, regardless of culpability'.[8] More precisely, under the statute, 'no culpability is required for the deadly result. A defendant is guilty whether the defendant intends the death or has absolutely no idea that it may occur.'[9]

Why did the court find this strict liability drug homicide statute to be constitutional? Some passages suggest that the court recognized virtually *no* limits to the authority of the legislature to dispense with culpability in creating offences.[10] 'Case after case, almost without exception, has upheld the power of the states to impose strict criminal liability not only in a regulatory setting but for serious offences as well.'[11] In particular, the imposition of strict liability has played a prominent role in combating the dangers of drug abuse.[12] Most states prohibit drug possession and/or distribution in proximity to a school zone;[13] none appears to require that a defendant believe or have any reason to believe that his possession or distribution took place within the proscribed area.[14] New Jersey is among these states.[15]

Not surprisingly, the court's reasoning in favour of constitutionality relied heavily on similarities between the strict liability drug homicide statute and the

---

[6] *New Jersey Statutes Annotated*: 2C:35-9 (2004).

[7] Above, n. 1. The opinion includes a companion case—*N.J.* v. *Maldonado*—in which the facts are not quite so unusual or distressing. With only slight hyperbole, the court described *Maldonado* as 'a straightforward drug distribution and strict-liability-death case'. Ibid. 1169.

[8] Ibid. 1170.      [9] Ibid.      [10] But see the exception discussed below in n. 66.

[11] *Rodriguez*, at 1171.      [12] See *US* v. *Balint*, 258 US 250 (1922).

[13] Federal law (21 USC § 860 (1994)) originally prohibited drug distribution near a 'school yard', but was subsequently amended to include public housing projects, public or private youth centres, public swimming pools, or video arcades. Several commentators have complained that these designated areas are so numerous that in many cities it is virtually impossible to find a place that is not covered by the statute.

[14] See Tracey Bateman, 'Annotation, Validity, Construction, and Application of State Statutes Prohibiting Sale or Possession of Controlled Substances Within Specified Distance of School' (2000) 27 *ALR 5th* 593.

[15] In *New Jersey* v. *Ivory*, 592 A 2d 205 (1991), a defendant riding his bicycle near a public park was convicted under a statute proscribing possession of drugs within 1,000 feet of a school with intent to distribute even though the state did not prove that he intended to sell drugs near school property, nor

felony-murder rule. These comparisons are unlikely to persuade those many commentators who believe that the felony-murder rule is equally objectionable.[16] Indeed, the court noted that even though the felony-murder rule demonstrated 'the power of the states to create strict liability crimes', it has been 'bombarded by intense criticism and constitutional attack' since its inception.[17] None the less, the court concluded that the continued survival of the felony-murder rule served as 'a strong indicator of states' power to impose strict criminal liability'.[18]

The *constitutionality* of strict liability offences is not the issue I will address.[19] Still, it is important to notice two differences between the felony-murder rule and the strict liability drug homicide statute upheld in *Rodriguez*. First, the application of New Jersey's felony-murder rule, like that in many states, is restricted to a small number of specifically enumerated felonies—robbery, sexual assault, arson, burglary, kidnapping, or criminal escape.[20] All jurisdictions that have retained the felony-murder rule construe it more narrowly than the broad formulation found in Blackstone.[21] Why have they done so? Whatever considerations led states to restrict the rule to enumerated felonies—perhaps the view that these felonies are 'inherently dangerous'—should have militated against applying the rule in the facts of *Rodriguez*. The dangers inherent in crimes such as arson and robbery need not be belaboured. But persons manufacture, distribute, or dispense Schedule I or II substances on literally billions of occasions, and serious harm rarely ensues.[22] Indeed,

---

that he had any reason to know the park was school property, and even though the park, owned by a parochial school, had been leased to the city and regularly used for general recreational purposes. In *New Jersey* v. *Ogar*, 551 A 2d 1037 (1989), a defendant was convicted under the same statute even though she distributed drugs within a prison that happened to be near a school. It is hard to imagine that the user would break out of prison to sell drugs to schoolchildren, or that schoolchildren would break into prison to buy drugs.

[16] The felony-murder rule is extremely unpopular among criminal theorists. According to some commentators, 'criticism of the rule constitutes a lexicon of everything that scholars and jurists can find wrong with a legal doctrine'. Nelson E. Roth and Scott E. Sundby, 'The Felony-Murder Rule: A Doctrine at Constitutional Crossroads' (1985) 70 *Cornell LR* 446, 446.

[17] *Rodriguez*, at 1171.          [18] Ibid.

[19] Most commentators would agree that *Rodriguez* was decided correctly as a matter of constitutional law. The statute satisfies tests recently articulated by commentators who have sought to assess the constitutionality of strict liability. See Alan C. Michaels, 'Constitutional Innocence' (1999) 112 *Harvard LR* 828. For a more sceptical view of the constitutionality of strict liability, see Richard Singer, 'The Resurgence of Mens Rea III—The Rise and Fall of Strict Criminal Liability' (1989) 30 *Boston College LR* 337.          [20] See *New Jersey Statutes Annotated*: 2C:11-3(3) (2004).

[21] 'And if one intends to do another felony, and undesignedly kills a man, this is also murder.' William Blackstone, *Commentaries on the Laws of England*, iv (1765–9), 200–1.

[22] The court may disagree. In a statement of extraordinary hyperbole, it noted that 'the conduct sought to be deterred—illegal drug manufacturing and drug distribution—is also widely regarded as constituting the most substantial threat to public safety that now exists.' *Rodriguez*, at 1172. To support this claim, the court indicated that in 1986 'more than 37,000 people suffered drug-related deaths'. Ibid. 1173. In 1988, the names of Susan Hendricks and Fred Bennett were added to this total. Notice that this rationale emphasizes *aggregate* rather than *relative* risk. This train of thought would allow traffic offences that result in death to give rise to strict liability as well. In a typical year since *Rodriguez* was decided, more than 40,000 Americans die in traffic accidents. If aggregate figures make rational a legislative determination that draconian measures are needed to protect the public, persons who cause

the consumption of some Schedule I substances (such as marijuana) has never been known to kill anyone.[23]

Second, the felony-murder rule, unlike the challenged strict liability drug homicide statute, preserves the usual test of causation applied elsewhere. New Jersey's statute governing causation provides that 'when causing a particular result is a material element of an offense for which absolute liability is imposed by law, the element is not established unless the actual result is a probable consequence of the actor's conduct.'[24] Had this statute applied, the court might have concluded that Rodriguez's act of selling cocaine did not cause the death of Hendricks or Bennett. After all, the victims would not have died but for their own decision to consume the drugs in order to avoid arrest—a situation that Rodriguez could not have been expected to anticipate. But the ordinary statute governing causation was *not* applied in Rodriguez's strict liability drug homicide prosecution[25]—an important point to which I will return.[26] At this juncture, I simply mention that the policy considerations included in most tests of proximate causation can function as a surrogate for culpability under many applications of the felony-murder rule.

Without contesting the authority of the state to impose strict liability in (so-called) regulatory offences, Rodriguez argued that strict liability was objectionable in cases of serious crime. Since he faced a lengthy term of imprisonment, Rodriguez contended that liability without culpability was especially unjust. The court's reason for dismissing this contention is surprising:[27] 'The Constitution places a lesser burden on the states to justify strict liability for serious criminal offenses than for regulatory offenses.'[28] Apparently, all that is needed to uphold strict liability is 'the legislator's rational conclusion that the safety of the public requires such draconian measures.'[29] In this case, the court entertained no doubt about the rationality of the legislature's conclusion.[30]

---

death by driving could be treated as guilty of strict-liability homicide. To be sure, state courts are not alone in exaggerating the dangers of illicit drugs; the US Supreme Court does so as well. See Douglas Husak and Stanton Peele, ' "One of the Major Problems of Our Society": Imagery and Evidence of Drug Harms in U.S. Supreme Court Decisions' (1998) 25 *Contemporary Drug Problems* 191.

[23] See Mitch Earlywine, *Understanding Marijuana: A New Look at the Scientific Evidence* (Oxford 2002), 143–4.      [24] *New Jersey Criminal Code*, 2C:2-3(2)(e) (2004).

[25] Under the strict liability drug homicide statute, a defendant can be liable even if death is *not* a probable consequence of his manufacture, distribution, or dispensing of drugs. See *N.J* v. *Martin*, 573 A 2d 1359, 1372 (1990).      [26] See § 3 below.

[27] This claim is surprising because concerns about the severity of punishment have been a persistent theme among courts and commentators who express reservations about strict liability. See A. P. Simester and G. R. Sullivan, *Criminal Law: Theory and Doctrine* (Oxford 2000), 165. The Model Penal Code does not allow strict liability in cases in which defendants are subject to imprisonment. See § 6.02(4).      [28] *Rodriguez*, at 1171.

[29] Ibid. 1172.

[30] This statute was said to have a rational basis because legislatures are entitled to conclude that greater deterrence would result from holding drug offenders strictly liable for deaths they cause. Ibid. 1172. Without questioning the minimal rationality of this judgment, many commentators express scepticism that such rules produce any marginal gains in deterrence. See Paul H. Robinson and John M. Darley, 'The Role of Deterrence in the Formulation of Criminal Law Rules: At Its Worst When Doing Its Best' (2003) 91 *Georgetown LJ* 949.

## 2. Formal and Substantive Strict Liability

Many commentators object to the offence upheld in *Rodriguez*, and express shock at the factual circumstances that allowed the defendant to be convicted of the mode of homicide it creates. What exactly is the nature of their complaint? Superficially, of course, they are unhappy that the statute imposes strict liability. But what exactly *is* strict liability? And what is alleged to be *unjust* about it? Clearly, we cannot hope to resolve the latter question without answering the former. In this section, I will make a number of observations about the *concept* of strict liability. It turns out to be surprisingly difficult to specify *when* liability is strict.[31] How should we decide which of several competing conceptions is best? I believe that we should prefer that conception that allows us to appreciate what many commentators have thought to be unjust about strict liability.

I hope to make progress in understanding both the nature of strict liability and the crux of the problem with it by contrasting what I will call *formal* from *substantive* conceptions of strict liability.[32] This distinction corresponds to a more familiar contrast between two conceptions of *mens rea*,[33] although I am painfully aware that neither distinction is quite as sharp as one would like. Still, I believe that some such distinction is crucial to the topic at hand. According to a *formal* conception, a mechanical test can be applied to decide whether a given statute is or is not an instance of strict liability.[34] The most familiar such test is that an offence qualifies as an instance of strict liability if and only if a defendant can be convicted despite lacking culpability for one or more of its material elements.[35] If negligence is the lowest form of culpability—as I will henceforth assume[36]—an offence imposes formal strict liability if and only if a defendant can be convicted

---

[31] Andrew Ashworth, *Principles of Criminal Law* (4th edn., Oxford 2003), 164.

[32] A somewhat similar distinction is developed in Kenneth W. Simons, 'When Is Strict Criminal Liability Just?' (1997) 87 *Journal of Criminal Law and Criminology* 1075.

[33] For a discussion, see Joshua Dressler, *Understanding Criminal Law* (3rd edn., New York 2001), 116–18.

[34] Unfortunately, the mechanical test I have described is not always so easy to apply. In the first place, the formal conception requires a canonical account of the offence in question. When the offence is codified, a statute provides this canonical formulation. When the precise description of an offence is controversial, however, it can be difficult to decide whether any of its elements dispense with negligence. In addition, it may be hard to subdivide a given offence into its component parts or elements. As far as I am aware, there is no authoritative device for deciding how to individuate or enumerate the elements of offences. Finally, there may be uncertainty about whether a given element qualifies as a *material* element. In particular, material elements may be easily confused with jurisdictional elements. For a sensitive treatment of these issues, see Richard Singer, 'The Model Penal Code and Three Two (Possibly Only One) Way Courts Avoid Mens Rea' (2000) 4 *Buffalo Criminal LR* 139, 195–206.

[35] Ibid. 143. See also Philip E. Johnson, 'Strict Liability: The Prevalent View', in Sanford Kadish (ed.), *Encyclopedia of Crime and Justice* (New York 1983), iv. 1518.

[36] This assumption has frequently been challenged, even by commentators who write about strict liability. According to one theorist, 'strict liability offence' and 'negligence offence' are 'interchangeable'. Alan Brudner, 'Imprisonment and Strict Liability' (1990) 40 *University of Toronto LJ* 738 n. 5.

even though he lacks negligence for one or more of its material elements.[37] I describe this test as mechanical because it is (or appears to be) value-free; commentators who purport to be unable to make any sense of normative discourse or inquiry can apply it.[38] According to a *substantive* conception, a normative test must be used to decide whether a statute is or is not an instance of strict liability. The most familiar such test is that an offence qualifies as an instance of strict liability if and only if a defendant can be convicted despite lacking fault. The beginning of wisdom in understanding most of the conceptual and normative controversy surrounding strict liability is to appreciate that these conceptions are different. A statute may be an instance of formal strict liability without imposing substantive strict liability; conversely, a statute may be an instance of substantive strict liability without imposing formal strict liability. In other words, a defendant may be at fault even though he is convicted of an offence that does not require negligence for one or more of its material elements, and a defendant may lack fault even though he is convicted of an offence that requires negligence for each of its material elements.[39]

These definitions contain several noteworthy features; I will explicitly mention only one.[40] We can conclude that a statute imposes formal strict liability after examining just one of its many material elements. A single material element for which negligence is not required is sufficient to transform the entire statute into an instance of formal strict liability.[41] By contrast, we cannot decide that a statute

[37] According to some commentators, approximately half of all existing offences in the United Kingdom satisfy the foregoing definition of formal strict liability. See Simester and Sullivan, *Criminal Law*, 165. Other commentators optimistically claim that the tendency to create strict liability statutes is 'on the wane'. Richard Singer, 'Strict Liability', in Joshua Dressler (ed.), *Encyclopedia of Crime and Justice* (2nd edn., New York 2002), 1541.

[38] Resisting normative discourse is regarded as an advantage of legal inquiry in some quarters. Although it is hard to know exactly how far their scepticism extends, some commentators claim that legal policies 'should be based exclusively on their effects on the welfare of individuals' and 'should not depend on notions of fairness, justice, or cognate concepts'. Louis Kaplow and Steven Shavell, *Fairness Versus Welfare* (Cambridge 2002), p. xvii.

[39] Examples from existing law are contentious, but imaginary examples are easy to construct. An offence of knowingly scratching one's head, for example, presumably does not proscribe faulty conduct, even though negligence is required for each material element.

[40] Other features of these definitions may be noteworthy as well. Determinations that a statute imposes strict liability (either formal or substantive) do not depend on the availability of defences or allocations of burdens of proof. Some commentators suggest that an offence is not an instance of strict liability if it allows for a defence of 'due diligence', or shifts the burden to the defendant to prove he acted without negligence. See Laurie Levinson, 'Good Faith Defences: Reshaping Strict Liability Crimes' (1993) 78 *Cornell LR* 401; Martin Wasik, 'Shifting the Burden of Strict Liability' (1982) *Criminal LR* 567. I do not insist that these alternative accounts are necessarily defective. At some point, theorists who seek to define strict liability must resort to stipulation.

[41] One might coin a phrase—say, *pure strict liability*—to describe an offence for which no material element requires negligence. Although the possibility of such an offence can easily be conceived, I am unaware of an existing offence that conforms to this description. Simons mentions this category as a logical possibility, but it is significant that he fails to provide a single example of a real statute that imposes pure strict liability. In all probability, such a crime would be a draconian exercise of state power. See Simons, 'When Is Strict Liability Just?', 1081–2.

imposes substantive strict liability without evaluating the offence as a whole. No inference can be drawn from separate elements.

I must say a good deal more about the nature of the *fault* involved in determining whether a given offence is an instance of substantive strict liability. Fault, as I propose to understand it here, involves a *moral, extra-legal* judgment about whether defendants deserve blame for engaging in the conduct proscribed by the statute.[42] These moral, extra-legal judgments are inherently controversial; reasonable minds may well differ about whether a given offence requires fault in the sense I have in mind.[43] I do not suppose that *moral* philosophers will reject my invitation to decide whether a person deserves blame for his conduct. After all, no theory of criminalization could hope to distinguish justified from unjustified impositions of the criminal sanction unless commentators were prepared to make extra-legal judgments about the morality of given types of conduct. The claim that behaviour should not incur criminal liability unless it causes *harm*, for example, imposes an external normative standard upon the law.[44] None the less, *legal* theorists may be more reluctant to make these judgments. Once a democratic state has duly enacted a criminal statute, on what grounds can we hope to decide that the prohibited conduct is blameless? I will not try to answer this difficult question here; my subsequent judgments about blame and innocence are wholly intuitive. I will, however, briefly digress to argue that the need to make and defend these judgments is unavoidable, since sensible statutory construction often requires extra-legal judgments about fault and innocence. Even positivists who subscribe to the slogan that 'law is one thing and morality another' must be willing to decide whether persons who engage in given kinds of conduct deserve blame. I will argue that the task of interpreting a statute that is written may require recourse to a moral code that is not.[45]

In several recent opinions, the court has indicated that statutes should be construed to require culpability in order to avoid convicting persons who lack fault in the sense I have in mind.[46] Two cases should suffice to illustrate this point. In *US v. X-Citement Video, Inc.*[47] the defendant was charged with 'knowingly transport[ing] and ship[ping] . . . a visual depiction [which] . . . involves the use

---

[42] Of course, not all questions about whether a defendant deserves blame can be answered by determining whether he engaged in the conduct proscribed by the statute. Justifications and excuses also serve to undermine blame, even though they derive from considerations extrinsic to statutes.

[43] Much of the difficulty arises in the context of *malum prohibitum* offences. For a thoughtful discussion, see Stuart Green, 'Why It's A Crime to Tear the Tag Off a Mattress: Overcriminalization and the Moral Content of Regulatory Offences' (1997) 46 *Emory LJ* 1533. See also R. A. Duff, 'Crime, Prohibition, and Punishment' (2002) 19 *Journal of Applied Philosophy* 97.

[44] For the classic defence, see Joel Feinberg, *Harm to Others* (New York 1984).

[45] See John Shepard Wiley, Jr., 'The New Federal Defence: Not Guilty By Reason of Blamelessness' (1999) 85 *Virginia LR* 1021.

[46] Other cases establish the same point. See *Posters 'N' Things* v. *US*, 511 US 513 (1994), which cited *Staples* in construing a federal statute that proscribed the sale of drug paraphernalia to require the government to prove that the defendant knew the items he sold were likely to be used with illegal drugs—even though the statute itself included no culpability term.         [47] 115 S. Ct. 464 (1994).

of a minor engaging in sexually explicit conduct . . . '.[48] The Supreme Court interpreted this statute to include a *mens rea* element of knowledge as to the age of the actress. This case raised a straightforward issue of statutory construction: did the adverb 'knowingly' reach 'down the statute' to the phrase 'use of a minor'? That is, must the defendant know a minor was in the film, or was it sufficient that he knowingly transported a film that, as it turned out, contained a minor? Without committing itself to any of several possible approaches to statutory construction, the court concluded that 'knowingly' should modify 'use of a minor'.[49]

After reaffirming the existence of a 'presumption' in favour of requiring culpability in criminal statutes, the court spoke of the 'dangers' of convicting 'innocent' persons if 'knowingly' were held not to modify the element in question:

Some applications of respondents' position would produce results that were not merely odd but positively absurd . . . we would sweep within the ambit of the statute actors who had no idea that they were dealing with sexually explicit material. For instance, a retail druggist who returns an uninspected roll of developed film to a customer 'knowingly distributes' a visual depiction . . . [o]r a new resident of an apartment might receive mail for the prior resident and store the mail unopened. . . . Similarly, a Federal Express courier who delivers a box in which the shipper has declared the contents to be 'film' 'knowingly transports' such film.[50]

Unless 'knowingly' were interpreted to reach 'use of a minor', the court argued, many blameless persons would be subjected to criminal liability. Innocent people such as messengers and film developers could not be blamed for their failure to discover the contents of films. Truck drivers who deliver salt that turns out to be cocaine, or developers of microfilm that turns out to be stolen missile plans, would also be 'innocent' under the court's approach.

*X-Citement Video* is not the only example that demonstrates the need to resort to extra-legal judgments of fault in statutory construction. Consider *Staples* v. *U.S.*[51] Staples owned an AR-15 assault rifle, which, unless modified, is a *semi-automatic* weapon. The AR-15 is manufactured with a metal stop that is intended to prevent persons from converting it into an automatic device. Staples' gun, which had been semi-automatic when obtained, had somehow 'become' automatic, either through active human intervention or by normal wear and tear. Federal statutes require that all automatic weapons ('machine guns') be registered with the Secretary of the Treasury; semi-automatic and non-automatic weapons need not be registered.[52] When Staples was prosecuted for failing to register his AR-15, he alleged ignorance of the facts that caused the gun to become automatic.

---

[48] 18 USC § 2252 (1988 edn. & Supp. V).

[49] This conclusion is remarkable, since strict liability as to age first appeared in a case involving the sexual activity of a minor. The landmark case is *Prince* (1874) LR 2 CCR 154.

[50] *X-Citement Video*, at 467–8.     [51] 114 S. Ct. 1793 (1994).

[52] 18 USC § 922; 26 USC §§ 5495, 5841.

The Supreme Court, with only two dissents, construed the statute—which had no explicit *mens rea* term—to require *knowledge* of the nature of the weapon. Any other position, it argued, might capture too many innocent actors:

(T)hat an item is 'dangerous' in some general sense does not necessarily suggest . . . that it is not also entirely innocent. Even dangerous items can, in some cases, be so commonplace and generally available that we would not consider them to alert individuals to the likelihood of strict regulation. . . . (P)recisely because guns falling outside [limited] categories traditionally have been widely accepted as lawful possessions, their destructive potential . . . cannot be said to put gun owners on notice of the likelihood of regulation.[53]

These two cases express a strong commitment to protect the innocent and thus to resist substantive strict liability—even though the term 'innocent' is not defined in any of the opinions.[54]

I hope to have shown that extra-legal, moral judgments of fault are needed not only to categorize offences as instances of substantive strict liability, but also to provide sensible interpretations of existing statutes. If I am correct, even the most committed legal positivist should be prepared to make moral judgments about whether given offences involve fault. My main point, however, is that commentators must distinguish between formal and substantive conceptions if they hope to understand what is often (but not always) objectionable about strict liability. In the remainder of this section, I will illustrate the importance of this contrast by returning to *Rodriguez*, the case with which I began.

It is obvious that the drug homicide statute upheld in *Rodriguez* qualifies as an instance of strict liability according to the formal conception I described. The 'result' element of this statute—the death caused by drug distribution—does not require negligence. It is far less clear, however, that the statute qualifies as an instance of strict liability according to the substantive conception I described. I believe there is considerable room for doubt on this matter. The *Rodriguez* court, however, expressed no reservations about it, and I will tentatively assume it is correct.[55] As the court explained, 'to the extent moral culpability is a desirable element of a criminal offence, it is inextricably embedded in the drug death statute'.[56] Strict liability for death is not imposed when persons engage in innocent conduct that happens to result in a fatality; it is reserved for situations in which the underlying conduct that causes death is deemed to be blameworthy.

The court's judgment that fault is contained in the act of distributing cocaine was bolstered by the fact that virtually all states withhold liability unless a defendant

[53] *Staples*, at 1800.

[54] For further discussion of these issues, see Richard Singer and Douglas Husak, 'Of Innocence and Innocents: The Supreme Court and *Mens Rea* Since Herbert Packer' (1999) 2 *Buffalo Criminal LR* 859.

[55] For present purposes, I will not contest the blameworthiness of drug distribution. Even if the use and possession of cocaine were innocent, distribution is another matter. See Peter Alldridge, 'Dealing With Drug Dealing', in A. P. Simester and A. T. H. Smith (eds.), *Harm and Culpability* (Oxford 1996), 239.                                                    [56] *Rodriguez*, at 1174.

*knows* that the substance he is distributing is controlled.[57] Presumably, a drug distribution statute that dispensed with culpability for *this* element would qualify as an instance of substantive strict liability (as well as an instance of formal strict liability). Suppose, for example, that Rodriguez had reasonably believed that he was distributing peanut butter rather than cocaine, and the purchaser died from a reaction that could not have been foreseen. In this event, a statute that imposed liability for death would have punished him despite his innocence or lack of blame—which the actual strict liability drug homicide statute in *Rodriguez* (arguably) did not. As I hope this modification of the original offence illustrates, no one is entitled to conclude that a case of formal strict liability is a case of substantive strict liability unless he knows *which* material element dispenses with negligence. Then, he must ask the kind of question posed by the Supreme Court in *X-Citement Video* and *Staples*: does the statute impose criminal liability on persons who are innocent and do not deserve to be punished?

Again, I emphasize that there is no easy way to answer this question;[58] the task of making and defending moral judgments, although controversial, cannot be avoided. Still, the mere fact that a statute does not require negligence for each material element (i.e. is an example of formal strict liability) does not entail that it imposes liability without fault (i.e. is an example of substantive strict liability). No mechanical, non-normative test can show that persons who are punished do not deserve to be blamed. I suspect that the failure to distinguish formal from substantive conceptions of strict liability—or the mistaken assumption that the two conceptions are equivalent—helps to explain why commentators have divided about whether strict liability is always unjust.[59]

*Substantive* strict liability in the criminal law *is* always unjust. I have nothing especially novel to say in favour of the conclusion that the state should not punish conduct that is morally innocent and does not merit blame, but a brief sketch of my reasoning is as follows.[60] Impositions of criminal liability subject offenders to state punishment.[61] Inflictions of punishment must be justified. Since the rights infringed by punishment are important and valuable, the standard needed to

---

[57] The lone exception is Washington, where the absence of knowledge is an affirmative defence. See *State* v. *Cleppe*, 635 P 2d 435 (1981).

[58] In attempting to decide whether given statutes punish blameless conduct, Justice Ginsburg provides several peculiar examples of 'innocent' behaviour, including persons seeking to avoid an IRS audit, and husbands trying to conceal their wealth to avoid an increase in alimony payments. See *Ratzlaf* v. *US*, 510 US 135, 144 (1994).

[59] In a comprehensive survey, one commentator concludes that 'the dominant view appears to be that in the Anglo-American culture, the use of strict liability crimes is arbitrary and unreasonable'. Levinson, 'Good Faith Defences', 403 n. 7. But dissenting voices *are* heard. See e.g. James Brady, 'Strict Liability Offences: A Justification' (1972) 8 *Criminal Law Bulletin* 217; and Steven Nemerson, 'Criminal Liability Without Fault: A Philosophical Perspective' (1975) 75 *Columbia LR* 1517.

[60] For further thoughts, see Douglas Husak, 'Limitations on Criminalization and the General Part of Criminal Law', in Stephen Shute and A. P. Simester (eds.), *Criminal Law Theory: Doctrines of the General Part* (Oxford 2002), 13.

[61] Since the criminal–civil law demarcation is so hard to draw, many of the objections against substantive strict liability in the criminal law would seem to apply to the civil law as well. Consider,

justify criminal prohibitions must be high. Any acceptable justification of punishment presupposes desert, which requires blame or fault in the defendant.[62] Although debatable, I believe these claims are widely accepted. In any event, I will not endeavour to defend them here.[63]

Formal strict liability, on the other hand, may or may not be unjust. I will say more in § 3 about the injustice that infects many cases of formal strict liability. At this time, I simply call attention to a phenomenon that should puzzle criminal theorists who are familiar with the massive critical commentary about strict liability. Earlier, I indicated that one conception should be preferred to another if it helps us to understand why so many theorists have regarded strict liability to be objectionable. Substantive strict liability satisfies this desideratum better than formal strict liability. Still, the majority of theorists define strict liability formally—as any offence that allows a defendant to be convicted despite lacking culpability for one or more of its material elements.[64] Why is this definition so prevalent? I confess that I cannot answer this question, although I believe I can locate it in a larger context. Legal theorists have long been concerned with form rather than with substance. Issues of criminalization—which must be addressed by anyone who aspires to understand whether and to what extent strict liability is objectionable—tend to be neglected by theorists.[65] It is baffling how a commentator could hope to derive substantial conclusions about justice from purely formal characteristics of criminal statutes.

The *Rodriguez* court reached much the same position about the injustice of what I have called substantive strict liability. The authority it granted to legislatures to enact criminal offences was not unbounded. The court maintained that 'constitutional-due-process limitations on strict liability criminal statutes apply when the underlying conduct is so passive, so unworthy of blame, that the persons violating the proscription would have had no notice that they were breaking the law'.[66] Although the court came close to endorsing the view I am defending here by precluding substantive strict liability, I want to mention two significant differences. First, the court was anxious to probe the *constitutional* limitations on

---

e.g. *Department of Housing and Urban Development* v. *Rucker*, 122 S. Ct. 1230 (2002), in which tenants were evicted from public housing for failing to 'assure that . . . any member of the household, a guest, or another person under the tenant's control, shall not engage in . . . any drug-related criminal activity on or near the premises'. The regulations authorized eviction even if the tenant did not know, could not foresee, or could not control the drug-related activity of other occupants. In other words, Congress did not provide for an 'innocent owner' defence. Such proceedings seem to involve substantive strict liability in the *civil* law, and impose hardships and stigma that seem roughly equivalent to that of criminal sanctions.

[62] This claim, frequently called 'negative retributivism', is endorsed by the vast majority of criminal theorists.

[63] For a more extended defence, see Andrew von Hirsch, *Censure and Sanction* (New York 1993).

[64] See e.g. Johnson, 'Strict Liability: The Prevalent View', *Encyclopedia of Crime and Justice*, iv. 1518.

[65] Of course, there are many exceptions to this generalization. Most notably, see Ashworth, *Principles of Criminal Law*.                                    [66] *Rodriguez*, at 1174.

strict liability in the criminal law. I am concerned, however, to identify the conditions under which the imposition of strict liability gives rise to injustice. I would hope that the considerations of justice I will cite are consistent with our best theory of constitutional interpretation, but no such compatibility can be guaranteed. Second, the court seemed to indicate that conduct is unworthy of blame only when persons are 'passive' and 'had no notice' that their behaviour was illegal.[67] But neither of these two factors is essential. Conduct may be innocent in the substantive sense to which I am appealing even though it is active rather than passive. Moreover, adequate notice that conduct is prohibited hardly ensures that it is blameworthy.[68] Neither passivity nor the absence of notice is the problem with my (hypothetical) offence that proscribes the distribution of cocaine by persons who reasonably believe it to be peanut butter. The court was on firmer ground, I believe, when it said that strict liability is objectionable when imposed on persons whose conduct is 'unworthy of blame'. The nature of the blame to which the court referred, I think, is moral and extra-legal. It is hard to fathom how anyone could hope to find an offence to be unjust unless he is prepared to make moral judgments about whether persons merit blame for engaging in the proscribed conduct.

## 3. Strict Liability and Proportionality

Once we become aware that not all cases of formal strict liability are cases of substantive strict liability, the most straightforward objection to the former evaporates. We cannot say that all instances of formal strict liability convict the innocent, notwithstanding their lack of blame and absence of desert. As the strict liability drug homicide statute upheld in *Rodriguez* suggests, formal strict liability need not dispense with fault altogether. What, then, might be unjust about examples of formal strict liability—about statutes that allow conviction even though a defendant is not negligent with respect to each material element? I doubt that there *is* a single principle of justice violated by all instances of formal strict liability. Indeed, some cases of strict liability seem to violate *no* principle of justice at all.[69] Still, I will argue that the most general complaint about formal strict liability stems from concerns about proportionality in punishment. To support this conclusion, I will distinguish two related principles of proportionate punishment. But some instances of formal strict liability may not infringe *either* principle of proportionality.

[67] The obvious reference is to *Lambert* v. *California*, 355 US 225 (1957).
[68] Even when conduct *is* blameworthy, notice is not the heart of the problem. The real difficulty is that there may be little that persons can *do* with notice to avoid liability.
[69] It does not follow, of course, that instances of formal strict liability are unobjectionable simply because they violate no principle of justice. Commentators disagree about whether and under what conditions strict liability in the criminal law is *effective*. For a useful discussion, see Ashworth, *Principles of Criminal Law*, 167–9.

I will assume that punishment includes two distinct but related components that render it notoriously difficult to justify: censure and hard treatment.[70] Theorists disagree about how these ingredients cohere in a single rationale of punishment, but I hope to avoid this complex issue here.[71] Each of these components gives rise to its own distinctive principle of proportionality, as can be seen by returning to *Rodriguez*. What exactly is alleged to be unjust about the strict liability drug homicide statute? After all, it is unlikely that the offence dispenses with blame altogether by punishing wholly innocent conduct; it is not a paradigm example of substantive strict liability. The answer, then, must be that even though the statute requires fault, it does not require *enough* fault. But this answer raises the further question: *enough fault for what*? To my mind, this is the hardest question to answer in attempts to understand both the nature of strict liability as well as the normative problems theorists have associated with it.[72] The solution is clear when strict liability is substantive. In such cases, fault is insufficient to merit *any* degree of punishment; no hard treatment or condemnation can be justified. But this solution is unavailable when strict liability is formal but not substantive. The tentative answer I propose here is that the extent of fault in cases of formal strict liability is (typically but not necessarily) insufficient to merit the *degree* of hardship or condemnation inflicted upon the offender.

One plausible analysis of the injustice in *Rodriguez* is that the defendant's conviction misrepresents the nature of what he *did*—what he is blameworthy *for*. Clearly, Rodriguez distributed cocaine. But the statute holds him liable for something quite different: the death of Fred Bennett. No one should be criminally liable for a state of affairs for which he does not deserve to be blamed. Unless persons are culpable for a state of affairs—at least negligent—no censure *for* that state of affairs is deserved. My claim, then, is that Rodriguez's conviction involves a kind of deception. Rodriguez may not be blameless altogether, but he is not blameworthy *for* the result for which he was convicted.

Why does this misrepresentation matter? My answer presupposes that criminal liability and punishment have an *expressive* dimension.[73] Criminal sanctions

---

[70]   See Andrew von Hirsch, *Past Or Future Crimes?* (New Brunswick, NJ 1985), Ch. V.

[71]   See the exchange between R. A. Duff, 'Punishment, Communication, and Community', and Andrew von Hirsch, 'Punishment, Penance and the State', in Matt Matravers (ed.), *Punishment and Political Theory* (Oxford 1999), 48 and 69.

[72]   For more detailed thoughts, see Douglas Husak, 'Varieties of Strict Liability' (1995) VIII *Canadian Journal of Law & Jurisprudence* 198. In this piece, I claimed that each of the many kinds of strict liability allow a defendant to be convicted of an offence even though he is substantially less at fault than the paradigm perpetrator of that offence. I am no longer confident that this general characterization is adequate. Still, my present approach enables us to understand what would be worrisome about strict liability as so defined. When given defendants exhibit less fault than paradigm perpetrators of the same offence, the former are likely to be punished in excess of their desert, giving rise to the problems of proportionality I emphasize here.

[73]   Expressive theories are now familiar. The classic source is Joel Feinberg, 'The Expressive Function of Punishment', in his *Doing and Deserving* (Princeton 1970), 95. For a lengthy critique of expressive theories generally, see Matthew Adler, 'Expressive Theories of Law: A Skeptical Overview' (2000) 148 *University of Pennsylvania LR* 1363.

convey a message about offenders and their conduct. Responses to persons who perform blameworthy acts are governed by a principle of proportionality. More specifically, such responses are governed by a *principle of proportionality in censuring*: the amount of reprobation deserved by an offender should be a function of the blameworthiness of his offence.[74] Reactions to persons who distribute cocaine are far less severe than reactions to persons who commit homicides. The deception involved in *Rodriguez* is important, since it allowed the defendant to be blamed in excess of his desert.

The central premise in the foregoing argument is that Rodriguez was blamed more severely than he deserved to be. But why shouldn't he be blamed for Bennett's death? Is the only answer that Rodriguez is not culpable for this result? Thus far, I have barely mentioned a significant feature of the strict liability drug homicide statute that lends additional support to my hypothesis that Rodriguez's conviction violates the principle of proportionality in censuring. Moral and legal philosophers have long debated the precise nature of the relationship that must obtain between a defendant and a state of affairs before he deserves to be blamed for it. Typically, this relationship is said to be *causal*.[75] Assume this position is correct; assume that Rodriguez does not deserve to be censured *for* the death of Fred Bennett unless he *caused* that death. *Did* Rodriguez cause Bennett's death? No philosopher has defended a theory of causation that should inspire much confidence about how to answer this question.[76] None the less, I believe there are several reasons to doubt that it should be answered affirmatively.

First, suppose that the legislature is generally correct about the conditions under which persons cause consequences for which negligence is not required.[77] As we have seen, the applicable statute requires the actual result in such cases to be 'a probable consequence of the actor's conduct'.[78] But the strict liability drug homicide statute does not retain this general test; it relaxes the ordinary rules of causation that typically pertain to strict liability result crimes.[79] To be sure, the statute preserves the so-called 'cause in fact' component of causation; an act of drug distribution does not cause a death that would have occurred regardless of that act. Still, the legislature decided to fashion a wholly new rule of *proximate* causation for strict liability drug homicide cases. But if the usual test of causation

---

[74] See Dan Kahan, 'What Do Alternative Sanctions Mean?' (1996) 63 *University of Chicago LR* 591.

[75] But see Douglas Husak, 'Omissions, Causation, and Liability', (1980) 30 *Philosophical Quarterly* 316.

[76] For a recent discussion, see Michael Moore, 'For What Must We Pay? Causation and Counterfactual Baselines' (2003) 40 *San Diego Law Review* 1181.

[77] *New Jersey Criminal Code*, 2C:3(2)(e) (2004).     [78] Ibid. 2C:2-3(2)(e).

[79] Remarkably, the court did not appear to believe that the new statutory provision regarding causation was needed to impose liability. In commenting on the nature of the causal connection between Rodriguez's sale and the ensuing deaths, the court indicated that 'no case could be more direct . . . Rodriguez provided cocaine to Bennett, he died from the ingestion.' Ibid. 1178. According to this analysis, the intervention of the police or the effort of Bennett to avoid arrest did not break the causal chain from sale to death.

is adequate in other contexts—when a consequence is brought about by using
a gun, for example—I cannot comprehend why it would be *in*adequate when that
same consequence is brought about by using a drug.[80] Deaths frequently ensue
from ingesting medications, even when patients conform to the terms of their
prescriptions.[81] Why should the test of causation vary depending on whether
death followed from taking a drug the legislature has assigned to Schedule III
rather than to Schedule I or II? Unless the test of causation is defective across the
board, I believe we are entitled to conclude that it is defective in this case.

Ordinary language provides additional reason to doubt that Rodriguez's act of
distribution caused Bennett's death. Homicides, I assume, are cases of killing,
especially when acts rather than omissions are involved. Killing, I further assume,
is not solely a technical term of legal art. If these two assumptions are correct,[82] we
can inquire whether respondents proficient in English discourse would say that
the defendant killed the decedent in the facts of *Rodriguez*. Although I do not
pretend to have conducted a methodologically sophisticated study of this matter,
my informal surveys as well as my own opinion suggest that the answer is no.

This conclusion is important to the topic at hand because questions about
causation are not wholly independent from those pertaining to culpability. The
policy considerations many theorists contend to be inherent in tests of proximate
causation often serve to mitigate the harshness of doctrines in the criminal law
that dispense with culpability—such as the felony-murder rule. In other words,
proximate causation frequently functions as a surrogate for culpability. In *King* v.
*Commonwealth*,[83] for example, a felony-murder conviction was reversed when a
co-pilot survived after his airplane, transporting marijuana, crashed into a moun-
tainside in dense fog. The court reasoned that the felonious nature of the defendant's conduct was not the proximate cause of the pilot's death, since the plane
would have hit the mountain even if its cargo had not contained contraband. The
court noted that the outcome might have been different if the crash had occurred
because the airplane had been trying to avoid detection by flying at a low altitude.
I am not suggesting that the very same reasoning would support an acquittal in
*Rodriguez*. In suspending the usual test of proximate causation, however, some of
the kinds of considerations adduced in *King* became unavailable to Rodriguez.
After all, deaths such as that suffered by Bennett could not have provided the state
with a reason to proscribe drug distribution. No legislature would enact a drug
offence in order to prevent buyers from consuming large quantities of cocaine
to avoid arrest and prosecution. Indeed, Bennett's fate provides a reason *not* to
proscribe drug distribution and possession. The special provisions applicable to

---

[80] I take the fact that lesser standards of causation apply to drug offences as further evidence for
what might be called 'drug exceptionalism' in the substantive criminal law. See Erik Luna, 'Drug
Exceptionalism' (2002) 47 *Villanova LR* 753.

[81] See Jay S. Cohen, *Overdose* (New York 2001).

[82] Of course, we might question the relevance of ordinary language to legal argument. Generally,
see George Fletcher, *Rethinking Criminal Law* (Boston 1978).          [83] 368 SE 2d 704 (1988).

strict liability drug homicide cases limit our opportunity to employ causal language to express our scepticism that Rodriguez deserves to be blamed for Bennett's death.[84]

I conclude that Rodriguez probably did *not* cause death. If I am correct, and a defendant does not deserve to be blamed for an outcome he did not cause, Rodriguez does not deserve to be blamed for Bennett's death. At least, he does not deserve the *degree* of blame that is reserved for persons who kill. Therefore, the strict liability drug homicide offence infringes the principle of proportionality in censuring. I am dubious, however, that comparable misrepresentations need infect each and every case of formal strict liability. My charge of deception and undeserved blame seems plausible in *Rodriguez*, since we generally understand the nature of homicide and the quantum of reprobation that is appropriate for persons who bring about death with different degrees of culpability. Consider, however, instances of regulatory, *malum prohibitum* offences of formal strict liability.[85] In such cases, the charge of deception may be much more difficult to substantiate, since we are less likely to have views about the degree of censure that is appropriate for the kind of conduct in question.

In any event, I have not begun to exhaust the complaints that might be brought against the statute upheld in *Rodriguez*. A second and more important source of injustice is that the offence infringes a related but distinct principle of proportionality in punishment—what I will call the *principle of proportionality in hard treatment*. According to this principle, the severity of hard treatment deserved by the offender should be a function of the seriousness of his offence. Thus far, my description of *Rodriguez* has not provided sufficient information on which to base this allegation. Yet we naturally assume that the strict liability drug homicide offence for which Rodriguez was convicted involves a more severe deprivation than the several other crimes he unquestionably committed. Why *else* would the legislature have created an additional species of homicide—especially when its inclusion in the criminal code gives rise to the misrepresentation I discussed above? Indeed, this assumption is correct. In New Jersey, a defendant convicted of

---

[84] We might even say that the strict liability drug homicide statute upheld in *Rodriguez* is *doubly* strict. The offence not only fails to require that a defendant be negligent for a death, but also fails to require that he proximately cause the death according to the test that generally applies in cases of strict liability. We might infer that each of these two features of the statute imposes a different *kind* of strict liability. One might well imagine additional kinds of strict liability this statute could impose. In order for criminal liability to be imposed under the strict liability drug homicide statute, I assume that death must be caused by ingesting the drug *token* distributed by Rodriguez. In other words, Rodriguez would not be liable simply because death was caused by ingesting the *type* of drug he sold. This assumption is crucial. Suppose that Smith sells cocaine to Jones, who ingests it and subsequently dies from a cocaine overdose. When White sells cocaine to Black, who consumes it but is unharmed, might the statute allow *White* to be convicted of *Jones's* death? If so, the strict liability drug homicide statute would impose *vicarious* liability on White for the act of Smith. Such vicarious liability might be conceptualized as a distinct variety of strict liability. See Husak, 'Varieties of Strict Liability'.

[85] Consider some of the examples of strict liability regulatory offences of recent vintage described in Andrew Ashworth, 'Is the Criminal Law a Lost Cause?' (2000) 116 *Law Quarterly Review* 225.

distributing cocaine is guilty of an offence of the second or third degree, while a defendant who is convicted of strict liability drug homicide is guilty of an offence of the first degree.[86] More specifically, Rodriguez was sentenced to an additional eighteen years for his homicide.[87] The severity of hardship inflicted for this offence is comparable to that imposed on murderers—one of the few other crimes of the first degree in New Jersey.[88]

I claim, then, that the strict liability drug homicide statute is unjust because it subjects offenders like Rodriguez to terms of imprisonment in excess of their desert. I hope that most commentators will agree that the extent of his deprivation is excessive. Yet it would be hard to defend this judgment were a theorist to challenge it; the specific demands of the principle of proportionality in hard treatment are enormously difficult to identify.[89] There is no uniquely correct solution to the problem of how much hardship given offenders deserve; any answer invokes controversial views about how penalty scales should be anchored—a question that depends partly on vague and elusive matters such as social conventions.[90] Since judgments of proportionality in hard treatment are so problematic, it is not obvious that each instance of formal strict liability will involve an excessive punishment. We cannot rule out the possibility that the sentence imposed on a person convicted of a formal strict liability offence will involve no greater deprivation than is deserved.[91] I have no idea about whether this possibility is ever actualized, but I see no reason to insist that *all* offences of formal strict liability must violate the principle of proportionality in hard treatment.

I have argued that cases of formal strict liability that are not also cases of substantive strict liability are usually but perhaps not always unjust. I want briefly to digress to discuss a metaphor to help illuminate many of the conclusions I have reached thus far. This metaphor can be used to understand both why substantive strict liability is always unjust, and why formal strict liability may or may not be unjust. A 'thin-ice' principle sheds light on each of these issues.[92] According to one version of this principle, a person who skates on thin ice has no cause for

[86]  *Rodriguez*, at 1168.

[87]  The court initially merged the counts for possession and possession with intent to distribute into the distribution count, for which Rodriguez was sentenced to a five-year term. On the school zone count, Rodriguez was sentenced to an additional term of four years. The Appellate Division affirmed Rodriguez's convictions, merged the distribution conviction into the school zone conviction, and ordered that the sentences for the drug death and the school zone conviction run concurrently. The court rejected Rodriguez's contention that his school distribution conviction should merge into his strict liability drug homicide conviction. Ibid. 1170.

[88]  In the light of this fact, it is not an exaggeration to conclude that the strict liability drug homicide statute is a new species of murder.

[89]  This difficulty is compounded in the case of drug offenders. See Douglas Husak, 'Desert, Proportionality, and the Seriousness of Drug Offences', in Andrew Ashworth and Martin Wasik (eds.), *Fundamentals of Sentencing Theory* (Oxford 1998), 187.

[90]  See von Hirsch, *Censure and Sanction*, 36–46.

[91]  This possibility becomes more likely if too little hardship is generally imposed on defendants who commit the same crimes as Rodriguez (for example) but do *not* kill.

[92]  See Ashworth, *Principles of Criminal Law*, 71–2. The metaphor is drawn from an opinion by Lord Morris in *Knuller* v. *DPP* (1973) AC 435, 463.

complaint when he falls through.[93] An important qualification must be added before this principle becomes plausible. No one should be blamed for falling *through* thin ice unless he had reason to believe he was *on* it. Suppose a person lacks negligence for being on thin ice—that is, he reasonably believes (somehow) that he is not skating on ice at all, or (more plausibly) that the ice on which he is skating is not thin. Under these circumstances, I doubt that he deserves blame or hardship for his misfortune. Blame or hardship could only be inflicted by an analogue of substantive strict liability—a categorical injustice. Suppose, however, that our skater *is* at least negligent about whether he is on thin ice. On this assumption, he will merit little sympathy if he falls through.

How helpful is the thin-ice principle? I suspect that the metaphor may obscure as many questions as it illuminates, since the plight of our skater is inadequately described. What exactly *does* our skater deserve when he falls through thin ice? To get wet? To catch pneumonia? To pay for his own rescue? To drown? Can he deserve the latter fate even if he had no reason to believe that the waters were sufficiently deep to make drowning a realistic possibility? As far as I can tell, the thin-ice principle provides no guidance about how these questions should be answered; it does not specify the *amount* of censure or hardship our skater deserves. Surely there is *some* limit to the blame or suffering that persons merit when they fall through thin ice; I see no reason to deem them morally equivalent to thrill-seekers who *knowingly* or *purposely* plunge into icy waters, or who skate fully aware that the waters are deep enough to cause death. If my observations thus far are cogent, these questions of proportionality raise the central difficulty with offences of formal strict liability.

Suppose I am correct that infringements of proportionality in punishment are the central problem of justice infecting most cases of formal strict liability. Why might legal philosophers have failed to reach this conclusion? The short answer is that criminal theorists have shown little interest in sentencing generally or in the grading of specific offences in particular.[94] We should not lose sight of the fact that the most significant impact of the strict liability drug homicide statute on defendants such as Rodriguez is to triple the length of their terms of imprisonment.

## 4. Possible Reforms

I conclude that the punishment inflicted on persons who violate the strict liability drug homicide statute upheld in *Rodriguez* almost certainly infringes each of the

---

[93] I call a general version of this principle *taint* in Douglas Husak, *Philosophy of Criminal Law* (Totowa, NJ 1987), 69–72. According to this principle, persons who engage in conduct that the state permits but does not encourage must be prepared to accept responsibility for consequences that turn out worse than they expect.

[94] Homicide may appear to represent an exception to this claim. As one commentator has observed, however, teachers of criminal law expend great effort analysing the standards by which instances of killing should be categorized as manslaughter or murder, but rarely discuss the sentencing consequences of either verdict. See Gerald E. Lynch, 'Towards a Model Penal Code, Second (Federal?): The Challenge of the Special Part' (1998) 2 *Buffalo Criminal LR* 297, 301.

two principles of proportionality I have discussed. We should anticipate that persons who commit strict liability offences will be punished excessively. It is tempting to believe that the solution to this problem is straightforward: eliminate strict liability from the substantive criminal law. Indeed, this option may be preferable to any of the alternatives I will examine in the remainder of this chapter. Unfortunately, however, matters may not be quite so simple. After all, the injustice I have described is a function of the severity of the punishment imposed on such persons as Rodriguez, and is not due to the existence of the strict liability drug homicide statute itself. Moreover, the very same objections may apply to statutes that do *not* impose formal strict liability, so the repeal of such offences provides no assurance that the injustice will be reduced. No one needs to resort to formal strict liability in order to inflict draconian punishments that disregard principles of proportionality.

Can we speculate about *how* unjust formal strict liability is likely to be relative to other injustices in the substantive criminal law? No precise measure of degree of injustice is available. One possible way to shed light on this issue is by trying to decide whether and to what extent various statutory reforms would help to rectify the problem I have raised. In an effort better to understand the extent of injustice in formal strict liability, I will examine five separate scenarios that involve modifications of the strict liability drug homicide statute and accompanying offences. The issue to be addressed in each scenario is whether the modifications produce more or less injustice than the original statute upheld in *Rodriguez*. The question is how to *rank* the five scenarios from the perspective of justice. I will not pretend to resolve this issue. But I am certain that at least *some* legislative responses that dispense with formal strict liability actually *increase* the net injustice of the criminal law. I hope that the following exercise helps us to gain some perspective on the extent to which formal strict liability is unjust.

The first of my five scenarios retains the status quo. Defendants such as Rodriguez are strictly liable for a death that results from the manufacture or distribution of given drugs. They are liable for additional crimes (such as distribution and possession) as well. Scenario two adopts the solution preferred by many commentators: the insertion of a culpability requirement in the drug homicide offence so that negligence is needed before a defendant becomes liable for death. Notice that this second scenario is likely to be redundant with existing law in the United States. Most but not all jurisdictions punish negligent homicide;[95] there is almost no reason to create an additional species of homicide when the means of death happen to involve a drug.[96] In any event, scenario two should please commentators who are persuaded that formal strict liability is unjust.

[95] See Model Penal Code, § 210.4. It is noteworthy that New Jersey itself lacks a crime of negligent homicide.
[96] No reason, that is, unless the tests of causation are different depending on how death is brought about. In what follows, I assume that tests do not differentiate between drugs and other means of causing death.

The remaining scenarios are a bit more complex. In the third, suppose that legislators try to circumvent whatever problems infect strict liability by introducing the following two changes. First, they delete the strict liability element from the statute altogether. If this change were implemented, the amended offence would become the manufacture or distribution of a Schedule I or II substance.[97] This crime, of course, predates the strict liability drug homicide statute applied in *Rodriguez*. Second, they reclassify this offence as a crime of the first degree, so that perpetrators are subjected to a term of imprisonment that is equal to that imposed upon murderers.[98] Such severe punishments for cocaine offences are not unprecedented.[99] Imagine that a defendant—call him Smith—is convicted of this modified statute. The length of his imprisonment would be comparable to what was imposed in *Rodriguez*—even though the new statute would not qualify as an instance of formal strict liability.

It is hard to see why this change would satisfy critics of formal strict liability. Anyone who believed that Rodriguez was treated unjustly would have little reason to think otherwise of Smith. The revised statute may represent a modest improvement over its predecessor, since Smith is not convicted for causing death. No deception or infringement of the principle of proportionality in censuring need occur. Presumably, however, this benefit is offset by greater injustices; commentators would have much *more* reason to complain if the legislature dispensed with formal strict liability by introducing the two modifications I have described. Pursuant to these amendments, *all* persons who manufacture or distribute designated substances—not only those whose conduct results in death—would be incarcerated for the same duration as Rodriguez. Suppose that roughly one death is caused per million acts of cocaine distribution. If so, this modification magnifies the injustice in *Rodriguez* by a factor of one million. This cannot be the outcome sought by commentators who oppose formal strict liability. Scenario three, I am confident, is much worse than scenarios one or two, even though it dispenses with formal strict liability.

Consider, then, a fourth scenario. As in the third scenario, the legislature deletes the strict liability element from the statute so that defendants such as Rodriguez again become guilty only of the offence of distributing cocaine. In contrast to the third scenario, however, the quantum of punishment for this offence is not excessive. In addition, suppose that a *separate* sentencing provision, extrinsic to the statute itself, were enacted to provide for enhanced deprivations—for greater amounts of hard treatment—in those rare cases in which drug distribution

[97] For purposes of simplicity, I henceforth ignore the other statutes for which Rodriguez was prosecuted and convicted.

[98] Some commentators predicted that minimum sentences would become more severe in order to satisfy the concerns raised in *Apprendi* v. *N.J.* 120 S. Ct. 2348 (2001). See Nancy J. King and Susan R. Klein, 'Essential Elements' (2001) 54 *Vanderbilt LR* 1467.

[99] This draconian sentence would not infringe a principle of proportionality in punishment as the Constitution is presently interpreted, since the court has approved a sentence of life imprisonment without parole for the crime of cocaine possession. See *Harmelin* v. *Michigan*, 501 US 957 (1991).

happens to result in death. Suppose further that the sentence is enhanced regardless of the defendant's culpability with respect to death. This approach, like that of its predecessor, has ample precedent.[100] Notice that this modification contracts the net injustice to its original dimension in *Rodriguez*. Enhanced punishments are not imposed on typical distributors of cocaine, but are reserved for unusual cases in which such acts cause death. Imagine that a defendant—call him Jones—is convicted and sentenced pursuant to this statutory scheme.

Once again, I cannot believe that this result would mollify commentators who are upset about the strict liability drug homicide statute in *Rodriguez*. To be sure, Jones is convicted only of distribution; his crime is not mislabelled. But this advantage would seem to be relatively small. If the severity of the hardship for drug distributors who lack negligence for causing death (but not otherwise) is the crux of the problem, this fourth scenario demonstrates that a statute need not be an instance of formal strict liability to give rise to it. Obviously, this injustice persists regardless of whether the increased punishment is imposed because the defendant satisfies a strict liability element of the offence, or is imposed pursuant to a separate provision that enhances his sentence. Statutory schemes can be functionally equivalent to formal strict liability without literally imposing it. If I am correct, it follows that one cannot assess the relative justice of statutes that are not instances of formal strict liability unless he expands his focus to include sentencing provisions that are extrinsic to substantive offences.[101]

Consider a fifth and final scenario that is unlike its immediate predecessors in *not* dispensing with formal strict liability. Suppose that the legislature retains the strict liability drug homicide statute upheld in *Rodriguez*, but repeals the crime of possessing or distributing cocaine *simpliciter*. In other words, criminal liability is imposed only on defendants whose acts of distribution result in death. Imagine that a defendant—call him Green—is convicted of this offence. Like Rodriguez, Green complains that the statute is an instance of formal strict liability. If we confine our focus to these two offenders, Green's situation is comparable to that of Rodriguez. The important distinction, of course, is that this scenario spares criminal liability and punishment from the millions of cocaine distributors whose acts do not cause death.

The challenge is to rank each of these five scenarios from the perspective of justice. I lack confidence in my ability to complete this formidable task. Some

[100] Consider e.g. various state assault statutes that enhance punishments when 'elderly' or 'vulnerable' victims are attacked. Even when the age of the victim must be proved beyond a reasonable doubt, states typically do not require defendants to be culpable with respect to this sentencing factor. See e.g. *People* v. *White*, 608 NE 2d 1220 (Ill. App. 1993).

[101] A recent decision of the Supreme Court—*Apprendi* v. *N.J.*, 120 S. Ct. 2348 (2001)—precludes this modification when (at least) three conditions are satisfied: first, when the severity of the enhanced punishment is greater than the maximum provided by the base offence; second, when the factor that enhances punishment need not be proved beyond a reasonable doubt; and third, when that aggravating fact is not found by the jury. In my fourth scenario, we should suppose that the state is required to prove to the jury beyond a reasonable doubt that Jones's act of distribution caused death. In this event, the concerns that led to *Apprendi* would not arise.

matters seem relatively clear. Scenario two is preferable to one, which in turn is preferable to three. Scenario four is better than one, but worse than two. Notice that scenario three, which dispenses with formal strict liability, is almost certainly the worst of the five. The controversial issue is where scenario five should be located along this continuum. Might it be the best option of all? Perhaps. If so, the decision to retain offences of formal strict liability may actually *decrease* the net injustice of the criminal law relative to several other alternatives. One might anticipate that theorists who oppose formal strict liability on grounds of justice would choose my second scenario, and propose to rewrite statutes to require at least negligence for (what is otherwise) the strict liability element. A viable alternative, however, might be to repeal *other* offences—even though these offences are not instances of formal strict liability. Among the options canvassed here, this solution might well be preferable from the standpoint of justice.

The general predicament that gives rise to my uncertainty might be described as follows. People frequently engage in conduct—such as drug distribution—that creates a risk of harm. If *all* such conduct were subject to punishment, officials would be forced to exercise discretion in arrests and prosecutions, or prisons would soon be filled beyond their capacities—outcomes that resemble the situation for drug offenders in the United States today.[102] Punishing *no* such conduct, however, may be unacceptable as well. A middle ground between prohibiting drug distribution *simpliciter* and refraining from using the criminal law altogether is to criminalize such conduct only when its risks materialize. The case for criminal liability and punishment seems especially strong when the conduct leads to serious harms such as death—even though defendants are not negligent for the consequences they cause. If my reasoning is sound, instances of formal strict liability may not be the unmitigated injustice they sometimes are portrayed to be. The strict liability drug homicide statute upheld in *Rodriguez* might involve a defensible compromise between unpalatable extremes.

Some ways to avoid the difficulties associated with formal strict liability actually lead to a net reduction in the overall justice of the substantive criminal law. We should be cautious about adopting a quick fix to the problems of proportionality I have described by demanding that these offences be abolished. The local injustice of many cases of formal strict liability cannot always be separated from broader injustices in the substantive criminal law. We lack a clear standard to gauge the relative injustice of various alternatives. But we should remain mindful of the possibility that repealing offences of formal strict liability may make our predicament worse.

---

[102] See Husak, *Drugs and Rights* and *Legalize This!*

# 5

# Whose Values Should Determine When Liability is Strict?

*Jeremy Horder*

## 1. Three Ways of Construing Criminal Statutes

The question of whether or not liability should be strict—whether, in other words, it should be possible to incur it without fault—is one of the most hotly debated issues within criminal law. As the title of this chapter implies, however, even if strict criminal liability can, morally speaking,[1] legitimately be imposed, there can be more than one answer to the question of whose values should inform the decision to impose it. In this chapter I will discuss different ways of answering that question. Most strict liability crimes are created by statute; but that is just the beginning of the inquiry posed in the title. The fact that a crime created by a statute of a supreme legislature makes no express mention of a fault requirement is—notoriously—no reliable guide, almost anywhere in the common law world, to whether the courts will or will not find such a requirement to be implied.[2] Moreover, at least in some jurisdictions, even if a fault requirement, as such, cannot be implied into a statute that is silent on the matter, this may not prevent the courts from finding that it is none the less a *defence* to the crime to show that, say, one exercised 'due diligence' in seeking to avoid committing it.[3] The finding that a defence has an application to a crime is frequently regarded as a matter to be detached, at least to some extent, from the question whether a fault requirement is express or implied in the statute itself, even though the 'defence' in question is,

I owe a great debt of gratitude to Andrew Simester for all his work in helping to turn this chapter into something that might be worth reading (if it still isn't, that is my fault). I have almost certainly also failed to do justice to the penetrating criticisms of Victor Tadros, Antony Duff, and Adam Tomkins, to whom I am also very grateful. Timothy Owen, QC, also provided helpful background to the *Barnfather* case.

[1] Few doubt that Parliament has the *legal* right to impose strict liability in civil or criminal law. See further in this volume, Alan Michaels, Ch. 9; G. R. Sullivan, Ch. 8.

[2] For general discussion, see A. P. Simester, and G. R. Sullivan, *Criminal Law: Theory and Doctrine* (2nd edn., Oxford 2003), 169–77.

[3] See *Proudman* v. *Dayman* (1941) 67 CLR 536; *R.* v. *City of Sault Ste Marie* (1978) 85 DLR (3rd) 161.

in effect, a requirement of fault (albeit one respecting which the defendant bears some kind of evidentiary burden).[4]

Assuming that strict liability is, at least on some occasions, rightly imposed, there are at least three ways in which one might decide whose values should inform the decision to construe a particular crime as one of strict liability. First, there is what can be called the theory of 'legislative positivism'. On this view, broadly speaking, the issue is whether an ordinary or purposive reading of the words of the offence demonstrates that a fault requirement is expressly or impliedly required by Parliament itself.[5] Secondly, there is what can be called the 'common law' theory, according to which even if Parliament has not expressly or impliedly provided for a requirement of fault, such a requirement can be imposed—through the device of the application of a 'due diligence' defence, if need be—where justice and good conscience require it.[6] Crudely understood, according to a familiar Benthamite caricature, the rivalry between these two well-known views may be characterized as the pitting of the values of a forward-looking, democratic legislature against the values of traditionally conservative (and unelected) judges. The clash of values occurs when judicial support for, in particular, the principles of 'negative' liberty (meaning, in this context, freedom from the stigma of conviction without individual fault[7]) cannot be reconciled with the absence of a fault requirement, on a purposive or ordinary reading of the wording of a statutory offence; and so something or someone has to give.[8] There can be a place for both such approaches, even in the same legal system, but there is a third way of approaching the question I have set myself to answer.

[4] N. Morris and C. Howard, *Studies in Criminal Law* (Oxford 1964), 221–2. The burden of adducing evidence is, at least tactically, on the defendant rather than on the prosecution, as it normally would be with a fault requirement.

[5] I shall not be much concerned with this theory here, since (as we shall see) it played no role in the case under discussion.

[6] This second view has been called 'liberal antipositivism': see David Dyzenhaus, 'The Politics of Deference: Judicial Review and Democracy', in M. Taggart (ed.), *The Province of Administrative Law* (Oxford 1997), 280. I shall not use this phrase, though, because it is unclear that the 'common law' view is really anti-positivist. Judges who adopt the 'common law' theory do not challenge, on merit-based grounds, the validity of the statutes they regard themselves as bound to interpret. They merely see the legislation against a different interpretative backdrop (one that presumes that the legislature did not intend to make inroads upon traditional liberties) to that employed by legislative positivists. By the 'common law' view, I mean the judicial perception that there is law-creating freedom to set the backdrop against which statutes are interpreted.

[7] I have explored the sense in which, in strict liability cases, the courts seek to defend negative liberty—the freedom 'from' certain kinds of evil, such as undeserved stigma of criminal conviction—in Jeremy Horder, 'Strict Liability, Statutory Construction, and the Spirit of Liberty' [2002] 118 *Law Quarterly Review* 458.

[8] That said, it is, of course, always possible that a statute will be silent on the issue of the mental element because the *legislature* is itself working on the assumption that the courts will at some point themselves imply appropriate fault or defence elements. This will be a rare case, as the legislature has as much reason to shape and determine the limits of defences *ab initio*, as it does to shape and determine the offence itself. Perhaps one can avoid the kind of clash of values referred to in the text, in a case where the wording of criminal statutes has become anachronistic. For then, there might be a constitutional competence in—and, indeed, a duty on—the courts to create defences to the relevant crimes, in the absence of statutory reform.

A statute may leave the development of important aspects of, say, education, policing, or health and safety at work policy to an executive agency, or to a number of agencies (perhaps including the courts) acting together. That devolution of policy-making power may expressly or impliedly include delegation of the power to develop a 'micro' policy, under the aegis of the broader policy strategy, concerning when it would be appropriate to prosecute those who contravene rules central to pursuit of the relevant policy strategy.[9] When this happens, there is an argument that the values that have informed the agency or agencies in the development of that prosecution policy should be decisive in determining whether strict liability should be imposed in, or a particular defence applied to, the offence in question. In the modern bureaucratic state, this is an argument that should be addressed and sometimes accepted by the courts, when they turn their minds to the age-old question of whether fault—in any form—has a legal bearing on criminal liability under statute.[10] Following Dyzenhaus, we can call this so-called third way of approaching the question the 'respectful deference' theory.[11] In the judicial review context, Dyzenhaus explains the respectful deference theory thus:

Deference as respect requires not submission but a respectful attention to the reasons offered or which could be offered in support of a decision, whether that decision be the statutory decision of the legislature . . . *or the decision of an administrative agency*. . . . [O]nly this principle can rearticulate the proper relationship between the legislature, administrative agencies and the courts.[12]

As I have just indicated, the respectful deference theory is of particular importance when statutes create criminal offences as part of a broader effort to bring official agencies (e.g. the courts, the police, local authority officials, and so forth) together, in a co-ordinated and coherent way, to promote citizens' co-operation with a policy. None the less, the respectful deference theory does not always provide a straightforward way of deciding whether, in a particular case, fault is a prerequisite for conviction. This is because the courts have a responsibility to ensure that the 'global' moral significance of conviction does not become lost from view when criminal prosecution is deployed in a particular context, even when the deployment is part of a legitimate attempt to enforce the policy that the legislature has authorized the relevant agency or agencies to formulate and carry through.[13] As we shall see, discharging that responsibility may sometimes involve the courts in

[9] For example, it may be the agency responsible for implementing the policy that also decides when to prosecute, rather than some separate prosecution agency.

[10] This is one of the conclusions that might be drawn e.g. from Keith Hawkins's magisterial survey of prosecution decision-making by executives from the Health and Safety Commission: Keith Hawkins, *Law as a Last Resort* (Oxford 2002), Chs. 12, 13.

[11] See Dyzenhaus, 'Politics of Deference', 286. He in fact calls it, 'the principle of deference as respect'; but I hope my rewording does no violence to the ideas he is trying to express. The principle is meant to be contrasted with 'submissive deference' (ibid.), an attitude to the exercise of legislative power that follows from siding with the legislative positivism theory.       [12] Ibid. (my emphasis).

[13] The 'global' significance of a conviction is its significance for the defendant in spheres of his or her life outside the context that gave rise to it: see Joseph Raz, 'Autonomy, Toleration and the Harm Principle', in Ruth Gavison (ed.), *Contemporary Issues in Legal Philosophy* (Oxford 1987), 331: 'The coercion of criminal penalties is a global and indiscriminate invasion of autonomy.'

implying fault requirements into—or in applying defences to—crimes under statute, even though to do so entails preferring something like the 'common law' view of statutory interpretation to the respectful deference approach. In short, what turns out to be problematic about treating the respectful deference approach as mandatory, in the way that Dyzenhaus would undoubtedly have the courts do, is the difficulty the courts will encounter in ensuring that 'respectful' deference does not (as it all too easily can) slide into mere 'submissive' deference. Avoiding this danger requires courts to treat the respectful deference approach purely as what John Gardner has called an 'advisory' (as opposed to mandatory or permissive), supervisory principle of the general part of the criminal law.[14]

In this regard, I shall use as an example the decision of the Divisional Court in *Barnfather* v. *London Borough of Islington Education Authority*.[15] In that case, the defendant (a mother of four children) was convicted of failing to ensure that her 13-year-old son attended school regularly, an offence contrary to section 444(1) of the Education Act 1996.[16] She did not attend the hearing, and was convicted without proof of *mens rea*. Following her conviction, the defendant challenged the imposition of strict liability on the grounds that this involved a breach of Article 6(2) of the European Convention on Human Rights, which guarantees the presumption of innocence in criminal proceedings. She claimed that (*a*) the court could review the status of the offence as one of strict liability in virtue of Article 6(2), and that (*b*) the court could and should go on to find that it was unjustified to make the offence one of strict liability, given that—as she claimed—she had been doing her best to ensure that her son attended school. On point (*a*), she failed in her appeal,[17] on the grounds that Article 6(2) was concerned with matters of procedure and evidence rather than with substantive (criminal law) questions, such as whether to impose strict liability. The court had no power to revisit a decision by Parliament to impose strict liability.[18] The court went on, however, to consider (*b*) in considerable detail, the hypothetical question whether, had it been possible in law to review the status of the offence as one of strict liability, strict liability would have been justifiably imposed.[19] On this question,

---

[14] See John Gardner, 'On the General Part of the Criminal Law', in R. A. Duff (ed.), *Philosophy and the Criminal Law* (Cambridge 1998), 208.

[15] [2003] EWHC 418 (admin.); Case No: CO/4139/2002.

[16] By s. 444(1) of the 1996 Act, 'if a child of compulsory school age who is a registered pupil at a school fails to attend regularly at the school, his parent is guilty of an offence'. The defendant was fined £75.

[17] On this point, the decision was, perhaps predictably, welcomed by the National Union of Teachers: see the comments of the Union's General Secretary in the *Highbury & Islington Express*, 14 March 2003, at 11.

[18] For further discussion of the point, see Ben Emmerson and Andrew Ashworth, *Criminal Justice and Human Rights* (London 2001), paras. 9.63–9.65; Mary Arden, 'Criminal Law at the Crossroads: The Impact on Human Rights from the Law Commission's Perspective and the Need for a Code' [1999] *Criminal LR* 439.

[19] The court saw this as a substantive question that would have arisen directly, had (*a*) been answered in the appellant's favour. In focusing on the answer to this hypothetical question, thus, the court did not proceed by the more usual route of asking whether (to use Lord Nicholls' words, in

the court was evenly divided.[20] Maurice Kay J held that there was sufficient justification for the imposition of strict liability, whereas Elias J held that there was insufficient justification. Elias J would have found that, if a parent discharged a burden of showing that all reasonable steps were taken to ensure his or her child's attendance, the parent was entitled to an acquittal.[21] Notwithstanding that a plausible argument for strict liability can be constructed on the basis of the 'respectful deference' approach, I shall suggest that Elias J was ultimately right in this case to take what I referred to above as the 'common law' view. I argue that— had the court had the power to review the strict liability status of the offence—it would have been right to create a general excuse to the offence under section 444(1), by placing a burden on parents to show 'due diligence' in seeking to ensure a child's regular attendance at school. Why?

First, in virtue of the procedures adopted in these kinds of cases to ensure a child attends school regularly, it need *not* remain peculiarly within a parent's own knowledge whether sufficient efforts have been made to ensure regular attendance (something that otherwise would put the prosecution at an unfair disadvantage).[22] Secondly, on what has been called the 'active' account of human well-being,[23] a parent's efforts to ensure a child's regular attendance at school should be regarded as activities with intrinsic value, because they are partly constitutive of the intrinsically valuable activity of good parenting. In this context, there are thus powerful reasons to ensure that the value of this activity is acknowledged through the provision of a 'due diligence' defence, rather than compromised by strict criminal liability. Finally (a point with more general moral significance), although this is an offence in relation to which Parliament has itself provided a limited number of defences,[24] the courts have a continuing responsibility to ensure, especially in a case where the stigma attaching to conviction may adversely affect the defendant in fields beyond the specific context in which the offence arises, that the defences

---

*B (a minor)* v. *DPP* [2000] 2 AC 428, at 460), 'putting aside human rights considerations, Parliament had indicated that the offence should be one of strict liability by necessary implication, if not expressly'. It was taken for granted that, were it not for the effect of human rights considerations, the balance of authority favoured the imposition of strict liability. See text below, at n. 31.

[20] Unusually, the Divisional Court was comprised of two High Court Judges, Maurice Kay J and Elias J, there being no available Lord Justice. Delay being thought undesirable, permission was obtained from the Lord Chief Justice to sit with two High Court Judges.

[21] In *Barnfather*, para. 52, Elias J speaks of imposing a 'reverse burden', which suggests that he has it in mind that, if a defendant can show 'due diligence' on the balance of probabilities, he or she is entitled to be acquitted. This course of action was looked on with disfavour by the House of Lords in *Sweet* v. *Parsley* [1970] AC 132. Alternatively, it may be that he has it in mind that D bears only an evidential burden with respect to showing 'due diligence'; whereupon, if discharged, it will be for the prosecution to prove beyond reasonable doubt that 'due diligence' was not shown.

[22] The relevance of this issue has traditionally been in determining who bears the burden of proof, but it can equally be presented as an argument bearing on the propriety of strict liability: Ben Emmerson and Andrew Ashworth, *Human Rights and Criminal Justice*, Ch. 9.

[23] For an examination of this concept, see John Gardner, 'On the General Part of Criminal Law', in R. A. Duff (ed.), *Philosophy and the Criminal Law* (Oxford 1998), 220. Gardner is drawing on Joseph Raz, *The Morality of Freedom* (Oxford 1986), 308–13.      [24] See the text below, following n. 30.

available are adequate in nature and scope to prevent such stigma from being unjustly borne.

## 2. Tough on the Causes of Truancy: The Iron Fist and the Velvet Glove

The respectful deference approach is capable of generating a highly plausible prima facie argument in favour of strict liability under section 444(1), and it is to this that I will turn my attention in this section. First (in § 2.1 below), I will briefly consider the legislative context and history, a matter of relevance under any interpretative theory. Beyond this, the legislation in which the offence created by section 444(1) takes its place needs to be understood both as the punitive part of a wider response to truancy; as a matter of growing social and political concern (addressed in § 2.2 below); and as the 'long stop' conclusion to a delegated process of intervention to reduce the incidence of truancy, a conclusion to be reached only when the delegated process has failed (a matter considered in § 2.3).

### 2.1. The Legal Background

A criminal law requirement that parents ensure their children attend school was first imposed by the Elementary Education Act 1870.[25] The Act was a reflection of the late-Victorian perception that adherence to the treasured belief in economic laissez-faire did not entail a belief in moral laissez-faire. Hence, it could be appropriate through law to require rational moral behaviour of parents (amongst others), in order to benefit those, such as children, who could not help themselves.[26] The modern equivalent of the 1870 Act is now the Education Act 1996. By section 444(1) of that Act, 'if a child of compulsory school age who is a registered pupil at a school fails to attend regularly at the school, his parent is guilty of an offence', an offence punishable with a fine of up to £1,000 (level 3 on the standard scale).[27] This offence has now been buttressed by a further offence, created by the

---

[25] 33 & 34 Vic, c. 75 (the so-called 'Foster' Act), described, along with the Industrial Schools Act 1866, by Sir James Stephen, as 'one of the most characteristic and most important sets of laws enacted in our days', in Sir J. F. Stephen, *History of the Criminal Law of England* (London 1883), iii. 264.

[26] See José Harris, *Private Lives, Public Spirit: A Social History of Britain 1870–1914* (Oxford 1993), 196–201. Another product of this thinking was the Vaccination (Amendment) Act 1867, under which there was a duty on parents, backed by the threat of criminal proceedings, to ensure that their children were vaccinated. Other similar measures from a slightly later period are discussed in Sir Leon Radzinowicz and Roger Hood, *The Emergence of Penal Policy* (Oxford 1986), 655–7.

[27] Both as regards offence and defence, the Education Act 1996, s. 444 is strikingly similar to the equivalent provisions in the Australian State of Victoria: Community Services Act 1970, s. 74(C)(1)–(3). In England and Wales, prior to 2000, about 9,000 parents were prosecuted annually under s. 444(1). Some 80% did not attend the court proceedings, and those convicted received very low fines (rarely exceeding £200). This doubtless reflects the fact that most such parents will be poor and on benefits.

Criminal Justice and Court Services Act 2000. Section 72(1) of this Act inserted a new section in the Education Act 1996, section 444(1A), which makes it an offence, 'if, in the circumstances mentioned in [s. 444(1)], the parent *knows* that his child is failing to attend regularly at school and fails *without reasonable justification* to cause him to do so . . . '[28] By way of contrast with the penalty available for the offence contrary to section 444(1), the penalty following conviction under section 444(1A) can be a fine of up to £2,500 (level 4 on the standard scale), or three months' imprisonment, or both.[29] In May 2002, single mother Patricia Amos became the first person to be imprisoned following a conviction under section 444(1A). She received a sentence of 60 days' imprisonment (reduced, on appeal, to 28 days) after her two teenage daughters were found to be persistent truants.[30]

Although the lesser offence contrary to section 444(1), unlike the offence contrary to section 444(1A), contains no explicit mention of a mental element, specific defences to the lesser offence are set out in section 444. So, by section 444(3), a child registered at school is not to be taken to have failed to attend school regularly by reason of his absence with leave, when prevented by 'reason of sickness or any other unavoidable cause', for religious reasons, or if the parent can show that the school at which the pupil is registered is not within walking distance (defined in s. 444(5)). Historically, previous incarnations of these specific defences were interpreted in a restrictive way. For example, in *Jenkins* v. *Howells*,[31] a child had been continuously away from school because her mother was a chronic invalid and (it was said) the girl consequently had to help her at home. In response to the charge under section 444(1), the mother sought to plead 'sickness or other unavoidable cause'. The Divisional Court held that this could be no excuse. In the court's view, not only the sickness but also the 'unavoidable cause' must relate to the child, not to the parent (a harsh conclusion, perhaps, given that it is the parent

---

[28] My emphasis. A similar renewal of interest in doing more to punish parents for the sins of their children, as well as the children themselves, can be found in some US states; see e.g. Wisconsin (1995, Laws, Act 77 § 118, § 939, 103.72; 1998, Laws, Act 239), Pennsylvania (1995, Laws, Act 29) and Minnesota (1995, Laws, Chapter 226, Article 3, §§ 8, 13, 31, 48), which have recently added to or increased the penalties for violating compulsory school attendance laws. The Minnesota law also makes it possible for a court to order a parent to deliver a truant child to school. See also Ohio Laws, SB 181 (2000), under which, *inter alia*, the concept of a delinquent or unruly child is expanded to include a 'habitual truant', and the original juvenile court is given jurisdiction over all cases where the parent is alleged to have contributed negligently to a child's habitual truancy. This mixing of criminal and educational concerns is likely increasingly to become a feature of English law. On the whole, the maximum penalties that may be imposed in US states are often considerably lower than those now available under s. 444(1) and ss. 444(1A) of the Education Act 1996.

[29] By way of contrast with the offence under s. 444(1), a warrant can be issued compelling a parent to attend court when charged under s. 444(1A).

[30] Ms Amos had previously broken a parenting order imposed by the courts under the Crime and Disorder Act 1998, in an attempt to make her ensure that her daughters attended school, and she had failed to appear at a court hearing in connection with her case. She has since received a further 28 days' imprisonment, following a second conviction under s. 444(1A), for failing to ensure that her younger daughter attended school regularly.   [31] [1949] 2 KB 218.

who stands to be convicted).[32] With this background in mind, it might be thought that the case for a restrictive approach, more generally, can now only have been strengthened by the insertion of the more serious offence in section 444(1A) that explicitly requires a mental element. It is, of course, not unknown for the courts to imply *mens rea* requirements into lesser offences which sit cheek-by-jowl with more serious offences that explicitly require proof of a mental element.[33] Moreover, even though there is some (somewhat dated) authority for the view that a 'due diligence' defence may not be 'read in' to a criminal statute in English law,[34] to take this course in relation to the section 444(1) offence, where the defendant bears an evidentiary burden, would not be to grant scope for rebutting the prosecution's case as broad as that afforded by the mental element in section 444(1A). For, under section 444(1A), the prosecution must ultimately show both that the defendant knew his or her child was not attending school regularly, and that there was no 'reasonable justification' for having failed to ensure the child's attendance. None the less, we are not dealing here with a mere consolidation statute. The balance of authority suggests that the juxtaposition in the statute of an offence making no mention of a mental element, and an offence that explicitly requires proof of a mental element, is a factor weighing against the implication of such an element into the former offence.[35] First, though, we must consider the 'punitive' dimension to the background against which the enactment of section 444(1A) can be explained. Does the adoption of a more punitive approach to parents' failure to ensure that their children attend school regularly strengthen or weaken the case for strict liability in section 444(1)?

## 2.2. The Iron Fist

The revised section 444 is part of a recent renaissance of interest in using the criminal law to enforce rational moral behaviour by parents. It is part of a network of statutory measures that have been built up over the last fifteen years or so, designed to force parents to take more responsibility for their children's deviant

---

[32] The court relied on the 'floodgates' bogey of invalids having a blank cheque to prevent their children going to school at all, in so far as there was no one else to care for them. A more principled 'tough' approach would have been to hold that the defence applied to the parent, but then to find that it was not made out on the facts, either because the mother could have found—even though she had hitherto had no success in finding—home help, or because her three grown-up sons who worked on the farm could have taken turns to assist her: D's perception of appropriate 'men's work' hardly amounts to an unavoidable cause sufficient to justify keeping her daughter at home. Cases of this kind might well now not come to court, because prosecutions under s. 444(1) are now subject to the restriction in s. 447(1): see text below, following n. 58.                        [33] See *Sherras* v. *De Rutzen* [1895] 1 QB 918.

[34] *Sweet* v. *Parsley* [1970] AC 132; queried on this point by Arden, 'Criminal Law at the Crossroads'.

[35] See *Pharmaceutical Society of Great Britain* v. *Storkwain* [1986] 1 WLR 903, at 908 (*per* Lord Goff). Strict liability was imposed in this case even though it involved an offence respecting which a sentence of two years' imprisonment could be imposed. Other offences under the relevant statute did, though, already have a 'due diligence' defence expressly applied to them by Parliament.

behaviour.[36] Where truancy is concerned, measures forming part of this network are being justified (as in other jurisdictions[37]) by the claim that there is a significant connection between truancy and criminal behaviour; it is not just the educational disadvantage to the child that is in issue. In *Barnfather* itself, it was claimed that, on any one school day, around 50,000 pupils take unauthorized absences from school, resulting in a loss of 7.7 million school days a year.[38] In *Barnfather*, an expert witness statement given on behalf of the Department for Education and Skills indicated that as well as performing much worse at school (and thereafter) educationally, two-thirds of habitual truants had offended against the criminal law, compared with less than one-third of those children who attended school regularly.[39] Seeking to address the supposed problem, between 1998 and 2002 the government provided approximately £100m for local initiatives to cut truancy by one-third, including 'truancy sweeps' involving joint operations in city and town centres by police and Local Education Authority officers to find those playing truant.[40] In May 2003, for

---

[36] See e.g. Criminal Justice Act 1991 (Requiring attendance of parents at court when their children are in court; Binding over of parents to control their children); Crime and Disorder Act 1998 (Parenting Orders); Powers of Criminal Courts (Sentencing) Act 2000 (Binding over of parents to take proper care of a child). These Acts are essentially revamped versions of measures taken just after the turn of the twentieth century, to secure parental responsibility for delinquent children: see the Youthful Offenders Act 1901 and the Children Act 1908. It has been said, of the Crime and Disorder Act 1998, that it is, 'the first piece of criminal justice legislation in England and Wales (at least since the Vagrancy Acts of the early nineteenth century) to act explicitly against legal and moral/social transgressions': J. Muncie, 'A New Deal for Youth? Early Intervention and Correctionalism', in G. Hughes, J. Muncie, and E. Mclaughlin (eds.), *Crime Prevention and Community Safety: New Directions* (London 2001), 21.

[37] See e.g. Ohio Laws, SB 181 (2000), that includes provisions that expand the definition of delinquent child and unruly child to include 'habitual truants', and grant original juvenile court jurisdiction over all cases where the parent is alleged to have contributed directly or negligently towards a child's habitual truancy. Parents are required to attend all court proceedings related to the child.

[38] Unauthorized absence has remained constant at 0.7% since attendance data were first published in 1994. See, in general, *Barnfather*, para. 27 (Witness Statement of Sheila Scales). In 1999, the Audit Commission estimated that at least 40,000 pupils are absent without school permission each day: see the Audit Commission briefing, *Missing Out: LEA Management of School Attendance and Exclusion* (1999).

[39] See *Barnfather*, para. 27, and <www.dfes.gov.uk/schoolattendance/truancysweeps>. At a conference on 29 April 2002, the then Secretary of State for Education, Ms Estelle Morris, estimated that 40% of street crimes, 25% of burglaries, 20% of criminal damage, and 33% of car thefts are carried out by children aged between 10 and 16, in school hours (it is hard to know how reliable these figures really are). The political concern is largely with what has been called 'adolescent-limited' antisocial behaviour: see T. E. Moffitt, ' "Life-Course Persistent" and "Adolescent-Limited" Antisocial Behaviour: A Developmental Taxonomy' (1993) 100 *Psychological Review* 674. In terms of crime, most such offending does take the form of burglary, criminal damage, and, to a lesser extent, theft: K. Soothill, B. Francis, and R. Fligelsone, 'Patterns of Offending Behaviour: A New Approach', Home Office Research Findings No 171. However, 43% of prisoners claimed that they left school before the age of 16 (as compared with 11% of the population generally), and the same percentage had no educational qualifications at all. Some 60–70% of prisoners have literacy and numeracy levels so low that they are ineligible for 96% of jobs: see R. Morgan, 'Imprisonment: A Brief History, The Contemporary Scene, and Likely Prospects', in M. Maguire, R. Morgan, and R. Reiner, *The Oxford Handbook of Criminology* (3rd edn., Oxford 2002), 1138–9.

[40] 'Truancy sweeps' were made possible by s. 16 of the Crime and Disorder Act 1996.

example, there was a nationally co-ordinated 'truancy sweep' involving operations by the police and 141 out of 150 English Local Educational Authorities, under the auspices of the Prime Minister's 'Street Crime Action Group'.[41] The sweep revealed that one child in three out of school was absent without permission (half of these were actually with their parents).[42] Significantly in this context, it has been claimed that a week-long truancy sweep in 1999 in East London saw recorded crime drop by 50 per cent, and the Education Department in York has claimed that its anti-truancy measures, including a 'truant-watch' scheme and regular truancy sweeps, have cut recorded crime by 67 per cent.[43]

It is important to note that, in using their powers, most Local Education Authorities have more-or-less formal non-attendance procedures in several stages that, if followed by the Local Education Authority and complied with by the parents, are in part meant to ensure that prosecutions are not undertaken where there has been no fault. These procedures are significant, in that a prosecution under section 444(1) may be brought only by a Local Education Authority, not by the police or by a private citizen.[44] A more formal four-step procedure is likely to be involved,[45] such as: (i) an office interview with the parents; (ii) a Governors' meeting to discuss the case; (iii) a meeting with a 'non-attendance panel'; (iv) Magistrates' or Family Court Proceedings.[46] Local Education Authorities' stated prosecution policy is often phrased in terms that assume prosecution would

---

[41] Department for Education and Skills, *Attendance Update*, 27 June 2003.

[42] Other studies have indicated that up to 80% of school-age children out of school during school hours do not have a valid reason for absence from school: *National Foundation for Educational Research* (1993), 'What Do Students Think About Schools?' In a truancy sweep conducted in Salford, in two-thirds of all cases, children were out shopping with their parents, who frequently said that the children were ill but where no official notification had been given to the school of this 'fact'. See P. Curtis, 'Truancy Sweeps Reap Rewards', *The Guardian*, Tuesday, 18 June 2002, p. 10.

[43] Duly flushed with enthusiasm, however, the government has amended s. 444 once again, through s. 23 of the Anti-Social Behaviour Act 2003, to make it possible to issue a penalty notice to parents where an authorized officer (police constable, Local Education Authority Officer, or school staff member) has 'reason to believe' that an offence under s. 444(1) has been committed. The Penalty Notice offers the parent in question a chance to discharge liability under s. 444(1) by paying the penalty, thus avoiding prosecution for such period as the notice itself indicates. A parent will pay £25 if he or she agrees the absence was unauthorized (£50 otherwise) and pays within 14 days, but this can rise to £100 if the parent does not agree that the absence was unauthorized and pays within 28 days. The development ties in with the policy of some Local Education Authorities to 'fast-track' prosecutions against parents, so that they appear in court charged under s. 444 in under twelve weeks: Salford City Council, Press Release 11/02/03, 'Salford Leads the Way in Tackling Truancy'. As we shall see, though, this tough, crime-prevention focused approach has been coupled at local level with a more compliance-orientated welfare approach to the stages leading up to prosecution.

[44] Education Act 1996, s. 446. In *Barnfather* (para. 29), this was thought to be an important factor weighing in favour of strict liability by Maurice Kay J.

[45] Typically, of course, this would only follow if, for example, oral warnings and letters to parents had failed to produce an effect.

[46] V. G. McEwan, *Education Law* (2nd edn., Welwyn Garden City 2000), 70–1. Further, under provisions analysed below, under s. 447 of the 1996 Act the Local Education Authority is duty-bound to consider applying for an 'Education Supervision Order', in lieu of prosecution under s. 444(1) or of care proceedings, if that is in the child's best interests because he or she is not being properly educated.

not be undertaken unless fault had been shown.[47] Important, in this regard, is the relatively new fast track to prosecution under section 444. In cases where parents do not seem disposed to co-operate with the school and/or the Education Welfare Service, a fast-track framework for prosecution has now been devised by the Department for Education and Skills,[48] under which, where there is evidence of non-co-operation, parents are given a specified time (typically, twelve weeks) to co-operate with the school and the Education Welfare Service to improve their child's attendance, and must be informed at the beginning of this process that prosecution under section 444 may result if they do not co-operate. The parents will be required to sign an 'action plan' to improve the child's attendance, and any failure to do so is recorded. Close monitoring of attendance, and of the parents' 'level of engagement', by the school and the Education Welfare Service then follows during the specified period. If an improvement is not forthcoming a prosecution may follow, in which information about the parents' (non-)co-operation is to be brought to the attention of the court.[49] If anything, then, the toughening up of governmental and Local Education Authority attitudes to parental non-co-operation has led to an *increased* emphasis on ensuring in various ways that parents receive adequate warning that their children are not attending regularly at school, and that they face prosecution if they fail to exercise 'due diligence' to change the child's behaviour.[50]

So, three rather different factors, in relation to the 'iron fist' approach to the reduction of truancy, converge to suggest that the offence contrary to section 444(1) should be regarded as one of strict liability. One is the evident social concern with which parental neglect of truancy (alongside truancy itself) is now regarded, the social concerns underpinning a criminal statute being a factor identified at the highest level as capable of rebutting any presumption of *mens rea*.[51] The second factor (considered earlier) is the insertion alongside the offence under section 444(1) of the more serious section 444(1A) offence, which explicitly

---

[47] So e.g. Devon County Council's prosecution policy is stated to be that, 'in cases where parents/carers wilfully withhold a pupil from school, or persistently refuse to co-operate with efforts to effect a return to regular attendance, the [Education Welfare Service] will begin legal Proceedings': see <www.devon.gov.uk/eal>, accessed 25 Sept. 2004.

[48] Department for Education and Skills Guidance, 'Ensuring Regular Attendance at School', paras. 53–9.                                                                          [49] Ibid. 53–7.

[50] To date, out of c.1,500 instances in which prosecution under s. 444 has been threatened, about half the parents involved have agreed to co-operate in order to avoid prosecution: see *The Times*, 22 December 2003, p. 7. Under the Anti-Social Behaviour Act 2003, further provisions are now in place that should in theory ensure that parents are given fair warning that a criminal prosecution may result from continued failure to ensure that their children attend school regularly. Under s. 19 of the Act, there is a power granted to Local Education Authorities and to the governing body of schools to enter into 'parenting contracts' with a parent or with parents, the 'consideration' for the contract provided by the parent or parents being a promise to ensure that a child attends school regularly, exchanged for a promise on the part of the Local Education Authority or governing body that it will support the parent's or parents' efforts in that regard. It is not currently intended, however, that breach of a parenting contract will give rise to civil liability: see Anti-Social Behaviour Act 2003, s. 19(8).

[51] See *Gammon Ltd.* v. *A-G of Hong Kong* [1985] 1 AC 1, at 14 (*per* Lord Scarman).

incorporates a mental element. Finally, of crucial importance to the 'respectful deference' view described in the final section, there is the fact that fair warning that they are failing in their responsibilities must inevitably be given to parents, by Local Education Authority officers, in the strategies they are required by the Authority to adopt. This creates a formidable argument that when criminal prosecution under section 444(1) is used as a last resort, to use Lord Scarman's words in *Gammon* v. *A-G of Hong Kong*,[52] 'strict liability will be effective to promote the objects of the statute by encouraging greater vigilance to prevent the commission of the prohibited act'.[53] On the 'respectful deference' analysis, sensitivity to questions of fault comes at the stage of what Hawkins calls 'private [or semi-private] ordering by negotiation'[54] between parent and school, or between parent and Local Education Authority. When a case crosses the boundary into the public sphere of prosecution, however, and '[n]egotiated problem-solving gives way to the imposed and uncompromising rigours of adjudicated justice',[55] the imposition of strict liability can be an important way of marking this transition: it can be an acknowledgement that, in the judgment of the relevant experts who are most familiar with the case at hand, the time has come 'to bring a particular defendant to book'.[56] That brings me to the measures that have been put in place for Local Education Authorities to take positive action that is more 'welfarist' in nature, long before any prosecution is undertaken, to ensure that parents exercise 'due diligence' in ensuring that their children attend school regularly.

## 2.3. The Velvet Glove

A substantial body of research has established links between family 'dysfunction' and criminal or antisocial behaviour, the link being strongest in cases in which parents neglect children by failing to provide adequate supervision.[57] There is considerable related evidence indicating that what might broadly be called 'parent training' (such as encouraging parents to monitor children's behaviour, and to make children's rewards and punishments dependent on behaviour judged in the light of house rules) can be effective in reducing deviant behaviour, including truancy and offending.[58] In that regard, under the 1996 Act, parental 'due diligence' is something to be promoted and developed *ex ante*, by co-operation between parents and Local Education Authority officers, and not (or not just) used *ex post facto* as a defence to a section 444(1) prosecution. Under section 447(1) of the 1996 Act, 'Before instituting proceedings . . . a local education authority

[52] *Gammon Ltd.* v. *A-G of Hong Kong* [1985] 1 AC 1.      [53] Ibid. at 14.
[54] Keith Hawkins, *Law as a Last Resort*, 422.      [55] Ibid.
[56] The words of an Area Director working for the Health and Safety Commission, cited by Keith Hawkins, ibid. 408.
[57] David J. Smith, 'Crime and the Life Course', in Maguire, Morgan, and Reiner, *The Oxford Handbook of Criminology*, 726. Smith explains what I am calling family 'dysfunction' at 727–8.
[58] See D. Farrington, 'Developmental Criminology and Risk-Focused Prevention', ibid. 684.

shall consider whether it would be appropriate (instead of or as well as instituting the proceedings) to apply for an education supervision order with respect to the child.' Further, under section 447(2), the court may itself direct the local authority to take this course when a charge comes before it.

Section 36 of the Education Act 1989 provides the legal basis for such orders, by which a child is placed under the supervision of the Local Education Authority if he or she is not being properly educated.[59] Under the 1989 Act, once an Education Supervision Order has been made, the designated Supervisor is under a duty, 'to advise, befriend and give directions to the child, the parents and any person with parental responsibility . . . in order to ensure that the child is properly educated'.[60] Highly intrusive though it is, when compared with the prospect of criminal conviction section 447(1) represents the relatively 'tender' side, in the form of encouragement and support for better parenting, of what is meant to be a 'tough-and-tender' approach to parental neglect of children, self-consciously designed to be more sophisticated than its supposedly cruder Victorian predecessors.[61] Section 447(2) shows, moreover, the extent to which Parliament is now willing, in the interests of better executive practice in discharging the responsibility for implementing a 'tender' approach, to depart from a strict view of the separation of powers. No longer confined to their traditional role of impartially reviewing the administrative decisions taken by members of the executive, by virtue of section 447(2) the courts can become directly involved in substantive decisions about the conduct of prosecutions. They can require Local Education Authorities to consider (before or alongside prosecution) pursuing constructive programmes, e.g. by making an Education Supervision Order, instead of prosecuting.[62] In practice, whilst some Local Education Authorities have certainly adopted tough language about vigorously pursuing prosecutions against the parents of persistent truants,[63] the primary emphasis remains on support and guidance for such parents, whether or not provided through the formal mechanism of an Education Supervision Order, to ensure that children resume regular

[59]  The welfare of the child is the paramount consideration, and an Education Supervision Order must be in the child's best interests.                    [60]  Section 36 of the Education Act 1996.
[61]  See text above, at n. 25. However, it should be noted that it is a criminal offence punishable by a fine to fail to comply with the Supervisor's directions.
[62]  By s. 447(2) of the Education Act 1996, 'The court . . . may direct the local education authority instituting the proceedings to apply for an education supervision order with respect to the child unless the authority, having consulted the appropriate local authority, decide that the child's welfare will be satisfactorily safeguarded even though no education supervision order is made.' See further, Nick Barber, 'Prelude to the Separation of Powers' [2001] *Cambridge LJ* 59. See also s. 20(3) of the Anti-Social Behaviour Act 2003. Under Magistrates' Association guidelines for sentencing offenders under s. 444(1), 'co-operation with the Education Authority' is a factor to be considered as mitigating the offence.
[63]  See e.g. the press release by East Sussex County Council, 5 June 2002, 'Court Action Over Non-Attendance at School . . . East Sussex County Council's Education Welfare Service is continuing with its policy of prosecuting parents who do not fulfil their legal responsibility regarding their children's attendance at school.'

attendance as soon as possible (with the possibility of prosecution under section 444 very much in the background).[64]

The primacy of the 'tender' ethos, where truancy is concerned, has come about through the emerging prominence of 'Education Welfare Services' in Local Education Authorities, whose task it is, in part, to bridge the gaps in responsibility for truants and their parents that can develop between the policy and practice respectively of schools, social services, and the police. In some Local Education Authorities, it will be the Education and Welfare Service that has the responsibility for initiating a prosecution under section 444 (although this may on occasion be solely the responsibility of the council's legal department).[65] However, the primary duties of Education and Welfare Services in relation to truancy are (i) in individual cases, to develop a predominantly non-confrontational 'inclusive' policy towards truanting whose aim is to improve the attitudes and practice of parents and children (as well as the attitudes and practices of schools, where appropriate) and (ii) in general, to develop a co-ordinated strategy followed by all concerned official agencies (including schools) towards the reduction of truancy.[66] In an individual case, where letters to parents, or other relatively informal means of securing regular attendance by a child have failed, the case may then be referred to the Education and Welfare Service of the Local Education Authority.[67] The Education Welfare

---

[64] See e.g. the education (welfare, and attendance information) sections of the Brent Council website (<www.brent.gov.uk>, accessed 25 Sept. 2004); also the statement of the Senior Education Welfare Officer for East Sussex in the Press Release cited in the previous note; 'The Education Welfare Service aims to provide support and guidance to parents on school attendance issues. However, if children remain out of school and parents continually fail to co-operate to resolve the problems, the legal options available to us will be pursued.' See also the Devon County Council statement of its policy on school attendance: 'The County Council is committed to: supporting parents/carers to ensure that children attend school regularly in order to benefit from education; reducing levels of unauthorised absence . . . through a strategy which focuses on raising levels of overall attendance; informing and supporting parents/carers and school staff in fulfilling legal responsibilities; taking action when appropriate to discharge its statutory duties.'

[65] See Department for Education and Skills Guidance, 'Ensuring Regular Attendance at School', para. 82, and the Department for Education and Skills Update, 27 June 2003, <www.dfes.gov.uk>, accessed 25 Sept. 2004.

[66] See e.g. the list of services the Education Welfare Service that Brent Council, in London, purports to provide: <www.brent.gov.uk/education>, accessed 25 Sept. 2004. The process begins with regular (weekly; and sometimes more frequent) visits by the Education Welfare Service to each school, in part to check the adequacy and efficiency of attendance registers and of the collection and categorization of data in relation to non-attendance by pupils. Also within the Service's supervisory purview is the way in which each school deals with unauthorized absence, respecting which there is an obligation to ensure that parents are contacted at an early stage, and chased up where necessary according to a 'standard letter system', alongside or followed by meetings with parents to develop a strategy or action plan to improve a child's attendance. See Department for Education and Skills Guidance, 'Ensuring Regular Attendance at School', paras. 25 and 37. Devon County Council indicates that there should be no referral of a case to the Education Welfare Service unless 'reasonable steps' have been taken to secure regular attendance, especially contacting parents on the first day of absence: see <www.devon.gov.uk/eal>, and <www.salford.gov.uk>, Press Release, 'Salford leads the way in tackling truancy', both accessed 25 Sept. 2004.

[67] There are other, non-confrontational possibilities, such as that a 'learning mentor' may be appointed to work with the family of a persistent truant, under an initiative announced by the then Secretary of State for Education, Ms Estelle Morris, MP, on 1 November 1999.

Service may act first as a kind of intermediary, seeking to discover whether the problem lies principally with the school and its policies, or with the parents. If the problem lies with the parents, then the Education Welfare Service casework will be directed towards working constructively with parents and children to secure regular attendance, liaising where appropriate with the Social Services, the Health Service, and the Police, amongst others.[68] As one Councillor with responsibility for education policy put it, 'our approach is not confrontational but . . . to explain to parents the importance of school attendance and gain their co-operation'.[69] With an eye on possible subsequent litigation, the Education Welfare Officer assigned to an individual case is obliged to keep documentary evidence to show what she or he has done to discover and address the reasons for a child's non-attendance, including parental attitudes.[70]

## 2.4. Respectful Deference, and the Policy of 'Joined-up' Government

The great strength of 'respectful deference' as a normative frame of reference is its sensitivity to integrated approaches by official agencies within a legislative framework. We have seen how government policies concerning the complex and widespread social problem of truancy have been implemented by constructing a joint enterprise between parents, schools, education authorities, and even the courts, to promote co-operation with those policies. Within the context of the legislative policy, the management of that joint enterprise has been delegated by the legislature to local agencies. It may therefore seem appropriate, when construing the terms of section 444(1), to take into account the values that have informed the micro-policies of local agencies in securing co-operation with the legislative aims, and which underpin the resort to prosecution. Understood in this way, as so often in the regulatory context, the criminal offences in section 444 appear as backstops, to be deployed only when other mechanisms have failed. In these circumstances, it can be taken for granted that it was persistent fault on the part of defendants that led to a criminal prosecution (rendering the requirement of fault

---

[68] See Department for Education and Skills Guidance, 'Ensuring Regular Attendance at School', para. 51. The aforementioned Patricia Amos (above, n. 30), jailed for failing without reasonable justification to secure the regular attendance of her daughters at school, was visited 71 times in twelve months by the social services, in an effort to ensure that her daughters attended school: *The Guardian*, 21 May 2002, p. 5. Interestingly, a year on from her mother's conviction, following improved attendance levels, her eldest daughter won a prize for English at school. Sadly, however, her mother was in jail once again almost two years later: see above, n. 30.

[69] <www.salford.gov.uk>. The Education Welfare Service meets parents and children to discuss attendance (as the school is meant to have done), but may go beyond this by offering support in key preventative parenting skills, such as behaviour management. This may involve agreeing with the family on a Personal Attendance Plan to be followed by the parent or parents and children. In the model action plan for securing regular attendance in Nottingham, approved by the Department for Education and Skills itself, prosecution of parents is barely mentioned as an effective way of reducing truancy: see <www.dfes.gov.uk/schoolattendance/press/>, accessed 25 Sept. 2004.

[70] Department for Education and Skills Guidance, 'Ensuring Regular Attendance at School', para. 50.

in the criminal offence itself effectively redundant). In this way, the respectful deference approach supports a strong prima facie case for interpreting section 444(1) as a strict liability offence.

As was said in § 1, however, a prima facie case for strict liability can be overridden by other considerations. Section 3 considers reasons why, in the context of section 444(1), the respectful deference analysis can, and should, be defeated by other values that ought to inform the courts' interpretation of criminal statutes, and of this criminal law in particular.

## 3. Criminal Law Values: The Courts, Legislators, and the Executive

### 3.1. The 'Mediating Influence' of the Courts

The 'velvet glove' processes described in § 2 can in fact be used as a way of meeting one argument in favour of strict liability, mentioned at the end of § 1. Suppose it were argued that a 'due diligence' defence, of the kind favoured by Elias J in *Barnfather*, would be unworkable because the efforts made by a parent to ensure their child attends school regularly are within his or her peculiar knowledge; and where that is the case, the prosecution is at an unfair disadvantage.[71] We can now see that, in this context, such an argument would have little weight. Before a case gets anywhere near the stage at which a prosecution is appropriate, the nature and extent of parental effort will have been fully documented, as a matter of official record. More significantly, however, the case against strict liability in *Barnfather*, and in favour of a due diligence defence, must meet the key argument in favour of the 'respectful deference' approach to decision-making by welfare authorities, set out above at the end of § 2.2. This is the argument that where negotiation to secure compliance—of a kind now guaranteed to parents through recent developments—has failed, strict liability quite properly facilitates bringing recalcitrant parents to book.[72] Strict liability does this, so the argument goes, while virtually eliminating the prospect that meretricious excuses and explanations, found by executive agencies to lack substance during the investigative compliance process, will simply be recycled in a form suited to (unmerited) success in the adversarial process.[73] Such recycling risks bringing the compliance process into undeserved disrepute, undermining the morale of those working in it, and so forth.[74] How can this argument be met?

---

[71] See text above, at n. 22.        [72] See text above, at n. 56.

[73] That this is not a remote possibility is argued by e.g. Keith Hawkins, who notes (*Law as Last Resort*, 409) the way in which the adversarial process 'imprints itself upon [the participants'] behaviour. . . . The nature of the legal method is to create its own reality by particularising, to allow the ready application of legal rules to produce an outcome, and an answer to a question posed in legal terms.'

[74] More generally, although perhaps not in this particular, welfare-focused context, low penalties upon conviction may be a more serious concern: see Hawkins, ibid. 288.

In many common law jurisdictions, and especially in those where the limits of judicial creativity in criminal cases have never been clearly marked out by the legislature, no one seriously doubts that the courts have an inherent legal power to imply mental elements into crimes ostensibly creating strict liability, or to apply defences to those offences, even if the power is rarely exercised. Speaking of English law, Lord Simon put the matter this way:

I am all for recognising frankly that judges do make law. And I am all for judges exercising this responsibility boldly at the proper time and place—that is, where they feel confident of having in mind, and correctly weighed, all the implications of their decision, and where matters of social policy are not involved which the collective wisdom of Parliament is better suited to resolve.[75]

In that regard, at least on some occasions judges have rejected a purely 'submissive deference' to bureaucratic decision-making,[76] and the implication (as some clearly see it) that such an approach would make them 'the mere handmaidens of public officials'.[77] By way of contrast, some judges have seen their role as being the development of a more proactive '*mediating influence* between the executive and the legislature on the one hand, and the citizen on the other',[78] an influence seemingly more consistent with respectful rather than submissive deference to decision-making by the executive. If this so-called mediating influence is, though, construed as being the straightforward judicial application of 'common law' values (such as negative liberty, in the form of freedom from unjustified stigma) to the interpretation of criminal statutes, it might be said that it is not really a *mediating* influence at all. It is an exercise of judicial discretion affirming the court's belief that Parliament, unless the contrary be clear, did not intend to prevent common law values from influencing the conditions in which convictions can be obtained, in the pursuit of welfarist bureaucratic policy. As has already been pointed out, in this context, the truly 'mediating influence' of the courts is in fact provided for by Parliament itself, in the form of an explicit statutory power (in effect) to stay a prosecution in circumstances where an Education Supervision Order respecting failing parents has not hitherto been sought.[79] Even so, the fact that the courts already have parliamentary authority to mediate in a specified form does not undermine the propriety of applying common law values to the interpretation of the criminal statute under which that influence is granted: as, for example, through the implication of a 'due diligence' defence at the trial stage. Like all bureaucrats within the legal system, judges can legitimately see themselves as 'wearing more than one hat': concerned, on the one

---

[75] *DPP* v. *Lynch* [1975] AC 653, at 695.

[76] For an explanation of this term, see above, text at n. 11.

[77] Lord Parker CJ's phrase, cited in G. T. Williams, 'The Donoughmore Report in Retrospect' (1982) 60 *Public Administration* 273, at 291.

[78] *Stock* v. *Frank Jones (Tipton) Ltd.* [1978] ICR 347, at 353, *per* Lord Simon (my emphasis).

[79] Education Act 1996, s. 447(2) and (4), discussed above, at n. 62.

hand, to ensure that priority is given to negotiation and support in order to secure compliance and a change of attitude (here, in parents), but also determined, on the other hand, to ensure that a proper regard for fair labelling is not set aside when, whether in sorrow or in anger, prosecution takes the place of continued negotiation.[80] There should be nothing inconsistent in that approach with the ideal of respectful deference.

Seen in this light, it is possible to make sense of the idea that judges exercise a truly mediating influence between citizens and the state when they apply common law values to the interpretation of criminal statutes, implying a mental element or a defence such as due diligence. A criminal statute must be interpreted in such a way that it fits, morally, with other legal obligations and permissions, and with other social or political phenomena (such as each citizen's standing in the community) on which it may have a bearing.[81] In this context, recognition that significant stigma attaches to conviction for a failure to ensure that a child attends school regularly ought to lead judges to give a high moral priority to the implication of a mental element or to the application of a defence of due diligence (for which, as we now know, there will be ample documentary evidence[82]), because the negative impact of that stigma may disadvantage the defendant in a number of contexts going well beyond the area of conduct governed by the offence itself. Conviction under section 444 of the Education Act 1996 may, for example, have an adverse impact stretching beyond the defendant's relationship with schools and Local Education Authorities during the rest of the child's school years, perhaps by affecting—in the eyes of the relevant authorities—his or her suitability to work in education or childcare, to foster or adopt children, and so forth. As Elias J put it, in *Barnfather*:

> I recognise that the penalties are small . . . and that is a factor which can properly be considered when determining whether an offence of strict liability is justified. However, in my opinion there is nonetheless a real stigma attached to being found guilty of a criminal offence of this nature. It suggests either an indifference to one's children, or incompetence at parenting, which in the case of the blameless parent will be unwarranted.[83]

The duty to interpret criminal statutes with an eye to the impact that conviction may have beyond the immediate context reinforces the reasons judges have to make stigma a ground for the implication of a fault requirement, or for the application of a defence. In that regard, there is perhaps an inherent risk, in always seeking to adopt an attitude of respectful deference, that the relevant moral issues will wrongly appear to be wholly *bounded by* their context, as they clearly seemed to be to the expert witness from the Department of Education and Skills called by

---

[80] For an account of how this dual role affects the self-perception of regulatory prosecutors, see Hawkins, *Law as Last Resort*, Ch. 13.

[81] For an examination of the theoretical significance of this kind of 'fit', one that (*inter alia*) seeks to distance jurisprudential thinking from the assumption that statutes must be analysed as if they were legislative 'bolts from the blue', see J. M. Finnis, *Natural Law and Natural Rights* (Oxford 1980), 283.                                             [82] See the discussion in § 2.3 above.

[83] *Barnfather*, para. 57.

the Education Authority in *Barnfather*. To her, the argument in favour of strict liability was simply that, 'This straightforward, easily provable offence, with limited penal consequences, is considered to be a useful tool within the local authority armoury to assist them in making parents face up to and discharge their responsibilities.'[84] Respectful deference, in other words, might too easily become what the theorist who coined the term himself criticized as 'submissive deference', on the part of the judiciary.[85]

## 3.2. The Value in Parenting: The Case for a 'Due Diligence' Defence

Neither judge in *Barnfather* devoted much attention to the question whether, if a fault element were to be implied in the wording of the offence under section 444, it should—following traditional principles[86]—be a *mens rea* element of an orthodox kind (intention; foresight; knowledge). Elias J, who—had the argument about Article 6(2) succeeded[87]—would have implied a fault element, indicated that it would take the form of a requirement to show due diligence: '[I]n my opinion, any problems of proof could in large part be dealt with by imposing a reverse burden on the parent to require him or her to demonstrate what steps had been taken and to satisfy the court that they were reasonable.'[88] There are important reasons supporting this proposal, reasons that reinforce the case against permitting liability to be strict under section 444. A parent's efforts to ensure a child's regular attendance at school are activities with intrinsic value, because they are partly constitutive of the intrinsically valuable activity of good parenting. As John Gardner puts it, speaking more generally of the 'active' account of human well-being: '[O]ur well-being consists in the wholehearted and successful pursuit of worthwhile activities . . . [and, further] the value which our virtues and skills bring to our worthwhile activities is by its very nature intrinsic or constitutive value.'[89] Someone who becomes a parent but plays no part in the rearing of the child necessarily misses out on the intrinsic value of being a parent, because it is only through taking (wholehearted) part in parenting itself—and not through the mere status of being a parent—that one realizes or generates the value in that form of life.[90] By the same token, a court that is prepared to uphold criminal liability

---

[84] Evidence of Sheila Scales, cited in *Barnfather*, para. 29. This argument is robustly rejected by Elias J, ibid. para. 55, where he says, 'will it in general be an appropriate case [for prosecution] only if the authority considers that there is fault? If so, then it means that the authority instead of a court will be deciding as a matter of executive discretion whether there is fault. No doubt that is highly convenient to the prosecution, but it is constitutionally unacceptable to permit the executive to make the decision.'          [85] See text above, at n. 11.

[86] See *Sweet* v. *Parsley* [1970] AC 132 (HL); *B (a minor)* v. *DPP* [2000] 3 WLR 471 (HL).

[87] See the discussion in § 1 above.          [88] *Barnfather*, para. 52.

[89] Gardner, 'On the General Part of the Criminal Law', 223.

[90] Although, ironically, as Counsel for *Barnfather*, Mr Timothy Owen QC pointed out, on Maurice Kay J's strict liability approach, a parent could in theory be found liable under s. 444 even if there was a court order preventing the parent from playing any part in their child's educational development.

imposed on a parent for failing to ensure her or his child's regular attendance at school, without regard to whether or not the parent can reasonably be considered to have done their best to ensure their child's attendance,[91] disregards— 'betrays' is perhaps not too strong a word—the intrinsic value in the wholehearted pursuit of that endeavour. It follows, then, that that value is best honoured, as Elias J envisages, with a due diligence defence respecting which the defendant bears the burden of proof.

One important advantage of this approach is that a due diligence defence can be made sensitive, in a way that traditional subjective fault elements cannot, to the fact that seeking to ensure a child's regular attendance at school may involve a mountain to climb for (say) a single, working parent with a number of perhaps difficult and aggressive children, but only a molehill to surmount for an affluent couple with a nanny to assist in childcare responsibilities for, say, only one child at a private school.[92] Parents who fail to ensure that their children attend school regularly set back their children's interests, interests the parents are under a duty to promote. In that sense, parents harm their children by such a failure.[93] However, exactly when it amounts to a breach of parental duty not to provide a certain kind and degree of care and attention would seem to some extent inevitably to depend on the circumstances—such as the economic, social, and familial[94] position of a family—in which parents are being asked to provide these things. This just underlines the point that, in holding the offence under section 444(1) to be one of strict liability, and hence refusing to acknowledge through the provision of an excuse the Herculean task that some parents may face in seeking to avoid conviction of that offence, the courts officially degrade the intrinsic value of the great effort that may have gone into that task.[95]

---

[91] In this regard, it will be recalled that the defendant in *Barnfather* was a mother of four children, and the child in question a 13-year-old boy (no mere 7-year-old). As Elias J rightly observed, 'in this context, I make the obvious but nevertheless relevant observation that the parent is being made liable for the failure of a third party—the child—who has a mind of his or her own capable of frustrating the best of parental endeavours . . . '

[92] Although this point was not taken, the imposition of strict criminal liability for a failure to ensure a child attends school seems controversial when viewed in the light of Article 8 of the European Convention, which guarantees a right to respect for private and family life so far as 'interference by a public authority' is concerned. It must be at least arguable that *strict* criminal liability poses disproportionate risks of the stigma of conviction being visited on poor, single, disabled, or mentally subnormal parents (amongst other instances) who have—say—several, older children, in breach of Article 8. See Jason Coppel, *The Human Rights Act 1998* (Chichester 1999), para. 10.26.

[93] That one can, in some circumstances, harm someone by failing to improve their prospects is argued for by Joseph Raz: see Raz, 'Autonomy, Toleration and the Harm Principle'.

[94] That is, how many dependants and carers there are within a family.

[95] This point holds good even if one takes the older view, embedded in the Victorian predecessor of the Education Act 1996, that ensuring a child attends school regularly is a duty owed to the state to promote a public good (the quest for national 'efficiency') and not a duty owed to the child. The promotion of that good should not be permitted to be pursued at the expense of other important liberal values.

# 6

# Strict Liability, Legal Presumptions, and the Presumption of Innocence

*R. A. Duff*

## 1. Varieties of Strict Liability

Strict criminal liability is criminal liability without proof of fault. However, given the variety of meanings that have been attached to 'strict liability',[1] I should clarify my use of the phrase.

First, my concern is with liability that is 'strict' rather than 'absolute', in one sense of the latter term.[2] Liability would be absolute if it required no proof of fault as to *any* aspect of the offence: thus the offence of being found drunk in a highway would be an absolute offence if conviction did not require proof of any *mens rea* either as to getting drunk or as to being in a highway.[3] Liability is strict if it requires no proof of fault as to *an* aspect of the offence: while *mens rea* must be proved as to some elements in the offence definition, it need not be proved as to every fact, consequence, or circumstance necessary for the commission of the offence. I could be guilty of possessing an uncertificated firearm even if I am reasonably sure that it is an antique (which would not require a certificate), and perhaps even if I do not realize that it is a firearm: but whilst liability is thus strict

This chapter was written during my tenure of a Leverhulme Major Research Fellowship: I am very grateful to the Leverhulme Trust for this support, and to participants in the Cambridge workshop on strict liability, and especially to Kim Ferzan, Alan Michaels, and Andrew Simester, for helpful comments.

[1] On which see D. Husak, 'Varieties of Strict Liability' (1995) 8 *Canadian Journal of Law and Jurisprudence* 189; K. W. Simons, 'When is Strict Criminal Liability Just?' (1997) 87 *Journal of Criminal Law and Criminology* 1075, at 1075–93; and Green in this volume, Ch. 1.

[2] See e.g. J. C. Smith and B. Hogan, *Criminal Law* (10th edn., London 2002), 117.

[3] See Licensing Act 1872, s. 12; *Winzar* v. *Chief Constable of Kent* (1983) *The Times*, 28 March: Mr Winzar was carried into the highway by the police; it is not clear whether conviction required proof of fault as to getting drunk. *Larsonneur* (1933) 24 Cr. App. R. 74 is often cited in this context, since the offence of being 'found' in the UK as an alien to whom leave to land had been refused supposedly required no *mens rea* (Aliens Order 1920: see Smith and Hogan, *Criminal Law*, 58): but it required that she had 'landed'; and unless she was carried bodily from the ship (in which case it could be argued that she had not 'landed'—compare *Hill* v. *Baxter* [1958] 1 QB 277), she at least landed in the UK intentionally, albeit under duress.

as to the fact that the item is a 'firearm', I must have at least known that I had that item in my possession.[4]

Second, my concern is with liability that is 'absolute' rather than 'strict' in another sense of 'absolute'. Liability is in this sense absolute if it does not require proof of fault as to some aspect of the offence, and cannot be averted by disproof of fault; it is strict if, although it does not require positive proof of fault, it can be averted by evidence or proof of lack of fault, or of 'due diligence'.[5] Liability for the unauthorized possession of a scheduled drug under section 1(1) of the Drugs (Prevention of Misuse) Act 1964 was absolute as to the fact that the substance that I knew I possessed was a scheduled drug;[6] liability for the matching offence under the Misuse of Drugs Act 1971 is only strict, since someone who had possession of a controlled drug can secure an acquittal by proving 'that he neither knew nor suspected nor had reason to suspect' that it was such a drug.[7] Liability that is in this sense strict involves a rebuttable presumption: proof of what the prosecution must prove creates a presumption of guilt, which the defendant can rebut by proving lack of fault. I will discuss such presumptions later (in §§ 3–5), but my ultimate interest is in liability that is in this sense absolute; I will use 'strict liability' to refer to such liability.

Third, we can distinguish legally or formally strict liability from morally or substantively strict liability, and correlative formal from substantive notions of fault.[8] Liability is formally strict as to an aspect of an offence if it does not require any legally recognized species of fault—such as intention, knowledge, recklessness, or negligence—as to that aspect.[9] Liability is substantively strict if it does not depend on proof of some appropriate moral culpability as to some aspect of the offence— proof of some fault that would justify condemning the defendant for committing the offence. This distinction gives us four possible patterns of strict and non-strict liability.

(*a*) Liability can be both legally and morally non-strict. A conviction for criminal damage requires proof of intention or recklessness as to the damage to another's property that I cause; absent a 'lawful excuse', this constitutes proof of legal and moral fault—of *mens rea* and of a moral culpability that justifies condemning me for damaging the property.[10]

---

[4] Firearms Act 1968, ss. 1(1), 58; see *Howells* [1977] QB 614 (on antiques); *Hussain* (1981) 72 Cr. App. R. 143 (on not knowing it to be a firearm).

[5] See A. P. Simester and G. R. Sullivan, *Criminal Law: Theory and Doctrine* (2nd edn., Oxford 2003), 185–6; A. J. Ashworth, *Principles of Criminal Law* (4th edn., Oxford 2003), 165. General common law defences such as duress are still available for absolute liability offences: see Simester and Sullivan, *Criminal Law*, 178.        [6] See *Warner* v. *Metropolitan Police Commissioner* [1969] 2 AC 256.

[7] Misuse of Drugs Act 1971, ss. 5(1)–(2), 28: see *Ashton-Rickhardt* (1977) 65 Cr. App. R. 67.

[8] Compare Simons, 'When is Strict Criminal Liability Just?', 1087–93; also Husak, this volume, Ch. 4, and Simester, this volume, Ch. 2.

[9] See e.g. Smith and Hogan, *Criminal Law*, 115; I assume here that negligence-based liability need not be 'strict': see e.g. A. P. Simester, 'Can Negligence be Culpable?' in J. Horder (ed.), *Oxford Essays in Jurisprudence: Fourth Series* (Oxford 2000), 85.        [10] See Criminal Damage Act 1971, s. 1(1).

(*b*) Liability can be both legally and morally strict. If I caused 'any poisonous, noxious or polluting matter . . . to enter any controlled water', I am guilty of an offence even if I can prove that I took all reasonable care, in pursuing my legitimate activity, to prevent such pollution.[11] Liability is thus legally strict, and is also morally strict if a defendant who took such reasonable care should not be condemned for the pollution.[12]

(*c*) Liability can be legally non-strict but morally strict, if the legally defined *mens rea* does not constitute an appropriate kind of moral fault. A girl who destroyed a shed by lighting a fire in it was guilty of criminal damage under English law if the risk of damage would have been obvious to a 'reasonably prudent' person, even if she did not appreciate that risk and (given her age and intelligence) would not have appreciated it had she given the matter any thought, since she was in law 'reckless' as to that risk.[13] Her liability was not legally strict, but even those who find some merit in the *Caldwell* doctrine should agree that it was morally strict, since she did not display any fault sufficient to justify holding her as culpably responsible for the damage she caused as if she had foreseen it.[14]

(*d*) Liability can be legally strict but morally non-strict, if conviction does not require proof of any legally recognized *mens rea* as to an aspect of the offence, but proof of legal guilt also constitutes proof of an appropriate moral fault in relation to the complete offence. I cannot offer uncontroversial examples of this possibility, since I will need to argue that it is not an empty category, but it underpinned the argument that since 'a taking of a girl, in the possession of some one, against his wi[ll] . . . done without lawful excuse is wrong, . . . it should be at the risk of the taker whether or no she was under sixteen'.[15] Liability for unlawfully taking an unmarried girl of under 16 from the possession and against the will of her parent was legally strict as to her age: but the argument was that anyone who acted with the *mens rea* that the law required—as to her being an unmarried 'girl' in the possession of a parent who did not consent to her departure—displayed a moral fault as to the risk that she was under 16 sufficient to justify convicting him of the offence if that risk was actualized, even if he was sure that she was over 16.

[11] Water Resources Act 1991, s. 85(1); *R.* v. *Milford Haven Port Authority* (2000) 2 Cr. App. R. (S.) 423. But it might be hard to decide whether a defendant 'caused' the pollution without attending to matters of fault: see *Alphacell Ltd.* v. *Woodward* [1972] AC 824.

[12] It might be morally appropriate to hold him strictly liable to pay the costs of the pollution, but strict civil liability is a quite different matter from strict criminal liability; see P. Cane, *Responsibility in Law and Morality* (Oxford 2002), 105–10.

[13] *Elliott* v. *C* [1983] 1 WLR 939, applying *Caldwell* [1982] AC 341; overruled by *R.* v. *G* [2004] 1 AC 1034.

[14] Simons ('When is Strict Criminal Liability Just?', 1085–8) notes another kind of legally non-strict but morally strict liability, when the law requires full *mens rea*, but defines the offence so widely that it captures conduct that should not be criminal; see also D. Husak, 'Limitations on Criminalization and the General Part of the Criminal Law', in S. Shute and A. P. Simester (eds.), *Criminal Law Theory: Doctrines of the General Part* (Oxford 2002), 24–31.

[15] *Prince* (1875) LR 2 CCR 154, at 174–5 ( *per* Bramwell B); Offences Against the Person Act 1861, s. 55.

I will say no more here about (*a*) (which is unproblematic) or (*c*) (which is objectionable for the same reasons as (*b*) is). I will comment briefly on (*b*) in § 2, but my primary interest is in (*d*).

We can distinguish two more specific patterns within (*d*). One is that of 'constructive' liability, which involves legally strict liability as to a fact that transforms a less serious into a more serious offence. Under the doctrines of implied malice and felony murder, for instance, wounding with intent or arson (crimes for which liability is neither legally nor morally strict), can become murder if they cause death; liability is legally strict as to the victim's death.[16] In the other pattern, there is no lesser offence out of which liability for a more serious offence is constructed: so a man of 30 who has sexual intercourse with a girl who is under 16, believing her to be 16, is guilty of an offence that involves strict liability as to the girl's age, and there is no lesser offence for which liability is not strict and of which the prosecution must prove him guilty.[17] The justification of constructive strict liability is, we will see, (relatively) easy, and provides a model for the justification of at least some kinds of truly strict liability.

## 2. Morally Strict Liability

For a long time, discussions of strict liability concentrated on liability that is both legally and morally strict. The arguments for and against such liability are familiar.[18] Those who seek to justify it argue that, at least for offences that regulate voluntary, specialized activities that create significant risks to public health or safety (especially those motivated by profit), and conviction for which attracts neither serious moral or social stigma nor oppressive penalties, strict liability can be justified if it is necessary to make the law effective. Any injustice that this involves is 'comparatively minor', and with such 'quasi-criminal offences . . . it does not really offend the ordinary man's sense of justice that moral guilt is not of the essence of the offence'.[19] I will make only three comments on this debate here.

First, I take it that a *criminal* process purports to deal with wrongdoings that warrant the condemnation that criminal conviction and punishment communicate.[20] The simple objection to offences of morally strict liability is that they result either in the unjust condemnation of those who have not been proved to deserve it, or in the misuse of the criminal law to penalize without condemning (which

---

[16] For implied malice, see Smith and Hogan, *Criminal Law*, 359–61. For arson and felony murder, see W. R. LaFave, *Criminal Law* (3rd edn., St Paul, Minn. 2000), 671–87.

[17] Sexual Offences Act 1956, s. 6: see Smith and Hogan, *Criminal Law*, 476–7; *Kirk and Russell* [2002] Crim. LR 756. Contrast *R. v. K* [2002] 1 AC 462 (see below, n. 71), on indecent assault under s. 14(1).          [18] See Simester, Ch. 2 in this volume, for a useful critical survey.

[19] *Warner* v. *Metropolitan Police Commissioner* [1969] 2 AC 256 at 272 (*per* Lord Reid). See generally F. B. Sayre, 'Public Welfare Offenses' (1933) 33 *Columbia LR* 55, at 70–5; *Gammon* v. *Attorney-General of Hong Kong* [1985] AC 1, at 14 (*per* Lord Scarman).

[20] See my *Punishment, Communication, and Community* (New York 2001), 56–66, 79–82; A. von Hirsch, *Censure and Sanctions* (Oxford 1993), Ch. 2.

subjects the innocent to simulacra of criminal punishment, and allows the guilty to escape the condemnation they deserve).[21]

Secondly, an obvious way to avoid this objection is to rely on a system of administrative tribunals to administer non-criminal penalties for breaches of non-criminal regulations. This would raise further issues that I cannot discuss here, about the justice of strict liability under such a system, but we should note a different objection to it. Many who are guilty of existing offences for which liability is both legally and morally strict are in fact culpable in ways that would if proved warrant criminal condemnation; they act with a carelessness of public health and safety that deserves the public condemnation of a criminal conviction: to transform all such offences into merely regulatory violations would be to fail appropriately to address the culpable wrongdoing that they often involve.

Thirdly, another way to avoid the simple objection to strict criminal liability is to insist on negligence as to all aspects of the offence as a minimal condition of liability, in particular for 'regulatory' offences; and to meet the argument that proof of negligence will often be so difficult that the law's efficacy will be vitiated by freeing the prosecution from the burden of proving negligence, and laying on the defence the burden of proving (or adducing evidence of) absence of fault.[22] I will discuss this and other reversals of burdens of proof later, but we should note the worry that this 'halfway house' concedes too much, too quickly, to advocates of strict criminal liability. This solution might be adequate if we could say that in discharging its probative burden, the prosecution would have done enough to justify the presumption that the defendant was at least negligent, a presumption that could be rebutted by evidence of due diligence, but that absent such evidence would satisfy the demand for proof of fault beyond a reasonable doubt. But if we could not say that, this solution would sanction the conviction of defendants whose guilt had not been proved beyond reasonable doubt—which is to say that they would be held strictly liable in that they would be convicted without due proof of fault.

My primary interest, however, is in the possibility of liability that is legally (or formally) but not morally (or substantively) strict; but before discussing that, we should look at some closely related procedural provisions concerning burdens of proof and presumptions.

## 3. Presumptions and Burdens of Proof

'Every writer of sufficient intelligence to appreciate the difficulties of the subject matter has approached the topic of presumptions', warned E. M. Morgan, 'with a

---

[21] See e.g. Ashworth, *Principles of Criminal Law*, 166–7; Cane, *Responsibility in Law and Morality*, 109–10. A different objection, which does not rely on the condemnatory aspect of criminal convictions, is that by imposing strict liability we will punish some who did not have a fair opportunity to obey the law: see H. L. A. Hart, *Punishment and Responsibility* (Oxford 1968), 22–4.

[22] See e.g. Simester and Sullivan, *Criminal Law*, 184.

sense of hopelessness, and has left it with a feeling of despair.'[23] Despite the risk of exposing my lack of 'sufficient intelligence', however, and the risk of being accused of 'functionalist error',[24] I think that a discussion of presumptions will illuminate some of the issues raised by strict liability.

My interest is in presumptions that we can call (in the absence of an agreed terminology) 'derivative' (rather than 'foundational'), and 'legal' (rather than 'common sense'). Derivative presumptions depend on proof of some fact: if $p$ is proved, the court may, or must, presume that $q$. Foundational presumptions (which some deny should count as 'presumptions' at all)[25] obtain independently of any proof of fact during the trial: thus the foundational presumptions of innocence and of sanity require courts to approach each case with the presumption that the defendant is innocent, and sane, until sufficient evidence is adduced of her guilt or insanity. Common sense presumptions (sometimes called 'presumptions of fact') have no formal legal status: they simply express ordinary rules of extra-legal reasoning—if we see smoke, we have reason to presume that there is a fire, unless and until we receive contrary evidence. Legal presumptions (or 'presumptions of law'), by contrast, go beyond what is sanctioned by extra-legal common sense: they mandate courts to presume that $q$, given proof of $p$, even if without such a legal rule, proof of $p$ might not give us good enough reason to take $q$ as true. If, in a corruption trial, it is proved that a government contractor gave a civil servant a present this might, as a matter of common sense (depending on the context), lead jurors to wonder if the gift was corrupt; but they might reasonably think that it cannot by itself prove corruption beyond reasonable doubt. As a matter of law, however, given such proof they must presume that the present was 'given and received corruptly . . . unless the contrary is proved'.[26]

Legal presumptions are typically rebuttable: they require courts to treat $q$ as true, given proof that $p$, unless sufficient evidence is adduced to rebut the presumption. Rebuttable legal presumptions in the prosecution's favour lay on the defendant the formal burden of rebuttal; if they are not rebutted, the court must find that part of the prosecution case proved beyond reasonable doubt.[27] That burden might be merely evidential, to adduce evidence sufficient to raise a reasonable doubt whether $q$; thus if it is proved that the defendant sexually penetrated someone whom he knew to be unlawfully detained, the court must presume that that person did not consent to the penetration, and that the defendant did not believe that she

[23] E. M. Morgan, 'Presumptions' (1937) 12 *Washington LR* 255, at 255. See more generally E. Ullmann-Margalit, 'On Presumption' (1983) 80 *Journal of Philosophy* 143.
[24] See Roberts, Ch. 7 in this volume. On the other side, see V. Tadros and S. Tierney, 'The Presumption of Innocence and the Human Rights Act' (2004) 67 *Modern LR* 402.
[25] See e.g. A. A. Zuckerman, *The Principles of Criminal Evidence* (Oxford 1989), 110; C. F. H. Tapper, *Cross and Tapper on Evidence* (9th edn., London 1999), 120.
[26] Prevention of Corruption Act 1916, s. 2.
[27] Rules that permit, but do not require, the court to conclude that $q$ given proof that $p$ belong with common sense presumptions: see A. J. Ashworth and M. Blake, 'The Presumption of Innocence in English Criminal Law' (1996) *Criminal LR* 306, at 312–13.

consented, 'unless sufficient evidence is adduced to raise an issue as to' either of those facts.[28] But the burden is sometimes persuasive, to prove that not-$q$ (on the balance of probabilities): a civil servant who receives a gift from a government contractor must prove that she did not receive it corruptly.[29] Apart from statutorily explicit legal presumptions, we can also talk of implicit presumptions, created by statutes that directly allocate an evidential or persuasive burden to the defence: thus someone who sells food that 'fails to comply with food safety requirements' is guilty of an offence, but has a defence if he proves 'that he took all reasonable precautions and exercised all due diligence to avoid the commission of the offence';[30] the statute, we can say, creates a rebuttable presumption of negligence, given proof that the defendant sold unfit food. Whether the presumption is explicit or implicit, what the prosecution must prove might not count, by the standards of common sense extra-legal thought, as proof beyond reasonable doubt that the defendant is guilty: but the presumption requires the court to treat it as (or as if it were) proof beyond reasonable doubt, unless the presumption is rebutted.

There are also so-called 'irrebuttable presumptions of law', requiring courts to presume that $q$ given proof that $p$, and leaving no room for the presumption to be rebutted by adducing evidence or even proof that not-$q$. Thus given proof that the defendant 'intentionally deceived the complainant as to the nature or purpose' of a sexual act that he committed on her, 'it is to be conclusively presumed' that she did not consent to that act and that he did not believe that she consented.[31] Now it is often said that these are not properly 'presumptions' that mandate an inference from a proven fact $p$ to a further fact $q$; they are, instead, disguised substantive rules of law that help define the relevant offence, and should be honestly expressed as such.[32] The presumption that a deceived complainant did not consent does not mandate an inference from deception to some further, separate fact about consent or its absence. Rather, it partially defines 'consent' for the purposes of the Act: assent obtained by deception does not amount in law to consent of a kind that could render the act in question non-wrongful.[33] Similarly,

---

[28] Sexual Offences Act 2003, ss. 1, 75.

[29] Prevention of Corruption Act 1916, s. 2 (see text at n. 26 above); see also e.g. Dangerous Dogs Act 1991, s. 5; Proceeds of Crime Act 2002, s. 10. I leave aside here the question of whether such persuasive burdens are consistent with Article 6(2) of the European Convention on Human Rights (defendants 'shall be presumed innocent until proved guilty according to law'): see *R.* v. *DPP, ex parte Kebilene* [2000] 2 AC 326; *Lambert* [2002] 2 AC 545; *Sheldrake* v. *DPP* [2003] 2 All ER 497; A. J. Ashworth, 'Article 6 and the Fairness of Trials' (1999) *Criminal LR* 261, at 265–8; Tadros and Tierney, 'The Presumption of Innocence and the Human Rights Act'; and Sullivan, Ch. 8 in this volume.

[30] Food Safety Act 1990, ss. 8, 21: for other examples see Ashworth and Blake, 'The Presumption of Innocence in English Criminal Law', 308. I comment later (text at nn. 52–4 below) on whether we should distinguish burdens relating to an element of the offence from burdens relating to 'defences'.

[31] Sexual Offences Act 2003, s. 76.

[32] See Zuckerman, *The Principles of Criminal Evidence*, 113; Tapper, *Cross and Tapper on Evidence*, 66; Ashworth and Blake, 'The Presumption of Innocence in English Criminal Law', at 311–12; also Roberts, Ch. 7 in this volume, p. 184–5.

[33] For a useful discussion of legal conceptions of consent, see P. Westen, *The Logic of Consent* (Aldershot 2004).

the English rule that a voluntarily intoxicated agent who fails to notice a risk that
he would have noticed if sober is reckless as to that risk might be described as
creating an irrebuttable legal presumption that he 'is to be treated as having been
aware of' that risk,[34] which suggests that the court is required to take as true, to
the defendant's detriment, something that the evidence suggests might well be
false. We can, however, make more plausible moral sense of this rule by seeing it as
declaring that recklessness can be constituted *either* by awareness of a relevant risk,
*or* by unawareness that is due to voluntary intoxication:[35] recklessness must be
'presumed', given proof of such unawareness, not because it can be inferred from
such unawareness, but because it is constituted by such unawareness. Such
'presumptions' do mandate conclusions that go beyond the evidence that grounds
them, but that 'going beyond' is normative, rather than factual: the court is
required to conclude that V's 'consent' was not such as to legitimize D's sexual act,
or that D was as culpable in relation to that risk as he would have been had he
taken it consciously. We should perhaps call such provisions constitutive or
definitional rules rather than 'presumptions'; but they are relevant to my purposes
because, I will argue, we can usefully portray some strict liability provisions (those
that are to make any claim to justice) as having a similar logic.

We can arrange the various legal doctrines concerning proof of guilt along a
spectrum. At one end is the orthodox default position that gives simple expression
to the 'golden thread' of English criminal law—that 'it is the duty of the prosecution to prove the prisoner's guilt', and to prove it beyond reasonable doubt.[36] At
the other end lies formally strict liability, relieving the prosecution of any need to
prove the defendant's fault as to an element of the offence. In between lie legal
presumptions that seem to greater or lesser degrees to lighten or qualify the prosecution's probative duty. Thus if we are formulating a statutory definition of the
offence committed by an adult who engages in sexual activity with an under-age
child,[37] we can deal in a range of possible ways with the question of what *mens rea*
should be required as to the child's age.

We could decide that, for such an offence, the adult should be guilty unless he
reasonably believed the child to be over the relevant age (since one who acts
without such a belief shows a culpable lack of concern for an important aspect of
his action), and require the prosecution to prove the lack of such belief along
with other elements of the offence.[38] Or we could create a rebuttable legal
presumption: given proof that the child was under-age, it must be presumed that
the defendant lacked a reasonable belief that the child was over the relevant age

---

[34] J. C. Smith, commenting on *Bennett* [1995] Crim. LR 877, at 878.
[35] See Simester and Sullivan, *Criminal Law*, 145; *Majewski* [1977] AC 443, at 474–5 (*per* Lord
Elwyn-Jones), 479 (*per* Lord Simon), 496–7 (*per* Lord Edmund-Davies), 498 (*per* Lord Russell).
[36] *Woolmington* v. *DPP* [1935] AC 462, at 481 (*per* Viscount Sankey).
[37] See further, text at nn. 93–99 below.
[38] As the Sexual Offences Act 2003 (ss. 9–12) does for certain offences involving children
under 16.

unless he adduces evidence that 'raise[s] an issue as to whether he reasonably believed' the child to be over age (if we want to place only an evidential burden on the defence),[39] or unless he proves that he reasonably believed the child to be over age (if we want to place a persuasive burden on the defence).[40] Or we could create an irrebuttable legal presumption: given proof that the child was under-age, 'it is to be conclusively presumed' that the defendant had no reasonable belief that the child was over age.[41] Finally, we could make liability formally strict as to the child's age: given proof of intentional sexual activity with someone who was in fact under-age, the defendant is to be convicted regardless of his beliefs about the person's age.[42]

There are, for my purposes, two significant points about this spectrum. First, as we move along it, the prosecution's probative burden is progressively lightened: this raises the question of whether both legal presumptions and strict liability provisions undermine the presumption of innocence by freeing the prosecution from the burden of proving guilt (taken as including some appropriate type of fault) beyond reasonable doubt. Secondly, the effect of the last two stages (of irrebuttable presumptions and of strict liability) is the same: in neither case can any evidence concerning the defendant's beliefs about or attempts to determine the other person's age secure him an acquittal—if his sexual partner was under-age, he is guilty. This raises the question of whether the way in which that effect is achieved matters: what, if anything (other than procedural convenience) hangs on whether the defendant is convicted via the procedural route of an irrebuttable presumption, or the substantive route of a strict liability provision?

## 4. The Presumption of Innocence and its Implications

The bare presumption of innocence, the requirement that 'everyone charged with a criminal offence shall be presumed innocent until proved guilty according to the law',[43] does not of itself require either that guilt be proved beyond reasonable doubt, rather than on the balance of probabilities, or that guilt involve fault as to all aspects of the offence. Those two further requirements can, however, be generated from the values that underlie the presumption.[44]

To be convicted of a crime is not just to suffer some loss or costs; it is to be condemned for committing a wrong. This gives us reason to make it quite hard to

[39] See Sexual Offences Act 2003, ss. 16–19, on sexual activity involving children under 18.
[40] Compare Sexual Offences Act 2003, ss. 23, 28, 43 on the 'marriage exception'.
[41] Compare Sexual Offences Act 2003, s. 76, on 'conclusive presumptions' about consent; see text at n. 31 above.
[42] See Sexual Offences Act 2003, ss. 5–9, on sexual activity with children under 13. Intention is formally required as to the activity, but not as to its being 'sexual' (see s. 78 on what counts as 'sexual').
[43] European Convention on Human Rights, Art. 6(2).
[44] For a useful summary see P. Roberts, 'Taking the Burden of Proof Seriously' (1995) *Criminal LR* 783; see also Simester, Ch. 2, p. 31–2, and Roberts, Ch. 7, in this volume.

convict defendants, by defining proof 'according to law' as proof beyond reasonable doubt. Civil liability, involving no more than liability to pay the costs of harm that has occurred, might be justly allocated to the defendant if it is proved only on the balance of probabilities that she was responsible for the harm; but proof that the defendant is 'probably' guilty is not enough to justify his formal condemnation and punishment by the state. We must also therefore interpret 'innocence' and 'guilt' in substantive, not merely formal, terms. What should matter is whether a defendant has been proved to merit the condemnation that conviction conveys; a statute that so defined 'guilt' as to capture those who were clearly innocent of anything that could plausibly count as wrongdoing might satisfy a formal presumption of innocence, by requiring the prosecution to prove what it defined as guilt, but would not satisfy the substantive presumption that a person is innocent until proved guilty of wrongdoing.[45]

The presumption of innocence thus requires that defendants be convicted only on proof beyond reasonable doubt of what the law legitimately defines as culpable wrongdoing. It also implies a conception of the duties of citizens as criminal defendants or suspects, expressed in the right of silence: suspects and defendants have no duty to assist in their own prosecution; they can legitimately remain silent, and challenge the prosecution to prove their guilt without their co-operation. The right of silence is controversial as to its status and grounds,[46] and has been to at least some degree undermined in England by statutory provisions allowing courts sometimes to draw adverse inferences from silence.[47] Nor indeed do citizen-defendants have no duty to assist the criminal process; and although many of their duties are negative (not to interfere with a lawful police search, for instance), some are positive—for instance to appear for trial when summoned to do so, or to provide certain kinds of evidence to the police.[48] But there is a general presumption that, though a criminal charge calls a defendant to answer to an allegation of wrongdoing, the defendant has no *duty* to play an active role in the trial; it is for the prosecution to prove guilt, not for the defendant to disprove it.

Of course if the prosecution case, relying only on common sense presumptions, is strong enough to persuade a jury of a defendant's guilt beyond reasonable

[45] See Ashworth and Blake, 'The Presumption of Innocence in English Criminal Law', 317; *Salabiaku* v. *France* (1991) 13 EHRR 379, at 388, on reading 'according to the law' as referring not merely to the local domestic law, but to 'the fundamental principle of the rule of law'; and my *Trials and Punishments* (Cambridge 1986), 153–5.

[46] See A. J. Ashworth, *The Criminal Process* (2nd edn., Oxford 1998), 96–108.

[47] See e.g. Criminal Justice and Public Order Act 1994, ss. 34–7 (on which see I. H. Dennis, 'Silence in the Police Station: The Marginalisation of Section 34' (2002) *Criminal LR* 25; Ashworth, *The Criminal Process*, 100–8); Criminal Procedure and Investigation Act 1996, s. 5 (see R. Leng, 'The Exchange of Information and Disclosure', in M. McConville and G. Wilson (eds.), *The Handbook of the Criminal Justice Process* (Oxford 2002), 205, at 213–18).

[48] See e.g. Road Traffic Act 1988, s. 7; and Production Orders under Schedule 1 of the Police and Criminal Evidence Act 1984 (see M. Levi, 'Economic Crime,' in McConville and Wilson, *The Handbook of the Criminal Justice Process*, 423, at 427–30), or 'information contained in a computer' under s. 20 of that Act.

doubt, she acquires the de facto burden of rebutting that case if she is to avoid conviction; that follows from the idea of proof. But legal presumptions and strict liability provisions appear to go further than this, and to undermine the presumption of innocence, by mandating the conviction of those who have not been proved substantively guilty beyond reasonable doubt. Many who are convicted of an offence of formally strict liability might in fact be culpable if prosecutors have exercised their discretion wisely,[49] but they have not been proved to be culpable. Irrebuttable presumptions similarly seem to mandate convictions without what would otherwise count as proof of guilt beyond reasonable doubt, since (if they are to make any substantive difference) they require courts to treat as conclusive proof of culpability facts that might not otherwise constitute such proof.[50] Even rebuttable legal presumptions, whether explicit or implicit, appear to fray the 'golden thread', in so far as they mandate conclusions about guilt, which the defendant then has the burden of rebutting, on the basis of what might not otherwise count as proof beyond reasonable doubt.

It might be argued that this concern about rebuttable presumptions applies only to those that bear on an element of the offence, not to those that concern (the absence of) a defence—and that many of the shifts of burden that I have described as creating implicit presumptions are of the latter kind.[51] If the prosecution proves all the elements of the offence (i.e. proves that the defendant committed the offence), without relying on any presumptions, it is surely not then unreasonable, or inconsistent with the presumption of innocence, to lay on the defendant the onus of showing why she should none the less be acquitted. I cannot discuss the merits of this suggestion (or the viability of the offence–defence distinction on which it depends) here, but I should note three points. First, when the burden allocated to the defence is merely evidential, it would be wholly consistent with the presumption of innocence if proof of all the elements of the offence would itself, by the canons of ordinary extra-legal reasoning, amount to proof of guilt beyond reasonable doubt—i.e. if, given such proof, a jury would have reason to doubt the defendant's guilt only when offered evidence of a defence (which will at least very often be true): but this cannot justify laying a persuasive burden on defendants, since evidence of a defence that falls well short of proof (even on the

---

[49] See e.g. S. Nemerson, 'Criminal Liability Without Fault: A Philosophical Perspective' (1975) 75 *Columbia LR* 1517, at 1560–77; I. Paulus, 'Strict Liability: Its Place in Public Welfare Offences' (1977) 20 *Criminal Law Quarterly* 445. But see Lord Bingham's comments in *R.* v. *K* [2002] 1 AC 462, at 475; also Brooke LJ in the court of Appeal in *B* v. *DPP* [2000] AC 428, at 444.

[50] That is why both irrebuttable presumptions, and rebuttable presumptions that place a persuasive burden on the defence, are unconstitutional in the USA: for the 'due process' required by the Fourteenth Amendment requires the prosecution to prove all elements of the offence beyond reasonable doubt (*In re Winship*, 397, US 358 (1970)), and such presumptions violate that requirement (*Sandstrom* v. *Montana*, 442 US 510 (1979)). The substantive force of this doctrine is, however, reduced by the fact that the state can simply remove the element in question from the definition of the offence, either by making liability strict in that respect or by making it a matter of defence, for which defendants can carry a persuasive burden; thanks to Alan Michaels for this point.

[51] See text at nn. 30 and 50 above.

balance of probabilities) could still be sufficient to create a reasonable doubt. Second, if presumptions or shifts of probative burdens that are not consistent with the canons of ordinary, extra-legal reasoning are to be justified, this will need to be in terms of an argument about citizens' responsibilities similar to that sketched below in § 5: although citizens have no general responsibility to prove their innocence, it is properly up to them to do so if they are proved to have committed an offence; and if that responsibility is properly laid on them, they must discharge it if it is to become reasonable to doubt their guilt. Third, if the offence–defence distinction is to do this kind of normative work, justifying such shifts of probative burden, it must be drawn in substantive, not merely in formal, terms: what counts as 'the offence' must be something that could plausibly count as a criminal wrong. An example will show the force of this point.

According to section 57 of the Terrorism Act 2000, 'possess[ion of ] an article in circumstances which give rise to a reasonable suspicion that his possession is for a purpose connected with' terrorism is an offence, to which it is a defence to 'prove that his possession of the article was not for a purpose connected with' terrorism. Ormerod argues that this does not create '"a presumption" of guilt' that the defendant must then rebut; it defines an offence, he thinks, of possessing an article in circumstances that give rise to a reasonable suspicion, and allows a defence that it is for the defendant to prove.[52] Even if the argument sketched in the previous paragraph is sound, however, it cannot save this provision: for if we look to substance rather than to legal form, we must realize that the possession of an article in circumstances that give rise to even a reasonable suspicion of terrorist purposes cannot plausibly be counted a criminal wrong; the wrong, the offence, should be possession for terrorist purposes. This provision therefore lays on the defendant the onus of disproving (what should be) an element of the offence; it creates an implicit presumption of guilt, which prima facie violates the presumption of innocence.[53]

One common response to such concerns about strict liability and legal presumptions is to accept that such provisions clearly do fray, or break, the golden thread, and to ask whether such derogations from the presumption of innocence can be justified in the interests of public health and safety.[54] There is, however, another possibility: that at least some such provisions do not infringe the requirement of proof of guilt beyond reasonable doubt, but rather specify what can or cannot count, in particular contexts, as 'reasonable doubt' and as 'guilt'. If those specifications are justified, those provisions are then legitimate ways of spinning

---

[52] [2000] Crim. LR 486, commenting on *Kebilene* [2000] 2 AC 326, and on the precursor to this provision.

[53] See also Sullivan, Ch. 8 in this volume, p. 212–13; Tadros and Tierney, 'The Presumption of Innocence and the Human Rights Act'.

[54] See text at n. 19 above; *Kebilene* [2000] 2 AC 326 (e.g. Lord Hope at 387, on striking a 'balance between the needs of society and the presumption of innocence'); *A-G of Hong Kong* v. *Lee Kwong-Kut* [1993] AC 951, at 962–75 (Lord Woolf); Ashworth, 'Article 6 and the Fairness of Trials', 265–6.

out the golden thread, rather than threats to it. This is the possibility that I will explore in the following two sections: in § 5 I will argue that rebuttable legal presumptions can be consistent with the requirement that guilt be proved beyond reasonable doubt if they can be interpreted as legitimate specifications (based partly on a conception of citizens' responsibilities) of what constitutes such proof, whilst in § 6 I will argue that irrebuttable legal presumptions and strict liability provisions are consistent with that requirement if proof of what the prosecution must prove can be shown to constitute proof beyond reasonable doubt of a suitable kind of fault as to the complete offence (including aspects as to which liability is legally strict).

## 5. Justifying Rebuttable Legal Presumptions

My suggestion is that rebuttable legal presumptions are specifications of what is to count, in a particular context, as proof 'beyond reasonable doubt': but how could it be legitimate for the law thus to redefine 'beyond reasonable doubt' in ways that disadvantage defendants? The answer has to do with citizens' responsibilities.

Suppose that someone engages in an activity that is known to create risks of serious harm beyond those accepted as unavoidable features of ordinary life: she runs a factory, perhaps, in which employees use machinery that can cause serious injury.[55] She is under a legal duty, as a matter of criminal law, 'to ensure, so far as is reasonably practicable, the health, safety and welfare at work of all [her] employees', which includes 'the provision and maintenance of plant and systems of work that are, so far as is reasonably practicable, safe and without risks to health'.[56] An employee is injured by a machine, and the employer faces a criminal charge based on the fact that the machine was clearly not 'safe and without risks to health'. Now the statute does not impose strict liability as to either risk or harm: a non-negligent employer who took all 'reasonably practicable steps' to make the machinery safe can avoid liability, and the fact that an employee was injured does not prove that she had failed to take such steps. Under English law, however, that fact does implicitly create a rebuttable legal presumption of lack of due care: given proof that the machinery was not entirely safe, the defendant must prove that she had taken all 'reasonably practicable' steps if she is to avoid conviction.[57] Can such a presumption be justified?

It might be easier for an employer to prove that she had taken all 'reasonably practicable' steps than it would be for the prosecution to prove that she had not—which is often cited as a legitimate reason for placing a probative burden on

---

[55] For simplicity's sake I focus here only on individual, not corporate, liability.
[56] Health and Safety at Work etc. Act 1974, s. 2.
[57] See *Nimmo* v. *Alexander Cowan & Sons* [1968] AC 107; *Hunt* [1987] AC 352, at 373–5 (Lord Griffiths).

defendants.[58] Its legitimacy also depends, however, on larger considerations concerning the employer's, and citizens', responsibilities. The employer's statutory duty is to 'ensure' that she provides a workplace that is, as far as is reasonably practicable, safe. On a plausible reading of 'ensure' this means that she must not only take all reasonably practicable steps, but must also be able to (re-)assure her employees, and anyone with a legitimate interest, that she has done so; the Act recognizes the importance of *assured* safety.[59] To be able to offer such assurance, she must be able to explain what steps she took and why it was not reasonably practicable to do more: if she has done her duty under the Act, she will therefore be well placed to show at her trial that she had taken all reasonably practicable steps; if she cannot do this, she has not done her duty.[60]

This might seem too quick: to require an employer not just to be able to explain herself to her employees and the factory inspectors, but to prove her innocence at trial, might still seem to deny her the benefit of the presumption of innocence. We can show that it does not do so by attending to her responsibilities as a citizen.

Citizens are not in general required to prove their innocence in a criminal court. Even if someone has caused serious, potentially criminal, harm, the prosecution must prove not just the *actus reus* (the causation of harm), but *mens rea*; proof of the *actus reus* cannot by itself mandate an inference to guilt.[61] In this employer's case, however, the harm flowed from an activity known to create risks more serious than those involved in the ordinary course of life. One responsibility that the law imposes on those who engage in such activities is a stringent duty of care, to ensure as far as is reasonably practicable that they minimize the risks of harm. To require them to bear the burden of proving in court that they did so, if someone is harmed, is to impose a further responsibility—to explain themselves to a criminal court (and to their fellow citizens) if things go wrong in this way. It does not seem unreasonable to impose this additional responsibility on citizens who choose to engage in such activities, especially since it is one that they will be easily able to discharge if they have done their duty.

Furthermore, placing such a burden on the defendant will not sanction the conviction of anyone who is not proved guilty 'beyond reasonable doubt' (this meets the objection that one who fails to discharge her responsibility to explain herself should be convicted only for that failure, not for failing to take due care). Proof constitutes proof 'beyond reasonable doubt' if, given such proof, the factfinder has no good reason to doubt the conclusion: but what counts as a good

---

[58] See *Nimmo* v. *Alexander Cowan & Sons* [1968] AC 107, at 122 (Lord Guest), 125–6 (Lord Upjohn), 132 (Lord Pearson); also Tapper, *Cross and Tapper on Evidence*, 129–30; Simester and Sullivan, *Criminal Law*, 54. What matters is not (as some put it) whether the fact is 'peculiarly within the defendant's knowledge', but whether it is one that it would be far easier for the defendant to prove than for the prosecution to disprove; these two criteria can diverge.

[59] Compare J. Braithwaite and P. Pettit, *Not Just Deserts* (Oxford 1990), 63, on liberty and the assured absence of constraint.

[60] See *Nimmo* v. *Alexander Cowan & Sons* [1968] AC 107, at 126 (Lord Upjohn).

[61] *Woolmington* v. *DPP* [1935] AC 462; see text at n. 36 above.

reason, and thus what would render doubt 'reasonable' or 'unreasonable', depends on the responsibilities of the prosecution and the defendant. If the law imposed no responsibility on the defendant to show that she had done all that was reasonably practicable, proof that her machinery was not entirely safe would not prove her guilt beyond reasonable doubt, even if she said nothing: her failure to offer a defence could not, absent such a responsibility, be treated as evidence that she had not done all that was reasonably practicable, and the inferential gap between 'the machinery was unsafe' and 'it would have been reasonably practicable to make it safer' is too large for the former to constitute proof beyond reasonable doubt of the latter. But in making it her responsibility to explain herself, the law requires the court to treat a failure or inability to explain herself as evidence that she had failed in her duty: it would then not be reasonable to doubt her guilt if it was proved that the machinery was unsafe, and she offered no evidence that she had taken all reasonably practicable steps to make it safe. Proof that the machinery was not safe grounds a presumption that she had not taken all reasonably practicable steps, and thus constitutes proof beyond reasonable doubt of her guilt unless she rebuts it.

It might seem that this argument can at most justify laying an evidential, not a persuasive, burden on the defendant.[62] But what kind of evidence could create a reasonable doubt? In this kind of case it would surely need to be evidence proving, on the balance of probabilities, that the employer had taken all reasonably practicable steps to render her machinery safe, since if she had discharged her responsibility to 'ensure' the safety of her factory, she would be able to produce such evidence.[63] Or is this too quick? We can imagine circumstances (perhaps a fire that destroyed the relevant records) in which it would be impossible for a defendant who had discharged her responsibilities to prove that she had done so: to allow for such cases, we should require defendants either to prove that they had taken all reasonably practicable steps, or to show why they were non-culpably unable to provide such proof. With that qualification, we can say that in cases such as the employer's the defendant would normally be able to create a reasonable doubt about her guilt only by proving her innocence; it is therefore not in principle inconsistent with the presumption of innocence to lay that persuasive burden on her.

How far can this line of argument reach? Can it apply not only to specialized commercial undertakings, but to non-specialized activities in which many citizens ordinarily engage? Driving is such an activity that creates serious risks, but it would surely be unreasonable to lay on drivers the kind of legal burden that the

---

[62] Compare Criminal Law Revision Committee, 11th Report: *Evidence (General)*, HMSO (London 1972); Ashworth and Blake, 'The Presumption of Innocence in English Criminal Law'; *Kebilene* [2000] 2 AC 326.

[63] And the law can of course partially specify what will count both as 'all reasonably practicable steps', and as suitable assurance that they have been taken (see e.g. Health and Safety at Work etc. Act 1974, s. 2(3), on the written statements employers must produce).

factory owner bears—to say that, given proof that a vehicle driven by the defendant caused harm, it must be presumed that he was driving dangerously unless he proves that he was driving with due care. Two factors distinguish the driver from the factory owner. First, driving is seen as an ordinary rather than a specialized activity, creating a 'normal' level of risk that we must accept as part of ordinary life. Second, drivers who fully satisfy their responsibility to drive with due care and attention do not thereby equip themselves, as the factory owner who fully discharges her safety-related responsibilities does equip herself, to prove that they have done so. However, drivers also have some responsibilities analogous to those of the factory owner. They must, for instance, have driving licences and insurance, and must produce the documents that prove that they are licensed and insured, when properly asked to do so:[64] such provisions specify ways in which drivers can ensure that they satisfy minimal conditions (of competence and ability to pay for damage, for instance) for legitimate driving; they impose duties to meet, and to be able to prove that one has met, those conditions.[65]

This suggests the following picture. Citizens have a general duty to take care not to cause harm to others. That duty generates both civil liabilities, to pay for harms that we negligently cause, and criminal liabilities for harmful or dangerous actions that are defined as constituting 'public' wrongs.[66] If my conduct does cause harm of a kind that concerns the criminal law, I might then be called to answer a criminal charge. Given the presumption of innocence, I need not offer any substantive answer to such a charge (any answer beyond a plea of 'Not Guilty') until the prosecution has produced evidence that could, if it is not rebutted, be taken to prove my guilt beyond reasonable doubt; only once such evidence has been produced should I face the threat of conviction if I do not rebut it by adducing evidence of my innocence. Normally what this requires is that the prosecution produce prima facie persuasive evidence—evidence that is persuasive by the standards of ordinary, extra-legal reasoning—of both *actus reus* and *mens rea*, before a legal or de facto burden falls on me to produce evidence of my innocence: this both protects innocent citizens against hasty or mistaken convictions and spares citizens the burden of having not just to take care, but to collect evidence that they are taking care, in their ordinary activities. Sometimes, however, the law does effectively impose such a burden on citizens: in particular, if someone is engaged in an especially dangerous activity,[67] *and* if it would not be unreasonably burdensome for her to take care in such a way that she would also be able to

---

[64] Road Traffic Act 1988, ss. 87, 143, 164–5; see also ss. 47, 165 on MOT certificates.

[65] See also Magistrates' Courts Act 1980, s. 101, *Edwards* [1975] QB 27, on proving that one is licensed to engage in an activity; gun ownership would be another good example here.

[66] Much more clearly needs to be said about the grounds for criminalizing harmful or dangerous conduct, but cannot be said here: see my 'Crime, Prohibition and Punishment' (2002) 19 *Journal of Applied Philosophy* 97, and 'Criminalizing Endangerment', in R. A. Duff and S. Green (eds.), *Defining Crimes* (Oxford 2005).

[67] What should count as 'especially' dangerous is, of course, a matter of normative judgment, and is subject to both disagreement and change.

produce evidence that she had taken it, then the law might declare (either explicitly by the creation of a legal presumption, or implicitly by allocating a probative burden) that, once the prosecution has proved a significant part of the case against her, it would be 'reasonable' to doubt her guilt only if she offered evidence in her own defence.

Why should the law (and the state) exercise such restraint in the demands it makes, or the responsibilities it lays, on its citizens? Why should the law not hold instead, for instance, that *anyone* who is proved to have caused a kind of harm that concerns the criminal law must be prepared to answer to a criminal charge by offering evidence that he caused it innocently, on pain of facing conviction if he offers no such evidence (evidence that might often consist simply in his offering an explanation in court); why, that is, should we not adopt the general presumption that, given proof of any *actus reus* involving the causation of criminal harm, the defendant is to be presumed to have been at least negligent as to that harm unless he adduces evidence sufficient to cast doubt on that presumption?[68] This would match what we expect of each other in our ordinary extra-legal dealings: if a friend causes me harm, I would expect her to offer a suitably apologetic or regretful explanation without even being challenged; and if a stranger causes me harm, I would at least expect him to answer for it if I challenge him. Why then should such an expectation not be enshrined in the criminal law?

Any complete answer to this question would need to articulate a theory of the state and of the proper responsibilities of citizenship. Some types of communitarian theory would, no doubt, justify transforming the moral expectation that we answer to each other for the harms we cause into some such formal legal requirement (which is not to say that they would reject the presumption of innocence; only that they would generate a different account of what does or does not make doubt about guilt 'reasonable'). On the other hand, the central elements of the kind of liberal theory that would ground a rejection of any such general legal requirement are quite familiar. Given the significance of a criminal conviction (and thus of the harm done to one who is mistakenly convicted); the burden that such a requirement would impose on citizens in their ordinary activities; the danger that innocents would be convicted because they were not articulate or confident enough to give credible evidence in the daunting context of the court:[69] we should make the presumption of innocence much stronger than this.

One more kind of example, the presumptions created by the Sexual Offences Act 2003,[70] will have to suffice to illustrate the issues here. Sexual activity is neither a specialized activity like the factory owner's, nor one that (like driving) involves special dangers. How then can it be consistent with the presumption of innocence to lay such probative burdens on the defendant: should we not instead

---

[68] I am grateful to Kim Ferzan for forcing me to think more carefully about this question.

[69] Even if giving evidence does not allow the prosecution to introduce one's prior convictions (as it can in the US; thanks to Alan Michaels for this point).                [70] See text at nn. 28, 40 above.

follow the lead of *B* v. *DPP* and *R.* v. *K*,[71] and require the prosecution to prove fault as to each aspect of the offence without relying on legal presumptions or on shifts of probative burdens?

The presumptions concerning consent, and reasonable belief in consent, in section 75 of the Act are grounded in facts (that the complainant was subject to violence or the threat of violence, or that s/he was unlawfully detained, or that s/he was unconscious, or that s/he was unable to communicate consent or non-consent, or that s/he had involuntarily ingested a stupefying drug) that, if known, raise a particular question about consent: even if it is sometimes legitimate, depending on the context, to take acquiescence or lack of dissent as adequate evidence of (or even as constituting) consent, these facts preclude such a taking. That they preclude it is a normative, not merely an epistemological, matter; it depends on a view of citizens' responsibilities, both in relation to making clear their lack of consent to sexual activities, and in relation to verifying their intended partner's consent. If a defendant was aware of such a fact (the presumption depends on proof that he was aware), he should have doubted whether the other person consented, and should therefore have persisted only after taking steps to make sure that she did consent; to persist without taking such steps would display a serious lack of that minimal regard for others' rights that the law demands of us. If he took such steps he would be well placed to adduce 'sufficient evidence . . . to raise an issue' as to whether the other person consented and as to whether he reasonably believed that she consented; his account as a witness of the steps that he took and the evidence that he had would normally be sufficient to raise those issues. Moreover, it seems quite reasonable to require a person who persists in sexual activity in the face of such evidence of lack of consent not only to make sure that the other person does consent, but also to be ready to account for himself in this way—to offer evidence either that his conduct was not wrong, because the alleged victim did consent, or that he was not culpable because he reasonably believed that she consented.

The rebuttable presumption created by section 16 (that if D engaged in sexual activity with a person to whom he stood in a position of trust, and who was actually under 18, D did not reasonably believe the person to be over 18)[72] can be rationalized in a similar way. The context of D's conduct (the position of trust, the other's youth) raises a question about the permissibility of the conduct—a question that a reasonable person would recognize and take steps to answer by checking on the other's age; if D had checked, he would now be able to give evidence, to offer an explanation, that would at least create a reasonable doubt about whether he reasonably believed the other to be over 18; and given his responsibilities as someone in a position of trust, it is proper to demand that he be

[71] *B* v. *DPP* [2000] 2 AC 428; *R.* v. *K* [2002] 1 AC 462: the prosecution must prove that the defendant did not believe the other person to be over the legally specified age.
[72] See also ss. 17–19 and 38–41 on care workers and those with mental disorders.

ready to account for himself in this way, if it is proved that the other person was in fact under 18.

My aim has not been to prove that such provisions are justified, but simply to sketch the kind of argument that would reconcile them with the presumption of innocence; and thus to show how rebuttable legal presumptions (both explicit and implicit) could be justified, not as justified derogations from the presumption of innocence, but as legitimate interpretations of that presumption. I must now turn to provisions that seem even more obviously inconsistent with that presumption.

## 6. Justifying Formally Strict Liability

Rebuttable legal presumptions give the defendant the chance to avert conviction, by offering adequate evidence of her innocence. Irrebuttable presumptions and strict liability provisions do not even give her such a chance: given proof that $p$ (as specified in the offence definition), the court must presume that $q$, which is a necessary element of the offence; or it must convict without further proof or explicit presumptions of fault, even though $p$ does not formally include legally relevant fault as to every aspect of the offence. If we are to show such provisions to be consistent with the presumption of innocence, we must show that although there is a formal gap between the $p$ that must be proved and the $q$ that is presumed, or that would constitute an appropriate kind of fault, there is no substantial gap: there is no real normative space for a defendant to admit that $p$ and still deny that $q$, since proof that $p$ constitutes irrefutable proof that $q$.

This possibility can be readily illustrated by doctrines of constructive liability in murder. Consider a narrow version of the English doctrine of 'implied malice'. If someone attacks a victim, intending to cause serious bodily harm; and the attack creates an obvious risk of death (a risk that would be obvious to anyone with a minimally reasonable concern for human life); and the attack kills the victim: that is murder.[73] This is an instance of formally strict liability, since no *mens rea* need be explicitly proved as to the death that is an essential element of the offence,[74] but we could achieve the same result by creating an irrebuttable legal presumption: drawing on Scots law, and on the Model Penal Code, we could say that, given

---

[73] See Smith and Hogan, *Criminal Law*, 359–61. On the need for an attack, for the action to be 'aimed at' someone, see *DPP* v. *Smith* [1961] AC 290, at 327 ( *per* Viscount Kilmuir); and *Hyam* [1975] AC 55, at 79 ( *per* Lord Hailsham). The requirement that the attack create an obvious risk of death is not currently part of English law, but see n. 75 below.

[74] The requirement that there be an obvious risk of death has clear echoes of the *Caldwell* definition of recklessness, but does not formally involve even *Caldwell*-recklessness, since the prosecution need not prove that the defendant either gave no thought to the possible risk or took the risk advertently: [1982] AC 341, at 354 ( *per* Lord Diplock); see n. 13 above. If an awareness of the risk was required (as suggested by the Criminal Law Revision Committee, 14th Report *Offences against the Person* (London 1980), para. 31; Ashworth, *Principles of Criminal Law*, at 265–6), liability would of course not be even formally strict.

proof of such an attack and such a risk, it is to be irrebuttably or conclusively presumed that the defendant was reckless as to the risk to his victim's life, and that such recklessness suffices to make him guilty of murder if the victim dies.[75]

That irrebuttable presumption is justified if proof that the defendant was engaged in such an attack leaves him no room to argue that he was not reckless of his victim's life. He could not argue that he exercised 'due diligence' to avoid killing his victim:[76] due diligence would have involved refraining from the attack. This does not yet justify a conviction for anything more than manslaughter— manslaughter committed, we might say, by gross negligence in an unlawful act.[77] But we can also argue that such an assailant is reckless of his victim's life. For either he noticed the risk of death or he did not. If he noticed it, even subjectivists would call him reckless. If he did not notice it, we must ask how he could not have noticed something so obvious, and so closely (morally) connected to his intended action. The only possible answer is that he did not care about his victim's life: he acted with the kind of 'practical indifference' as to whether his victim lived or died that properly counts as recklessness.[78] His attack on his victim thus grounds an irrebuttable legal presumption that he was reckless of his victim's life. This also shows why the formally strict liability involved in the doctrine of implied malice is not substantively strict: for what must be proved (an intentional and actually life-threatening attack) also proves the appropriate kind of fault as to death.[79]

Does it matter whether we achieve this result by making liability formally strict, or by an irrebuttable legal presumption?[80] One merit of the presumption method is that it spells out the fault that is required, and how it can be proved; one draw-back is that it might suggest that the court must make an inference from what is proved to some *further* fact—an inference that we would then be hard put either to explain or to render plausible as a non-defeasible inference.[81] Perhaps then we need a different legislative device—the definitional or constitutive rule. The legal

[75] On the Scottish doctrine of 'wicked recklessness', see G. H. Gordon and M. G. A. Christie, *The Criminal Law of Scotland* (3rd edn., Edinburgh 2001), ii. 295–310; such wicked recklessness is displayed if death is 'within the range of the natural and probable consequences' of the attack (ibid. 304, quoting Lord Wheatley in *Miller and Denovan* (1960)). See also Model Penal Code, § 210.2(1)(b) on what grounds a presumption of 'extreme indifference to the value of human life' (but see n. 50 above).

[76] On defences of 'due diligence', see text at n. 30 above.

[77] See Simester and Sullivan, *Criminal Law*, 361–71.

[78] This is not an (inadequately based) causal explanation of his failure to notice the risk, but an interpretation of what that failure means: the failure is related constitutively, not causally, to the lack of care.

[79] On constructive liability see also Simons, 'When is Strict Criminal Liability Just?', 1105–20; A. Michaels, 'Constitutional Innocence' (1999) 112 *Harvard LR* 828, at 891–3; J. Horder, 'A Critique of the Correspondence Principle in Criminal Law' (1995) *Criminal LR* 77; Simester, Ch. 2 in this volume, p. 44–6. My example would have been simpler had it omitted the requirement for an obvious risk of death (see nn. 74–5 above); but without that requirement the doctrine is less plausible as an acceptable species of constructive liability (see my *Intention, Agency and Criminal Liability* (Oxford 1990), 173–9).                    [80] See Roberts, Ch. 7 in this volume, p. 185.

[81] See text at nn. 32–6 above; compare also the confusions caused in English law by judicial talk of 'inferring' an intention to bring *x* about from foresight of *x* as a virtually certain effect of my action (see Smith and Hogan, *Criminal Law*, 71–2).

definition of constructive murder would then require recklessness as to the risk of death, and would explicitly provide that such recklessness is displayed by one who attacks another, intending to cause serious injury, and in fact creating an obvious risk of death.

Constructive liability is constructed out of an underlying crime, for which fault is proved in the usual way: constructive liability for murder depends on non-constructive liability for a violent attack, whose criminal wrongfulness consists partly in the risk of death that it creates—the risk of that more serious harm that would turn it from wounding into murder.[82] But can we justify strict liability which is not thus constructed out of an existing crime?

Suppose that the legislature decriminalizes the supply (as well as the possession) of drugs that are now 'controlled' under Schedule 2 of the Misuse of Drugs Act 1971—not because it has been persuaded that drug dealing is not wrong, or not a 'public' wrong that can properly concern the criminal law, but because it comes to believe that attempts to enforce the existing law are not only ineffective, but probably do more harm than good. However, drug dealing is not put wholly beyond the reach of the criminal law: new offences are created in relation to a specified set of dangerous drugs—an offence of supplying drugs that are impure in ways that make them more dangerous to users, an offence of supplying drugs that in fact cause death or serious injury; and liability for such offences is legally strict as to the impurity of the drug, or to the death or injury that it causes. Conviction thus depends on proof of intentional supply of what the defendant knew to be one of those specified drugs, but no other or further *mens rea* need be proved. Could such provisions be justified?[83]

We have laws that criminalize recklessly dangerous conduct, but only if it actually causes the relevant harm: an agent who is reckless as to whether her conduct will damage another's property is guilty of criminal damage if it causes damage, but might be guilty of no offence if it does not.[84] This is not an offence of strict liability: but it exemplifies a pattern that will help to make sense of certain types of strict liability.

---

[82] See Simester and Sullivan, *Criminal Law*, 187–91, on 'intrinsic' as against 'extrinsic' luck. This is not the place to defend the claim that criminal liability can properly depend on such matters of moral luck: see my *Criminal Attempts* (Oxford 1996), 327–47.

[83] Compare Husak's discussion, Ch. 4 in this volume §§ 1,4, and Simester's at Ch. 2, p. 46–9. Such provisions cannot be straightforwardly justified by the 'greater-includes-the lesser' doctrine (see J. C. Jeffries and P. B. Stephan, 'Defences, Presumptions, and Burden of Proof in the Criminal Law' (1979) 88 *Yale LJ* 88 1325, at 1336–7)—that if the legislature could in principle criminalize drug dealing as such, it can legitimately criminalize the sub-category of drug dealing that involves impure drugs or serious bodily harm; this does not yet justify convicting the dealer of supplying impure drugs, or of causing death or bodily harm (see Husak's argument, Ch. 4 in this volume, § 3, about proportionality).

[84] See Criminal Damage Act 1971, s. 1(1): only 'might' because she might be guilty of a specific offence of endangerment (see the examples collected in P. R. Glazebrook, *Blackstone's Statutes on Criminal Law* (12th edn., Oxford 2002), Ch. 4); but she would not be guilty of the general endangerment offences in the Model Penal Code (§ 211.2) or in Scots law (see Gordon and Christie, *The Criminal Law of Scotland*, 427–30).

First, there is a type of conduct—recklessly endangering property—that we have reason to criminalize. Second, our reasons for not criminalizing that type of conduct as such have to do not with its not being wrongful in a way that properly concerns the criminal law, but with more pragmatic concerns about the difficulties and costs of enforcement, and about whether the benefits of creating such an offence would outweigh its costs.[85] Third, we do criminalize that type of behaviour under the further condition that it actually brings about some harm the prospect of which provided an important part of the reason for criminalizing it (actual damage to another's property). What the criminal law now says to those who engage in such conduct is that they do so at their own (as well as at their prospective victims') risk: if they are lucky, and cause no damage, they escape liability; if they are unlucky, and cause damage, they are criminally as well as civilly liable. They are given fair warning of their potential liability, on what is surely an uncontroversial version of the 'thin-ice' principle that 'those who skate on thin ice can hardly expect to find a sign that will denote the precise spot where [they] will fall in'.[86] Although the law does specify 'the precise spot where they will fall in', the spot at which damage is caused,[87] that specification does not enable agents to identify it precisely in advance: but they can avoid criminal liability by refraining—as they anyway should refrain—from their reckless conduct.

The drug dealer's position is analogous to this, *if* we can say that intentional drug dealing in any of the specified drugs already involves an appropriate kind of fault as to the harm that this might cause, and whose causation makes a dealer criminally liable. But we surely can say this, so long as the dangers involved in such drugs are sufficiently well publicized that anyone engaged in drug dealing could reasonably be expected to be aware of them. Anyone who then deals in such drugs thereby shows herself to be at least negligent as to the risk they create: for whereas in other activities one can take 'due care' in carrying them out, in this case (the law tells us) one takes 'due care' only by abandoning the activity. A defendant cannot admit that she was dealing drugs, and claim that she was taking due care not to endanger life: there can be no such thing as 'duly diligent drug dealing'. Drug dealers are therefore given fair warning that if they embark on this activity they do so at their own, as well as their customers', risk: if they are lucky, they will escape liability; but if they are unlucky, they will be criminally liable—and cannot complain that this is unfair.

This argument depends, of course, on judgments about the character of drug dealing and about whether or why it properly concerns the criminal law which are at best controversial,[88] but my claim here is only that it exemplifies a pattern of

---

[85] It thus passes the first of Schonsheck's three 'filters' on the way to criminalization, but not the second or third filter: J. Schonsheck, *On Criminalization* (Dordrecht 1994), esp. 63–83.

[86] *Knuller* v. *DPP* [1973] AC 435, at 463 (*per* Lord Morris); see Ashworth, *Principles of Criminal Law*, 74–5.

[87] Whereas the worry in *Knuller* was that it was not clear what kind of conduct would fall under the offence of 'conspiracy to corrupt public morals' (an offence that I am not seeking to justify).

[88] See D. Husak, *Drugs and Rights* (Cambridge 1992); P. Alldridge, 'Dealing with Drug Dealing', in A. P. Simester and A. T. H. Smith (eds.), *Harm and Culpability* (Oxford 1996), 239.

argument that could justify imposing formally strict liability, by showing that the liability is substantively non-strict.[89] We identify a type of conduct that we have reason to criminalize, but that we do not criminalize in itself, for reasons unrelated to its wrongfulness. We show that anyone intentionally engaged in such conduct thereby displays a relevant kind of fault as to a harm that it is liable to cause, and that provides part of the reason for criminalizing it. We can then define an offence of causing such harm by such conduct, making liability for that offence formally strict as to the occurrence of the harm. But this is a formal, not a substantive, strictness, since any intentional engagement in the conduct constitutes (or creates an 'irrebuttable presumption' of) substantive fault as to that harm: those convicted of the strict liability offence have been proved, beyond reasonable doubt, to be substantively guilty.[90]

(This shows why it is unjust to hold a shopkeeper who sells unfit food strictly liable. It might be legitimate to create a rebuttable legal presumption of negligence, given proof that the food was unfit:[91] but defendants must be given a chance to prove due diligence, since we cannot say that we have reason to criminalize selling food, or that to engage in that activity is to display a lack of due diligence, or that shopkeepers could avoid liability by refraining, as they anyway should, from selling food.)

I have space to consider only one further example. The Sexual Offences Act 2003 (ss. 5–12) makes liability as to the victim's age formally strict in offences involving children under 13. To justify these provisions, we must identify an underlying intentional activity that we have good reason to criminalize (i.e. one that could properly be condemned as a 'public' wrong),[92] and engagement in which displays an appropriate kind of fault as to the mischief at which the law is aimed (a mischief connected to the aspect of the offence as to which liability is strict). In the example of drug dealing, the activity is dealing in one of the specified drugs, which displays at least negligence as to the risk of bodily harm, the mischief at which the law is (according to this argument) aimed. In the case of sexual activity with under-age children, however, the initial task of identifying the mischief presents two problems.[93]

First, 'under 13' is an artificial stipulation of the aspect of the offence as to which liability is strict, which does not purport to define the mischief. That

[89] For an actual example, though I cannot discuss its complexities here, see the money laundering provisions in 18 USC § 1956 (thanks to Alan Michaels for pointing me towards this example).

[90] My argument has obvious affinities with Michaels's account ('Constitutional Innocence') of when strict liability is constitutionally permissible: his concern, however, is constitutionality, whereas mine is with justice, and whether we have good reasons of principle to criminalize the relevant kind of conduct; and constitutionality is not, regrettably, a guarantee of justice.

[91] See Food Safety Act 1990, ss. 8, 21; and text at nn. 56–64 above.

[92] See further S. E. Marshall and R. A. Duff, 'Criminalization and Sharing Wrongs' (1998) 11 *Canadian Journal of Law and Jurisprudence* 7.

[93] See J. Horder, 'How Culpability Can, and Cannot, Be Denied in Under-age Sex Crimes' (2001) *Criminal LR* 15.

mischief is the danger of psychological or moral harm to those who are led into sexual activity before they have gained sufficient maturity to cope with it or to make rational decisions about it, but for good reasons the law does not define the offence in those terms. It instead stipulates a precise age, although we know that some below that age are precociously mature, while some over that age are still immature—though those between 13 and 16 are also protected. Second, there are at least two different paradigms of sexual activity involving children.[94] One is of children of similar ages engaged in mutual sexual experimentation; the other is of an older person exploiting a much younger person. Since the cases for criminalization, and for strict liability as to the victim's age, are stronger in relation to the second paradigm, I will focus on that.[95]

'The man who has connexion with a child, relying on her consent, does it at his peril, if she is below the statutable age'.[96] So is 'sexual activity with a child' the relevant underlying activity? This is too vague a specification to meet 'rule of law' demands for certainty, whilst more precise specifications—'fornication', for instance—might not pick out conduct that we have reason to criminalize. However, this is not a fatal problem: the impossibility of precise specification of the conduct is a reason against criminalization that figures at the second, not the first, stage. Why then should we not say that an adult who engages in sexual activity with someone he knows to be a child can be held strictly liable if the child is under 13, since he thereby displays a negligent, or even reckless, lack of care for the possibility that . . . but that what? That the child is under 13? But that is not the mischief.[97] That the child is not mature? But perhaps he has good reason to believe that she is mature enough.

This problem might be resolved by a suitable account of why citizens should respect laws that contain such artificial stipulations of criminal conduct:[98] if part of the rationale for such stipulations is that citizens should not trust themselves to make such substantive judgments as to whether their intended sexual partner is mature enough, the child's age becomes a guiding reason, to which the would-be sexual partner should pay careful attention. But can we really say that any adult who intentionally engages in sexual activity with a child thereby culpably fails to attend as he should to the possibility that the child is under 13, and so properly takes the risk of criminal liability if the child is actually under 13—a risk he could avoid by refraining, as he anyway should refrain, from that activity? Can the thin-ice principle save us from the charge that such a specification of the activity from which people should anyway refrain is intolerably vague?

[94] See the comments in *B v. DPP* [2000] 2 AC 428 by Lord Nicholls (at 464) and Lord Steyn (at 472).

[95] This suggests that the law should specify not just the child's age, but also the defendant's age: see e.g. the Washington Criminal Code 9A 44.073, 076, 079; and compare Sexual Offences Act 1956, s. 6(3).    [96] *Prince* (1875) LR 2 CCR 154, at 172 (*per* Blackburn J); and see text at n. 15 above.

[97] Compare Horder, 'How Culpability Can, and Cannot, Be Denied in Under-age Sex Crimes', on how the child's being under or over 13 is not a 'guiding reason'.

[98] See my 'Crime, Prohibition and Punishment'.

We could rely on that principle only if 'child', despite its vagueness, would be generally so understood that anyone who was actually under 13 would obviously count as a child: only then would the potential defendant be put on notice, by the character of his intentional activity, that he should attend carefully to the child's age. We must, however, doubt whether this condition is met: not just because 'child' is vague, but because the appearance, clothes, and behaviour of children can be quite misleading as to their true age.

One solution, given that there are also offences of sexual conduct with children of under 16, for which the prosecution must prove that the defendant did not reasonably believe the victim to be 16 or over,[99] would be to make liability as to the age of a child who is actually under 13 constructive rather than strict: that is, a defendant should be guilty of an offence involving a child under 13 only on proof that he had engaged in the relevant sexual activity, and had not reasonably believed the child to be 16 or over. For we have good reason to criminalize sexual activity by an adult with children under 16, and to hold liable those who engage in such activity without a reasonable belief that the child is 16 or over (assuming, as I am assuming for the sake of the argument, that we share the view of the dangers of such sexual activity that the law embodies, and that 16 is a reasonable age to stipulate). Anyone who engages in that activity thereby displays an appropriate fault not only as to the risk that the other person is under 16, but also as to the risk that they are under 13; he thus takes the risk of being liable not just for an offence involving a child under 16, but for a more serious offence involving a child under 13—a risk that he could have avoided by refraining, as he anyway should have refrained, from that activity.

I have sketched lines of argument that could, in principle, justify legal presumptions that shift a probative burden (evidential or persuasive) on to the defendant; so-called 'irrebuttable' presumptions, which are better understood as constitutive specifications; and provisions that impose formally constructive or even strict liability. More precisely, I have shown how such provisions can be justified not as necessary derogations from the presumption of innocence, but as being quite consistent with that presumption, since they amount to legal specifications of what can count as proof of guilt beyond reasonable doubt. As the examples discussed in this section should suggest, I do not suppose that it will often be appropriate to make liability even formally strict, rather than constructive; but it is important to be clear about the way in which it can, in principle, be justified.

---

[99] See ss. 9–12 of the Act; and text at n. 38 above.

# 7

# Strict Liability and the Presumption of Innocence: An Exposé of Functionalist Assumptions

*Paul Roberts*

## 1. Substantive and Procedural Dimensions of Strict Liability

Strict liability is generally conceived as a topic within the substantive law of crimes. The many varieties of 'strict liability'[1] share the defining feature of authorizing conviction of an offence where the accused's moral fault in some measure falls short of the full extent of his legal liability. There are several typical patterns to which the label 'strict liability' could conceivably be applied. Sometimes a reduced level of *mens rea* is required for the offence as a whole, as where the law equates reckless disregard with intentionality,[2] or culpable ignorance is equated with guilty knowledge.[3] On other

This chapter has benefited from discussion at the two Cambridge colloquia on strict liability held in May 2002 and May 2003. I am particularly grateful to Jeremy Horder, Alan Michaels, and Andrew Simester for providing detailed written comments on previous drafts.

[1] Cf. Douglas N. Husak, 'Varieties of Strict Liability' (1995) 8 *Canadian Journal of Law and Jurisprudence* 189, 199, 223, identifying seven discrete forms of strict liability by way of illustration, without any pretensions to an exhaustive analysis: 'Clearly there exist additional kinds of substantial deviations from the fault paradigm, and thus additional varieties of strict liability. . . . There are as many different kinds of strict liability offenses as there are ways that defendants can be convicted despite being substantially less at fault than the typical perpetrator of those offenses.' Also see the contributions to this volume by Stuart Green, Ch. 1 (identifying 'six senses of strict liability', but recommending only one) and R. A. Duff, Ch. 6, § 1 (suggesting 'four possible patterns of strict and non-strict liability').

[2] Subjective recklessness is frequently equated with intention for the purposes of assigning criminal liability in English law, both in modern statutes such as the Criminal Damage Act 1971 and in older pieces of legislation—including, notably, the Offences Against the Person Act 1861, wherein the key concept of 'malice' is interpreted to embrace both advertent recklessness and intention (purpose): see *R.* v. *Cunningham* [1957] 2 QB 396, CCA.

[3] As in the principle *ignorantia juris non excusat*—ignorance of the law affords no excuse: see e.g. *Attorney-General's Reference (No 1 of 1995) (B and F)* [1996] 2 Cr. App. R. 320, CA; *Warner* v. *Metropolitan Police Commissioner* [1969] 2 AC 256, 296, HL; *R.* v. *Jacobs* [1944] KB 417, CCA. For illuminating meditations on the limits of the *ignorantia juris* doctrine, see Andrew Ashworth,

occasions the lack of correspondence[4] between legal guilt and moral fault relates just to one or more key elements of the offence definition. In the offences against the person, for example, the accused who foresees injury is liable for the full extent of the injuries he causes, even if such injuries turn out to be very much graver than he ever contemplated.[5] For these offences, the *mens rea* standard of subjective recklessness attaches to a coarse-grained category of injury, but not to its extent. Again, liability for offences against minors has been notoriously strict regarding age limits: until the English courts' recent retreat from the strict *Prince* rule,[6] even a reasonable mistake as to the age of a minor would not avail an accused charged with offences designed to protect the young, not only from the depredations of adults, but also from their own youthful folly.[7] A third species of strict liability might justifiably be labelled 'absolute', as where the offender can be convicted of a crime without even voluntarily performing the acts constituting the *actus reus* of the offence.[8] In each scenario, however, the objection to strict liability is essentially the same: that the accused's legal liability exceeds his moral culpability.

'Testing Fidelity to Legal Values: Official Involvement and Criminal Justice', in Stephen Shute and A. P. Simester (eds.), *Criminal Law Theory: Doctrines of the General Part* (Oxford 2002), 302–10.

[4] See Jeremy Horder, 'A Critique of the Correspondence Principle in Criminal Law' [1995] *Criminal LR* 759; Barry Mitchell, 'In Defence of a Principle of Correspondence' [1999] *Criminal LR* 195; Jeremy Horder, 'Questioning the Correspondence Principle—A Reply' [1999] *Criminal LR* 206.    [5] *R. v. Mowatt* [1968] 1 QB 421, CA; *R. v. Savage; Parmenter* [1992] 1 AC 699, HL.
    [6] *B (A Minor) v. DPP* [2000] 2 AC 428, HL, effectively overruling *R. v. Prince* (1875) LR 2 CCR 154 (see the speeches of Lord Nicholls at 465–6; Lord Steyn at 476; and Lord Hutton at 482). This important decision was followed by *R. v. K* [2002] 1 AC 462, HL, where Lord Bingham dismissed 'the now discredited authority of *R. v. Prince*' (para. 21). The Sexual Offences Act 2003, which in material part entered into force on 1 May 2004, replaces these authorities with a systematic legislative framework. In essence, the 2003 Act reinstates strict liability regarding the victim's age for offences against children under 13, but allows a reasonable belief that the victim had attained the statutory age of consent to exculpate in relation to offences against children who are between 13 and 16 (for certain offences, 18) years of age: see ss. 5(1)(b), 6(1)(c), 7(1)(c), 8(1)(c), 9(1)(c), 10(1)(c), 11(1)(d), 12(1)(c), 15(1)(c)–(d), etc.
    [7] Cf. *B (A Minor) v. DPP* [2000] 2 AC 428, 441, DC, *per* Tucker J ('Parliament has for many years recognised the need to protect young women from the undesirable attentions of men of all ages, and also from their own inclinations').
    [8] The paradigm example typically dredged up to illustrate this highly exceptional form of liability is *R. v. Larsonneur* (1933) 24 Cr. App. R. 74, CCA; also see *R. v. Blake* [1997] 1 Cr. App. R. 209, CA; *Winzar v. Chief Constable of Kent, The Times,* 28 March 1983. In *R. v. Secretary of State for Home Affairs, ex p. Soblen* [1963] 1 QB 829, 836, DC, Lord Parker CJ cites *Larsonneur* as an instance of 'absolute liability [which] did not depend upon *mens rea*'. However, whether Mlle Larsonneur's conviction of being an illegal alien 'found in the United Kingdom' was truly imposed on an 'absolute' basis has spawned long-running controversy: see J. C. Smith, *Smith and Hogan: Criminal Law* (10th edn., London 2002), 58–9; A. P. Simester and G. R. Sullivan, *Criminal Law: Theory and Doctrine* (2nd edn., Oxford 2003), 83–5, 117–18; C. M. V. Clarkson and H. M. Keating, *Criminal Law: Text and Materials* (5th edn., London 2003), 90–3; William Wilson, *Criminal Law: Doctrine and Theory* (2nd edn., Harlow 2003), 73–5; Glanville Williams, *Textbook of Criminal Law* (2nd edn., London 1983), 157–8; Rakesh C. Doegar, 'Strict Liability in Criminal Law and *Larsonneur* Reassessed' [1998] *Criminal LR* 791; J. C. Smith and Rakesh C. Doegar (Correspondence), 'R v. Larsonneur' [1999] *Criminal LR* 100; David Lanham, 'Larsonneur Revisited' [19/6] *Criminal LR* 276.

Whether the objection succeeds with regard to any particular strict liability offence raises controversial issues in the overlapping fields of morality, politics, and jurisprudence.

Behind the understandable prominence of substantive moral and legal considerations in this sphere of criminalization, the topic of strict liability has cultivated a long-standing, if subsidiary and intermittent, affinity with evidentiary questions of proof and procedure.[9] This affinity has a straightforward, but it soon transpires superficial and unsatisfying, explanation: *coincidence*. Even cursory perusal of the English statute-book confirms that strict liability offences are frequently qualified by affirmative defences imposing 'reverse onus' burdens of proof on the accused. This is apparently a favourite technique of English criminal legislation. Such offences proscribe designated conduct, such as dumping hazardous waste,[10] selling liquor to minors,[11] or carrying an offensive weapon in a public place,[12] and then invite the accused to prove that he falls within a specified exception or excuse, for example that he took all reasonable precautions and exercised all due diligence to avoid illegal dumping,[13] that he had no reason to suspect that his alcohol-purchasing patron was under 18,[14] or that his employment as a butcher gives him a lawful excuse for carrying knives to work.[15] But perhaps there is more to the relationship between strict liability and criminal procedure than the contingent proximity of affirmative defences and reverse onus clauses in statutes imposing criminal liability in the absence of fully coextensive moral fault. Might this recurrent pattern of association imply a more profound conceptual symbiosis between substantive criminal prohibitions and procedural devices bearing on the presumption of innocence? Some writers think it does. In certain recent commentaries and judicial pronouncements, elements of strict liability and procedural mechanisms such as reverse onus clauses appear to be conceptualized as doctrinal counterparts, or even as functional equivalents. I would prefer to see these functionalist tendencies

---

[9] For an example from over twenty years ago, see Martin Wasik, 'Shifting the Burden of Strict Liability' [1982] *Criminal LR* 567 (discussing a comparatively unusual model of affirmative defence by which the accused is able to transfer his own prima facie strict liability to a negligent third party).

[10] Environmental Protection Act 1990, s. 33(1).

[11] Licensing Act 1964, s. 169A(1) (as substituted by s. 1 of the Licensing (Young Persons) Act 2000).     [12] Criminal Justice Act 1988, s. 139.

[13] Environmental Protection Act 1990, s. 33(7)(a).

[14] Licensing Act 1964, s. 169A(2). Also see s. 169C(4).

[15] This provision is examined more closely in § 3, below. For further examples of reverse onus defences to strict liability crimes, giving a flavour of their staggering diversity, see Terrorism Act 2000, s. 57 and sch. 13, para. 4(2) (possession of otherwise innocent articles for a terrorist purpose; employment of unlicensed security services); Merchant Shipping Act 1995, ss. 132–3 (discharges of oil); Trade Marks Act 1994, s. 92 (fraudulent use of trade marks); Protection of Badgers Act 1992, s. 7 (killing, taking, or injuring a badger); Water Resources Act 1991, s. 48 (unlicensed abstraction or obstruction of watercourse) and s. 80 (breach of drought order); Human Fertilisation and Embryology Act 1990, subss. 41(10) and (11) (unlawful use of human embryos or gametes); Environmental Protection Act 1990, s. 80(4) (non-compliance with notice to abate statutory nuisance); Road Traffic Act 1988, s. 5 (being drunk in charge of a motor vehicle); Medicines Act 1968, s. 46 (unauthorized manufacture of medicinal products).

nipped in the bud, before they are allowed to run riot in the garden of English criminal jurisprudence.

This chapter examines the conceptual, jurisprudential, and moral foundations of the argument for functional equivalence between strict criminal liability and procedural doctrines implicating the presumption of innocence. It does not launch an indiscriminate (and ill-conceived) broadside against functionalism *tout court*. Rather, the exclusive concern of this chapter is with a specific contextual application of functionalist reasoning. The conceptual structure of these particular functionalist arguments is subjected to microscopic analysis in § 3, before § 4 turns to critical evaluation. In reaction to the functionalist tendency to treat substantive criteria of criminal liability and procedural doctrines of evidence and proof as essentially fungible functional equivalents, § 4 stresses the distinctive meaning, inherent value, and practical division of labour differentiating elements of substance and procedure in criminal legislation and in the administration of criminal justice. On my account, substance and procedure are independent, incommensurable dimensions of penal law that cannot be reduced to interchangeable tokens and traded like currency. To the extent that it overlooks or denies these subtleties of meaning and value, the argument for functionalist equivalence perpetrates a reductionist fallacy that misleadingly oversimplifies the task of criminal legislation and cheapens our traditional ideals of criminal justice.

The first thing to stress about functionalist conceptualizations of the relationship between strict liability and procedural doctrines, however, is that their functionalist orientation is typically *assumed* rather than asserted, much less justified by coherent and fully elaborated arguments.[16] Functionalism creeps into discussions of the presumption of innocence unannounced and unnoticed, sometimes apparently unbidden. So before stripping down the conceptual engineering of functionalist approaches and evaluating their normative significance, whether as would-be advocates or critics, it is first necessary to describe the status and treatment of strict liability's procedural dimensions in modern criminal jurisprudence. Just what is at stake in this debate? How widely are the issues known, and to what extent are their implications fully appreciated? To set the scene for this chapter's principal tasks of the conceptual analysis and normative critique, § 2 exposes the nature and prevalence of functionalist assumptions that lurk in much contemporary scholarship (and some judicial pronouncements) grappling with the presumption of innocence and its relationship to criminal liability without fault. Even if substantive elements of strict liability and procedural mechanisms could legitimately be regarded as functional equivalents in certain contexts, which this essay trenchantly disputes, it is surely incumbent on advocates of functionalism to take the trouble to articulate and defend their presuppositions.

---

[16] A rare exception, expressly arguing for a functionalist conception of procedural devices, is Ronald J. Allen, 'Structuring Jury Decisionmaking in Criminal Cases: A Unified Constitutional Approach to Evidentiary Devices' (1980) 94 *Harvard LR* 321.

## 2. Exposing Functionalist Assumptions

Discussions of strict liability frequently mention reverse onus clauses and related procedural mechanisms. These implicit references to a burden or standard of proof necessarily engage the presumption of innocence, whether or not that terminology is expressly invoked. Though hardly an alien concept to English lawyers, the presumption of innocence has not attracted systematic conceptual or doctrinal analysis in English criminal jurisprudence. Traditionally, English law has focused instead on the more prosaic notions of the burden and standard of proof, though the advent of the Human Rights Act 1998 may in time revise conventional patterns of thought and language in this respect.[17] Article 6(2) of the European Convention on Human Rights (ECHR), guaranteeing to every person facing a criminal charge the right to be 'presumed innocent until proved guilty according to law', is now, via the Human Rights Act, a source of English legal rights and duties.[18] In the absence of much pertinent local experience with a human rights-based approach to the presumption of innocence, comparative perspectives may be especially valuable. British lawyers and legislators might learn from the experience of jurisdictions such as South Africa, where a constitutional presumption of innocence modelled on Article 14(2) of the International Covenant on Civil and Political Rights[19] has been written into section 35(3)(h) of the 1996 national constitution,[20] as well as from jurisdictions, including most prominently the US federal legal system, where courts rather than legislatures have elevated the burden and standard of proof in criminal proceedings to constitutional status.[21] However, comparative inquiries soon confront the functionalist tendencies which this chapter fixes squarely in its sights.

An unremittingly functionalist conception of the presumption of innocence is implied, for example, by Andrew Paizes' analysis of section 35(3)(h) of the South African Constitution.[22] According to Paizes, all forms of strict liability breach the presumption of innocence if they truly involve criminal liability without fault (as opposed to merely requiring lesser, but still potentially culpable, standards of liability such as inadvertent recklessness or gross negligence).

---

[17] See, generally, Paul Roberts and Adrian Zuckerman, *Criminal Evidence* (Oxford 2004), Ch. 8.

[18] Human Rights Act 1998, ss. 1–2 and sch. 1. Section 2(1) also qualifies the jurisprudence of the Strasbourg-based European Court of Human Rights as a source of English law.

[19] Article 14(2) of the ICCPR is in identical terms to Article 6(2) of the ECHR: 'Everyone charged with a criminal offence shall have the right to be presumed innocent until proved guilty according to law.'

[20] For an informative guide to the South African position, which also incorporates discussion of Canadian and English authorities, see P. J. Schwikkard, *Presumption of Innocence* (Kenwyn, RSA 1999).        [21] *In re Winship*, 397 US 358, 90 S. Ct. 1068 (1970).

[22] Andrew Paizes, 'A Closer Look at the Presumption of Innocence in our Constitution: What is an Accused Presumed to be Innocent *of* ?' (1998) 11 *South African Journal of Criminal Justice* 409.

He maintains without qualification that:

[C]rimes of strict liability offend against the right to be presumed innocent. All that remains is to consider the extent to which they may be said—if ever—to constitute a reasonable and justifiable limitation of that right . . . Even if one accepts that it is almost entirely in respect of so-called regulatory offences . . . that strict liability tends generally to be employed, it is my view that there is no justification for its existence . . . Strict liability constitutes a violation of the right to be presumed innocent which cannot, in my view, be defended in the ordinary course.[23]

Later, in § 3, this chapter will carefully retrace each step in the functionalist thinking implicit in such conceptualizations of the presumption of innocence, but from this passage we can already infer the argument's rough outline. Crypto-functionalists typically advocate a 'substantive' rather than a 'procedural' conception of the presumption of innocence, according to which the presumption is violated as much by a statute dispensing with moral fault as by a statute formally trans-ferring an onus of proof to the accused. In both scenarios, the functionalist reasons, an accused who is innocent may none the less be convicted at law without moral culpability of the requisite kind or degree. Strict liability and reverse onus provisions are implicitly regarded as functional equivalents, and both are imagined to embarrass the presumption of innocence, for essentially the same reason.

Paizes' analysis of the presumption of innocence affords an unusually clear glimpse of functionalism at work. More commonly, functionalism lurks in the background or insinuates itself mid-argument for unexpected cameo appearances, as it does in Jeffries and Stephan's celebrated article discussing the status of the burden of proof in American constitutional law.[24] Two decades before Paizes extended the argument to the South African context, Jeffries and Stephan also criticized a 'purely procedural' conception of the presumption of innocence. However, in contrast to Paizes' uncompromisingly 'purist' thesis, Jeffries and Stephan denied that every legislative provision imposing a burden of proof on the accused must necessarily violate constitutional rights. For Jeffries and Stephan, the scope of federal restraint on the power of individual US states to impose criminal liability could only be determined, following the Supreme Court's landmark decision in *In re Winship*,[25] by reference to a substantive conception of constitutional innocence protected by federal law: 'The issue, in short, is not whether the state has proved with requisite certainty whatever facts it chooses to regard as relevant. The issue, rather, is whether the state has proved beyond a reasonable doubt a just basis for punishment.'[26] This contention obviously calls for further clarification of the principles for determining 'a just basis for punishment', if not for a fully articulated theory of penal legislation. Undeterred

[23] Ibid., 414–15, 417.
[24] John Calvin Jeffries, Jr. and Paul B. Stephan III, 'Defences, Presumptions, and Burden of Proof in Criminal Law' (1979) 88 *Yale Law Journal* 1325.
[25] *In re Winship*, 397 US 358, 90 S. Ct. 1068 (1970).
[26] Jeffries and Stephan, 'Defenses', 1382.

by the enormity of the task, Jeffries and Stephan gamely set out to sketch, albeit in rather faint outline, the contours of constitutional innocence. We will return to the substance of their main theme later. Our immediate interest lies with the arguments deployed by Jeffries and Stephan to reject procedural or 'formal' interpretations of *In re Winship* in favour of their substantive conception.

As a fixed first point of departure, Jeffries and Stephan rejected out of hand the possibility that the constitutional demand for proof beyond reasonable doubt might be limited to criteria expressly designated as offence elements in state criminal legislation. In probing the limits of constitutional constraints on state criminal law, the proposition that individual states might be able to oust federal oversight simply by redefining offence elements in penal statutes as 'defences' was regarded as patently inadequate. The principle reasserted with great fanfare by the Supreme Court in *In re Winship*[27] would hardly be worth boasting about, Jeffries and Stephan quickly concluded, if the states could circumvent its strictures so effortlessly: 'There is no reason in policy to limit *Winship* to essentially formal distinctions among the facts relevant to criminal liability. Indeed, there is good reason to try to make more of the decision, for it is a singularly shallow constitutional principle that is subject to defeat by a single stroke of the drafter's pen.'[28]

Proponents of procedural conceptions of the presumption of innocence might concur in rejecting this puny minimalist interpretation of constitutional federal oversight. In the absence of any other readily available alternatives, however, proceduralists who rejected the theory of substantive constitutional innocence were apparently then forced into the arms of a maximalist interpretation of the Supreme Court's judgment, which Jeffries and Stephan also criticized and denounced. Proponents of a procedural conception of the presumption of innocence were seemingly presented with an all-or-(almost) nothing choice. On a maximalist reading, the logical implication of *In re Winship* was that no reverse onus clause or burden-reversing evidentiary presumption could ever be compatible with constitutional due process. This is precisely how Paizes interprets section 35(3)(h) of the South African constitution; but Jeffries and Stephan recoiled from ascribing similarly maximalist intentions to the US Supreme Court: 'Read this way, *Winship* . . . launched a sweeping, though probably unintended, attack on the constitutionality of many familiar aspects of the criminal law.'[29]

---

[27] Brennan J, delivering the opinion of the court (Burger CJ and Stewart and Black JJ dissenting), enthused: 'The requirement that guilt of a criminal charge be established by proof beyond a reasonable doubt dates at least from our early years as a Nation. . . . Expressions in many opinions of this Court indicate that it has long been assumed that proof of a criminal charge beyond a reasonable doubt is constitutionally required': *In re Winship*, 397 US 358 (1970), 361, 362. Also see *Speiser* v. *Randall*, 357 US 513 (1958), 525–6 (Brennan J); *Davis* v. *US*, 160 US 469 (1895); *Coffin* v. *US*, 156 US 432 (1895), 452 *et seq*. ('The principle that there is a presumption of innocence in favour of the accused is the undoubted law, axiomatic and elementary, and its enforcement lies at the foundation of the administration of our criminal law. It is stated as unquestioned in the textbooks, and has been referred to as a matter of course in the decisions of this court and in the courts of the several states').        [28] Jeffries and Stephan, 'Defenses', 1333.
[29] Ibid.

Jeffries and Stephan's rejection of the (unintentionally) subversive maximalist interpretation of *In re Winship* turns on the proposition that 'the greater power includes the lesser': that is to say, according to Jeffries and Stephan, if state legislatures are constitutionally free to dispense with a particular culpability requirement altogether, by enacting offences containing elements of strict liability, then it stands to reason that states must also be empowered to take the less drastic step of legislating a reverse onus defence or rebuttable presumption to regulate the proof of an equivalent aspect of moral culpability that would otherwise be legally strict. The greater power of dispensing with proof altogether—requiring the prosecutor to prove *absolutely nothing at all* in relation to some aspect or degree of culpability—must surely include the lesser power of utilizing procedural devices to transfer a corresponding evidentiary burden to the accused.

The 'greater includes the lesser' argument does not rest merely on a formal logic of (constitutional) legal competence, but also evinces a robustly pragmatic appreciation of the politics of criminal legislation. Many state legislatures—then as now, and over here as well as over there—are nervous about overburdening the prosecutor with proof requirements or conceding too many liability-negating 'defences' that could be exploited to secure unmerited acquittals by devious professional criminals, aided and abetted by their huckster lawyers. A legislature might be prepared to concede a reverse onus defence as an acceptable compromise between imposing criminal liability without fully commensurate moral fault, by enacting offences of strict liability, and the alternative of prescribing more elaborate, culpability-sensitive, offence definitions which increase the prosecutor's probative burden and, by extension, the likelihood that the guilty will evade their just deserts. If the compromise reverse onus option is withdrawn, however, this would 'force the state to choose between the extremes of proving more or proving less';[30] and both legislative history and the general drift of contemporary penal policy[31] suggest that legislatures committed to being 'tough on crime' would regularly opt for less rather than more proof of moral culpability. Jeffries and Stephan concluded that to 'contradict this logic and deny the validity of the greater-includes-the-lesser argument'[32] would be perverse. Yet procedural conceptions of the presumption of innocence seemed to them to court just such perversity, by purporting 'to preserve individual liberty and the societal sense of commitment to it by forcing the government *either* to disprove the defence beyond a reasonable doubt *or* to eliminate the defence altogether':

The latter solution results in an extension of penal liability despite the presence of mitigating or exculpatory facts. It is difficult to see this result as constitutionally compelled and harder still to believe that it flows from a general policy, whether actual or symbolic, in favour of individual liberty. When a constitutional commitment to individual liberty is construed

---

[30] Ibid., 1345.
[31] For insightful surveys, see David Garland, *The Culture of Control* (Oxford 2001); Jock Young, *The Exclusive Society* (London 1999).          [32] Jeffries and Stephan, 'Defenses', 1345.

to induce harshness in the penal law, something is plainly amiss . . . [W]e think it likely, that a rule barring reallocation of the burden of proof would thwart legislative reform of the penal law and stifle efforts to undo injustice in the traditional law of crimes. Even if one were to believe that rigid insistence on proof beyond a reasonable doubt might in some purely symbolic sense reaffirm the 'presumption of innocence', it would do so at the risk of a harsh and regressive expansion in the definition of guilt.[33]

If strictly procedural conceptions of the presumption of innocence erode the moral foundations of criminal liability and, in their rejection of 'the greater includes the lesser' argument, contradict the logic and sensible practical strategy of criminal legislation, the pressure to adopt some version of the substantive alternative might seem irresistible. Before we begin to expose the pitfalls of their latent functionalism, however, it bears observation that substantive conceptions of the presumption of innocence are no quick-fix solution to the real or imagined shortcomings of more orthodox procedural interpretations. Far from it. Substantive conceptions of constitutional innocence ultimately demand nothing less than a systematically elaborated account of the moral limits of the criminal law; in short, a complete theory of criminal legislation.[34] Jeffries and Stephan recognized the enormity of the jurisprudential endeavour they were advocating, but felt that a productive start could, and should, be made on the construction and elaboration of a constitutionally mandated federal criminal law. These radical implications of propounding a substantive conception of the presumption of innocence were stated with admirable clarity:

[P]roof beyond a reasonable doubt is a procedural standard designed to protect the innocent. Innocence, however, is not a procedural concept. Its meaning under law derives from the exercise of legislative authority over the definition of criminal conduct. A constitutional rule governing procedural allocation of the burden of proof, therefore, should take account of the substantive content of crime definition as well as the degree of certainty with which specified facts are established. In other words, the constitutional guarantee of proof beyond a reasonable doubt should be premised in part on a constitutional conception of what must be proved.[35]

Jeffries and Stephan made a lasting contribution to the literature on the presumption of innocence by drawing attention to the basic dichotomy between procedural and substantive conceptions, and by starting to tease out what might be at stake in adopting either mode of interpretation. Now that the presumption of innocence has become a hot topic in English criminal jurisprudence, pursuant

[33] Ibid. 1347, 1353.
[34] It would undeniably be desirable and useful to have such a theory: see, further, Alan C. Michaels, 'Constitutional Innocence' (1999) 112 *Harvard LR* 828. The question is whether one must make substantial progress on this notoriously difficult and controversial task as a precondition to developing a theoretically coherent conception of the presumption of innocence with meaningful practical purchase. This is the claim I dispute. Michaels wisely distinguishes his substantive strict liability version of the greater-includes-the-lesser argument from procedural variants, and thus deftly insulates himself against my critique of functionalist equivalence: ibid. 846–7 n. 84.
[35] Jeffries and Stephan, 'Defenses', 1327.

to Article 6(2) of the ECHR and the Human Rights Act 1998, it is no surprise to find broadly similar arguments and debates resurfacing in this new constitutional context. Thus, Victor Tadros and Stephen Tierney have recently made the case for a substantive interpretation of Article 6(2),[36] partly in response to my own previously expressed preference for a procedural conception of the presumption of innocence.[37] Like Jeffries and Stephan before them, Tadros and Tierney reject 'formalistic' or 'technical' approaches to the interpretation of criminal statutes and insist, instead, that courts must scrutinize the substantive moral basis of criminal liability in order to determine the scope of the presumption as a Convention-based right. Were it otherwise, they—quite correctly—observe:

[I]t would always be open to Parliament intentionally to evade the implications of Article 6(2) by creating new criminal offences. In that case, the presumption of innocence would provide citizens with no protection against the state whatsoever. It would be capable of evasion merely by reconstructing the surface of the offence, leaving the underlying evidential requirements unchecked. For this reason, our reading of Article 6(2) is to be considered preferable: it provides citizens with real protections against state power.[38]

Tadros and Tierney do not expressly invoke the 'greater includes the lesser' argument deployed by Jeffries and Stephan, but their analysis is consistent with it. Tadros and Tierney are quite explicit, and perfectly unabashed, in insisting that strict liability offences usually infringe (their conception of) the presumption of innocence, even though the legislature has simply dispensed with a pertinent fault requirement altogether, rather than employing any of the constitutionally dubious procedural devices, such as reverse onus clauses or evidentiary presumptions, that more obviously engage Article 6(2):

Often, the reason why an offence is made an offence of strict liability is the difficulty of proving *mens rea*. In such circumstances, warranting conviction of some individuals who are not morally at fault may be regarded as justified, by the legislature at least, in order to ensure conviction of more of those who are morally at fault. On the argument presented here, that trade-off, if it is being made, interferes with the presumption of innocence. This is a point not properly recognised either by the European Court of Human Rights or the courts of England and Wales as yet.[39]

Inverting Jeffries and Stephan's idiom, we might say that Tadros and Tierney's argument amounts to the complementary proposition that 'the lesser excludes the greater': Article 6(2) not only prevents state parties to the Convention from utilizing onus-shifting procedural devices, but also invalidates the more drastic step of imposing strict liability through substantive criminal law. At the same time, Tadros and Tierney concede that particular reverse onus clauses might in principle be consistent with moral innocence and therefore compatible with

---

[36] Victor Tadros and Stephen Tierney, 'The Presumption of Innocence and the Human Rights Act' (2004) 67 *Modern LR* 402.

[37] Paul Roberts, 'The Presumption of Innocence Brought Home? *Kebilene* Deconstructed' (2002) 118 *Law Quarterly Review* 41.          [38] Tadros and Tierney, 'Presumption of Innocence', 413–14.

[39] Ibid. 423.

Article 6(2).[40] This position is at least reminiscent of the 'greater includes the lesser' argument pioneered by Jeffries and Stephan—though it must be stressed that accepting the constitutionality of particular reverse onus provisions is *not* necessarily premised on 'greater includes lesser' reasoning. So it is an open question on this evidence how far Tadros and Tierney would in fact be prepared to go along with Jeffries and Stephan in combining a substantive conception of the presumption of innocence with a 'greater includes lesser' justification of particular onus reversing procedural devices.[41]

When we turn our attention from commentary to jurisprudence, substantive conceptions of the presumption of innocence would not appear on the face of it to have made much headway with English courts thus far. A procedural interpretation of Article 6(2) was strongly preferred in *Barnfather*,[42] where the strict liability offence of failing to ensure that one's children attend compulsory schooling, contrary to section 444(1) of the Education Act 1996, was challenged on grounds of incompatibility with the presumption of innocence. Neither judge comprising the Administrative Division of the High Court on that occasion was favourably impressed by the applicant's contentions. Dismissing the Strasbourg authorities invoked by the applicant as indications of an evolving substantive approach to the presumption of innocence in European human rights law,[43] Maurice Kay J endorsed the strictly procedural interpretation of Article 6(2) previously advocated by Lord Justice Auld in *Daniel*.[44] Elias J stated simply:

Article 6(2) does not impose any restrictions on the power of Parliament to create strict liability offences. It follows that the courts are not entitled to use Article 6(2) to import a defence into a strict liability offence where Parliament has not done so, nor can they make

---

[40] Ibid. 418–20. Also see Duff, Ch. 6 in this volume, purporting 'to show how rebuttable legal presumptions (both explicit and implicit) could be justified, not as justified derogations from the Presumption of Innocence, but as legitimate interpretations of that Presumption'.

[41] If Tadros and Tierney reject the logic of 'greater includes lesser', they expose themselves to Jeffries and Stephan's original pragmatic objection to reducing the legislature's options. If strict liability is, *ex hypothesi*, compatible with Article 6(2), what objection could there be to a reverse onus clause that is *more favourable* to the accused than the alternative of a strict liability offence would have been? The answer to this question proposed in § 4 of this chapter involves abandoning the functionalist assumptions that Tadros and Tierney share with Jeffries and Stephan.

[42] *Barnfather* v. *London Borough of Islington and Secretary of State* [2003] EWHC Admin. 418; [2003] 1 WLR 2318. See Jeremy Horder's contribution to the present volume, Ch. 5, for detailed commentary on this decision.

[43] See *Salabiaku* v. *France* (A/141-A) (1991) 13 EHRR 379; *Hansen* v. *Denmark*, App. No 28971/95, ECtHR (admissibility decision) 16 March 2000. In *Barnfather*, para. 22, Maurice Kay J commented that 'counsel have not been able to find any subsequent case in which *Hansen*, to the extent that it purports to expand *Salabiaku*, has been followed. Indeed, if I may say so, it appears rapidly to have achieved a degree of obscurity. Having taken account of it . . . I am not disposed to follow it.'

[44] See *R.* v. *Daniel* [2002] EWCA Crim. 959, para. 34, where Auld LJ observed: 'In determining the essentials of an offence, courts should also keep in mind the distinction between the *procedural* guarantees provided by Art 6(2) and the *substantive* elements of the offence, a distinction that the Strasbourg Court has now acknowledged in the civil sphere in *Z v United Kingdom* (2002) 34 EHRR 97, paras. 100–101. . . As Paul Roberts has argued, in an article entitled 'The Presumption of Innocence Brought Home? *Kebilene* Deconstructed' (2002) 118 LQR 41, 50: "Article 6(2) has no bearing on the *reduction or elimination* of *mens rea* requirements, and is therefore perfectly compatible with offences of strict or even absolute liability".'

any declaration of incompatibility because of the absence of any such defence. On this fundamental ground this application must fail.[45]

Yet all is not quite as it seems. English judges have in reality been more receptive to substantive conceptions of the presumption of innocence than at first meets the eye, but judicial sponsorship has been indirect and implicit rather than openly acknowledged. The incremental insinuation of substantive conceptions of the presumption of innocence into English criminal jurisprudence has consequently hardly been noticed, let alone evaluated or justified.

The first task that any court must undertake when invited to consider the applicability of Article 6(2) is to ascertain the scope and content of the relevant criminal prohibition. Although the common law continues to play a significant residual role in defining criminal offences, this task is for the most part a labour of statutory interpretation in modern English law. The challenge of interpreting criminal statutes should never be underestimated. Even in relation to well-conceived and expertly drafted offences, the precise wording and structural topography of statutory provisions frequently leave considerable room for rival interpretations and no little controversy.[46] Judges approach their interpretative task within a normative framework of conventional assumptions and expectations, in the form of institutional constraints (e.g. higher courts will not tolerate radical innovation or excessive idiosyncrasy from inferior tribunals; dissenting judgments are never given in the Criminal Division of the Court of Appeal) and principles of statutory construction (e.g. penal statutes should be construed narrowly; serious criminal offences normally require *mens rea*;[47] in the absence of express provision to the contrary, Parliament intends its legislation to be compatible with the UK's international legal obligations including, with particular relevance to our current topic, obligations enshrined in the European Convention on Human Rights[48]), all of which import further layers of complexity, judicial discretion (judgment), and controversy into the equation. But we can set aside such fascinating issues within the context of the present discussion, because ascertaining the authentic

---

[45] *Barnfather* v. *London Borough of Islington and Secretary of State* [2003] EWHC Admin. 418, para. 34.

[46] Controversy that flares up from time to time: see *R.* v. *Hunt* [1987] AC 352, HL; *Westminster City Council* v. *Croyalgrange Ltd.* (1986) 83 Cr. App. R. 155, HL; and associated commentaries: A. A. S. Zuckerman, 'No Third Exception to the *Woolmington* Rule' (1987) 104 *Law Quarterly Review* 170; Glanville Williams, 'The Logic of "Exceptions"' (1988) 47 *Cambridge LJ* 261; Francis Bennion, 'Statutory Exceptions: a Third Knot in the Golden Thread?' [1988] *Criminal LR* 31; Peter Mirfield, 'The Legacy of *Hunt*' [1988] *Criminal LR* 19; D. J. Birch, 'Hunting the Snark: The Elusive Statutory Exception' [1988] *Criminal LR* 221; Peter Mirfield, 'An Ungrateful Reply' [1988] *Criminal LR* 233; Alex Stein, 'After *Hunt*: The Burden of Proof, Risk of Non-Persuasion and Judicial Pragmatism' (1991) 54 *Modern LR* 570.

[47] *R.* v. *K* [2002] 1 AC 462, HL; *B (A Minor)* v. *DPP* [2000] 2 AC 428, HL.

[48] *R.* v. *Secretary of State for the Home Department, ex p. Brind* [1991] 1 AC 696, 747–8, HL, *per* Lord Bridge: 'it is already well settled that, in construing any provision in domestic legislation which is ambiguous in the sense that it is capable of a meaning which either conforms to or conflicts with the Convention, the courts will presume that Parliament intended to legislate in conformity with the Convention, not in conflict with it.'

definition of a criminal offence through statutory interpretation is a discrete exercise quite separate from applying the presumption of innocence, or at least it should be.

The definitional clarity of this picture may become blurred, however, after Parliament's intention has been ascertained and a determinate, stable, agreed definition of the relevant offence has been extracted. If at this point in the analysis the presumption of innocence is invoked to alter that definition—that is, to rewrite the criminal statute—a substantive conception of the presumption must now be at work. On this approach, the presumption of innocence is capable of amending the substantive definition of a criminal offence, and only a substantive conception of (moral) innocence could invalidate and supersede the court's original, considered, interpretation in this way. But how, one might well ask, does such a novel feat of interpretational revisionism even get off the ground? A criminal offence with a settled definition in one paragraph of the court's judgment, but which acquires a different definition in the next, sounds suspiciously like *Law Through the Looking-Glass*. Just as the vaporizing Cheshire Cat bamboozled Alice, now you see a criminal prohibition, now you don't.

A solution to this riddle can be found in a fleet-footed doctrinal two-step, showcased in several recent appellate decisions. The manœuvre features an impressively versatile distinction between the 'technical' or 'formal' definition of an offence and, reproducing Lord Bingham's terminology in *Kebilene*,[49] its 'gravamen'. The gravamen of the offence is understood to be the underlying harm or wrong at which the offence is aimed.[50] With the aid of this distinction, a previously identified ('technical') offence definition can subsequently be reinterpreted, utilizing a substantive conception of the presumption of innocence under Article 6(2), to harmonize the definitional scope of a criminal prohibition with its underlying gravamen. After Lord Bingham had premiered this presumption-of-innocence shuffle[51] in the Divisional Court in *Kebilene*, an equivalent analysis was subsequently incorporated into influential *obiter dicta* by the House of Lords in *Lambert*.[52] Doctrinal assimilation has been swift and, apparently, unopposed. By the time of the *Sheldrake* decision,[53] just two years later, these passages were already being hailed as instant classics,[54] and references to 'the gravamen' of an offence were seemingly institutionalized as boilerplate notation in the application of Article 6(2)'s presumption of innocence to English criminal statutes.[55]

[49] *R.* v. *DPP, ex p. Kebilene* [2000] 2 AC 326, 344, DC. Laws LJ echoed these references to the 'gravamen' of criminal offences (at 356). For discussion, see Roberts, 'Innocence Brought Home?', Part V.
[50] Tadros and Tierney, 'Presumption of Innocence', 410–13, propose an alternative interpretation of 'gravamen' as 'the conduct which it is the purpose of the offence to control'. This modification has certain merits, but also potential drawbacks. Overall, I do not think that it advances the debate in the way that Tadros and Tierney claim.
[51] Cf. Bruce L. Ackerman, 'The Conclusive Presumption Shuffle' (1977) 125 *University of Pennsylvania LR* 761.       [52] *R.* v. *Lambert (Steven)* [2001] UKHL 37; [2002] 2 AC 545.
[53] *Sheldrake* v. *DPP* [2003] 2 Cr. App. R. 206, DC.       [54] Ibid. para. 27 (Clarke LJ).
[55] Ibid. para. 31, *per* Clarke LJ ('. . . likelihood of driving is part of the gravamen of the offence'); para. 92 (Henriques J); para. 142, *per* Jack J ('The essence of the offence . . .').

Elsewhere I have set out at some length my reasons for regarding their Lordships' reasoning (but not necessarily their conclusions) in *Kebilene* and *Lambert* as misconceived.[56] Extended critique raises discrete issues of statutory interpretation, legal jurisdiction, and constitutionality that are beyond the scope of this chapter (though I will briefly revisit these themes in the concluding section). This essay focuses on the functionalist assumptions that lurk, unacknowledged, behind all the commentaries and judicial pronouncements surveyed in this section.

Substantive conceptions of the presumption of innocence, whatever their generic strengths or idiosyncratic peculiarities, all share the assumption that an ostensibly procedural presumption, which for all the world looks as though it should belong to the adjectival law of evidence and proof rather than the substantive law of crimes, is essentially fungible with substantive criteria of criminal liability. Functionalists tend to be preoccupied with achieving ultimate objectives, often to the detriment of moral and legal distinctions in the ways in which particular outcomes are generated. From a functionalist perspective, it will naturally appear perverse that the presumption of innocence might be neutralized by strategic legislative drafting, empowering Parliament 'by a single stroke of the drafter's pen' to achieve *the very same* objective that the presumption notionally prohibits. By the same token, if the presumption of innocence is construed broadly to invalidate all liability without full moral fault, the legislature's residual power to create (morally justifiable) strict liability offences should logically include the lesser power of ameliorating those crimes of strict liability with reverse onus defences (provided only that such defences are independently morally appealing).[57] The greater must include the lesser, as Jeffries and Stephan insisted, just as the right to vote implies a right of access to campaign literature, to travel on the appointed day to a polling booth, to make the designated mark on the ballot paper, etc. But notice that certain crucial assumptions are built into this 'logic'. What if the presumption of innocence is *not* fungible with substantive criteria of criminal liability? What if it performs a unique procedural function with an inherent or constitutive value that is *not* reducible to substantive criteria of moral or legal fault? In that case the greater (on reflection, in what sense *greater?*) would not include the lesser (in what sense *lesser?*), any more than the right to vote implies the right to call elections or to appoint judges. Each of these responsibilities could be specified as part of a richer conception of constitutional democracy, just as substantive moral fault and the presumption of innocence might both be indispensable components of a comprehensive theory of criminal justice. But none of this implies, still less does it entail, that individual components of comprehensive theories can always be derived in hierarchical fashion, one from another, as the lesser from the greater.

---

[56] Paul Roberts, 'Drug-dealing and the Presumption of Innocence: the Human Rights Act (Almost) Bites' (2002) 6 *Evidence & Proof* 17; Roberts, 'Innocence Brought Home?'
[57] Acting from motives of self-preservation or under fear of reprisals might be acceptable reasons for mitigating strict criminal liability with reverse onus defences, for example, whereas foolish or bigoted motivations would not be compelling grounds for leniency.

It will be argued in § 4 of this chapter that the presumption of innocence does indeed perform a unique procedural function, such that its value cannot be collapsed into, or straightforwardly traded-off against, substantive criteria of criminal liability as though substance and procedure were fully commensurable items on a single, scalar, metric. What is more, creeping functionalist assumptions tend to cloud the popular meaning and institutional legal significance of the presumption of innocence, and this confusion in turn threatens to undermine the presumption's practical virtues—contrary to most commentators' stated best intentions. The time is therefore ripe to blow the whistle on functionalist assumptions and to call a halt to their insidious infiltration into post-Human Rights Act analysis of the presumption of innocence in English law. The descriptive dimension of this exposé should be welcomed by potential proponents of functionalism as much as by critics. For functionalist claims to pass the minimum threshold of justification, the case for a functionalist presumption of innocence must be brought out into the open where its merits can be examined and evaluated. Cogent arguments must replace blithe assumptions. In the cause of greater transparency, those functionalist assumptions exposed in this section will now be placed under the microscope of conceptual analysis.

## 3. A Microscopic Anatomy of Functional Equivalence

Perhaps it should occasion no surprise that the relationship between strict liability and the presumption of innocence has failed to attract much explicit elucidation, let alone systematic reconsideration, in English law and legal commentary. After all, substance is substance and procedure is procedure, and how could the one ever be equated to the other? The answer, contrary to initial appearances, is that the functionalist equation can be reached by taking either of two, independent, doctrinal routes.

The first route to functional equivalence, examined in § 3.1, I will call 'the reverse onus argument'. It is quite straightforward to demonstrate, in terms of the reverse onus argument, that one particular procedural mechanism—the reverse onus clause—can be deployed as the functional equivalent of substantive elements of criminal liability. More ambitiously, an extension of the reverse onus argument purports to show that an offence subject to a reverse onus clause might in practice impose criminal liability that is substantively strict, at least in certain circumstances. The qualification 'in practice' is crucial to the success of this complex argument for functional equivalence. Without making significant assumptions about the practicalities of proof in criminal trials—assumptions that will later be challenged in § 4.2—the argument would run into a conceptual brick wall.

Quite independently of the reverse onus argument, proponents of functional equivalence may opt for a second, considerably more direct route to their desired destination. What I will call 'the irrebuttable presumption argument' is sketched out in § 3.2. The irrebuttable presumption argument boasts an elegant simplicity calculated to be superficially attractive to proponents of functional equivalence. Through all the twists and turns of the first argument's manipulation of reverse onus clauses, the functionalist holds the irrebuttable presumption argument in reserve, like an ace up her sleeve.

## 3.1. The Reverse Onus Argument

The reverse onus argument is best explained by way of illustration. We will therefore proceed by considering some typical examples of strict liability offences qualified by reverse onus clauses, starting with the offence of carrying an offensive weapon in public.

Section 139 of the Criminal Justice Act 1988, as amended by the Offensive Weapons Act 1996, provides in material part:

(1)  Subject to subsections (4) and (5) below, any person who has an article to which this section applies with him in a public place shall be guilty of an offence.

(2)  Subject to subsection (3) below, this section applies to any article which has a blade or is sharply pointed except a folding pocket-knife.

(3)  This section applies to a folding pocket-knife if the cutting edge of its blade exceeds three inches.

(4)  It shall be a defence for a person charged with an offence under this section to prove that he had good reason or lawful authority for having the article with him in a public place.

(5)  Without prejudice to the generality of subsection (4) above, it shall be a defence for a person charged with an offence under this section to prove that he had the article with him—
    (a)  for use at work;
    (b)  for religious reasons; or
    (c)  as part of any national costume.

The motivation behind section 139 is obviously to stop people with no good reason to do so from carrying knives or other bladed or sharply pointed instruments in a public place. A prohibition against carrying an offensive weapon in public is a member of the 'substantive-inchoate' family of offences.[58] It adopts the doctrinal formula and characteristics of a substantive crime, rather than the outward appearance of a (true) inchoate offence such as criminal attempts, conspiracy, or incitement. But its purpose is equally prophylactic, in authorizing law enforcement officials to intervene and disarm a potentially dangerous individual before any real harm is done. Merely carrying a knife is not harmful in itself nor even inherently immoral, yet experience shows that people armed with knives in public have a tendency to get involved in fights or confrontations, or to intimidate

---

[58]  Roberts, 'Innocence Brought Home?', Part V.

others. Criminal offences are more likely to be perpetrated and, sooner or later, somebody will end up getting seriously hurt or even killed. The English criminal prohibition on being in possession of a knife (or similar bladed or pointed object) in a public place is justified by reference to the harm that would probably result if people were entitled to carry dangerous weapons with them wherever they went. Whether this rationale is sufficient to justify a substantive-inchoate criminal prohibition along the lines of section 139, or any criminal prohibition at all, is obviously a controversial question of political morality and penal policy.[59] The acceptability of such restrictions may vary between different societies and political cultures, depending in part on the extent to which individual choice and personal autonomy are regarded as important political values in any given society. Official assessments and popular fears of the risks posed by leaving the possession of offensive weapons unregulated by criminal law will also be influential.

With this prophylactic objective in contemplation, Parliament might simply have enacted that 'it shall be a criminal offence to possess a knife (or similar bladed or pointed object) in a public place'. However, this proscription would patently have been unacceptably broad. It might have criminalized supermarket butchery, tradesmen conveying their tools from one job to the next, and knitting-needle toting maiden aunts, as well as the activities of knife-gangs and hoodlums with a short fuse at which the offence is really aimed. A simple revision would be to limit the offence to those in possession of a knife (etc.) 'without lawful authority or reasonable excuse', or some equivalent formula. This would have given the police, prosecutorial authorities, and courts ample latitude to ensure that people with a genuine reason for possessing potentially dangerous implements in public were not unintentionally swept up into the net of criminality. In essence, this drafting technique turns normative standards of unlawfulness and unreasonableness into circumstantial elements of the *actus reus* of the substantive offence.

If section 139 had straightforwardly criminalized possessing a knife (etc.) in a public place without lawful authority or reasonable excuse, it would have been subject to the established procedural default rule, classically restated in *Woolmington* v. *DPP*,[60] requiring the prosecution to prove each and every element of the offence charged to the criminal standard, beyond reasonable doubt.

---

[59] Note that liberal Harm Principle arguments can be used to justify substantive-inchoates such as s. 139 because 'the Harm Principle is capable of applying to actions that lead only indirectly to harm and not just to actions that are intrinsically harmful': A. P. Simester and Andrew von Hirsch, 'Rethinking the Offense Principle' (2002) 8 *Legal Theory* 269, 283–7.

[60] *Woolmington* v. *DPP* [1935] AC 462, 481–2, HL, *per* Viscount Sankey: 'Throughout the web of the English Criminal Law one golden thread is always to be seen, that it is the duty of the prosecution to prove the prisoner's guilt subject . . . to the defence of insanity and subject also to any statutory exception. If, at the end of and on the whole of the case, there is a reasonable doubt, created by the evidence given by either the prosecution or the prisoner, as to whether the prisoner killed the deceased with malicious intention, the prosecution has not made out the case and the prisoner is entitled to an acquittal. No matter what the charge or where the trial, the principle that the prosecution must prove the guilt of the prisoner is part of the common law of England and no attempt to whittle it down can be entertained.'

*Woolmington* does not imply that the prosecutor is obliged to rebut every conceivable defence or counter-claim theoretically open to the accused, irrespective of the state of the evidence. It means only that the prosecutor must assemble cogent proof that the accused committed the offence charged, and rebut any ostensibly exculpatory evidence that the defence actually adduces in the trial. The accused is said to bear the 'evidential burden' of producing evidence or asking questions in cross-examination capable of raising any new issues going beyond those presented to the fact-finder by the prosecution's case in-chief. Unless and until the defence 'passes the judge' by discharging its burden of production in relation to particular supplementary issues, the prosecutor can safely ignore merely hypothetical defence arguments lacking any foundation in evidence.

The statutory provisions previously excerpted show that, in enacting section 139, the UK Parliament rejected the straightforward substantive approach to criminalizing possession of an offensive weapon in public. Instead, subsections (1)–(3) establish the broad scope of the offence and identify the articles covered by the prohibition, but are immediately qualified by subsections (4) and (5), setting up a reverse onus defence in favour of the accused. All the prosecutor has to demonstrate is that the accused was found in a public place in possession of any bladed or sharply pointed article (with the exception of a folding pocket knife with a blade of three inches or less). It is then down to the accused to prove, if he can, albeit to the lower balance-of-probabilities standard,[61] that he had 'good reason or lawful authority' for having a proscribed article in his possession. Subsection (5) elaborates by providing an explicitly non-exhaustive list of legislatively authorized good reasons. Being in possession of the tools of one's trade is included, as perhaps the most obvious and frequently encountered good reason, although at least one equally plausible explanation—being in the process of taking the item home having just purchased it—is not expressly mentioned. Good reasons (b) and (c), which one would not necessarily expect to encounter in a piece of legislation criminalizing possession of offensive weapons, are an interesting digression. In going out of its way to accommodate religious practices and national dress, Parliament demonstrates its fundamental commitment to liberal tolerance and non-discrimination in a multi-cultural, multi-ethnic, and religiously diverse society.

We can now begin to see how reverse onus provisions might be regarded as the functional equivalents of substantive elements of criminal liability. Subsections (4) and (5) seem to function in a similar way to the alternative 'without good reason or lawful authority' clause that might have been inserted into section 139's substantive definition of the offence, the only apparent difference between these two alternative strategies of criminalization being the location of the burden of proof.

---

[61] *R. v. Hunt* [1987] 1 AC 352, 374, HL, *per* Lord Griffiths: '[I]f a burden of proof is placed on the defendant it is the same burden whether the case be tried summarily or on indictment, namely, a burden that has to be discharged on the balance of probabilities.' Also see *R. v. Carr-Briant* [1943] KB 607, CCA.

If this is accepted, the question then arises as to how the legislature should choose between two (or more) 'functionally equivalent' drafting techniques. The standard functionalist answer is that the choice should be dictated by pragmatic considerations of proof: whichever party could most easily discharge the burden should bear it. This, indeed, has traditionally been a well-worn justification for imposing reverse onus burdens on the accused in English law.[62] Since, for example, the accused himself is in the best position to know if he possesses a relevant licence (to keep a vehicle on public roads, sell liquor, watch TV at home, etc.), it is the accused who should bear the burden of proof on that issue if charged with a criminal offence of keeping a vehicle, selling liquor, or watching TV without a licence.[63] The same rationale could be extended to the section 139 offence, for surely (runs the argument) the accused himself is best placed to know whether he had a good reason for carrying in public an article capable of being misused as an offensive weapon. If a good reason truly existed, the accused will be able to explain to the court's satisfaction why he had the article in his possession; if not, he will rightly be found guilty. But in neither case will the accused be the hapless victim of an excessively broad offence, any more than if he had been charged with the functionally equivalent substantive crime of 'being in possession of a knife (etc.) in a public place without good reason or lawful authority'.

At a pinch, the reverse onus argument can be pressed still further in the service of a functionalist analysis. Section 139 provides an example of a reverse onus clause operating to ameliorate strict liability in the substantive definition of an offence, transforming what on first examination appears to be a strict basis for penal censure into a fault-based crime more closely congruent with moral standards of culpability. On this drafting model, the reverse onus clause assumes the role of the accused's saviour, providing an opportunity for exculpation where otherwise none would exist. Genuine strict liability presents an altogether different scenario. Could a reverse onus clause ever be part of a legislative scheme imposing strict criminal liability on an unqualified basis? The functionalist claim that it might rests on the

---

[62] See e.g. *R.* v. *Drummond* [2002] 2 Cr. App. R. 352, CA, para. 31; *L* v. *DPP* [2001] 1 Cr. App. R. 420, DC, para. 27; *R.* v. *Ewens* [1967] 1 QB 322, 330, CCA; *John* v. *Humphreys* [1955] 1 WLR 325, DC; *R.* v. *Oliver* [1944] KB 68, CCA; *R.* v. *Schwartz* [1988] 2 SCR 443, SCC. For critical commentary, see Glanville Williams, 'The Logic of "Exceptions"' (1988) 47 *Cambridge LJ* 261, 267–9, 274–5; J. C. Smith, 'The Presumption of Innocence' (1987) 38 *Northern Ireland Legal Quarterly* 223.

[63] Respectively, Vehicle Excise and Registration Act 1994, s. 29: see *Guyll* v. *Bright* (1987) 84 Cr. App. R. 260, DC; Licensing Act 1964, s. 160: see *R.* v. *Edwards* [1975] QB 27, 31, CA ('those who practise and sit in criminal courts have long thought that the burden of proving that a licence has been granted to authorise the doing of an act which is prohibited by statute unless a licence to do it is held rests upon the defendant'); Communications Act 2003, s. 363. Note, however, that the imposition of a reverse onus burden on the accused often follows directly from the court's interpretation of the wording of the relevant offence read in conjunction with s. 101 of the Magistrates' Courts Act 1980, without the need to invoke practical considerations of relative ease of proof: *R.* v. *Edwards* [1975] QB 27, 40, CA (citing Wigmore to the effect that 'this concept of peculiar knowledge furnishes no working rule'). Section 101 provides that: 'Where the defendant to an information . . . relies for his defence on any exception, exemption, proviso, excuse or qualification . . . the burden of proving the exception . . . shall be on him.'

further, pragmatic, contention that there are some things that it is nigh impossible ever to prove, practically speaking, even on the balance of probabilities. If this pragmatic condition could be established in relation to one or more subsisting criminal offences, functionalism would appear vindicated to that extent. An offence qualified by a reverse onus clause which can never be satisfied in practice is, to all intents and purposes, an offence of strict liability in the relevant respect.

To construct a test-case for this argument we need to identify the kinds of facts which present the greatest practical difficulties of proof. A negative empirical proposition which also relates to an intangible fact, like a person's state of mind, would be an ideal candidate. Lack of knowledge, for example, is often (though always subject to context) amongst the hardest of all negatives to prove. Knowledge can be acquired in any number of ways and from all manner of sources, and its acquisition in the ordinary course of life generally leaves no permanent visible trace or audit trail confirming when, how, or why one came to be informed. Conversely, it would usually be a very tall order to supply a convincing retrospective demonstration of one's genuine ignorance of facts allegedly known at the material time, when the ways in which one might have acquired incriminating knowledge are, almost literally, limitless. We can concretize this probative dilemma, and illustrate its significance for extending a functionalist analysis of reverse onus clauses, by exploring a series of variations on a second modern statutory offence.

Section 1(1) of the Computer Misuse Act 1990 criminalizes the activity popularly known as 'computer hacking' in the following terms:

A person is guilty of an offence if—

(a) he causes a computer to perform any function with intent to secure access to any program or data held in any computer;

(b) the access he intends to secure is unauthorised; and

(c) he knows at the time when he causes the computer to perform the function that that is the case.

Computer hacking thus only becomes an offence in English law when perpetrated by a person who *knowingly* secures unauthorized access to computer data; and, in accordance with *Woolmington*, the onus is on the prosecution to prove that an alleged hacker knew that the digital access attempted or secured was unauthorised. In most cases, however, the reality of the situation will be patently obvious, either way. People who hack into the Pentagon's missile defence systems or the on-line customer records of major retail banks generally know that they lack authorization for the havoc they wreak, and are too proficient in doing so plausibly to claim otherwise. Conversely, the prosecution is unlikely to be able to persuade a fact-finder beyond reasonable doubt that the accused knew he was accessing unauthorized data unless it is evident from the context that access was meant to be restricted.[64]

---

[64] Unless the accused happens to possess special knowledge of the conditions of access not available to ordinary hackers, a contingency that can be disregarded for present purposes.

The offence would extend to cover carefully encrypted data, for example, but not material freely available on the internet (regardless, it should be emphasized, of the actual intentions of the data-owner, who might in fact have wanted to restrict access to a limited group of users but lacked the technological competence to do so effectively).

On the assumption that a hacker's knowledge of authorization is evidentially trivial, the legislature might have been tempted to condense section 1(1) into a simpler form:

**Variation 1**
A person is guilty of an offence if he intentionally causes a computer to perform any function securing unauthorized access to any program or data held in any computer.

Variation 1 would make computer hacking a strict liability offence to the extent that the hacker would no longer have to know that his access was unauthorized.[65] Of course, the hacker would still need to act intentionally in operating the computer equipment which secured unauthorized access. Neither the Variation 1 offence, nor the section 1(1) original, could be committed involuntarily by, for example, accidentally falling on the keyboard and causing unanticipated computing operations or random program launches.

Alternatively, the legislature might have followed its frequent practice of qualifying a substantively strict liability crime with a reverse onus clause, suggesting a second variation on the section 1(1) computer hacking offence:

**Variation 2**
(1) A person is guilty of an offence if he intentionally causes a computer to perform any function securing unauthorized access to any program or data held in any computer.

(2) In proceedings for an offence under this section, it is a defence for the defendant to prove that he did not know at the material time that his access to the relevant program or data was unauthorized.

In this variation, the accused is equipped with an affirmative 'no knowledge' defence, modelled on the vast array of similar defences attached to strict liability crimes in English penal statutes.

Can it plausibly be contended that Variation 2 is the functional equivalent of Variation 1? If so, this would substantiate the functionalist claim that an offence qualified by a reverse onus clause in respect of a particular aspect of criminal liability could be the functional equivalent of an offence for which that aspect

---

[65] To be sure of achieving this result, it was also necessary to reposition the requirement of intentional computer use, to avoid the phrase 'with intent to secure unauthorised access'. The natural interpretation of this formulation would have been that the accused must intend to secure *authorized* *access*. But one can only intend to secure unauthorized access if one knows, or at least believes, that the access being attempted is unauthorized. Hence, leaving the requirement of intent in its original form and place would have defeated the point of the variation.

of liability is unequivocally strict. Yet there are obvious conceptual and juridical distinctions to be drawn between these two models of criminalization. The functionalist claim must be that liability under Variation 2 is strict *in spite of* the legislature's inclusion of a reverse onus clause, rather than because of it. In Variation 1 the accused's knowledge or lack of knowledge of authorization is quite simply not in issue, and any evidence proffered in order to prove or disprove such knowledge should be rejected by the judge as irrelevant and therefore inadmissible.[66] Under Variation 2, by contrast, the accused is entitled to adduce evidence to show that he never knew his access was unauthorized in an effort to establish an affirmative 'no knowledge' defence. These evidential discrepancies ought fatally to undermine any suggestion of functional equivalence between the two alternative strategies of criminalization and associated drafting styles exemplified by Variations 1 and 2.

But look again. How, exactly, is the accused supposed to discharge the onus of proof resting on him under Variation 2? He can always choose to go into the witness box and swear to his innocence, and the fact-finder will evaluate what he says, and the demeanour with which he says it, for whatever such information might be worth. However, the simple fact of the accused's testifying that he never appreciated the need for authorization is unlikely to count for very much. Many accused decline to testify in their own defence for tactical reasons,[67] but for the rest, fact-finders will routinely discount the value of an accused's self-serving testimony in recognition of the natural human inclination for guilty people to lie through their teeth in the cause of self-preservation. To the extent that computer hacking is the solitary pastime of bedroom-dwelling techno-nerds or professional organized criminals, there will probably be no eyewitnesses, still less will physical evidence settle the issue of the accused's knowledge, or lack of it. And whereas the guilty hacker might have betrayed himself by incautious remarks to third parties, prior or subsequent to the commission of his offence (an admissible confession of guilty knowledge), the innocent accused can hardly have alerted any potential witness to his ignorance of what later turn out to be crucial facts, prior to engaging in conduct that he never imagined could constitute a criminal offence![68] The only way in which the accused is seemingly going to be able to establish an affirmative 'no knowledge' defence is if the surrounding circumstances lend plausibility to his

---

[66] It is conceivable that evidence that D knew his access was unauthorized could still be admissible to rebut a claim that D's computer usage was unintentional, the result of an accidental fall or uncontrollable spasm. Under all three scenarios, liability rests on *intentional* computer usage, and evidence of knowledge of authorization must therefore remain admissible just in so far as it goes to prove, or disprove, that intent.

[67] In a detailed survey of Crown Court trials conducted for the Runciman Royal Commission on Criminal Justice, approximately 30% of accused declined to testify in their own defence: Michael Zander and Paul Henderson, *Crown Court Study*, RCCJ Research Study No 19 (London 1993), para. 4.5.

[68] If the force of this point is still unclear, consider: when was the last time that you informed someone of your ignorance of a fact in preparation for a contingency that you did not foresee?

plea of ignorance—if, for example, the data or program in question appear, on an objective view, to be freely available to all-comers.

This is at first a surprising conclusion. We seem now to be saying that objective circumstantial factors in practice eclipse the accused's subjective knowledge or intention, in which case the location of the burden of proof apparently becomes inconsequential. Objective circumstantial factors are in principle equally amenable to proof by either prosecution or defence. But this conclusion is too radical to advance the argument for functional equivalence between procedural mechanisms and substantive strict liability. The pragmatic realities of proof seemingly turn Variation 2 into the functional equivalent of the original, supposedly non-strict-liability, section 1(1) offence, implying an equivalence in the diametrically opposite direction to that predicted by the functionalist reverse onus argument. Variation 1 appears isolated as the only scenario in which a person could be found guilty of criminal hacking even though he did not know, *and lacked reasonable grounds for believing*, that his access to data was unauthorized. If the circumstances were such that, on an objective view, a reasonable person would have concluded that access to particular data was unrestricted, then an accused charged with the Variation 2 offence should be able to lead circumstantial evidence to establish an affirmative 'no knowledge' defence ('How was I supposed to know something that nobody else could reasonably have known?'). Conversely, in the absence of such circumstances, the prosecution should be able to satisfy section 1(1)(c) of the 1990 Act by inviting the fact-finder to infer the accused's guilty knowledge from the fact that the absence of authorization would have been obvious to any reasonable person ('The accused must have known what any reasonable person would have known in those circumstances'). Variation 1 emerges as the only version of the computer hacking offence for which liability would be strict in the relevant sense.

There is a blind spot in this line of reasoning, however, which a functionalist analysis can exploit. For 'authorization' is not, as we have been assuming, an exclusively subjective concept. As well as reflecting the data-owner's subjective desires, authorization operates in the external, objective, world of appearances and events.[69] As a general proposition, authority can be granted by conduct without conscious animadversion, and even where authorization actually frustrates one's unarticulated wishes. Suppose that Anne, flushed with the enthusiasm of a first encounter with internet web-page design, decides to mount photographs of herself and her friends on her newly created homepage. The photographs depict party antics of a personal, potentially mildly embarrassing nature, and it is Anne's intention to distribute them only within her intimate circle of close friends (none

---

[69] Thus, English courts have approached the concept of 'unauthorized access' in s. 1 of the 1990 Act as a mixed question of law and fact: see *R. v. Bow Street Metropolitan Stipendiary Magistrate, ex p. Government of USA* [2000] 2 AC 216, HL, departing from the interpretation adopted in *DPP v. Bignell* [1998] 1 Cr. App. R. 1, 12–13, DC. For illuminating analysis of the concepts of 'access' and 'authorization' in US computer misuse statutes, see Orin S. Kerr, 'Cybercrime's Scope: Interpreting "Access" and "Authorization" in Computer Misuse Statutes' (2003) 78 *New York University LR* 1596.

of whom has exhibitionist tendencies). Unfortunately, being an internet novice, she does not realize that placing material on a web-page, without protective encryption, extends access to all and sundry. Anne is mortified when she later discovers that Billy has downloaded her private images and disseminated them amongst his very wide circle of teenage net-head voyeurs. Could Billy be convicted of the Variation 1 hacking offence? Surely not. By uploading her pictures on to an unprotected internet site, Anne *has*, objectively speaking, authorized access to them, whatever her subjective desires might have been. Billy cannot therefore be guilty of hacking, even under Variation 1's strict liability regime, because he has not secured '*unauthorized* access to any program or data held in any computer.'

This further twist in the analysis appears to vindicate the functionalist reverse onus argument after all, to the extent that *all three* versions of the hacking offence amount to more or less the same thing when the pragmatics of proof have been factored into the equation. The decisive factor in every case is the objective appearance of authorization. In the original section 1(1) and Variation 2 scenarios, circumstantial appearances constitute evidence from which the accused's knowledge or ignorance of authorization may be inferred, whilst under Variation 1—in which the accused's knowledge is strictly irrelevant—outward appearances settle the issue of authorization as a question of conceptual logic and statutory interpretation. Three ostensibly divergent strategies of criminal legislation conduce to the same practical regime of criminalization. Functionalist analysis has substantiated the claim it set out to demonstrate, and more. An offence qualified by a reverse onus provision can be the functional equivalent of a strict liability crime, and both may be indistinguishable in their practical effect from a non-strict-liability offence subject to a traditional burden of proof.

Many readers will doubtless share my intuition that something must have gone seriously wrong with the 'logic' of this (suspiciously elaborate) argument for functionalist equivalence if it carries such radically heretical implications for the imposition of burdens of proof, and by extension significantly devalues the presumption of innocence. The functionalist reverse onus argument reconstructed in this section is tackled head-on in § 4, with a rebuttal lending renewed conviction to legal orthodoxy. However, in case the counterintuitive possibility of comprehensive functional equivalence should appear too far-fetched to be worthy of serious consideration, it should be noted that traces of such functionalist heresies can already be discerned in post-Human Rights Act jurisprudence addressing the presumption of innocence.

In *L* v. *DPP*[70] the Divisional Court rejected an Article 6(2)-based challenge to the reverse onus clause in section 139(4) of the Criminal Justice Act 1988 which, as we have seen, requires an accused to prove that he had 'good reason or lawful authority' for carrying a knife or other bladed or pointed instrument in public. The court's principal conclusion was that section 139(4) strikes an acceptable balance

---

[70] *L* v. *DPP* [2002] 1 Cr. App. R. 420, DC.

between justice and security, in view of the palpable risk of harm presented by those who carry dangerous weapons in public, and was therefore compatible with Article 6(2). This might be regarded as a perfectly predictable conclusion.[71] In the course of argument, however, Pill LJ opined that in the majority of cases nothing of any consequence would turn on the formal allocation of the burden of proof:

> In the great majority of cases, I would expect the fact-finding tribunal to make a judgment as to whether there was a good reason without the decision depending on whether it has to be proved that there is a good reason or that there is not a good reason. The present case is a good illustration. The fact-finding tribunal will need to make a value judgment as to whether, upon all the evidence, the reason is a good one. Either there is or there is not a good reason though I accept that there will be cases in which the fact-finding tribunal may attach significance to where the burden of proof rests.[72]

This passage betrays textbook functionalist assumptions. In particular, Pill LJ seems to countenance the type of functionalist argument illustrated in this section by hypothetical variations on the offence of computer hacking; though it is right to add that, in conceding marginal significance to the allocation of the burden of proof in certain—presumably exceptional—cases, Pill LJ stops short of implying *complete* functional equivalence between procedural mechanisms and substantive criteria of criminal liability.

## 3.2. The Irrebuttable Presumption Argument

Functionalism's final gambit is the irrebuttable presumption argument, that still-sleeved ace. Bypassing entirely the rigmarole of manipulating reverse onus clauses, this argument appears to provide a much more direct and secure route to establishing the functional equivalence of procedure and substance in strict liability. The Computer Misuse Act 1990 will again serve to illustrate the general legislative technique.

Consider a final variation on the section 1(1) offence of computer hacking:

**Variation 3**

(1)  A person is guilty of an offence if—

    (a)  he causes a computer to perform any function with intent to secure access to any program or data held in any computer;

    (b)  the access he intends to secure is unauthorized; and

---

[71]  Or not, depending on one's perspective. It is perfectly predictable that the courts will err on the side of caution by promoting security over liberty in troubled times. On the other hand, in the absence of clear or settled principles to guide judicial applications of Article 6(2), litigation contesting the scope of the presumption of innocence might currently be regarded as something of a lottery. Who can tell which way the court will jump next time when rulings in relation to particular statutory offences have little or no precedent value beyond their immediate legislative context? See *A-G's Reference (No 1 of 2004)* [2004] EWCA Crim. 1025; *R. v. Johnstone* [2003] UKHL 28; *Sheldrake* v. *DPP* [2003] 2 Cr. App. R. 206, DC; *R. v. S (Trademark Defence)* [2003] 1 Cr. App. R. 602, CA; *R. v. Lang and Deadman* [2002] EWCA Crim. 298; *R. v. Carass* [2002] 1 WLR 1714, CA; *R. v. Drummond* [2002] 2 Cr. App. R. 352, CA; *Davies* v. *Health and Safety Executive* [2002] EWCA Crim. 2949.

[72]  *L* v. *DPP* [2002] 1 Cr. App. R. 420, para. 27.

     (c) he knows at the time when he causes the computer to perform the
         function that that is the case.

   (2) For the purposes of this section, it shall be assumed for all purposes that
     a person who causes a computer to perform any function with intent to
     secure access to any program or data held in any computer knows that the
     access he secures is unauthorized.

Subsection (2) of Variation 3 sets up by operation of law an irrebuttable presumption regarding a fact in issue. The substantive offence requires the accused to know
that his access to data or programs was unauthorized, but the effect of subsection (2)
is that the fact-finder must assume that a person who has hacked into unauthorized
data or programs was fully cognizant of the restricted status of the material he
accessed. An irrebuttable factual presumption, like subsection (2)'s irrebuttable
presumption of knowledge, is a procedural device for transforming fault-based
elements of a substantive criminal charge into liability without fault. This operation
epitomizes the core functionalist claim examined in this chapter: that procedure can
serve as the functional equivalent of substance in strategies of criminalization
imposing strict liability.

    The irrebuttable presumption argument is not afflicted by the tortuous
complexities of the reverse onus argument, neither does it depend for its success on
contestable assumptions concerning trial tactics and the pragmatics of proof in criminal litigation (of which, more in a moment). To the contrary, it might be counted
a significant strength of the irrebuttable presumption argument that it purports to
offer a direct, conceptually secure, route to functional equivalence. None the less,
despite these comparative advantages, the irrebuttable presumption argument is still
a variant of the type of functionalism that this chapter set out its stall to expose
and reject. Akin to the reverse onus argument, in the final analysis, functionalism's
resort to irrebuttable presumptions ultimately stands or falls by the strength of its
underlying commitments and presuppositions, which must now be examined.

## 4. What's Wrong with Functionalism?

Advocates as much as critics of functionalism might concur with the analysis
developed in §§ 2 and 3 of this chapter. We began in § 2 by exposing the prevalence
of functionalist assumptions in comparative commentary and jurisprudence
addressing the relationship between strict liability and the presumption of innocence. Against this backdrop, § 3 projected a microscopic conceptual analysis of
two independent arguments for functional equivalence, each utilizing a different
procedural mechanism available to legislators: the reverse onus clause and the
irrebuttable presumption. The present section proceeds from exposé to critique.
We need to inquire just what, after all, is wrong with functionalism?

    Most readers, I suppose, will readily agree that unacknowledged, unreflective,
and untested assumptions should be brought out into the open, clearly articulated,

and subjected to critical scrutiny. But what is to prevent functionalist *arguments* from displacing and successfully superseding functionalist assumptions? The arguments for functional equivalence developed in the last section can claim a certain conceptual coherence and practical efficacy, and they have already begun to infiltrate post-Human Rights Act criminal jurisprudence, as we have seen.

Functionalism's fatal flaw, I contend, is that it is incapable of accommodating the morally significant sense in which procedure really is procedure, and substance really is substance, so that the one can never truly be the functional equivalent of the other in every material respect, whatever functionalist conceptual logic and reductive preoccupations might suggest to the contrary. This objection is fundamental and comprehensive. It applies to all forms and manifestations of the type of functionalism examined in this essay, though the principal target for purposes of illustration will continue to be the argument for functional equivalence between procedural devices and substantive strict liability. The critique developed in this section proceeds in two, cumulative stages. Section 4.1 explains the essential moral distinction between procedural and substantive norms and techniques. Section 4.2 then extends the analysis to take proper account of the principles and pragmatics of criminal evidence and proof. These discrete arguments converge on an important conclusion for English criminal jurisprudence. In rescuing the presumption of innocence from functionalist corruptions it becomes possible to reassert an orthodox interpretation of the *Woolmington* principle with renewed confidence and vigour.

## 4.1. The Meaning of Criminal Law

Language is, generally speaking, all the better and more valuable for being subtle and complex. All language systems—whether natural languages such as English or French, or artificial computer languages composed of mathematical signs and symbols—are ultimately self-referential. Definitions of words in dictionaries always refer back to other, epistemologically equivalent, dictionary definitions. However, within the 'hermeneutic' circle of meaning, communications of extraordinary complexity and subtle differentiation can be sent and received. Conversely, languages tend to contain few true synonyms because we do not need a variety of ways of expressing exactly the same thing. In ordinary conversation or writing, one's choice of words is usually intended to be significant, and will generally be interpreted as meaningful by one's audience. In the standard case people endeavour to say what they mean. If they had meant something different, they would have said something else. Of course the possibilities for misstatement, ambiguity, imprecision, malapropism, and so forth are endless (student essays supply a constant source of fresh examples), to say nothing of deliberate obfuscation, euphemism, or dissimulation. Yet language in all its complexity and subtlety remains an inexhaustibly rich resource for clarifying one's intended meaning by (for example) rephrasing, qualifying, or amplifying a previous communication that—judging by the response of one's audience—appears to have provoked an unexpected reaction or to have fallen on deaf ears.

Enacting criminal legislation is not a simple analogue of everyday conversation. Like ordinary communicative utterances, legislators mean to communicate certain things to the intended audience(s) of criminal statutes through the careful selection of words and phrases. But legislation is at once a simplified and more stylized mode of communication. It is simplified to the extent that good faith legislators have no use for commonplace paralinguistic inflexions such as empathy, humour, or irony. Legislators are meant to express themselves free of ulterior motives to impress, ingratiate, demean, persuade, menace, or deceive, etc. At the same time, legislation is enacted within a peculiar institutional framework of legal rules, informal conventions, occupational cultures, and reciprocal expectations that are in many ways more highly evolved and exquisitely mannered than the conventions of ordinary conversation.

Despite these important differences, a critique of functionalism in criminal legislation can usefully begin by recalling some basic facts about successful communication in any context. Intuitive suspicion of functionalism takes root, I believe, at this elementary level. Why would a legislator require two (or more) alternative drafting strategies for achieving exactly the same legislative result? If true functional equivalents were theoretically available, surely one would be chosen as the standard format, if only for simplicity's sake. The others would be expected to fall into legislative desuetude just as redundant synonyms, like 'an' meaning 'if', have slipped out of standard English usage. Conversely, a legislator has no reason to collapse distinct techniques of criminalization into a single functional equivalent. Such a reductive strategy could only serve to restrict the legislator's room for manœuvre in constructing complex patterns or subtle gradations of criminal liability. Even if one model drafting style—strict liability, reverse onus clauses, or whatever—were strongly favoured as the default option for regulating particular spheres of activity, it would be wise to preserve the integrity of viable alternative techniques in anticipation of as yet unknown future contingencies. A legislator opting for functional equivalence would be akin to a chess player agreeing to convert all four of her bishops and knights into rooks before making her opening move. Yet imprudence, inflexibility, and lack of strategic forward-planning are only the first charges that functionalism must answer. For if the distinction between substance and procedure is invested with moral salience, as I now seek to demonstrate, pursuing a reductive strategy of functional equivalence in criminal legislation would be morally objectionable as well as gratuitously impetuous.

We can begin to grasp the moral significance of differentiating between procedural and substantive norms by analogy to the moral distinction, well known to criminal law theorists, between positive fault elements and exculpatory 'defences' in criminal legislation.[73] The idea is frequently expressed in terms of 'fair labelling',[74] meaning that the criminal law should articulate as clearly and precisely as possible the nature of the moral judgments being passed on citizens' conduct. We should not, for example, say of an armed police marksman who shoots dead a would-be assassin to avert an imminent threat to the Prime Minister's life that the officer committed murder, but should be exonerated in these circumstances because he killed in the prevention of crime. We should rather say that, in responding proportionately to an imminent threat, the officer acted reasonably and commendably,[75] that his conduct was justified, and that he is *in no sense* a murderer, not even a murderer whose killing should be condoned in the circumstances. Likewise, we should not say of a person who absent-mindedly takes somebody else's umbrella from a restaurant's communal umbrella-stand, that he is a thief who should be let off because he acted without dishonesty. We should rather say that a person who innocently walks off with somebody else's property, though he might be a nuisance, is no kind of thief. The notion of an honest theft would be oxymoronic in English law, according to which the thief has *by definition* been judged dishonest according to the standards of ordinary decent people.[76]

There are, to be sure, hard questions that might be addressed to the institutional mechanisms for translating the law's penal judgments into comprehensible moral messages for the consumption of the offender, his victim, and society at large. Suffice it here to say that the criminal law should at least strive to communicate sound moral judgments as effectively as it can. One important way to promote effective communication is to build common sense moral distinctions into the structural design of criminal offences. Thus, in English law a killing can

[73] See, in particular, Kenneth Campbell, 'Offence and Defence', in I. H. Dennis (ed.), *Criminal Law and Justice* (London 1987), picking up the gauntlet thrown down by Glanville Williams, 'Offences and Defences' (1982) 2 *Legal Studies* 233. Also Paul Roberts, 'On the Preconditions and Possibilities of Criminal Law Theory' (1998) 11 *South African Journal of Criminal Justice* 285, 312–14.

[74] See Andrew Ashworth, *Principles of Criminal Law* (4th edn., Oxford 2003), 89–92. This compendious terminology is in general circulation and probably commands broad recognition, but may be somewhat unfortunate to the extent that it implies that 'labels', fair or otherwise, are consciously attached to pre-existing phenomena. In fact language partly *constitutes* reality, such that choosing the right 'label' is not merely a matter of words, but—as Foucault taught Marx—part of the process of changing the world. There is further potential for confusion between fair labelling in criminal jurisprudence and 'the labelling perspective' in the sociology of deviance, although this could admittedly only create major difficulties if criminal lawyers and criminologists started talking to each other more often.

[75] If it goes too far to say that the officer's conduct in killing another human being was praiseworthy (though some—including, presumably, the Prime Minister—would certainly want to insist that it was), we can at least say that the officer's conduct was morally permissible. For an account of justifications as 'contextual permissions', see Eric Colvin, 'Exculpatory Defences in Criminal Law' (1990) 10 *Oxford Journal of Legal Studies* 381.

[76] *R. v. Ghosh* [1982] QB 1053, CA; *R. v. Feely* [1973] QB 530, CA. See A. P. Simester and G. R. Sullivan, *Criminal Law: Theory and Doctrine* (2nd edn., Oxford 2003), § 13.8; Andrew Ashworth, *Principles of Criminal Law* (4th edn., Oxford 2003), 383–7.

only be murder or manslaughter if death was caused *unlawfully* (not in self-defence; in order to prevent crime, etc.), and a deprivation of property is incapable of constituting theft unless it amounts to an 'appropriation' made *dishonestly*.[77] Offence definitions such as these track widely held moral intuitions. Neither the heroic police marksman nor the absent-minded umbrella taker would be branded as criminals, or described as 'getting away with it', in ordinary parlance. If the umbrella purloiner later realized his mistake but dishonestly decided to keep what he now knows to be somebody else's property, *then* he would become a thief, both at law[78] and by common understanding.

Substantive criminal offences are consciously designed to encapsulate, in their detailed legal specifications, the particular moral wrongs proscribed by law, thereby clearly advertising the limits of penal regulation and potential criminal liability.[79] An offence definition should competently demarcate the boundary between lawful conduct and illegal activity liable on conviction to penal censure and punishment. That boundary must be staked out with clarity and precision, to reduce the risk of injustice arising from inappropriate penal censure, as well as for well-known 'rule of law' reasons: moral guidance, fair-warning, respect for personal autonomy, constitutional propriety in criminalization, and democratic accountability. Competent and legitimate criminal legislation is much more than threats-based deterrence or a schema for prudential reasoning ('Don't do *x* unless you want to risk punishment'). Offence definitions purport to signal the nature and limits of criminalized immorality, because legitimate criminal laws either reinforce pre-existing moral wrongs with legal sanctions, or create new institutional reasons for condemning morally neutral behaviour—as where, through a positive act of legislation, it becomes immoral, because dangerous, to drive on the wrong side of the road. So much is well known, and perhaps even relatively uncontroversial amongst theorists. It is less widely appreciated, however, that the distinction between substantive and procedural norms carries similar moral freight. Just as an unremittingly functionalist account of substantive criminal law would fail to do justice to the moral salience of criminalization,[80] so the

---

[77] Theft Act 1968, s. 1(1).

[78] *Attorney-General's Reference (No 1 of 1983)* [1985] QB 182, CA; *R. v. Gresham* [2003] EWCA Crim. 2070.

[79] For further illuminating analyses of the proper scope of a range of criminal prohibitions, including property crimes and offences against the person, see Alan L. Bogg and John Stanton-Ife, 'Protecting the Vulnerable: Legality, Harm and Theft' (2003) 23 *Legal Studies* 402; John Gardner and Stephen Shute, 'The Wrongness of Rape', in Jeremy Horder (ed.), *Oxford Essays in Jurisprudence: Fourth Series* (Oxford 2000); Stuart P. Green, 'Why It's a Crime to Tear the Tag Off a Mattress: Overcriminalization and the Moral Content of Regulatory Offenses' (1997) 46 *Emory LJ* 1533; John Gardner, 'Rationality and the Rule of Law in Offences Against the Person' (1994) 53 *Cambridge LJ* 502; Jeremy Horder, 'Rethinking Non-Fatal Offences Against the Person' (1994) 14 *Oxford Journal of Legal Studies* 335; Stephen Shute and Jeremy Horder, 'Thieving and Deceiving: What is the Difference?' (1993) 56 *Modern LR* 548.

[80] As Antony Duff has shown in his critique of Paul Robinson's unremittingly functionalist conception of criminal law: see R. A. Duff, 'Rule-Violations and Wrongdoings', in Stephen Shute and A. P. Simester (eds.), *Criminal Law Theory: Doctrines of the General Part* (Oxford 2002), comprehensively rejecting 'the austerely descriptive simplicities of a Robinsonian code'.

argument for functional equivalence between strict liability and procedural devices undermines the moral significance of the presumption of innocence.

When the criminal law is recognized for what it is, an institutionalized system of morality designed in part to communicate moral judgments on the conduct of the accused, functionalism becomes untenable. Procedural mechanisms are not freely interchangeable with definitional elements of substantive offences, because the moral messages each conveys are distinct, and sometimes mutually incompatible. It follows that, when their distinctive meanings are properly appreciated, the respective functions of procedural and substantive aspects of criminalization are *not* fungibly equivalent in either their design or consequential impact. From a functionalist perspective, it is a contingent matter of legislative strategy and convenience whether the most effective tools of law enforcement in any particular case will be procedural or substantive. But the criminal law's ambitions are more lofty and demanding than functionalism allows. Criminal law and its administration serve justice, and achieving justice is not only a matter of arriving at the right destination, but of taking an approved route to get there and behaving appropriately along the way.

A moralized analysis exposes the harshness of much contemporary penal law, which should be counted an analytical strength of this approach. It is criminally wrongful in English law, for example, to possess a controlled substance, and it makes no difference whether or not that substance's particular narcotic properties were appreciated[81] or even, in certain circumstances, whether the existence of any narcotic was known. If drugs were concealed in a box, bag, or other container, the accused need only know that he has the container and that there is *something* in it. If that something turns out on inspection to be a prohibited substance, he is guilty of the offence.[82] In these respects, possession can be regarded as a strict liability concept under the Misuse of Drugs Act 1971. Now, a functionalist analysis would maintain that the same practical result could be achieved by an irrebuttable factual presumption of guilty knowledge, or (possibly less comprehensively, depending on the contextual pragmatics of proof) by a reverse onus clause. But here's the rub.

---

[81] By s. 28(3)(a) of the Misuse of Drugs Act 1971, an accused 'shall not be acquitted of the offence charged by reason only of proving that he neither knew or suspected nor had reason to suspect that the substance or product in question was the particular controlled drug alleged'.

[82] *R. v. McNamara* (1988) 87 Cr. App. R. 246, CA; *R. v. Lambert* [2002] 2 AC 545, HL, esp. para. 61 *per* Lord Hope ('The mental element involves proof of knowledge that the thing exists and that it is in his possession. Proof of knowledge that the thing is an article of a particular kind, quality or description is not required. It is not necessary for the prosecution to prove that the defendant knew that the thing was a controlled drug which the law makes it an offence to possess'); and para. 126 *per* Lord Clyde ('Where the drug is in a container, it is sufficient for the prosecution to prove that the defendant had control of the container, that he knew of its existence and that there was something in it, and that the something was in fact the controlled drug which the prosecution alleges it to be. The prosecution does not require to prove that the accused knew that the thing was a controlled drug'). This interpretation of the meaning of 'possession' in s. 5 of the 1971 Act remains somewhat controversial: cf. *Warner* v. *Metropolitan Police Commissioner* [1969] 2 AC 256, HL. However, a strict liability approach to the meaning of 'possession' has also been extended to the offence of possessing an unlicensed firearm contrary to s. 1 of the Firearms Act 1968: see *R. v. Steele* [1993] Crim. LR 298, CA; *R. v. Waller* [1991] Crim. LR 381, CA.

*The same practical result would not be achieved by either of these procedural devices,* because the law's moral message is changed, or distorted, when a different medium for its expression is employed.

Criminal law is not taxation. Substantive criminal prohibitions speak in the imperative voice of 'Thou shalt not . . . ', not in the pricing idiom of the shop-keeper or accountant ('It will cost you *y* to do *x*'). The message conveyed by an offence of strict liability is that the conduct it proscribes is morally wrongful, and should not be engaged in or tolerated, notwithstanding an offender's lack of fault in relation to the matter on which liability is strict. Criminal law should not, on pain of self-contradiction, transmit one message about the nature and scope of criminal wrongs, and then act as though it had said something else. But this is exactly what it does if the law announces that only those who knowingly possess drugs act wrongfully, yet then proceeds to authorize the conviction of both knowing and inadvertent drug-possessors without distinction. The legislator's deliberate choice to employ procedural devices qualifying the primary scope of liability conveys the impression that the targeted substantive wrong is '*knowingly* possessing a controlled substance'. It follows by implication that it is not wrong, in the eyes of the law, to possess a controlled substance in ignorance. Yet the argument from functional equivalence still purports to sanction the conviction of ignorant possessors, on the basis that procedural mechanisms can be used to achieve the same result as substantive criteria of liability. Under the procedural alternative, the law's message would appear to be that, although it is not wrong to possess drugs in ignorance, an accused whose conduct is beyond reproach can be treated in exactly the same way as somebody who, by knowingly possessing drugs, unquestionably deserves condemnation by the law's advertised standards. Both categories of accused might be convicted of a serious criminal offence carrying substantial penalties. The law giveth to the ignorant possessor with the substantive right hand, and taketh away with the procedural left.

When a person who conscientiously satisfies the law's articulated moral standards can still none the less be condemned and punished as a criminal wrongdoer, the presumption of innocence is reduced to a fatuous empty promise. Anybody who cares about criminal justice and human rights should be dismayed by that prospect. However, penal statutes creating strict liability crimes, whatever other objections might be levelled against them, do not necessarily cross this line. In the standard case, a criminal statute imposing strict liability does exactly what it threatens to do. Unless one ignores their communicative dimension, the use of procedural devices cannot, therefore, be regarded as the functional equivalent of a substantive liability rule, in the particular context of drugs possession offences or in any other. In reality, the 'functionally equivalent' procedural alternative is a manifestly inferior means of communicating mixed moral messages, which mystifies criminalization policy and blurs the moral boundaries of criminal liability.

It is tempting, but misconceived, to think that English law's substantive liability rule in drugs possession cases, whereby a person can be convicted of possessing drugs without knowing he has them, is no worse than the 'functionally equivalent' procedural alternatives of irrebuttable presumption or reverse onus of proof. Confusion is understandable, since the English rule is (to put it no higher) patently morally dubious, and distracting just on that account. To be sure, not everybody who inadvertently comes into the possession of drugs necessarily lacks moral culpability. People who agree to carry packages on behalf of shady-looking strangers whom they met in a pub, for example, arguably *ought to* ascertain the nature of the packages they receive, and might reasonably be said to assume the risk of being treated by the criminal law as a drugs courier if caught in possession of what turns out to be narcotics. But wholly blameless people, too, can be caught with drugs in their possession. Think of the innocent stooge of a drug-dealer on whom unwanted merchandise is foisted with a menacing 'Just look after this package for me, will you mate?', or the hapless target of a deliberate frame-up. In treating such moral innocents as presumptive drugs offenders, English law casts the net of criminality too widely. A dragnet will inevitably ensnare individuals who could never legitimately be described as criminal wrongdoers, either in serious philosophical scholarship or in popular moral discourse.

To argue as a general proposition that the use of procedural mechanisms to define the scope of criminal liability is always inferior to substantive legislation is not yet to endorse any particular substantive offence. If the English crime of drugs possession is over-broad it should be criticized, and if necessary recast, on its own substantive terms. A functionalist procedural variation would not only perpetuate excessively broad liability for innocent possessors (if that is what the 1971 Act, as judicially interpreted, does), but compound that primary defect by garbling the criminal law's intended moral messages into the bargain. Whatever the substantive merits of the English rule, it at least promises clarity and certainty: *designated forms of knowledge are simply irrelevant to the question of possession*.[83] If this is the right moral message, it is effectively conveyed; if it is the wrong moral message, there is a clearly advertised target for reform. Compare this state of affairs to the implications of the procedural alternative, which starts by announcing that drugs must be possessed knowingly, and then abandons the knowledge requirement mid-stream. This approach still authorizes the conviction of moral innocents, as before, but in addition inflicts doctrinal incoherence, ineffective communication of penal messages, confusion of citizens and criminal justice professionals, and the appearance of legislative incompetence or—arguably worse—hypocrisy. Whilst isolated instances of faulty communication are tolerable and perhaps inevitable in any human system of criminal law,

---

[83] In the event, the promise of clarity and certainty was defeated by the reasoning adopted in *R. v. Lambert* (*Steven*) [2002] 2 AC 545, HL, turning what appeared on its face to be an affirmative defence into a mere burden of production. The pay-off was mitigation of an otherwise very harsh rule of liability, an undeniably attractive compromise in pragmatic terms, but only those exclusively preoccupied with outcomes could regard the House of Lords' reasoning and decision in *Lambert* as entirely satisfactory. For extended critical discussion, see Paul Roberts, 'Drug-Dealing and the Presumption of Innocence: The Human Rights Act (Almost) Bites' (2002) 6 *Evidence & Proof* 17.

systematic failings would begin to erode the legislature's moral authority to legislate for criminal sanctions.

It is in this sense that functionalism's procedural 'equivalent' is always inferior to the substantive alternative in defining the scope of criminal liability: *the functionalist's use of procedural mechanisms is compromised by additional procedural deficiencies over and above the potential shortcomings of substantive legislation*, and this remains the case even where the 'equivalent' substantively defined offence would itself be morally indefensible, because it imposes criminal liability in the absence of coextensive moral fault or for some other (substantive) reason. Whether morally objectionable liability without fault is an *exclusively* substantive defect in criminal legislation, or whether it also necessarily implies procedural infirmity as a breach of the presumption of innocence, is a question to which we will briefly return in this chapter's concluding section.

In an ideal world, the boundaries of criminal liability would remain within the parameters of moral culpability. To the extent that citizens' conduct must be regulated and their choices influenced in the absence of fault, the legislature should ideally employ regulatory mechanisms that are not intended to import moral blame and censure, such as taxation, social welfare policy, planning and design of the built environment, education, and, of course, the civil law of actionable entitlements and compensation. In the real world, we can at least insist, as a matter of transparency and integrity in criminal legislation, that if moral innocents are going to be criminalized by operation of law, that fact should be advertised openly in substantive offence definitions, rather than insinuated through the procedural back door. Any government wishing to enact such legislation, moreover, should present it to Parliament with candour and solicit open parliamentary debate and informed assent, rather than trying to sneak new criminal offences on to the statute-book using diversionary tactics or argumentative make-weights. Relying on smoke and mirrors in the legislative process is hardly the hallmark of the conscientious democratic legislator, and might even be invested with rather sinister connotations.

The morality of criminal legislation has particular salience for irrebuttable factual presumptions. An argument can be made for retaining a legitimate, if strictly delimited, role for reverse onus clauses in a morally defensible system of criminal justice. Where Parliament, after due consideration, is willing to criminalize on a strict liability basis, the provision of a genuine affirmative defence subject to a reverse onus clause may be morally justifiable. Antony Duff's contribution to this volume indicates how such an argument might be developed without necessarily impinging on the presumption of innocence.[84] Irrebuttable presumptions, by contrast, appear to serve no other purpose than to enact substantive criteria of criminal liability in procedural disguise. At least, I cannot envisage any circumstances in which a straightforward substantive provision would not be

[84] R. A. Duff, 'Strict Liability, Legal Presumptions, and the Presumption of Innocence', this volume, Ch. 6.

preferable to the circumlocutory procedural 'equivalent'. Perhaps demagogues seeking to conceal the ideological content of their criminal legislation would find merit in the use of an irrebuttable presumption. For the conscientious legislator, however, irrebuttable factual presumptions are at best superfluous, and at worst a menace. Parliamentary draftsmen should renounce them altogether, as the US Supreme Court has sometimes intimated.[85]

This is my answer to the question posed by Duff, as to whether choice of legislative technique matters: 'what, if anything (other than procedural convenience) hangs on whether the defendant is convicted via the procedural route of an irrebuttable presumption, or the substantive route of a strict liability provision?'[86] Accordingly, I can readily concur with Duff's remark that 'so-called "irrebuttable" presumptions . . . are better understood as constitutive specifications'[87] of substantive criminal fault. However, I am bound to take issue with his twice-repeated assertion that the effect of alternative procedural and substantive drafting devices in criminal legislation can be 'the same',[88] at least if this choice of words is intended to be more than a loose, albeit convenient, *façon de parler*. In my submission, the critique of functional equivalence developed in this subsection is conclusive. When called upon to play her procedural 'ace', the functionalist was holding only a busted flush.

## 4.2. The Pragmatics of Proof Revisited

The foregoing argument is surely persuasive *in principle*. Who will insist, in reply, that the legislature should strive to send garbled moral messages rather than speaking clearly and unequivocally when enacting criminal prohibitions? Who will maintain that a legislature is best served by having fewer, rather than more, legitimate tools and techniques of criminalization at its disposal? A critique of functionalism confined to the desirability of communicating unequivocal moral messages and fair labelling in criminal legislation might none the less be accused of overindulging rather fine distinctions. Although an irrebuttable presumption or reverse onus clause might be a rather circuitous and clumsy way of implementing a particular legislative agenda, it is often possible to reconstruct the intended scope of the offence through judicial interpretation. The message that designated knowledge is not required to be convicted of possessing drugs, for example, could

---

[85] A judicial instruction is unconstitutional in the USA if it might mislead jurors into thinking that the law allows an irrebuttable presumption of fact to reduce the prosecutor's burden of proof in relation to any element of the offence: *Sandstrom* v. *Montana*, 442 US 510 (1979); *Morissette* v. *US*, 342 US 246 (1952). For discussion, see Bruce L. Ackerman, 'The Conclusive Presumption Shuffle' (1977) 125 *University of Pennsylvania LR* 761 (observing that, following a 'conclusive presumption invalidation spree' in the early 1970s, the Supreme Court became more selective in striking down state legislation employing irrebuttable presumptions).

[86] Duff, this volume, Ch. 6, p. 133. Also see ibid. 144, suggesting the need for 'a different legislative device—the definitional or constitutive rule'.                    [87] Ibid. 149.

[88] Ibid. 133, 143.

be conveyed directly by the substantive offence definition, or indirectly by a definition ostensibly incorporating a knowledge requirement coupled with an irrebuttable presumption or reverse burden of proof. With a bit of interpretative effort, even obscure meanings can be recovered. Yet if no real harm is done either way, the vaunted moral distinction between substance and procedure might begin to look like an exclusive preoccupation of theorists with unrealistically purist expectations of legislative drafting.

But that conclusion would be premature and, it turns out, mistaken. Against the charge of scholasticism, it should be maintained both that ill-conceived or badly designed criminal offences are a blot on the statute-book, which per se dilutes the moral integrity of penal law, *and* that such legislative shortcomings impose tangible additional risks of miscarriages of justice occurring in practice. To see why, it is necessary to delve more deeply into the normative and practical implications of the distinction between substance and procedure.

Recall that, according to the argument for functional equivalence apparently entertained by Pill LJ in *L* v. *DPP*, the location of the burden of proof in relation to particular offence elements frequently has little or no bearing on the outcome of a trial. Although, as an empirical description of criminal litigation, this is probably often true in the circumstances of particular cases, as a proposition of law it is nothing short of apostasy. English lawyers, before[89] and after *Woolmington*, have always thought that the location of the burden of proof in criminal proceedings is a matter of very great, indeed of constitutional, significance. That the prosecution must prove by admissible evidence each element of the offence(s) charged is supposedly cherished as English law's most visible manifestation of the presumption of innocence. Yet, despite its exalted status in the theory of criminal process, it seems that in practice the *Woolmington* principle is in danger of being eclipsed.

How could legislators, let alone experienced judges steeped in the traditions of the common law, be so careless with the presumption of innocence? One feature of functionalist thinking might be partly to blame. Functionalism fosters a preoccupation with the manipulation of abstract concepts to achieve 'functional equivalence'. Yet this tendency towards an arid conceptualism may serve to distract attention from the prosaic realities of criminal evidence and proof, at the same time as it strips away the broader moral context of criminal legislation.

Conceived as an abstract proposition, the primary objective of a trial is to expose the truth behind criminal charges. Trials settle disputed facts so that justice may take its course. From that postulate it might appear to follow that either party to the litigation might reasonably bear the burden of adducing evidence, so long as, one way or another, the fact-finder secures access to all relevant information

---

[89] Though one should add that the scope of the principle, particularly in relation to common law defences requiring the accused to make any positive averment, does not appear to have been finally settled until *Woolmington* (hence the significance of that decision): see George P. Fletcher, 'Two Kinds of Legal Rules: A Comparative Study of Burden-of-Persuasion Practices in Criminal Cases' (1968) 77 *Yale LJ* 880; J. C. Smith, 'The Presumption of Innocence' (1987) 38 *Northern Ireland Legal Quarterly* 223.

and adjudication is consequently fully informed to the greatest possible extent. Designing a system of proof for criminal litigation becomes a strategic question of sanctions and rewards to 'incentivize' the parties to locate, generate, and organize relevant information and present it, in the form of evidence admissible at trial, to the fact-finder. The allocation of probative burdens is relegated to a subsidiary practical detail, to be governed exclusively by pragmatic considerations.[90]

However, real-world criminal litigation belies such scholastic abstractions. Trials are typically a messy, uncertain, hit-and-miss affair, from which an unequivocal, comprehensive 'truth' seldom emerges. Criminal trials begin, for the fact-finder, in total ignorance of the facts of the case, and proceed through the presentation of evidence, not to absolute certainty, but to a reduced measure of uncertainty. Frequently such uncertainty is reduced to the point at which the fact-finder is prepared to dismiss any residual doubts as unreasonable flights of fancy, and the accused is convicted; only somewhat less frequently in English Crown Court trials,[91] the jury's lingering uncertainty results in an acquittal. In either event, uncertainty is managed rather than eliminated.

Burdens of proof are procedural mechanisms for allocating the risk of non-persuasion under conditions of uncertainty. They can be conceptualized as litigation default-rules, determining what will happen in the event of an evidential 'tie', where the fact-finder is simply unable to decide, after hearing all the evidence and arguments presented by the litigants, where the truth of the disputed matter lies. When the fact-finder says 'We still don't know what happened', the law says to the party bearing the burden of proof: 'You lose.' So far as the appropriate *standard* of proof is concerned, proof on the balance of probabilities has an intuitively logical attraction.[92] A party who 'more likely than not' has established the truth of his contentions has done enough to persuade the fact-finder that his cause is superior to his opponent's, whilst anything less than proof on the balance of probabilities is not 'proof' of anything. Even 51 per cent proof tips the scales,

[90] This is the functionalist line predictably pursued by law-and-economics theorists such as Judge Posner: see Richard A. Posner, 'An Economic Approach to the Law of Evidence' (1999) 51 *Stanford LR* 1477, 1481, proposing that one should 'model factfinding as a problem in search, analogous to searching for a consumer durable, with the correct answer to the question of (say) "Did X shoot Y?" corresponding to the utility-maximizing choice between two brands of dishwasher'. An immediate qualification is that 'the incentives of the participants [are] not the same in the two search processes'.

[91] In 2003 over 67% of accused who pleaded 'not guilty' to all charges in the Crown Court were acquitted, but less than 1 in 3 of these acquittals were 'jury acquittals' after a full trial. Excluding judge-ordered and judge-directed acquittals, 8,254 'not guilty'-pleaders were convicted as against 5,262 acquitted on the jury's verdict after a full trial: Department of Constitutional Affairs, *Judicial Statistics 2003* (London 2004), 72–3, on-line at: <http://www.dca.gov.uk/judicial/jsar03/contents.htm>, accessed 25 Sept. 2004.

[92] The logic of the balance-of-probabilities standard is instructively expounded by Mike Redmayne, 'Standards of Proof in Civil Litigation' (1999) 62 *Modern LR* 167. Also see D. H. Kaye, 'Clarifying the Burden of Persuasion: What Bayesian Decision Rules Do and Do Not Do' (1999) 3 *Evidence & Proof* 1; Ronald J. Allen, 'Clarifying the Burden of Persuasion and Bayesian Decision Rules: A Response to Professor Kaye' (2000) 4 *Evidence & Proof* 246; D. H. Kaye, 'Bayes, Burdens and Base Rates' (2000) 4 *Evidence & Proof* 260.

but 50 : 50 is an even balance, representing the fact-finder's inability to choose between two (or more) equally plausible scenarios, either of which could equally well represent the truth.

Although proof on the balance of probabilities has been adopted as the governing standard of proof for nearly all civil proceedings, and as the applicable standard whenever an onus of proof lies on the accused in a criminal trial,[93] the prosecution must, as everybody knows, attain the significantly more demanding standard of 'proof beyond reasonable doubt' in order to secure a criminal conviction. This steeply asymmetric standard[94] reflects, as it concretizes and operationalizes, English law's commitment to protecting the innocent from wrongful conviction, which is the core value animating the presumption of innocence. The accused should have the benefit of any real doubt still remaining after a criminal trial, not because criminal litigation is a game in which the human quarry is entitled to a sporting chance,[95] still less because government and criminal justice professionals love offenders and despise victims of crime, but because wrongful conviction, censure, and punishment are such grave injustices that strenuous efforts must be made—sometimes involving sacrifices of other interests and values—in order to minimize the risk of condemning the innocent. Howsoever the trade-off might be quantified (if quantification is indeed desirable at all),[96] most people share the intuition that it is worse for an innocent person to be wrongly convicted than for a guilty person to escape their just deserts. The steeply asymmetric criminal standard of proof is formulated precisely so that the risk of wrongful conviction is minimized, even at the cost of allowing some guilty offenders to slip through the net. A tangible implication of espousing the presumption of innocence is that a political community commits itself in the administration of criminal justice to treating unconvicted citizens *as though they were* innocent, even if—or rather, especially when—the finger of suspicion is pointing their way. The presumption's normative significance lies in the moral imperative of expressing official censure of criminal wrongdoing, and the correspondingly grave injustice of wrongfully convicting a person who is innocent.

The allocation of burdens of proof in criminal proceedings must be evaluated against this normative backdrop. Tie-breakers do not affect the outcome of every case, nor even a majority of cases. Their practical purchase, as default rules, is limited to trials in which the litigation contest is otherwise too close to call on the evidence available to the fact-finder. Allocating a probative burden to the

[93] *R.* v. *Hunt* [1987] 1 AC 352, 374, HL; *R.* v. *Carr-Briant* [1943] KB 607, CCA.
[94] See Paul Roberts, 'Double Jeopardy Law Reform: A Criminal Justice Commentary' (2002) 65 *Modern LR* 393, 402–4; Roberts and Zuckerman, *Criminal Evidence*, § 8.4(b).
[95] As Bentham's mocking reference to the Foxhunter's Reason implied: see William Twining, *Theories of Evidence: Bentham and Wigmore* (London 1985), 85.
[96] Blackstone shared the conventional view that it is 'better to let ten guilty men go free than to convict one innocent', though ratios of 5 : 1 (Hale), 20 : 1 (Fortescue), and even 100 : 1 (Bentham) can be found in the older literature. See Glanville Williams, *The Proof of Guilt* (3rd edn., London 1963), 186–8. But the precise figures hardly matter, because the commitment to safeguarding the innocent which they symbolize is moral and political, not numerical.

accused is always morally problematic in any case where there is neither clear-cut proof of guilt nor adequate suggestion of innocence to sustain an acquittal, because the risk of an erroneous verdict is transferred from the prosecution to the defence. This transfer of risk is admittedly also asymmetrical, because the accused shoulders a lower standard of proof than the prosecutor. Whereas, for example, the accused might have to establish that he had lawful authority for carrying an offensive weapon in public only on the balance of probabilities, in the absence of a reverse onus clause the prosecutor would have to demonstrate the accused's lack of lawful authority beyond reasonable doubt. But this discrepancy only mitigates what is nearly always a major sacrifice of principle. Rather than accepting that some guilty people will benefit, albeit wholly undeservedly, from a rule safeguarding innocence, reverse onus clauses typically operate to sacrifice some innocents in order to penalize more of the guilty. This trade-off is, in plain words, a betrayal of a political community's commitment to the presumption of innocence.

A tempting off-the-cuff retort is that a person is not necessarily 'innocent' just because the prosecution would have been unable to *dis*prove an affirmative defence, the proof of which has instead, and for precisely that reason, been assigned by the legislature to the accused. But this misguided response proves far too much. By that peremptory logic, one might as well say that every prosecution should automatically result in a conviction, without ever troubling to go through the motions of adjudication, because if the police and prosecution are performing conscientiously the vast majority of accused called to account will probably be guilty as charged. Whilst empirically plausible in relation to criminal prosecutions in England and Wales, this proposition is the normative nemesis of the presumption of innocence. Genuine affirmative defences aside, reverse onus clauses involve a normative[97] presumption *of guilt*.

In tie-breaker situations, in which by definition the fact-finder remains uncertain where the truth lies regarding some aspect of liability, a reverse onus clause operates as a short-cut to conviction. The law effectively announces: 'though the fact-finder cannot be sure of your guilt to the advertised standard, we will convict you anyway, to be on the safe side, since we are not convinced you are innocent and we wouldn't want such crimes to go unpunished'. This is a disturbing message to receive from a system of criminal justice supposedly committed to the presumption of innocence. That message erodes the moral integrity of a conviction *even if the accused is truly guilty*, because it authorizes conviction

---

[97] Not to be confused with the—highly plausible—*empirical* proposition that criminal investigators typically adopt a practical hypothesis of guilt and then look for confirmatory evidence around which to 'construct' a case: see Mike Redmayne, *Expert Evidence and Criminal Justice* (Oxford 2001), Ch. 2; Paul Roberts, 'Science in the Criminal Process' (1994) 14 *Oxford Journal of Legal Studies* 469; A. A. S. Zuckerman, 'Miscarriage of Justice—A Root Treatment' [1992] *Criminal LR* 323; Mike McConville, Andrew Sanders, and Roger Leng, *The Case for the Prosecution* (London 1991); Andrew Sanders, 'Constructing the Case for the Prosecution' (1987) 14 *Journal of Law and Society* 229. Such investigative practices may be perfectly compatible with a normative presumption of innocence, and are in any case analytically distinct.

without *proof* of guilt; and the significance of public proof, in preference to unsubstantiated police theories or official accusations, for the maintenance of an open, free, and democratic society hardly needs to be laboured. Indeed, one might insist that the mere presence in English criminal legislation of reverse onus clauses contravening the presumption of innocence *ipso facto* debases the quality of justice dispensed in English courts, whether or not such clauses are actually ever invoked.

As it happens, however, reverse onus clauses are surprisingly common in English criminal law,[98] and readily available in practice to ease the prosecution's evidential burdens. The mere prospect of having to respond to such tactics must sometimes induce defence counsel to advise their clients to plead guilty when they would otherwise have gone to trial. In addition, there are bound to be contested cases in which the fact-finder cannot discount the truth of an accused's explanation, but is willing to take refuge in a reverse onus clause to bring in a conviction. Some accused will be the victims of prejudicial stereotyping, which is all the more likely if the accused's previous convictions or other bad character become admissible as a consequence of legal[99] and tactical pressures to forego the privilege against self-incrimination. A reverse onus clause will often force the accused to testify in his own defence, or risk almost certain conviction. Other individuals are just not very convincing witnesses in their own cause, even when they are telling the truth. Remember that, in *L* v. *DPP*, Pill LJ went on to acknowledge that 'there will be cases in which the fact-finding tribunal may attach significance to where the burden of proof rests'.[100] However, this enigmatic coda scarcely hints at the nature or significance of the constitutional principles under attack from the corrosive functionalist assumptions implicit in his Lordship's analysis. Conviction without proof is both inherently morally decrepit, and an instrumental threat to innocence and justice.

## 5. Reasserting a Meaningful Presumption of Innocence

The previous section presented a systematic critique of the argument for treating substantive elements of criminal liability and procedural devices, such as reverse onus clauses and irrebuttable presumptions, as 'functional equivalents' in strategies of criminalization. Against the reductionist, one-dimensional argument for functional equivalence, I stressed the inherently meaningful, communicative dimension of criminal legislation that invests the legislature's choice of statutory

---

[98] N. 15, above, contains a miscellany of examples. For a more systematic survey, see Andrew Ashworth and Meredith Blake, 'The Presumption of Innocence in English Criminal Law' [1996] *Criminal LR* 314.

[99] Including the threat of adverse inferences being drawn from the accused's silence under ss. 34–7 of the Criminal Justice and Public Order Act 1994.

[100] *L* v. *DPP* [2001] Cr. App. R. 420, para. 27.

language, patterns and models of offence structure, conceptual distinctions, and drafting tools and techniques with nuanced moral salience. Against the functionalist tendency towards arid conceptualism, I urged realistic appreciation of the pragmatic contingencies of proof, which inform the allocation of probative burdens and reinforce the moral value, as well as the practical purchase, of the presumption of innocence. Functionalism, § 4 concluded, is neither normatively appealing nor empirically robust.

Corresponding to the intuition, now reinforced in the crucible of critical reflection, that substance is substance and procedure is procedure, two distinct grounds for criticizing criminal legislation have been identified: (1) *the substantive defect*—an offence may be excessively broad in imposing criminal liability in the absence of coextensive moral fault; and (2) *the procedural defect*—an offence may be accompanied by a procedural mechanism contravening the presumption of innocence, that is to say, reneging on a political community's commitment to protecting the innocent from wrongful conviction. Strict liability offences are often said to suffer from the first, substantive, defect, but—in the absence of a reverse onus clause or another procedural mechanism potentially infringing the presumption of innocence—there is no *ex facie* reason to regard strict liability as procedurally defective. In conclusion, I must briefly revisit a previously deferred question: are the substantive and procedural defects truly independent grounds for criticizing criminal legislation, or is there a deeper conceptual connection between them, extending beyond the merely contingent possibility that a particular offence might conceivably betray both defects simultaneously?

Substantive conceptions of the presumption of innocence, such as those propounded by Paizes, Jeffries and Stephan, and in other commentaries canvassed in § 2, purport to forge a conceptual link between (in my terminology) the substantive and procedural defects in criminal legislation. Their (implicitly) functionalist argument boasts an elegant simplicity when expounded *in abstracto*. Excessively broad criminal offences authorize the conviction of accused who lack moral fault in the requisite type or degree. This necessarily implies that such accused may be convicted *without proof* of moral fault, since the prosecutor obviously does not have to prove something that is not an element of the offence. But if an accused can be convicted of a criminal offence without proof of fully corresponding moral fault, such convictions must contravene the presumption of innocence, which supposedly encapsulates a guarantee against conviction and punishment without full proof of guilt. *Ergo*, all morally unjustifiable offences of strict liability, including those drafted without any trace of a reverse onus clause or evidentiary presumption, are incompatible with the presumption of innocence.

The critique of functionalism developed in this chapter was pitched at the level of general principle. It implies a moral theory of criminal legislation. The application of that theory to the law and practice of particular legal jurisdictions raises a further set of distinctively political and jurisprudential issues. Those who in principle reject the argument from functionalist equivalence still need to consider how best to translate philosophical principle into legislative and judicial practice. But this burden of explanation is perfectly ecumenical. Opponents who would prefer to embrace functionalism and dismiss my critique are in no way exempt from the demand for reasons. Even if one thinks that § 4 gushes moralizing claptrap, whilst the arguments for functional equivalence developed in § 3 were really quite smart, it still remains to be explained how and why functionalist analysis should be encouraged to advance from the beachhead in English criminal jurisprudence that it has thus far established predominantly by stealth.

The status and meaning of the presumption of innocence *in English law*, as opposed to the free-floating ideal, must be grounded in authoritative legal sources, judicial culture, and traditions of constitutionalism. The interpretational challenge has lately become vastly more complex and demanding, since what has always been to some extent a dynamic institutional environment is currently undergoing revolutionary reconstruction, in terms of expanding EU competence (not to mention other political, economic, and social consequences of globalization), radical parliamentary reform, devolution to the regions (not to mention other manifestations of political, social, and cultural fragmentation in a pluralistic society), and the unfolding impact on all spheres of public policy of the Human Rights Act. Constitutional history must today be reckoned an uncertain and incomplete guide to the present demands of constitutionalism. Yet we need to retain a firm grasp on the values embedded in our constitutional traditions, and an appropriate regard for the institutions, cultures, and practices that preserve and transmit those traditions, if we are to orientate ourselves in the present without bewilderment and to face the future with any measure of confidence.

It would be unwise at this time of flux and uncertainty to be dogmatic about the role of the senior English judiciary in developing norms of constitutional criminal procedure within the framework of the Human Rights Act. But here I want to qualify my previously expressed enthusiasm for comparative analogies with a note of caution. Substantive conceptions of the presumption of innocence advanced by American scholars, in particular, must be placed in the institutional context of a federal system of law incorporating substantive judicial review, and a tradition of constitutional criminal procedure stretching back at least forty years to the 'procedural revolution' inaugurated by Chief Justice Warren's Supreme Court. In stark contrast, there is, to my knowledge, no explicit doctrinal foundation whatsoever for a substantive conception of the presumption of innocence in English law. The traditional theory of parliamentary sovereignty stands in opposition to such an idea,[101] and could only accommodate it with

---

[101] As David Lanham once summarized the doctrine of unlimited parliamentary sovereignty in this context, 'If Parliament were to enact that any baby found in the street having been thrown thereon from a second storey window was guilty of an offence, a baby found in such circumstances would in theory be liable despite the absence of any normal form of *actus reus*, any *mens rea* and the presence of infancy and physical compulsion': [1976] *Criminal LR* 276, 277. Also see J. R. Spencer,

significant adjustment (which is still not to say that constitutional fundamentals are completely static or carved in granite). If in future there is to be substantive judicial review of the grounds of criminal liability in English law, development of the common law's 'presumption of *mens rea*'[102] into a fully fledged constitutional principle precluding criminal liability without moral fault would be the logical, direct, and therefore morally principled route to take. At all events, this is a task for which Article 6(2) ECHR's presumption of innocence was never intended, and could not readily be adapted. Either Parliament will in due course be prepared to concede to the judges a roving brief to inspect the morality of criminal prohibitions, or it will not. The presumption of innocence can only be an unhelpful distraction in this power-struggle for the conscience of criminal legislation.

In the meantime mounting criticism of Parliament's failings as a custodian of penal law has been richly deserved,[103] but it is unlikely that a kind of low-intensity guerrilla warfare through extravagant judicial interpretation will conduce to a stable constitutional settlement. Nor will the quality of criminal legislation be improved in the long run by judges taking it upon themselves to rewrite criminal statutes under cover of the Human Rights Act. Quite apart from the confusion, obfuscation, and error that are the inevitable sequel when statutory words are warped to assume meanings that stretch their normal everyday or even technical-legal usage to the boundaries of credulity, Parliament will not be encouraged to concede genuinely affirmative excuses if creative judicial interpretation threatens to broaden the scope of a defence beyond its intended parameters, or to result in an unwarranted 'declaration of incompatibility' under section 4 of the Human Rights Act. Like the doctor who, fearing a medical malpractice suit for lending incompetent assistance, leaves an accident victim bleeding by the roadside, governments will be tempted into 'defensive practices'—which ironically enough,

'English Criminal Procedure and the Human Rights Act 1998' (1999) 33 *Israel LR* 664, 668: 'What could a UK court do when confronted with a convicted prisoner if a future Parliament, tiring of legislation to safeguard human rights, had re-enacted the Act for the Boiling of Prisoners [22 Hen VIII Ch 9, 1530]? Surprisingly, perhaps, the answer seems to be that the court would have to sentence the prisoner to be boiled. If there is one matter of principle on which British politicians of all shades of opinion seem invariably to agree, it is the importance of preserving the sovereignty of Parliament.'

[102] See *R.* v. *K* [2002] 1 AC 462, HL; *B (A Minor)* v. *DPP* [2000] 2 AC 428, HL. The modern *locus classicus* is *Sweet* v. *Parsley* [1970] AC 132, 148–9, HL, *per* Lord Reid: 'there has for centuries been a presumption that Parliament did not intend to make criminals of persons who were in no way blameworthy in what they did. That means that whenever a section is silent as to *mens rea* there is a presumption that, in order to give effect to the will of Parliament, we must read in words appropriate to require *mens rea* . . . it is firmly established by a host of authorities that *mens rea* is an essential ingredient of every offence unless some reason can be found for holding that that is not necessary.' But cf. *Harrow London Borough Council* v. *Shah* [1999] 2 Cr. App. R. 457, DC, where the presumption was rebutted in relation to the 'quasi-criminal' offence of selling a national lottery ticket to a minor.

[103] See e.g. Andrew Ashworth, 'Is the Criminal Law A Lost Cause?' (2000) 116 LQR 225; Martin Wasik, 'Legislating in the Shadow of the Human Rights Act: The Criminal Justice and Police Act 2001' [2001] *Criminal LR* 931.

in this context, involves enacting exceptionless strict liability offences devoid of any dedicated affirmative excuses.[104]

In principle, Parliament should have at its disposal a wide range of conceptual tools and legislative techniques, so that it may strive to reflect more faithfully in its criminal legislation the contours of pertinent moral distinctions. Penal law will always be a relatively crude translation of more finely grained codes of public and private morality, but the legitimacy of state conviction and punishment hangs on the thread of continuity between applicable ethical standards and the practical administration of criminal justice. Preserving this thread intact is a collective effort that makes various demands on criminal justice professionals, one of which is judicial fidelity in statutory interpretation. Statutory interpretation faithful to Parliament's intention is perfectly compatible with judicial creativity in answering any question genuinely left open by legislative design or omission, and it is within these circumscribed parameters that the judges must demonstrate their commitment to defending human rights and promoting criminal justice. Moreover, if a statutory offence does directly contravene the presumption of innocence, and cannot realistically be 'read down' under section 3 of the Human Rights Act, the judges now have at their disposal the procedural means for clearly signalling Parliament's dereliction through a section 4 declaration of incompatibility. Less is sometimes more. The future prospects for the presumption of innocence in English law may depend as much on calculated judicial restraint, disappointing the inflated expectations of some of the presumption's most avid supporters, as it will on isolated instances of judicial activism and the residual liberal instincts of elected politicians.

---

[104] Cf. Lord Woolf's remark in *Attorney-General of Hong Kong v. Lee Kwong-kut* [1993] AC 951, 975, PC, echoing the concerns expressed by Jeffries and Stephan fifteen years before (nn. 30–3 above), that 'It would not assist the individuals who are charged with offences if, because of the approach adopted to "statutory defences" by the courts, the legislature, in order to avoid the risk of legislation being successfully challenged, did not include in the legislation a statutory defence to a charge.'

# 8

# Strict Liability for Criminal Offences in England and Wales Following Incorporation into English Law of the European Convention on Human Rights

*G. R. Sullivan*

## 1. Strict Liability Prior to Human Rights Act 1998

In 1798 Lord Kenyon CJ in *Fowler* v. *Padget* delivered what might have become a canonical text: '[I]t is a principle of natural justice, and of our law, that *actus non facit reum nisi mens sit rea*. The intent and the act must both concur to constitute the crime . . . '[1] Taken at face value, these words might have reflected a fundamental principle of English law, namely that the criminal law, with its language and practice of accusation, blame, and punishment, was not to be employed against blameless defendants. No doubt the regulatory and co-ordination requirements of a rapidly industrializing society required forms of state coercion not dependent on proof of any form of culpability. Yet those forms of coercion need not have involved direct recourse to the criminal law. One can imagine a counterfactual historical narrative where the resolute refusal of judges to entertain criminal liability without fault led to the creation of regimes of administrative regulation of industrial and other dangerous activities, regimes which did not culminate in an adversarial trial and were not dependent, at least in the first instance, on the imposition of fines and imprisonment.

The reality, as it proved, was very different. Even when spoken, Lord Kenyon's words contained an element of misleading rhetoric. If we understand, as we should, the concept of strict liability to include situations where liability may be imposed without proof of culpability as to one or more elements of the offence,

---

[1] (1798) 7 Term Rep. 509, 101 ER 1103.

the phenomenon of strict liability was already present.[2] By the mid-nineteenth century strict liability was well established. Moreover, the judges did not dispense with a requirement to prove some form of culpability only if required to do so by the clearly expressed intention of Parliament: from the very inception of regulatory criminal law, the courts were prepared to infer strict liability from the absence of any explicit requirement for proof of *mens rea* in the statutory specification of the offence.[3]

In large part, the incidence of strict liability has been confined to regulatory law; law where the emphasis is on the preservation of standards of safety, hygiene, and environmental integrity across the relevant industry or activity rather than the imposition of just deserts for individual offenders. Moreover, many of the defendants in such cases will be corporations rather than individuals.[4] That said, the division between crimes *mala in se* and *mala prohibita* is far from exact and is subject to the conventions and concerns of the time and place.[5] Furthermore, in English law, strict liability has strayed into areas incontestably, according to the mores of the time, *mala in se.*[6] Moreover, many regulatory offences carry the sting of possible imprisonment. The main bulwark against the encroachment of strict liability has been a presumption in favour of *mens rea* when interpreting a statute.

---

[2]  On the view expressed in the text, a crime such as constructive manslaughter is a crime of strict liability in one of its crucial aspects, namely the causing of death: a conviction for that form of manslaughter may follow without any culpability whatever for the causing of death, e.g. *Mallet* [1972] Crim. LR 260. That version of manslaughter was well established by the time of Lord Kenyon's words. Strict liability also existed, albeit exceptionally, at common law for contempt of court, criminal libel, and employer's liability for public nuisance.

[3]  As in *Woodrow* (1846) 15 M & W 404, 153 ER 907, the case considered by commentators to mark the inception of the modern statutory form of strict liability.

[4]  The European Convention for the Protection of Human Rights does protect companies, which have equal protection with individuals in the enjoyment of rights such as fair trial, presumption of innocence, and non-retroactive law. In our discussion of Art. 3, below in § 5, it will be assumed that the interdiction of inhuman and degrading treatment has no application for corporate defendants. While companies do have Convention-protected rights, when determining questions of proportionality under the Convention consequentialist concerns may be allowed more weight in the balance when the applicant is a company.

[5]  Driving while the worse for drink or despoiling the environment may have been perceived to fall on the regulatory side of the line some time ago but will be widely perceived as *mala in se* today. And, of course, regulatory crimes that allow for conviction without proof of culpability may be committed with great culpability; as when, say, a construction company deliberately flouts safety standards in the construction of tall buildings: *Gammon (Hong Kong) Ltd.* v. *A-G for Hong Kong* [1985] AC 1.

[6]  *Howells* [1977] QB 614 (possession of a firearm); *Vann and Davis* [1996] Crim. LR 52 (carrying a firearm in a public place); *K* [2001] 3 All ER 897 (sexual intercourse with a girl under 13). Moreover many serious drug offences under the Misuse of Drugs Act 1971 will be crimes of strict liability mitigated by defences following the meaning given to the term 'possession' by the House of Lords in *Warner* [1969] 2 AC 256. However, the severity of the Act may now be much mitigated by the decision of the House of Lords in *Lambert* [2001] 3 All ER 577, where a reverse burden placed on D to prove that he neither knew nor suspected or had reason to suspect that the item possessed was a controlled drug was, in the light of Art. 6(2) of the European Convention on Human Rights (presumption of innocence), reduced merely to an evidential burden entailing a full burden of proof of knowledge etc., on the part of the prosecution.

At the present time, the presumption is more salient than in the recent past but the leading cases that have reinvigorated this presumption nevertheless acknowledge a significant role for strict liability in the imposition of criminal responsibility.[7]

Currently, if we for the moment disregard the incorporation of the European Convention of Human Rights (ECHR), English law has no rule that criminal liability is precluded by a state of blamelessness (however that may be defined) at the time of the offence. The point may be made with particular force in respect of offences that do require *mens rea*. It has been ruled at the highest level that proof of *mens rea* is a formal principle and may, or may not, be indicative of fault in any substantive sense.[8] There has been a preparedness to countenance the conviction of individuals for serious stigmatic offences despite the court's own finding that the individual was without culpability. A fortiori, blamelessness per se cannot preclude conviction for an offence of strict liability—the very nature of strict liability precludes any defeasibility of a conviction because of blamelessness.[9] Further, strict liability has been imposed in circumstances where fundamental principles relating to the *actus reus* (or what should be regarded as fundamental principles) have been overridden. What has been called the *status offence* has been allowed full rein: it is possible to be convicted of an offence by meeting a statutory description—e.g. being an alien to whom leave to land has been refused—without perpetrating any voluntary act or omission.[10]

The question arises whether laws and practice relating to strict liability offences have been affected by the incorporation of the ECHR into domestic English law, following the passing of the Human Rights Act (HRA) 1998. In determining the nature and extent of any effect, the focus in this chapter will be on particular articles of the Convention rather than on the at large justifiability, in whole or in part, of strict liability. But before turning to those particular articles, we need briefly to discuss the implications of strict liability for justice and fairness to individuals. In particular, attention must be paid to arguments that emphasize the primacy, in terms of moral and legal responsibility, of the outcomes attributable to an agent's conduct rather than the disposition and motivation of the agent when causing those outcomes. If such arguments are persuasive, strict liability may be taken to be less problematic than has commonly been held to be the case. If this is

---

[7] *Sweet* v. *Parsley* [1970] AC 132; *B (a minor)* v. *DPP* [2002] 2 AC 428; *K* [2001] 3 All ER 897.

[8] *Yip Chiu-cheung* [1995] 1 AC 111 (PC); approved in *Kingston* [1995] 2 AC 355. In *Yip* an undercover policeman was praised for his resource and courage in bringing to justice a group of drug-traffickers but the policeman, apparently, was guilty of drug trafficking.

[9] Conversely, because culpability is irrelevant to liability for an offence of strict liability, evidence that the defendant acted in a blameworthy fashion cannot be put at the trial of an offence of strict liability: *Sandhu* [1997] Crim. LR 288.

[10] *Larsonneur* (1933) 24 Cr. App. R. 74; *Crump* v. *Gilmore* [1970] Crim. LR 28; *Winzar* v. *Chief Constable of Kent, The Times*, 28 March 1983.

so, there may be less intensity in the scrutiny applied to strict liability under the terms of the Convention.

## 2. Primary Outcome Responsibility

On the question of the responsibility of agents for the outcomes of their conduct, a line of thought strongly associated with Tony Honoré stresses the primacy of agency over issues of motive and disposition.[11] For Honoré, this 'primary outcome responsibility'[12] is an unavoidable concomitant of being human: we are, in large part, what we do. I am the man who scored the winning goal in the key cup-tie even if I am not a particularly good footballer and my goal was something of a fluke. My opponent, a much better footballer, who was denied what would have been a wonderful winning goal by a freak gust of wind, did not score. For that match, I am in credit for scoring a goal and he is not.

Who are eligible for credit and debit accounts based on outcomes? Persons who possess the normal range of competencies sufficient to participate as autonomous individuals in organized society.[13] Persons who participate in potentially dangerous activities are a particular object of concern for Honoré.[14] I decide to become a butcher. This can be a dangerous trade—meat sold may contain the prion for BSE or *e.coli* bacteria. Yet I am a good, hygienic butcher and for many years I enjoy the financial profit and standing in my community that comes from being a good butcher. But then, as in *Hobbs* v. *Winchester Corporation*,[15] I sell meat unfit for human consumption despite my reasonable reliance on veterinary certification that the meat is fit for consumption. Despite my exemplary record to date, in social terms, I cannot deny the description that I am the butcher who sold the meat that, say, caused the death of V. That must go on the debit side whatever protestations I may make. Yet overall, according to Honoré, I could still be winning: even for the most careful butcher each sale of meat is something of a gamble and most of these bets will turn out well. And such, so Honoré claims, is the position for persons in

---

[11] A. M. Honoré, *Responsibility and Fault* (Oxford 1999), Ch. 2.

[12] Strict liability, of course, is not confined to causing outcomes as in 'result crimes': many offences of strict liability will be 'conduct crimes' involving responsibility for failure to obtain licences, ensuring the condition of vehicles, the safety of machinery, adequate specifications for buildings, the filing of accounts and returns, etc. Liability for these strict liability offences is, in terms of justice and fairness to offenders, not so problematic because, typically, the offender should be aware of the regulatory environment of the activity concerned and of what is needed to conduct the activity lawfully. Yet in the sphere of result crimes, untoward consequences may occur whatever the amount of care taken, undermining the important liberty of participating in worthwhile and socially beneficial activities: see further J. Horder, 'Strict Liability, Statutory Construction and the Spirit of Liberty' (2002) 118 *Law Quarterly Review* 458.

[13] Honoré, *Responsibility*, 27–9. Honoré accepts that certain classes of people, such as young children, the insane, and some of the elderly, are ineligible for primary outcome responsibility.

[14] Ibid. 17–18.     [15] [1910] 2 KB 471.

other spheres involved in seeking benefits from taking risks in the course of otherwise lawful working and private activities. When things go wrong, and those things are attributable to our agency, we must take the rough with the smooth.[16]

For Honoré, this accounting is pre-moral. And therefore, a fortiori, pre-legal and legal consequences do not necessarily follow from causing bad outcomes.[17] Yet, for him, it is not objectionable and may even be useful if adverse legal consequences do follow from causing, without more, untoward events. This allocation of legal sanctions is justifiable because, as noted, Honoré believes persons gain more than they lose in taking risks in otherwise lawful activities, provided they possess a general capacity for taking risks which is not markedly below average. Therefore, there may be a strong case for making even a blameless butcher responsible for paying compensation to persons injured by his meat. There may even be a case for holding him criminally responsible, as was done in *Hobbs*.

Theorists who may find the imposition of criminal responsibility problematic in circumstances such as *Hobbs* would point to the butcher's lack of intention to sell bad meat, his reasonable reliance on veterinary certification, and his sheer bad luck in unwittingly using the services of a negligent veterinary surgeon. Honoré would be particularly dismissive of any reference to bad luck. For Honoré luck—risk—is intrinsic to human agency; misfortune, even blameless misfortune, should not be characterized as some form of disruption of the natural order in order to deflect assignments of legal responsibility.

Honoré's stress on the primacy of outcomes will strike a resonant chord with the responses of many people to the vagaries of life. Causal involvement in a tragic incident, however blameless, is an episode which will feature thereafter in the agent's biography; something to be explained away, perhaps, but not to be set aside and forgotten. By contrast, a near miss, however blameworthy in terms of the agent's motivation and disposition, and however potentially catastrophic, will rapidly fade from individual and collective memories. That risk is endemic, and that certain roles carry with them legal and social responsibilities as a risk bearer, must in part explain why, even in the sphere of criminal law, strict liability is so long-standing a feature of Anglo-American criminal law. Honoré's defence of a basic responsibility for outcomes reflects deep community sentiments about

---

[16] That risk-taking outcomes balance out in credit for persons who are in the class of those eligible for outcome responsibility is something that Honoré presents as the fact of the matter without any attempt to warrant this claim in empirical terms. That good luck my predominate over bad luck may be true for particular individuals but there must surely be individuals for whom the converse is the case as well as individuals for whom the balance is approximately even. Moreover, even a very fortunate individual, running into an isolated pocket of bad luck, may justifiably raise objection to conviction, blame, and punishment for a strict liability offence if the circumstances of the offence reveal no culpability on her part. See further S. Perry, 'Honoré on Responsibility for Outcomes', in P. Cane and J. Gardner (eds.), *Relating to Responsibility* (Oxford 2001), 66–8.

[17] Honoré, *Responsibility*, 30–1.

the appropriate legal and social sanctions to be imposed on persons causally responsible for injurious outcomes.

On occasion, Honoré assumes uncritically the imposition of criminal liability on a strict basis;[18] and, at least until the advent of the HRA 1998, strict liability has had a secure place in English criminal law. None the less, the central focus of his analysis is the law of tort.[19] This emphasis on the law of tort is important because of the different legal consequences and social meanings that flow from the imposition of liability in tort and a conviction for crime. While there are major differences between those theorists who argue that we should give salience to considerations of morality and corrective justice in the law of tort, and other scholars who emphasize issues of efficient risk-bearing and loss allocation,[20] none the less there is unanimity that the appropriate outcome of tort proceedings is the payment of compensation to a successful claimant. Theorists may differ, say, on whether legal regimes for product liability should be negligence-based or strict; but even under a strict regime, the defendant manufacturer whose product has been responsible for causing injury or loss to the claimant will be liable merely for damages and, at least in the terms of the law, is not censured or blamed for producing a dangerous product.

Contrast the blameless butcher in *Hobbes* v. *Winchester Corporation*.[21] Despite his blamelessness, he is not merely liable for selling bad meat but is *guilty* of selling bad meat. Because of his guilt, he will be censured and punished for selling the meat. It is all too easy to imagine circumstances where, despite a butcher's blamelessness, disastrous consequences arise from the sale of tainted meat: the *e.coli* bacteria may be present, causing many deaths. It is entirely possible that the seller may receive a custodial sentence in such an event.

It is an all-too-human response for persons afflicted by loss and bereavement to feel anger and resentment against those who are in some sense responsible for their changed circumstances. Further, it would be entirely appropriate for an agent responsible, in whole or in part, for causing loss and bereavement to express concern and regret even if, all things considered, there was nothing that the agent could or should have done to avert the tragedy (apart from not being in that line of business in the first place). An agent who merely protested his blamelessness and offered no words of sympathy or regret would cause great offence. The very fact of causal involvement engenders social duties of tact and concern. Indeed, there may be no objection in appropriate circumstances to treating causal responsibility per se as a sufficient predicate for a legal duty to pay compensation. Yet, from the perspective of a non-consequentialist justification of punishment, the agent's blamelessness should preclude resort to criminal sanctions.

---

[18] Ibid., 9, 16.

[19] Moreover there are times when Honoré concedes that primary responsibility for outcomes does not and should not necessarily imply grounds for punishment: ibid. 138–42.

[20] For an excellent survey of the appropriate grounds for liability in tort, see S. Perry, 'The Moral Foundations of Tort Law' (1992) *Iowa LR* 449. See too the collection of essays in D. Owen (ed.), *The Philosophical Foundations of Tort Law* (Oxford 1995).                      [21] [1910] 2 KB 471.

Accordingly, the imposition of criminal liability on a strict basis cannot be justified on a theory of basic responsibility for outcomes—at least, not for anyone unprepared to countenance systemic injustice for the sake of consequentialist gains. Convictions and punishment of persons without proof of culpability as to one or more elements of a criminal offence can be a form of mistreatment, capable of giving rise to what may broadly be described as human rights concerns. These concerns now have more legal salience with the incorporation of the ECHR into English law.

## 3. Strict Liability and Human Rights—a Brief Survey

It would be naive to assume that one of the ultimate consequences of the incorporation of the Convention into English law will be the demise of strict liability in English criminal law. Such an outcome is not inconceivable: it may be that proof of negligence by the defendant will be the default position for all criminal offences as a consequence of the infiltration of human rights standards. Yet such a development is far from assured and, even should it occur, it is likely to be a lengthy process.

One reason for caution about the impact of the Convention on strict criminal liability is the longevity of this phenomenon and its familiarity as the default form of liability in regulatory criminal law. Industrialization, and with it a burgeoning range of activities that required regulation, came to England and Wales before anything that could be described as an administrative state was in being. In the nineteenth century, much governance was local and an important part of that governance was the magistracy, a body that had long held regulatory as well as judicial functions.[22] It followed that much of the regulation of industrial and commercial activity was devolved to magistrates and, thereby, the enforcement of regulations cast in strict form was through a criminal rather than an administrative law process.

The legacy is an uneasy coexistence between the requirements for effective regulation and the exposure of the regulated to the blame, punishment, and censure that are an intrinsic part of the criminal process (even in its summary form). From a purely regulatory perspective, strict liability is extremely useful. Predominantly, the aim of regulators is to negotiate compliance with regulatory law, with prosecution regarded as a costly and time-consuming last resort.[23] None the less, the threat of prosecution is an important factor in inducing compliance.[24] The threat is all the more effective if the regulator can insist on improvements and modifications without becoming entangled in discussions about the reasonableness of what is required. Professor Leonard Leigh, in his study of strict

---

[22] J. Redlich, *Local Government in England* (London 1903).
[23] K. Hawkins, *Law as a Last Resort*: *Prosecution Decision-Making in a Regulatory Agency* (Oxford 2002).                    [24] Ibid. Ch. 10.

liability, identified effective enforcement in the regulatory sphere as the principal reason why strict liability is so deep-rooted.[25] The European Court of Human Rights has stressed the public interest in effective enforcement of regulatory law, when rejecting the argument that strict liability, of itself, breaches articles of the European Convention.[26] Likewise, the Court of Appeal in *Barnfather* v. *London Borough of Islington* declined to hold that, of itself, strict liability for a criminal offence entailed a breach of Convention rights.[27]

None the less, while it is important not to overestimate the likely impact of the Convention on criminal strict liability, it would be equally facile to dismiss the Convention as having no relevance to the legitimacy of liability and/or punishment on a strict basis. Many regulatory offences are punishable by imprisonment. It will be argued that acute human rights concerns arise when a custodial sentence follows a conviction imposed on a strict basis. The same applies if any sentence that constitutes a significant setback to the interests of the defendant (a large fine, disqualification, confiscation, etc.) is imposed without considering the culpability of the defendant. Furthermore, human rights issues arise in relation to that extreme form of strict liability known as the 'status' offence; and, additionally, where strict liability strays out of the regulatory sphere and becomes the basis of liability for serious, stigmatic offences.

Shortly, we will examine articles of the ECHR and associated jurisprudence that lend support to these contentions. First, however, something needs to be said about the framework and methodology of the HRA 1998, in order to assist an understanding of the likely impact of the Convention on strict liability in English and Welsh criminal law.

## 4. The Human Rights Act 1998—the Framework

The major purpose of the HRA 1998 is, within the framework of parliamentary sovereignty, to bring English statutory and common law into compliance with the minimum standards set by the ECHR. In the rare instances where liability at common law is imposed on a strict basis, the position under the Act is straightforward. If any trial or appellate court considers that the imposition of strict liability on the facts of the instant case breaches one or more of the defendants' Convention rights, the court is obliged to bring the applicable common law into line with the Convention.[28]

The position for statutory offences is not so clear-cut. Should imposition of liability for an offence be perceived as infringing one or more of the defendant's

---

[25] L. Leigh, *Strict Liability: A Study in Administrative Criminal Law* (London 1982). See also G. Richardson, 'Strict Liability for Regulatory Crime? The Empirical Research' [1981] *Criminal LR* 295.
    [26] *Salabiaku* v. *France* (1998) 13 EHRR 379; *Hanson* v. *Denmark* (16 March 2000, No 28971/95).         [27] [2003] 1 WLR 2318; noted by J. R. Spencer [2004] *Cambridge LJ* 10.
    [28] Under s. 6 of the HRA 1998, courts are obliged as 'public authorities' to act in a manner compatible with Convention rights. Accordingly when courts are resolving an issue at common law, they must do so in accordance with established Convention rights.

Convention rights, the responsibility of the courts is 'as far as it is possible' to interpret the statutory provision in a way that is compatible with the Convention.[29] In that interpretative task the court must take into account not merely the terms of any Convention article implicated in the case but also any relevant jurisprudence of the European Court.[30] If an interpretation compatible with the Convention is impossible, the court has no power to strike down the offending domestic legislation. The impugned provision remains in force and must be applied. If the court in question is the High Court or an appellate court, a 'declaration of incompatibility'[31] may be made; the declaration puts an onus but not an obligation on the responsible minister to introduce reformative legislation that aligns domestic law with Convention obligations.[32]

What is the position under the HRA 1998 when a legislative provision cannot be interpreted in a manner compatible with a Convention right and when a conviction for the offence will constitute a serious violation of an important right? Suppose, for example, that the defendant has succeeded in arguing that his conviction for a particular offence will constitute inhuman or degrading treatment under Article 3, or that the exclusion of evidence denied the fair trial guaranteed by Article 6. There will be a palpable tension between the duty of the court to uphold the validity of domestic legislation if it cannot be interpreted in a manner compatible with the Convention and the duty of the court, as a public authority, to act compatibly with the Convention. On occasion, this tension has been resolved by courts going beyond interpretation and resorting to reformulation of domestic law to render the law Convention-compatible.[33] Should a declaration of incompatibility be made, it seems that domestic law is to be applied whatever the implications for the defendant's Convention rights.[34]

## 5. Articles of the Convention which May Have Implications for Strict Liability

The following articles of the Convention may restrain conviction for strict liability offences and/or the mode and quantum of punishment following conviction for a strict liability offence.

---

[29] HRA 1998, s. 3.    [30] Ibid. s. 2.    [31] Ibid. s. 4.    [32] Ibid. s. 10.

[33] As seemed to occur in *R.* v. *A* [2002] 2 AC 545 and, arguably, in *Lambert* [2002] 2 AC 545. It may be that these cases are the high-water mark of an interpretative approach that effectively allowed a degree of rewriting of provisions held to infringe Convention rights. Recent authority lays stress on confining the judicial task under HRA 1998 to the interpretation rather than the reformulation of statutory provisions and a greater emphasis on Parliamentary sovereignty: *R. (on the application of Anderson)* v. *Secretary of State for the Home Department* [2003] 1 AC 837; *Re S, Re W* [2002] 2 AC 291; *Bellinger* v. *Bellinger* [2003] 2 AC 437. See further A. Kavanagh, 'Statutory Interpretation and Human Rights after *Anderson*: A More Contextual Approach' [2004] Public Law 537. But see now *A-G's Reference (No 4 of 2002)* [2004] UKHL 43 where the House of Lords interpreted a provision requiring a defendant 'to prove' a statutory defence as imposing merely an evidential burden.    [34] *Lichniak* [2002] 4 All ER 1122.

*Article 3—Proscription of torture and inhuman and degrading treatment*
No one shall be subjected to torture or to inhuman or degrading treatment or punishment.

*Article 6(1)—Right to fair trial*
In the determination . . . of any criminal charge against him, everyone is entitled to a fair and public hearing within a reasonable time by an independent and impartial tribunal established by law.

*Article 6(2)—Presumption of innocence*
Everyone charged with a criminal offence shall be presumed innocent until proved guilty according to law.

*Article 7—Proscription of retroactive criminal law*
No one shall be held guilty of any criminal offence on account of any act or omission which did not constitute a criminal offence under national or international law at the time when it was committed.

*Article 1, First Protocol—Right to peaceful enjoyment of possessions*
Every natural or legal person is entitled to the peaceful enjoyment of his possessions. No one shall be deprived of his possessions except in the public interest and subject to the conditions provided for by law and by the general principles of international law.

[This] shall not, however, in any way impair the right of a State to enforce such laws as it deems necessary to control the use of property in accordance with the general interest or to secure the payment of taxes or other contributions or penalties.

The potential impact of these articles will now be examined.

## Article 3: Proscription of Torture and Inhuman and Degrading Treatment

Unquestionably, strong feelings of injustice arise on the part of persons who suffer criminal convictions for conduct they consider blameless, feelings that arise even when convicted for minor regulatory offences. Take the Shah family, who were found to have managed their convenience store in an exemplary fashion, taking every reasonable precaution to comply with law. Despite their care and circumspection, in the course of the business a lottery ticket was sold to a person under the age of 16. No negligence was involved; there was nothing about the purchaser to put anyone on notice that she was aged under 16.

In confirming the conviction of the proprietor, Mr Shah, for selling a lottery ticket to an under-age person, the Divisional Court took judicial notice of his sense of injustice and complimented him on the way his business was run. Yet the confirmation of his conviction was straightforward: on establishing the fact of the sale and the age of the purchaser, a conviction for the offence necessarily followed.[35] And Honoré might counsel Mr Shah not to feel his grievance too keenly. He wanted to profit from selling lottery tickets. Among potential purchasers will be that class of persons whose age on first scrutiny might be anything from, say, 13 to 18 years old. Doubtless Mr Shah took the profit from inadvertent under-age sales that did not result in prosecution. The risk of prosecution is just part of the territory, or so it might be argued.

Since the advent of the HRA 1998, could someone in the position of a Shah, blamelessly committing a regulatory offence, raise any objection to conviction within the terms of Article 3?[36] The threshold is high—does a conviction for a strict liability offence constitute inhuman or degrading treatment? One appellate judge, Arden LJ, writing extra-judicially, considers that the conviction of a blameless defendant for a regulatory offence might raise an Article 3 issue. She gives the example of a proprietor of a business who is prosecuted for causing pollution in the course of his business activities. The pollution occurred without fault on his part and he had taken all the steps required to rectify the damage caused. She raises as a serious possibility that a court, under the interpretative leeway allowed by section 3 of the HRA 1998, may write in a due diligence defence to avoid contravening Article 3.[37]

This seems a surprising conclusion. Although controversial, strict liability in the field of regulatory criminal law has been a familiar feature of Anglo-American legal systems for very many years. A considerable proportion of the defendants will have been corporations and no Article 3 concerns are raised by the conviction of corporations.[38] That leaves the question of blameless individuals convicted of strict liability offences. If the conviction per se of a blameless individual for a regulatory offence may implicate Article 3, then there have been widespread and long-standing infringements of a fundamental right. The familiarity and repetition of abuse in no way justify abuse, but it is important to retain perspective. The prevalence and longevity of strict liability might be said to reflect a general and stable judgment that acceptable standards of safety, hygiene, and environmental integrity require effective regulation and that the imposition of strict liability for regulatory crime is a proportionate response by legislatures in terms of what is at stake for the welfare of everyone. Even if not persuaded by that

---

[35] *London Borough of Harrow* v. *Shah* [2002] 1 WLR 83.

[36] It may be noted that the offence for which Shah was convicted carried a maximum penalty of two years' imprisonment.

[37] M. Arden, 'Criminal Law at the Crossroads: The Impact of Human Rights from the Law Commission's Perspective and the Need for a Code' [1999] *Criminal LR* 439. But see the cases at n. 33, deprecating 'writing in' rather than interpretation of the text.

[38] There is no direct authority for this conclusion but it is entailed by any conception of companies as non-natural entities. Conceivably, very harsh treatment of companies *qua* companies might raise Art. 3 concerns if companies are conceived of as natural entities, as some theorists contend. Yet even a theorist committed to a naturalistic conception of companies should accept they remain non-human entities.

line of consequentialist argument, the fact that so many judges and officials in representative democracies adhere to it should give rise to hesitation before castigating strict liability per se as inhuman and degrading. Even opponents of strict liability may concede that not every conviction on that basis involves a serious violation of human rights.

There is no case that directly raises the compatibility of strict liability with Article 3 but the indications are that the argument would fail. In *Muhammed* it was stated in the context of an Article 7 challenge that, in terms of the Convention taken as a whole, there was nothing objectionable in principle with strict liability.[39] That view was also taken in the Article 6 cases of *Barnfather* v. *London Borough of Islington Education Authority*[40] and *International Transport Roth GMBH and others* v. *Secretary of State for the Home Department*.[41] There is very little jurisprudence from the European Court on strict liability but what there is indicates that strict liability, without more, does not infringe any Convention right.[42]

A different verdict might be reached if liability for a serious stigmatic offence is imposed on a strict basis. The conviction for a serious drug offence upheld by the Court of Appeal in *Sweet* v. *Parsley*[43] would, arguably, implicate Article 3. Recall that, until the position was rectified by the House of Lords,[44] a perfectly innocent letting of property to tenants led to a conviction for being concerned in the management of premises on which cannabis was consumed. Article 3 could and should be invoked to stop that form of abuse. To turn blameless conduct into the stuff of an offence redolent of serious offending is to defame and degrade the defendant by the very fact of conviction alone. Had the conviction been sustained by the House of Lords, Ms Sweet would have been associated with an offence carrying a maximum penalty of 14 years, an offence strongly associated with the encouragement or condonation of drug taking for commercial gain. By disclosing such a conviction in, say, a job application form, she would surrender her status as a person of good character. To undermine her character in that fashion would, in the language of Article 3, be to degrade her and, in the light of the blameless circumstances associated with her conviction, would have been, again to use the terms of Article 3, an inhuman thing to do. To avoid such injustice, an appropriate *mens rea* term should be read into the statutory specification of the offence, as was done by the House of Lords in *Sweet* v. *Parsley*. The House inferred an intention by Parliament not to convict blameless persons for such a serious offence. This inference would now be fortified by section 3 of the HRA 1998.

---

[39] [2002] EWCA Crim. 1856.        [40] [2003] 1 WLR 2318.        [41] [2003] QB 728.
[42] In *Salabiaku* v. *France* (1998) 13 EHRR 379, a rebuttable presumption of an intent to smuggle based on mere possession of contraband in a customs area was upheld as legitimate on the facts; and in *Hanson* v. *Denmark* (16 March 2000, No 28971/95) the imposition of strict liability for an offence of driving an excessive number of hours was not seen to raise a Convention issue, the case being dismissed at the preliminary stage. In both cases, strict liability was seen as something that needed justification but which could be justified if liability on the facts under consideration was a proportionate response to the social mischief the offence engaged.        [43] [1968] 2 QB 418.
[44] [1970] AC 132.

Any breach of Article 3 by way of convicting a blameless defendant would be gravely compounded if the defendant were sent to prison following the conviction. It is notable that, in *Kebilene*, Laws LJ expressed concern that an offence that did not require *mens rea* carried a maximum prison term of 10 years.[45] The Canadian Supreme Court has curtailed some strict liability offences which may lead to imprisonment.[46] It would be a salutary principle if Article 3 were to be read as imposing a bar on the imprisonment of blameless persons.

It would be inappropriate, however, if such a prohibition on imprisonment of blameless persons were to take the form of a categorical refusal to allow imprisonment for offences of strict liability. A seller of food may commit the strict liability offence of selling food unfit for human consumption and do so by selling food he knows to be unfit, thereby demonstrating a serious form of culpability that may deserve to be punished by imprisonment. Because of the important decision in *Sandhu*,[47] evidence of his knowledge of the unfitness of the food must not be put at trial because of its irrelevance to the grounds of conviction and its prejudicial effect. But when sentencing the defendant, it would be crucial to resolve whether imprisonment was merited.[48]

## Article 6(1): Right to Fair Trial

The right guaranteed by Article 6(1) to a fair and impartial trial is a right of due process which has, it seems, no implications for the substantive law to be applied at the trial. English law has drawn a sharp line between the trial process on the one hand and the applicable law on the other. A trial may be fair notwithstanding the draconian quality of the substantive law that was applied.[49]

However, there is one extreme form of strict liability that may contravene the right to fair trial: where liability is imposed for the acquisition of a proscribed status—e.g. being an alien, present in the United Kingdom, after leave to land has been refused—if that status is acquired without any voluntary act or omission on the part of the defendant.

A striking illustration is the case of *Larsonneur*,[50] where the defendant was forcibly removed from what is now the Republic of Ireland and taken into police custody in England. As a French citizen, the defendant was, in the terminology then used, an alien. From police custody, she was taken to court to be tried for the offence of being an alien, present in the United Kingdom, after leave to land had been refused. The refusal of leave to land had occurred some weeks ago at

---

[45] [1999] 3 WLR 175, 201.
[46] *References re Section 94(2) of Motor Vehicle Act (BC)* (1986) 48 CR (3d) 289.
[47] [1997] Crim. LR 288.
[48] If facts material to sentence are disputed by the defence they would have to be established beyond reasonable doubt: *Newton* (1982) 77 Cr. App. R. 13.
[49] *Concannon* [2002] Crim. LR 213; *Gemmel* [2003] 1 Cr. App. R. 343.
[50] (1933) 24 Cr. App. R. 74.

Southampton; on being refused entry there, the defendant had made her way to Ireland. But what of the presence in England? Naturally, the defendant emphasized that her return to England was completely involuntary, a product of *force majeure*. This observation did not help her: according to Lord Hewart CJ, 'The circumstances of her entry are perfectly immaterial.'[51]

One might hope that conviction for an offence arising from such circumstances might sustain an Article 3 challenge. Yet success cannot be assured; the offence is regulatory and there is great political and social pressure for effective immigration law. Moreover, *Larsonneur* is by no means an isolated case.[52] None the less, there may be an argument under Article 6(1). The form of the argument proposed is that a fair trial requires a procedure that is truly a trial, whereas what is involved on facts such as *Larsonneur* is the mere simulacrum of a trial.

The argument can be sharply presented by what may seem an absurd example. Imagine it to be an offence to have green eyes. In what sense could *criminal* proceedings be held to determine whether or not a defendant is guilty of this offence? To be sure, the setting, language, and process of the standard criminal trial could be followed to the letter. A defendant might plead not guilty to the charge. Some legally applicable standard of greenness would have to be resolved. There could well be borderline cases, with a clash of expert testimony entailing long deliberation by the jury before a verdict could be given. But in what substantive sense would this fact-finding exercise correspond to a criminal trial, properly so called? To what extent can be a person be *guilty* of possessing a particular form of genetic endowment? It might be that the bizarre legislation we are discussing allows green-eyed persons to avoid conviction by wearing contact lenses of a colour other than green. Then it would not be incoherent to say of green-eyed persons who spurn the contact lens option that they are truly guilty of an offence. Their defiance (however justified in moral terms) is something to which they can be held to account. But absent that possibility, it is surely incoherent to find someone 'guilty' of being green-eyed.

This conclusion rests on the premiss that a criminal trial must involve a process leading to proof of some voluntary act or omission on the part of the defendant. As the contact-lens defence illustrates, satisfaction of this condition is still compatible with extreme forms of injustice. Yet the injustice, if such a defence were allowed, would at least be a form of injustice imposed through the process of a criminal trial. My argument is not that status offences are inimical to the holding of trials. Rather, it is that a criminal trial in any substantive sense requires that the proscribed status rests on proof of a voluntary act whereby the status was acquired, or proof of some omission whereby the defendant failed to divest himself of the status. To hold a criminal trial there must be something for which the defendant is held to account and, absent proof of some voluntary act or omission, that condition does not hold.

---

[51] Ibid. 75.        [52] See the cases below, at nn. 54, 55.

Determining whether the voluntary act or omission requirement is present may involve some difficult questions relating to the applicable base-line. For example, it is an offence under English law to be a parent of a child of compulsory school age who is not in regular attendance at school.[53] The courts have consistently ruled that no knowledge of the child's truancy or any other form of culpability is necessary to convict a parent of this offence, and liability on these terms has withstood challenge under the terms of Article 6(2).[54] Suppose that the defendant adopts a 10-year-old child known for persistent truancy. If, despite the best efforts of the adoptive parent, truancy persists, though liability on the terms accepted by English law is manifestly unjust, the voluntary act requirement is arguably satisfied—the act of adoption made acquisition of the proscribed status a possible outcome. More typical would be a case like *Crump* v. *Gilmore*,[55] where the blameless natural parent's liability was entirely a product of the devious plausibility of the child. The decision to have a child would be unlikely to be seen as a voluntary act that led to the acquisition of the proscribed status. And there will be clear-cut cases. In *Larsonneur*, there was nothing to put the defendant on notice that going to Ireland would lead to acquisition of a proscribed status in the United Kingdom.[56] Likewise, in *Lim Chin Aik*,[57] the defendant's status as a lawful resident in Singapore was changed to an illegal status by unpublished ordinance. For such cases, a ruling under section 3 of the HRA 1998 that Article 6(1) requires status offences to be premised on a voluntary act or omission would offer some protection against an extreme form of liability.

Status offences aside, Article 6(1) is likely to have no impact on convictions for strict liability offences provided what needs to be proved is proved by a fair procedure. None the less, Article 6(1) may have a significant impact on the sentencing process for strict liability offences. In *International Transport Roth CMBH and others* v. *Secretary of State for Home Department*,[58] the Court of Appeal considered a legislative provision that imposed a fixed penalty of £2,000 for each clandestine entrant brought into the United Kingdom by lorry. It was held that the provision, though cast in civil form, was in substance criminal and contravened Article 6(1). Liability to make payment could be triggered by blameless conduct and, *qua* liability, was held to be permissible under Article 6(1).

---

[53] Education Act 1996, s. 444(1).

[54] *Barnfather* v. *London Borough of Islington Education Authority* [2003] EWHC 418 (Admin.). From the incomplete version of the facts presented at the judicial review hearing, the mother of the child does not appear to have made any act or omission associated with her child's truancy. The argument proposed in the text was not put, but a similar argument was put and succeeded in the Scottish trial case of *O'Hagan* v. *Rea* [2001] SLT (ShCt) 30. For a penetrating discussion of the law and policy of this truancy offence see Horder, 'Whose Values Should Determine When Liability is Strict?', this volume, Ch. 5.    [55] [1970] Crim. LR 28.

[56] In '*Larsonneur* Revisited' [1976] *Criminal LR* 276, David Lanham has researched the background of the case and proposes that Mme Larsonneur was not quite a hapless victim of circumstances. Be this as it may, that is what she appears to be from the court record.

[57] [1963] AC 160.    [58] [2002] EWCA Civ. 158; [2003] 1 WLR 2318.

However, in terms of penalty, Article 6(1) was taken by the Court of Appeal to require an investigation of the culpability of defendants at the sentencing stage in order to make a punitive response that was proportionate to the wrongdoing involved. *International Transport* clearly has implications beyond fixed penalties. Punishment is not merely a function of the consequences—a lorry driver who has inadvertently carried into the country twelve clandestine entrants does not necessarily merit a greater punishment than a driver who has inadvertently transported only one. As the culpability of the defendant must not be examined at the trial stage of a strict liability offence,[59] the implication of *Roth* is that culpability must be properly examined at the sentencing stage. This reading of *Roth* is fortified by the earlier (pre-HRA 1998) case of *Newton*,[60] which decides that any fact disputed at the sentencing stage must be established by the prosecutor or judge beyond any reasonable doubt.

## Article 6(2): Presumption of Innocence

The presumption of innocence deals with the burden of proof regarding the elements of the offence and any defences: it has no necessary bearing on what those elements are or whether a defence should be provided. Accordingly, if there were an offence of selling food unfit for human consumption subject to a defence that the defendant neither knew, nor suspected or had reasonable cause to know or suspect that the food was unfit, Article 6(2) would be relevant to that defence.[61] If, however, the legislature were simply to proscribe the selling of unfit food, without more, Article 6(2) would be engaged only to the extent of proof of a sale of unfit food.

This proposition, that Article 6(2) relates solely to matters of proof and does not concern the definition and content of offences, is challenged in an interesting paper by Tadros and Tierney.[62] They argue that strict liability offences should not necessarily be taken, as it were, at face value, and advise looking beneath the 'surface' of strict liability offences to discern their 'true' nature and content. By way of example, they address the offence of being a parent of a child of compulsory school age who is not regularly attending school. As we have already noted, this offence has been interpreted in a draconian way, imposing a form of status liability on defendants who may be completely blameless in the matter of the child's non-attendance at school.

---

[59] *Sandhu* [1997] Crim. LR 288.          [60] (1982) 77 Cr. App. R. 13.

[61] The formulation in the text follows the drafting of s. 28 of the Misuse of Drugs Act 1971, a formulation found to offend Art. 6(2) in *Lambert* [2001] 3 All ER 577. A due diligence defence is provided by the Food Safety Act 1990 for the offence of selling unfit food with the onus of proof on the defendant. It may well be that that provision would survive Art. 6(2) scrutiny. Since the decision in *Lambert*, reverse burdens have been upheld as legitimate on the basis of a proportionality test (see the cases above at n. 33, especially *A-G's Reference (No 4 of 2002)* [2004] UKHL 43). It is noteworthy that the proportionality doctrine is taken to apply to issues arising under Art. 6(2) notwithstanding that the presumption of innocence is expressed in terms of an absolute right.

[62] 'The Presumption of Innocence and the Human Rights Act' (2004) 67 *Modern LR* 402.

By way of amelioration, I have suggested that Article 6(1) should be interpreted so as to demand that any form of status liability should require proof of a voluntary act or omission. Tadros and Tierney go further, and invoke Article 6(2) in order to remove the strictness of this and, by extension, other offences. Essentially, their position is that a legislature, acting in good faith, could not have intended blameless parents to be within the purview of this offence.[63] Using that assumption to go, in their terminology, beneath the surface of the offence, they conclude that the offence, properly conceived, must be limited to parents who are in some sense at fault in not ensuring the child's attendance. Therefore, they argue, a definitional element of the offence must include an element of culpability, entailing at least proof of a lack of due care on the part of the parents. Courts, in allowing convictions of blameless parents, will contravene Article 6(2) by dispensing with proof of this culpability; which, on the Tadros/Tierney analysis, is an integral part of the definition of the offence when its true nature is revealed.

The flaw in their analysis is the assumption that a legislature, acting in good faith, could never be taken to intend the imposition of criminal liability on blameless parents. In effect, their argument amounts to an assertion that proof of negligence should be the default position for the offence and that a breach of Article 6(2) will occur whenever liability is imposed without proof of, at least, negligence. But, of course, the statute book is replete with examples of the most explicit kind of strict liability offences fully intended by the legislature to operate in a strict fashion. A legislature may determine, in good faith, that a beneficient policy—universal education—will only be effectively implemented on a strict basis. It may well be that such a legislature is misguided, both in its own terms (proof of neglect on the part of the parents may not hamper effective implementation of the policy of universal education) and in principle (any policy, however worthwhile, should not be implemented by way of convicting blameless people). But good faith is compatible with error. Therefore, it cannot be assumed that the legislature intended some form of culpability to be an integral part of the offence and that an absence of proof of that culpability necessarily entails breach of Article 6(2).

None the less, Article 6(2) should be interpreted to protect against the imposition of what may be regarded as the ultimate form of strict liability, a liability that may be imposed without proof of anything, either *actus reus* or *mens rea*. Suppose a situation whereby any person licensed to sell food can be obliged, as a condition of the licence, to prove that the food he has sold was, in all cases, fit for human consumption. Failure to prove the fitness of all food sold entails liability for a criminal offence. To describe this offence as a crime of strict liability does not really do justice to the extreme form of liability involved. Strict liability, properly

---

[63] Ibid. 422–44. For further discussion of the form of culpability that should be required for this offence, see Horder's Ch. 5 in this volume, at n. 25 and associated text.

so called, is liability that may be imposed without proof of culpability as to one or more elements of the offence; as in the case of an offence which proscribes, without more, the selling of food unfit for consumption. Yet the offence conjectured here is even more objectionable: it dispenses with proof of anything, and places sellers of food under an obligation continually to prove that they should not be criminalized.

Such extreme forms of liability are rare.[64] More likely would be an offence obliging sellers to prove that food sold was fit for consumption once the prosecution has established a reasonable suspicion that the seller has sold unfit food. Licence-holders would be liable to conviction only if they failed to dispel a reasonable suspicion of selling unfit food. Yet they would still remain exposed to what I have described as the ultimate form of strict liability, a liability imposed without proof of any element of conduct or event capable of being the gravamen of the offence, merely proof that such an element might have occurred. Could Article 6(2) be invoked to require proof that the defendant had, in fact, sold unfit food?

In a trenchant article, Paul Roberts argues for a negative response to the question just posed.[65] Adapting his argument to our food-seller example, his essential premiss, with which I agree, is that Article 6(2) is concerned with the requirement to prove the elements of the offence charged; it has no bearing on what those elements should be. Roberts maintains that all Article 6(2) mandates in the case we have posed is that it is for the prosecution to prove a reasonable suspicion. By way of answer to the assertion we have made above—that the revised provision still allows liability to be imposed without proof of conduct or event—Roberts insists that the offence, as defined by the legislature, has been proved. On his view, the offence consists of selling food in circumstances that give rise to a reasonable suspicion that it is unfit for human consumption. Placing a probative burden on the seller to establish that the food is fit for consumption merely provides a defence that mitigates the rigour of the primary offence and does not contravene Article 6(2).

The target of Roberts's argument is the decision of the Divisional Court and *dicta* of the House of Lords in the *Kebilene* litigation.[66] The case concerned the serious offence of possessing any item in circumstances giving rise to a reasonable suspicion that it was connected with or used for terrorist activity. Should such a reasonable suspicion be established, a defendant was[66A] liable for the offence unless

[64] But see the Prevention of Bribery Ordinance 1980 (Hong Kong), s. 10(1): 'Any person who, being or having been a Crown servant—(a) maintains a standard of living above that which is commensurate with his present or past official emoluments . . . shall, unless he gives a satisfactory explanation to the court as to how he was able to maintain such a standard of living . . . be guilty of an offence.'

[65] 'The Presumption of Innocence Brought Home? *Kebilene* Deconstructed' (2002) 118 *Law Quarterly Review* 41. Roberts now elaborates his position in this volume: 'Strict Liability and the Presumption of Innocence: An Exposé of Functionalist Assumptions', Ch. 7.

[66] *R. v. DPP, ex p Kebilene* [2000] 2 AC 326.

[66A] But see now the Terrorism Act 2000, ss. 57, 118(2).

he could prove that his possession of the item was *not* connected with or used for terrorist activity. It was a majority view in the Divisional Court, and the House of Lords, that the gravamen of this offence was the possession of an item that, in fact, had a terrorist connection or use. Accordingly, requiring a defendant to disprove such a connection or use was to rebut the presumption of innocence, thereby contravening Article 6(2). For Roberts, by contrast, the gravamen of the offence was proof of possessing an article giving rise to a reasonable suspicion of such connection or use and there was, therefore, no contravention of Article 6(2).

Which view is to be preferred? It is submitted that the Roberts view is untenable. It would be a flagrant breach of the harm principle to penalize persons merely suspected of being associated with an immediate or more remote harm. The harm principle can accommodate the penalizing of conduct remote to a harm, provided it is shown to be associated with the ultimate harm.[67] Accordingly, there can be no objection to an offence that proscribes the possession of articles that the possessor *intended* to use in connection with terrorist activity. But where all that is required is proof of a reasonable suspicion of such use, conduct wholly innocent of any connection with the harm identified in the offence is swept into the net. Inevitably, certain circumstances will give rise to plausible suspicions against persons whose actual motivation and conduct are impeccable. It is an essential safeguard of liberal democracy that persons merely under suspicion should not be obliged, on pain of conviction and punishment, to clear their name. *Kebilene* gives ground for some optimism that, where an offence specifies some form of proscribed conduct (e.g. terrorist activity or assisting such activity), mere proof that the defendant may be reasonably suspected of such conduct will not satisfy the presumption of innocence guaranteed by Article 6(2).

Yet the jurisprudence on Article 6(2) does not absolutely guarantee that this approach will be taken. Although some decisions of English courts seek to maximize the impact of Article 6(2), there are other English decisions that attenuate and even override Article 6(2), where the laws at issue are considered a proportionate response to the public interest in the effective enforcement of particular laws. This relaxed approach to the presumption of innocence has, unfortunately, been extended to serious offences and to matters that go clearly to the gravamen of the offence. The English jurisprudence on Article 6(2) is in some disarray.[68]

---

[67] A. von Hirsch, 'Extending the Harm Principle: "Remote" Harms and Fair Imputation', in A. P. Simester and A. T. H. Smith (eds.), *Harm and Culpability* (Oxford 1996), 259.

[68] Contrast the firm assertion of the presumption of innocence by the House of Lords in *Lambert* [2001] 3 All ER 577 and *Kebilene* [2000] 2 AC 326 with the greater readiness to justify reverse burdens on a test of proportionality on the part of the House of Lords in *Johnstone* [2003] 1 WLR 1736. The most recent decision by the House of Lords in *A-G's Reference (No 4 of 2002)* [2004] UKHL 43 strikes a middle way between *Johnstone* and *Lambert* and *Kebilene*, a stance that does little to resolve the uncertainty in this area of law.

There is, however, one form of protection for cases where liability is imposed without proof of one or more elements of the offence or without disproof of any defence raised by the facts. Earlier, it was argued that Article 6(1) as interpreted by the Court of Appeal in *International Transport* required a proper examination of the culpability of offenders before passing sentence.[69] Article 6(1), as interpreted, reinforces the important case of *Newton*,[70] a case that obliges a sentencer to resolve any disputed fact that is relevant to the sentencing decision on the criminal standard of proof.

The protection provided may be illustrated by way of example. Take D, found in possession of a large quantity of fertilizer in his garden shed. It is established at trial that he is acquainted with persons who are engaged in terrorist activity, although there is no proof that he himself has any association with such activity. None the less, a trial judge, taking the approach advocated by Paul Roberts, has directed the jury that they may find D guilty of the offence of possessing articles in circumstances giving rise to a reasonable suspicion that they may be connected or used for terrorist activity unless D has persuaded them that his use or intended use of the fertilizer was innocent.

At his trial, let us say, D testified that he was a keen gardener and had bought fertilizer in such quantities for himself and gardening friends to obtain bulk discount. None the less, the jury found him guilty of the offence. On what basis can the judge pass sentence? All that she can take from the jury's verdict is that he failed to persuade the jury that his exculpatory story was true. But, of course, it has not been proved to be false on a criminal standard of proof.

If, at the sentencing hearing, D still stands by his gardening story, Article 6(1) (as interpreted in *International Transport*, reinforced by the pre-HRA Act case of *Newton*) will require the sentencing judge to assure herself, beyond reasonable doubt, that D's story is false. What if she thinks it is likely to be false but is unsure? In that event she is obliged under *Newton* not to pass any sentence on D which assumes the falsity of his story. Accordingly, the basis for any custodial sentence— indeed for any punitive response whatever—is completely undermined. A pyrrhic victory for the prosecution, and an additional reason for rejecting the analysis of Roberts and following the approach in *Kebiline*.[71]

## Article 7: Proscription of Retroactive Criminal Law

On its face, Article 7 offers protection merely against retroactive criminal law. However, the jurisprudence of the European Court extends Article 7 protection

---

[69] See above, text at n. 58.      [70] (1982) 77 Cr. App. R. 13.

[71] The conclusion just reached could be challenged on the basis that the law governing the factual basis for sentencing when liability is imposed under a reverse burden of proof does not seem to have been addressed   a wide search found no relevant authorities. Conceivably, the prosecution might contend that the reverse burden applied at trial should influence the sentencing stage. In our terrorist/gardener example, the argument might be made that D must be treated for sentencing purposes as a terrorist or assister of terrorism if he cannot prove that he is innocent of any terrorist

beyond strict retroactivity and requires of signatory states that their criminal law meets a 'quality of law' benchmark. Of particular concern to us is the understanding that Article 7 requires minimum standards of clarity and precision, enabling citizens[72] and their legal advisers[73] to ascertain with reasonable assurance where they stand in terms of the potential for their conduct to attract criminal liability.

It will be recalled that H. L. A. Hart identified the loss of autonomy and predictability as a major cost of dispensing with *mens rea*.[74] Take away the need for dishonesty and an intent to deprive permanently, and forgetting to return that borrowed book may constitute theft. Absent-mindedly bumping into a fellow pedestrian may open up liability for battery. As things stand now, with a degree of circumspection and luck, a life can be planned that will be free from charges of theft and assault.

Contrast that relative freedom and predictability with the situation of those responsible for the management of *Smedleys Ltd*. A caterpillar is found in a can of peas. It is rolled up into a ball and is the very size and density (as well as colour) of the standard issue pea. Sterilized by the canning process it is quite harmless, indeed edible. A state-of-the-art canning process backed up by eagle-eyed inspection could, according to evidence accepted by the court, only stop so many caterpillars—some were bound to get through. But if a caterpillar was found in a can bought by a member of the public, the company committed an offence whatever the level of care achieved: so the House of Lords confirmed in *Smedleys Ltd*. v. *Breed*.[75] What is the management of Smedleys to do? The only sure way to stop offending is to stop canning. But if the business is to carry on, as it did, further offences were inevitable. From one perspective, the company knew exactly where it stood. From another perspective, it was in a state of radical uncertainty. It could make some estimate of how many cans in its total production would have a caterpillar supplement. Yet how many trials and convictions might ensue would be impossible to pin down. A company such as Smedleys can absorb these uncertainties, and the costs of appellate litigation, into its risk assessments and financial contingencies. Yet the proprietor of a small business in similar circumstances might well not be able to sustain such costs and pressures.

Does the dilemma faced by Smedleys—stop canning or face criminal liability otherwise beyond avoidance and control—raise an Article 7 issue? Is the degree of legal stability guaranteed by Article 7 solely a matter of texts and their interpretation? If it is, the position of Smedley's could not be more clear-cut; what facts constituted an offence could be pellucidly stated. Surely, however, a richer

connection. But that is a non sequiter. The most that can be made of his conviction for sentencing purposes unless a terrorist connection is actually proved is that he can reasonably be suspected of connection with terrorist activity. And what, precisely, is the appropriate sentence for that?

[72] *G* v. *France* (1995) 21 EHRR 288.

[73] That legal advice may be necessary to elucidate the scope of an offence does not entail that it is not 'reasonably certain' for the purposes of Art. 7: *Cantoni* v. *France*, RJD 1996–V1614.

[74] *Punishment and Responsibility* (Oxford 1968), Chs. 1, 7.          [75] [1974] AC 839.

notion of fair warning could and should accommodate the perspective of persons who in the context of socially useful activities are seeking with all due diligence to organize their affairs in a way that complies with the law.

The Article 7 jurisprudence is (outside the context of temporal retroactivity) almost exclusively concerned with the clarity of text, standards, and interpretation.[76] The way in which clearly expressed yet strict offences may undermine freedom of choice and certainty in planning has hardly been addressed in the Article 7 jurisprudence.[77] The contribution that culpability elements can make to fair warning would be advanced if all offences of strict liability were subject to a due diligence defence. This would allow managers of businesses, among others, to plan their activities in such a fashion as to avoid criminal convictions. Such an argument is immanent in the constellation of values associated with the rule of law; it may yet be brought to the surface in arguments based on Article 7. Many strict liability offences are tempered by provision of a due diligence defence—but not consistently. To subject all strict liability offences to due diligence defences would greatly enhance predictability of liability for regulatory criminal offences.[78]

## Article 1, First Protocol: Right to Peaceful Enjoyment of Possessions

The core right guaranteed by Article 1 is the peaceful enjoyment of possessions. The term 'possessions' employed in the English text of the article is not to be read narrowly: the French text employs the expression '*biens*', which has been interpreted widely to cover such advantages as licences[79] and welfare payments.[80] As would be expected, there is no absolute right to the peaceful enjoyment of possessions and, in particular, contracting states are permitted laws that may require the surrender or liquidation of property.

The Article has given rise to few cases, such is its latitude for state action in respect of the taking or confiscation of property. None the less, the Article has been infringed in the context of criminal proceedings, most notably in the *Roth* case discussed earlier.[81] The Court of Appeal held that the fixed penalty of £2,000

---

[76] B. Emmerson and A. Ashworth, *Human Rights and Criminal Justice* (London 2001), Ch. 10.

[77] In *Muhammed* [2002] EWCA 1856, the Court of Appeal dismissed an argument that the offence of gambling or making rash and hazardous speculations in the two years preceding a petition in bankruptcy contravened Article 7. The appellant's contention was that the offence lacked a sufficient degree of certainty as the bankruptcy petition did not exist and might never have come into existence at the time of his speculative activity. Reasonably enough, the Court of Appeal held that the appellant was on fair notice at the time of his speculations that his conduct put his capacity to pay his creditors gravely at risk.

[78] Arden LJ considers that 'due diligence' defences can be 'read in' to strict liability offences under the terms of s. 3 of the HRA 1998 (above, n. 37). In terms of tempering strict liability yet acknowledging the need for effective regulation, a probative burden to establish due diligence might be compatible with Art. 6(2), applying the proportionality doctrine.

[79] *The Traktörer Aktiebolag* v. *Sweden* (1989) 13 EHRR 309.

[80] *Baygusuz* v. *Austria* (1996) 23 EHRR 365.　　　　[81] [2003] QB 728.

per clandestine entrant, and an ancillary power to seize and hold vehicles until the penalty was paid, breached Article 1. It should be remembered, however, that before turning to Article 1 the court had already decided that the fixed penalty scheme contravened the guarantee of fair trial under Article 6(1). The discussion of the Article 1 question is cursory: the breach of Article 1 occurred *because* the procedure that imposed the penalty was unfair in its failure to consider the varying circumstances of individual offenders. Likewise, in *Benjafield*,[82] the Court of Appeal indicated that a breach of Article 1 would have occurred had the challenged confiscation procedure been in breach of Article 6. However, the procedure was found to comply with Article 6, a finding that also entailed the conclusion that Article 1 of the First Protocol had not been transgressed. Accordingly, we may conclude that Article 1 has no sphere of autonomous operation in criminal proceedings. Fines, forfeiture, and confiscation imposed following strict criminal liability may breach Article 1, but only if the liability itself has been impugned under other articles of the Convention.

## 6. Conclusions

Our discussion of the ECHR has generated a number of conclusions. It is unlikely that the conviction of blameless defendants for regulatory crimes contravenes Article 3 per se. None the less, Article 3 may curtail the conviction of blameless defendants for serious, stigmatic, offences. Moreover, Article 3 should confine imprisonment as a sanction to those against whom a culpability commensurate with the term of imprisonment to be served can be proved. Culpability should not merely be a function of the gravity of the consequences caused by the defendant.

Article 6(1) does not impinge on the content of the substantive criminal law. Article 6(1) requires a procedure that constitutes a trial. A criminal trial properly so called requires proof of a voluntary act or omission on the part of the defendant otherwise there is nothing for which to hold the defendant to account. Article 6(1) requires proof to a criminal standard of the extent of the culpability of the defendant before passing sentence.

Article 6(2) has no bearing on the elements of offences or on the provision or denial of defences. If something short of proof of a fact such as establishing a 'reasonable suspicion' suffices for criminal liability then, effectively, the prosecution is relieved of the burden of proof. Particularly for serious offences, Article 6(2) should be construed to impose a full burden on the prosecution to prove facts otherwise merely suspected.

The jurisprudence on Article 7 has been concerned with the interpretation of texts and the clarity of the exegetical jurisprudence. It is an open question whether Article 7 can be deployed to lessen the loss of predictability that strict liability

---

[82] [2001] 3 WLR 75.

entails. The provision of due diligence defences for all strict liability offences would assist those subject to regulatory law in planning the avoidance of liability. It is to be hoped that such provision is seen to be within the spirit of Article 7 and within the interpretative scope of section 3 of the HRA 1998.

Finally, Article 1 of the First Protocol may be breached by the imposition of fines, forfeiture, or confiscation following conviction for a strict liability offence. Such will only be the case, however, if the procedure leading to the fiscal penalty has contravened an article of the Convention apart from Article 1.

# 9

# Imposing Constitutional Limits on Strict Liability: Lessons from the American Experience

*Alan C. Michaels*

## 1. Policy *v.* Constitutional Law

In the United States, the question of strict liability is really two questions: (1) is strict liability a good idea, and (2) is strict liability constitutional? The first question considers both the morality and utility of strict liability, and addresses whether legislatures ought to enact strict liability criminal statutes and how courts should interpret statutes that are ambiguous regarding strict liability. The second question asks whether, good idea or no, the United States Constitution permits the imposition of strict liability.

In this respect, strict liability is similar to many of the issues of interest to criminal justice scholars in the United States. Thus, criminal laws regarding acts such as sodomy,[1] abortion,[2] and euthanasia,[3] and more general questions such as capital punishment in particular circumstances,[4] and mandatory minimum sentences based on findings by a judge by a preponderance of the evidence,[5] for example, are debated in the United States both as policy questions—is such a law a good idea?—and as constitutional questions—does such a law have force?

Because of the tradition of parliamentary supremacy under English law, this second inquiry may be less familiar in general in English criminal law jurisprudence, and is certainly less familiar in the case of strict liability. This chapter focuses on the American answer to the second question, when is strict liability constitutional? and the possible lessons for English law as the Human

I am grateful to Antony Duff, Stephen Shute, Robert Sullivan, the participants in the Strict Liability Workshop at the Centre for Penal Theory and Penal Ethics of the Institute for Criminology in Cambridge and, especially, the editor of this volume, for comments on earlier versions of this essay.

¹ *Lawrence* v. *Texas*, 539 US 558 (2003); *Bowers* v. *Hardwick*, 478 US 186 (1986).
² *Roe* v. *Wade*, 410 US 113 (1973).     ³ *Washington* v. *Glucksberg*, 521 US 702 (1997).
⁴ *Atkins* v. *Virginia*, 536 US 304 (2002).     ⁵ *Harris* v. *United States*, 536 US 545 (2002).

Rights Act 1998 gives it 'a source of "higher law" that can be used as a benchmark of the constitutionality of criminal legislation'.[6]

After setting out some preliminaries about strict liability, the American approach is briefly described and defended, and its effects are summarized. From there, the chapter turns to consider the effect the American approach might have on English law after the 1998 Act.

## 2. Definition

In this chapter, a strict liability crime means a crime that authorizes liability no matter what the evidence would show about the actor's fault with regard to a particular material element. Thus, strict liability crimes are only those that contain a material element for which the actor's culpability is irrelevant.[7] This definition's emphasis on 'element analysis'[8] makes it a broad one. Under the definition, a law will qualify as a strict liability crime if strict liability is imposed as to *a single material element*, even if other elements of the offence do include culpability requirements or demonstrate an 'evil will'. Felony murder, for example, which consists of causing a death (even accidentally and non-negligently) during the commission of a felony, is a strict liability offence under this definition since no culpability is required with regard to the element of causing a death.

The famous case of *Regina* v. *Prince*,[9] which is required reading in many first-year criminal law courses in the United States, provides another example. Prince's conviction for taking a girl under the age of 16 out of the possession of her father was upheld, even though the defendant reasonably believed the girl was over 16. Those who ignore the element analysis perspective might not view this as a case of strict liability—because, as the Law Lords stressed in deciding the case, Prince's knowingly taking a girl out of the possession of her father demonstrated *mens rea*—the wicked mind, if you will—for the offence.[10] Under the definition used in this chapter, however, *Prince* was convicted of a strict liability offence, even if the intentional portion of his action violated both moral and legal strictures of the time.

---

[6] Andrew Ashworth, *Principles of Criminal Law* (4th edn., Oxford 2003), 63.

[7] In the words of a leading English authority, 'There is no clear convention about when criminal liability should be classified as "strict".' Ibid. 164. This is, if anything, an understatement. For a collection of definitions in the academic literature, see Alan C. Michaels, 'Constitutional Innocence' (1999) 112 *Harvard LR* 829, at 830 n. 11.

[8] Under 'element analysis', each element of an offence may have a different *mens rea*. This approach may be distinguished from 'offence analysis,' under which a given offence is understood as having a single *mens rea* requirement. See Michaels, 'Innocence', at 839 and n. 4.

[9] (1875) 13 Cox CC 138. The decision in *Prince* itself must now be regarded as unsound in English law following the House of Lords' decision in *B* v. *DPP* [2000] 2 AC 428.

[10] See Paul H. Robinson and Jane A. Grall, 'Element Analysis in Defining Criminal Liability: The Model Penal Code and Beyond' (1983) 35 *Stanford LR* 681, at 689 n. 37.

## 3. The American Approach

Strict liability in the United States has endured decades of withering academic criticism.[11] There are numerous and still-developing arguments both for and against strict liability, but the core of the most frequent arguments against strict liability crimes was well summarized by Professor Herbert Packer:

[Strict liability] is inefficacious because conduct unaccompanied by an awareness of the factors making it criminal does not mark the actor as one who needs to be subjected to punishment in order to deter him or others from behaving similarly in the future, nor does it single him out as a socially dangerous individual who needs to be incapacitated or reformed. It is unjust because the actor is subjected to the stigma of a criminal conviction without being morally blameworthy.[12]

Notwithstanding these arguments, however, strict liability crimes are commonplace in American criminal law.[13] They range from very serious felonies, such as felony murder, to minor crimes, such as licence violations, and the strict liability element may be at the core of what makes the conduct wrongful, as in statutory rape,[14] or it may be peripheral, as in the crime of selling drugs within 1,000 feet of a school, with strict liability imposed regarding the distance from the school.[15]

The United States Supreme Court's strict liability jurisprudence extends back to 1910 and covers many cases. Careful study of these opinions reveals the court's consistent adherence to an underlying principle that establishes the boundaries for strict liability under the United States Constitution. That principle, which I have previously labelled 'constitutional innocence', explains the cases in which the court has upheld a legislature's power to impose strict liability and those in which the court has rejected strict liability:

According to the principle of constitutional innocence, strict liability is constitutional when, but only when, the intentional conduct covered by the statute could be made criminal by the legislature. In other words, strict liability runs afoul of the Constitution if

---

[11]  See Michaels, 'Innocence', at n. 15 (collecting sources).

[12]  Herbert L. Packer, 'Mens Rea and the Supreme Court' [1962] *Supreme Court Review* 107, at 109.

[13]  See Michaels, 'Innocence', 887–900 (canvassing more than 136 separate decisions by state and federal courts in the United States between 1985 and 1998 adjudicating the constitutionality of strict liability crimes (about 75% state statutes and 25% federal statutes)); Model Penal Code § 2.05 comment, at 290 (1985) (noting that most states continue to use strict liability for some crimes carrying the possibility of imprisonment).

[14]  Statutory rape criminalizes engaging in sexual intercourse with a person below a certain age. Many United States jurisdictions impose strict liability with regard to the age element. See e.g. *United States* v. *Ransom* 942 F 2d 775, at 776–7 (10th Cir. 1991) (holding that defendant could not assert defence of reasonable mistake as to 12-year-old victim's age, statutory rape was a recognized exception to requirement of criminal intent).

[15]  Comprehensive Drug Abuse Prevention and Control Act of 1970, 21 USC § 860(a) (2000).

the other elements of the crime, with the strict liability element excluded, could not themselves be made a crime. Otherwise, strict liability is constitutional.[16]

Rather than creating an independent restriction on strict liability, the constitutional innocence principle draws on other constitutional limits on the legislature's ability to define crimes to establish the constitutional parameters for strict liability.

Two examples drawn from Supreme Court cases clarify the concept. In *Smith* v. *California*,[17] the defendant was a bookstore owner who had been sentenced to thirty days in jail for possessing an obscene book in a place where books were sold. The statute imposed strict liability with regard to the element of obscenity: according to the statute, if the defendant knowingly sold books, and a book in his store was obscene, then the defendant was guilty, regardless of the degree of care he took regarding the content of books in his store.

Under the principle of constitutional innocence, this statute would be unconstitutional. The question becomes whether a statute without the strict liability element—in this case, that would mean a statute that prohibited knowingly selling books—would be constitutional. Because the First Amendment to the United States Constitution would bar such a statute,[18] the constitutional innocence principle mandates that the statute in *Smith* be held unconstitutional, even though the First Amendment does *not* protect obscene material. This is the result the Supreme Court reached.

In contrast, consider *United States* v. *Freed*.[19] In *Freed*, the defendant was convicted under a statute that contained three material elements: (1) the accused possessed certain items; (2) that were hand grenades; and (3) that were not registered.[20] The statute imposed a knowledge requirement as to the first two elements, but strict liability as to the third; in other words, the prosecution needed to show that the defendants knew they possessed hand grenades, but not that they knew (or ought to have known) that the hand grenades were unregistered. The Supreme Court upheld this application of strict liability, as the constitutional innocence principle would suggest. If the strict liability element were removed, the statute would prohibit the knowing possession of hand grenades. Such a statute would clearly be constitutional. Therefore, under the principle of constitutional innocence, the statute with a strict liability element added is also constitutional.

Although the constitutional innocence principle provides a single coherent explanation for the multitude of Supreme court decisions related to the constitutionality of strict liability crimes, the court has not articulated the principle in any of its decisions, much less expressly adopted it. Neither do treatises recognize this

---

[16] Michaels, 'Innocence', 834.       [17] 361 US 147 (1959).
[18] See 361 US 147, at 152 (stating that there is no 'state power to restrict the dissemination of books which are not obscene').                                    [19] 401 US 601 (1971).
[20] 401 US 601, at 612 (Brennan J concurring in the judgment).

principle as the accepted constitutional limit on strict liability. The constitutional innocence view has begun to find its way into leading treatises and casebooks in the field, but as a theory, not yet as the settled law.[21] Instead, the court has simultaneously insisted that there is no general constitutional bar to strict liability crimes and suggested that the Constitution does place some, unspecified, limits on them.[22] Indeed, the court has expressly refused to delineate the constitutional limits on strict liability.[23] This jurisprudence is often summarized with Herbert Packer's aphorism, '*mens rea* . . . is not a constitutional requirement, except sometimes'.[24] Thus, the constitutional innocence principle provides a remarkable descriptive fit with the decided cases, but its claim to authority in the United States is, at this point, derived from that fit rather than from a declarative judgment of the Supreme Court.[25]

## 4. Justifications for the Constitutional Innocence Principle

Regarding attacks on strict liability, the constitutional innocence principle serves as both a sword and a shield. As noted earlier, it does not create an independent prohibition on strict liability as such, nor does it rely on the wrongness of strict liability itself. Instead, the principle restricts strict liability by using other constitutional norms. It serves as a shield by validating the legislature's power to include a strict liability element in a criminal statute if the statute would be constitutional without that element. It serves as a sword by declaring certain uses of strict liability off limits. Both aspects—the shield and the sword—have justifications within the law of the United States. One may consider whether these justifications would apply in the English context.

Legislative primacy in defining crimes is the most important justification for the 'shield' portion of the constitutional innocence principle, and one might well expect this justification to resonate in England, which has such a long tradition of unquestioned ultimate legislative authority in this area.[26]

The justification is most easily discussed with an example. Imagine a law that makes it a crime to sell alcoholic beverages to a minor—someone less than 18 years old—and imposes strict liability with regard to the age of the purchaser.

---

[21] See e.g. Joshua Dressler, *Understanding Criminal Law* (3rd edn., New York 2001), § 11.03 nn. 24, 33.

[22] See e.g. *United States* v. *Gypsum Co.*, 438 US 422, at 437–8 (1978); *United States* v. *International Minerals & Chem. Corp.*, 402 US 558, at 564–5 (1971); *Smith* v. *California*, 361 US 147, at 150 (1959); *Lambert* v. *California*, 355 US 225, at 228 (1957).

[23] See *United States* v. *Park*, 421 US 658, at 669–70 (1975); *Powell* v. *Texas*, 392 US 514, at 535 (1968) (Marshall J, plurality opinion); *Morissette* v. *United States*, 342 US 246, at 260 (1952); *United States* v. *Dotterweich*, 320 US 277, at 285 (1943).

[24] Packer, 'Mens Rea and the Supreme Court', 107.

[25] The details of that descriptive fit have been set out elsewhere; see Michaels, 'Innocence', 841–76.

[26] See generally, A. V. Dicey, *Introduction to the Law of the Constitution* (10th edn., London 1959).

In simple form, the argument is that, if the legislature can punish any sale of alcohol by prohibiting it entirely, it is hard to see why it cannot take the less extreme step of punishing it only when it leads to the resulting harm of a sale to a minor, assuming that choosing to limit liability for the sale of alcohol to sales to minors is not without some rational justification.[27]

If a court were to determine that creating this strict liability crime of selling alcohol to minors was beyond the legislature's power, the reason presumably would be either that the crime punishes conduct that is not 'blameworthy' or that such a law would have no value in diminishing the sale of alcohol to minors. While such arguments might have merit as policy, the problem is that, in a democratic society, it is usually the elected representatives of the people— rather than appointed judges or legal academics—who decide what conduct should be labelled 'blameworthy' and what the likely effects of legislation will be.[28] This argument has particular force if the law is passed by a subdivision (such as a state in the United States), where the decision regarding the legislature's power to enact is made by an authority covering many subdivisions. No doubt this concern—called federalism in the United States—would also be a concern in England to the extent that power to decide what conduct in England was blameworthy was shifted from Parliament to the European Court of Human Rights.

A second advantage of this shield limitation in United States law is that it limits courts to constitutional questions that they are already used to deciding. Rather than being forced to consider whether a particular strict liability crime is 'unjust' or inefficacious, the constitutional innocence approach limits courts to deciding issues about rights that are independently protected by the Constitution—such as the rights to free speech, association, and privacy. By pegging the limits on strict liability to an independent jurisprudence of restrictions on the legislature's ability to define crimes, this approach limits the encroachment on democratic values that comes with restricting legislative primacy in crime definition and directs courts to the kind of inquiries they have a demonstrated capacity (in addition to a positive constitutional duty) to undertake.

Notwithstanding this reasoning, some might find that any amount of punishment for an outcome that essentially depends on moral luck[29] is either so unjust or so pointless that a legislature not only would never be wise to enact strict liability crimes, but should also be prohibited from doing so, even if it so desires.

---

[27] While a statute with a wholly irrational strict liability factor would be problematic—for example, a crime of selling alcohol to left-handed people—the problem with that statute would not lie in its strict liability aspect. The statute would have the same difficulties even if the prohibition were on knowingly selling alcohol to a left-handed person.

[28] The legislature's ability to define 'blameworthy' or 'dangerous conduct' is subject to judicial review in the United States under the 'rational basis test' (see below nn. 56–8 and accompanying text), but that limit provides legislatures so much latitude that they have only rarely bumped up against it.                    [29] See Michaels, 'Innocence', at n. 337 (collecting views on moral luck).

Indeed, Canada has taken precisely this approach, prohibiting strict liability offences as a constitutional matter for offences involving imprisonment.[30]

Whatever one might wish from the process of judicial review, however, the experience in the United States has been that the Supreme Court has been extremely reluctant to impose constitutional rules regarding criminal responsibility, and its few efforts in that direction have always proved to be false starts.[31] The jurisprudence of the Strasbourg Court appears headed in the same direction—equivocal at times but refusing to impose a universal bar to strict liability.[32] Thus, from a practical perspective, because of its respect for legislative primacy and its reliance on independently established limits on criminal legislation, a constitutional innocence principle may be a more realistic and effective limit on strict liability than the broader, normative prohibitions that commentators have long urged in vain.

Regarding the 'sword' part of the constitutional innocence principle, the theoretical justification is tied to the control principle. To be subject to punishment, a person must have made some punishable choice—and by punishable, I mean a choice to act in some way that the legislature could prohibit. This notion is at the core of the 'voluntary' portion of the voluntary act requirement, and explains why a statute that, for example, made having a seizure a crime would not be constitutional in the United States.

[T]he voluntary act requirement is in large measure a requirement of culpability. It provides a '*locus potententiae*, a point of no return' beyond which a person may be punished, but before which she is 'free of the very specific social compulsions of the law.' By preventing the state from holding individuals accountable for conduct they plainly cannot control, the voluntary act requirement serves as the 'first line of defence' against punishment that would undermine personal autonomy and security.[33]

In the rare case that runs afoul of this principle, such as a statute creating punishment for being an addict, the United States Supreme Court has signalled that this principle has constitutional force.[34]

---

[30] See *Reference Re Section 94(2) of the Motor Vehicle Act* 23 CCC 3d 289 (1985).

[31] See Michaels, 'Innocence', at n. 297 and accompanying text.

[32] See Ben Emmerson and Andrew Ashworth, *Human Rights and Criminal Justice* (London 2001), 278–9; Lord Lester of Herne Hill and David Pannick (eds.), *Human Rights Law and Practice* (London 1999), para. 4.6.59; Richard Clayton and Hugh Tomlinson, *The Law of Human Rights* (Oxford 2000), para. 11.238; Bob Sullivan, 'Strict Liability for Criminal Offences in England and Wales following Incorporation into English Law of the European Convention for Human Rights', this volume, Ch. 8, § 3 and n. 42 with accompanying text.

[33] Michaels, 'Innocence', 878–9 (quoting Herbert L. Packer, *The Limits of the Criminal Sanction* (Stanford 1968), 75–7). See also A. P. Simester, 'On the So-Called Requirement for Voluntary Action' (1998) 1 *Buffalo Criminal LR* 403, at 407–18 (tying voluntariness principle to control principle and finding voluntariness provides the 'indispensable minimum' for the *actus reus* requirement).

[34] Michaels, 'Innocence', at n. 270 (setting out the US Supreme Court jurisprudence on this question). Cf. *Finau* v. *Dept. of Labour* [1980] 2 NZLR 396 (holding that, under New Zealand law,

Andrew Ashworth has made a similar point with regard to *mens rea* requirements:

> The essence of the principle of *mens rea* is that criminal liability should be imposed only on persons who are sufficiently aware of what they are doing, and of the consequences it might have, that they can fairly be said to have chosen the behaviour and its consequences. This approach is grounded in the principle of autonomy. . . . [R]espect for their autonomy means holding them liable only on the basis of their choices.[35]

Notwithstanding this close tie between *mens rea* and the control principle, most strict liability crimes do not run afoul of this core culpability requirement because, by voluntarily engaging in some act identified in the statute, the actor has chosen (by engaging in the other elements of the offence) to use less care than she could have to avoid the strict liability element. The actor is aware of her conduct and (if we accept the assumption that she knows the law) has chosen to risk the potential consequences. A felony murderer by engaging in the felony; a seller of alcohol to minors by selling alcohol: each provides the minimum culpability required by the United States Constitution and any similar document that would prohibit punishment of conduct utterly beyond the actor's control. The law provides a clear line of safety, and a defendant charged with a strict liability crime usually crosses that line by engaging in the intentional conduct covered by the statute.

Some might argue that the obscene bookseller similarly provides the minimum culpability by deciding to sell books and, by choosing to sell books, crosses the clear line of safety. Choosing to sell books or to engage in other constitutionally protected activity, however, cannot by itself count as a culpable choice. When the constitutional document prohibits designating conduct as punishable, courts and legislatures cannot rely on that conduct to supply the minimum culpability. The choice to sell books—like the 'choice' to have a seizure—cannot be the basis for punishment. 'If the other elements of the crime cannot be blamed themselves, then "voluntarily" engaging in them cannot serve as the basis of blame for the harm that results.'[36] Hence the principle of constitutional innocence: a strict liability statute is beyond the legislature's power when the other elements of the offence, without the strict liability element, would not be within the legislative power to punish.

prosecution for staying in the country after expiration of a visitor's permit was invalid where departure from New Zealand was impossible given the defendant's pregnancy). But cf. Simester, 'On the So-Called Requirement for Voluntary Action', 410–12 (discussing 'notorious' exception of the English case of *Larsonneur* and its relationship to voluntariness).

[35] Ashworth, *Principles of Criminal Law*, 158. See also Dressler, *Understanding Criminal Law*, 89; Douglas N. Husak, *Philosophy of Criminal Law* (Totowa 1987), 102–3; Larry Alexander, 'Reconsidering the Relationship Among Voluntary Acts, Strict Liability, and Negligence in Criminal Law' (1990) *Social Philosophy and Policy* 84, at 86.

[36] Michaels, 'Innocence', 880–1.

## 5. Constitutional Innocence and the Human Rights Act 1998

The Human Rights Act 1998 creates the possibility of a similar principle working in English law—with the European Convention on Human Rights serving as the constitutional document checking the use of strict liability. Under the Act, English courts must read and give effect to legislation so as to make it compatible with the Convention 'so far as it is possible to do so'.[37] Moreover, a court cannot act in a manner incompatible with the Convention, unless 'primary legislation'[38] forces it to do so.[39] Finally, if a piece of primary legislation cannot be read so as to make it compatible with the Convention, certain courts may issue a 'declaration of incompatibility',[40] though such a declaration does not itself affect the validity of the incompatible statute.[41]

In this last respect, of course, the Human Rights Act 1998 gives the European Convention less control over English law than the United States Constitution has over law in the United States. Under the American principle of judicial review, a statute that is incompatible with the Constitution is not valid. Notwithstanding that difference, however, the Human Rights Act 1998 provides ample ground for operation of the constitutional innocence principle through the European Convention.

'Convention rights . . . take precedence over rules of common law or equity, and over most, but not all subordinate legislation,'[42] and primary legislation must be read to comply with the convention if at all possible. The American experience suggests that this latter principle can have particular force. Under the principle of 'constitutional doubt', federal courts, faced with two possible meanings for a statute, will adopt one when there is a 'serious likelihood that the statute will be held unconstitutional' if the alternative construction is adopted.[43] This interpretative rule, which is *less* forceful than the one the Human Rights Act 1998 imposes, has considerable play regarding questions of strict liability, because those questions usually arise where a legislature has been silent with regard to a *mens rea* requirement, rather than expressly mandating strict liability. Such silence leaves courts the necessary interpretative room to read a *mens rea* requirement into the statute when the Constitution suggests that it should. As a result, in deciding strict liability questions under federal statutes, the United States Supreme Court has never actually used the power the Human Rights Act 1998 denies to English courts. Instead, when strict liability under a federal statute would or might violate

[37] Human Rights Act 1998 s. 3.
[38] Primary legislation is defined in s. 21 of the Act and includes any 'public general Act'.
[39] Human Rights Act 1998 s. 6(1)–(2).    [40] Human Rights Act 1998 s. 4.
[41] Human Rights Act 1998 s. 4(6)(a).
[42] Emmerson and Ashworth, *Human Rights and Criminal Justice*, 115.
[43] *Almendarez-Torres* v. *United States*, 23 US 224, at 238 (1998).

the Constitution, the court has found that the statute does not impose strict liability.[44]

Accepting that the principle of constitutional innocence could have force in English law under the Human Rights Act 1998, one might ask where in the European Convention the principle might plausibly be found. This question too may be answered by reference to the American experience: the principle may be found in the provision of the Convention that the statute would contravene if the strict liability element were excluded. The reason, as explained above, is that the statute pegs culpability on the choice to engage in conduct that the provision protects.

For example, recall the bookseller held strictly liable for selling obscene books. The authority for application of the constitutional innocence principle in that case would be the constitutional provision that would prohibit a statute that banned the selling of books. In the case of the US Constitution, it is the First Amendment, which guarantees freedom of speech and of the press. Because the only intentional conduct the statute punishes is the choice to sell books, the statute can be understood to violate the First Amendment. Similarly, the rejection of statutes that impose strict liability for unprotected circumstances surrounding otherwise protected acts, such as belonging to an organization (the organization is criminal)[45] or having an abortion (the foetus was viable)[46] may be understood as violating the provisions that bar a statute prohibiting belonging to an organization (the First Amendment) or having an abortion (the Due Process Clause).[47]

A suggestion of the constitutional innocence approach—in both its sword and its shield aspects—can be seen in the European Court of Human Rights' discussion in *Salabiaku* v. *France*,[48] the leading strict liability case in that court's jurisprudence. *Salabiaku* involved a defendant who was charged with smuggling, under a statutory scheme that presumed smuggling from the fact of possession. The court avoided deciding whether a mandatory presumption of this kind would violate the right of presumption of innocence by determining that the defendant had an opportunity to rebut the presumption and, in fact, had been warned about the contents of the trunk that held the drugs prior to his taking possession of it. In passing, however, the court noted that 'the Contracting States remain free to apply the criminal law to an act *where it is not carried out in the normal exercise of one of*

---

[44] See *United States* v. *X-Citement Video*, 513 US 64 (1998); *United States* v. *Robel*, 389 US 258, at 264–6 (1967); *Aptheker* v. *Secretary of State*, 378 US 500, at 509–12 (1964); *Scales* v. *United States*, 367 US 203, at 229 (1961).          [45] See *Scales* v. *United States*, 367 US 203, at 228–9 (1961).

[46] See *Colautti* v. *Franklin*, 439 US 379 (1979) (*dictum*), overruled in part on other grounds, *Webster* v. *Reproductive Health Services*, 492 US 490 (1989).

[47] Of course, if the control principle were not a part of the Convention, that fact would undermine the theoretical justification for the constitutional innocence principle. Although Bob Sullivan suggests that the control principle of the voluntary act requirement may not be a universal principle in English law (see Ch. 8 in this volume), even there, the only exceptions may be so-called 'status offences', which make no reference to conduct. Moreover, Sullivan believes that there may be a basis for asserting this principle under the Convention.          [48] 13 EHRR 379 (1988).

*the rights protected by the Convention* and, accordingly, to define the constituent elements of the resulting offense'.[49] The implication is that, while strict liability for an 'act' is permissible in general, if the 'act' results from the normal exercise of a protected right, it may not be so punished.

## 6. Application to the Law of England

What effects would this have on English law? Perhaps because there is something deeply troubling about punishment in a case where the only choice made by the accused was to engage in conduct worthy of constitutional protection, there may be cases where English courts have reached results consistent with the constitutional principle as an interpretative matter, even before application of the Human Rights Act 1998. At the outset, an American reader is struck by the principle's ability to reconcile two landmark English cases, one that rejects strict liability—*Sweet* v. *Parsley*[50]—and one that endorses it—*Howells*.[51] Although commentators understandably describe these cases as 'hard to reconcile',[52] the constitutional innocence principle can do so, at least regarding their results if not their rhetoric.

Of course, both cases were decided as matters of statutory construction. If the cases were examined as a constitutional matter in the United States, however, strict liability in *Howells* would probably have been upheld, and strict liability in *Sweet* would have been struck down—precisely the result the English courts reached as an interpretative matter. The same results would be likely to follow if the constitutional innocence provision were used alongside the European Convention.

*Howells* presented a question under the Firearms Act 1968, which prohibited possession of a firearm without a licence.[53] The issue was whether strict liability applied to the statutory exception that exempted antique firearms from the statute's coverage.[54] In other words, the statute had three elements: (1) possessing a firearm, (2) without a licence, (3) that was not an antique; and the question was whether strict liability applied to the last of these elements (the defendant claimed he reasonably believed the firearm was antique).

If strict liability applied to that element, such a statute in the United States would nevertheless pass muster under the constitutional innocence principle. The statute without the strict liability element would prohibit knowingly possessing a firearm without a licence. There is almost certainly no constitutional barrier in the United States to a criminal law requiring the licensing of firearms (indeed, there are many such laws), and it is hard to see how an 'antique' exception would be constitutionally mandated (indeed, many gun laws do not have such an

---

[49] Ibid. para. 27 (emphasis added; citations omitted).     [50] [1970] AC 132.
[51] [1977] 1 QB 614.     [52] Ashworth, *Principles of Criminal Law*, 171.
[53] Firearms Act 1968 s. 1(1).     [54] See Firearms Act 1968 s. 58(2).

exception).[55] Similarly, it is hard to see how a statute prohibiting possession of a firearm without a licence would run afoul of the European Convention on Human Rights.

In *Sweet* v. *Parsley*, by contrast, the statute criminalized: (1) being concerned in the management of premises, and (2) the premises are used for the purpose of smoking cannabis. The case involved a woman who had rented her house to people who smoked cannabis in it, and the issue was whether strict liability applied to the second element of the offence. The court held that it did not.

Under the constitutional innocence principle in the United States, a statute that did impose strict liability with regard to that second element would probably be unconstitutional. With the strict liability element eliminated, the statute would simply prohibit 'being concerned in the management of premises'. A criminal statute that broad would almost certainly fail the 'rational basis test' of the Due Process Clause of the US Constitution. Under the rational basis test, 'legislation must be rationally related to a legitimate governmental interest',[56] and, in the case of a criminal statute, the test means that the law must bear some relationship to injury to the public.[57] A statute prohibiting 'owning premises' or 'possessing anything' would, for this reason, almost certainly be beyond the legislative power.[58] Indeed, a survey of constitutional challenges to strict liability in the United States between 1985 and 1998 revealed three cases imposing strict liability for conduct occurring on the defendant's property in which, arguably, the only intentional conduct covered by the statute was owning the place or operating a business there.[59] In two of the three cases, the court indicated strict liability would be unconstitutional.[60]

I suspect a similar result would follow under the European Convention for a statute that prohibited 'having an interest in premises', perhaps on the basis that such a statute would, in practice, be impermissibly vague in violation of Article 7. Under the US Constitution, unconstitutional vagueness can occur not only when people can only guess at a statute's meaning, but also when:

[I]t provides so few guidelines that '[it] vests virtually complete discretion in the hands of the police to determine whether the suspect has satisfied the statute', Koleander v. Lawson, 461 U.S. 352, 358 (1983). A statute that 'permits and encourages an arbitrary and

---

[55] If strict liability were imposed regarding the other elements, it would be a different case. Strict liability with regard to the licence would be a harder case for the government, though I suspect the government would still prevail with a majority of the Supreme Court. If strict liability were imposed with regard to the possession element—e.g. the defendant had received an unopened birthday present that turned out to be a firearm—the statute would probably be unconstitutional in the US.

[56] Scott H. Bice, 'Rationality Analysis in Constitutional Law' (1980) 65 *Minnesota LR* 1, at 1.

[57] See Wayne R. LaFave, *Criminal Law* (4th edn., St Paul 2003), 142–8.

[58] See Michaels, 'Innocence', 896–7.      [59] Ibid. 897.

[60] See *State* v. *Larson* 653 So 2d 1158, 1164–7 (La. 1995) (upholding strict liability with regard to 'permitting' commission of a crime on the ground that the statute contained an additional element of intentionally selling alcohol on the premises); *State* v. *Brandner* 551 NW 2d 284, 286 (ND 1996) (construing a statute punishing ownership of land on which there are illegal fish traps to allow an affirmative defence of lack of knowledge of the fish traps' presence to avoid a constitutional problem);

discriminatory enforcement of the law,' Papachristou v. City of Jacksonville, 405 U.S. 156, 170 (1972), is unconstitutionally vague.[61]

Other possibilities might be that such statutes would run afoul of Article 1 of the First Protocol,[62] which provides the right to enjoyment of one's property, or, in cases where the intentional conduct in the statute comprised owning a home, as a violation of the right to respect for one's home and private and family life under Article 8.[63]

Regardless of legislative intent, if the statute in *Sweet* v. *Parsley* would be 'incompatible' with the European Convention if it entailed strict liability, the Human Rights Act 1998 would certainly direct that it be read not to impose strict liability, in order to avoid that incompatibility.

Review of the European Convention and the American experience can also provide a preliminary sense of the impact on English law that might follow from the adoption of the constitutional innocence principle. To be sure, the effect of the constitutional innocence principle on strict liability crimes would be considerably more limited than a principle mandating a defence of lack of culpability with respect to every material element of an offence. Nevertheless, opponents of strict liability may take solace from considering that, if experience in the United States is any guide, restrictions on strict liability consistent with the constitutional innocence principle are more likely actually to be enforced by courts, and their impact would not be insignificant.

The Convention articles most likely to curtail the use of strict liability in English law would be Article 8 (right to respect for private and family life), Article 10 (freedom of expression), Article 11 (freedom of assembly and association), and Article 1 of the First Protocol (protection of property).

## Article 8

Article 8 provides that 'Everyone has the right to respect for his private and family life, his home and his correspondence.' Even though the right it creates is a qualified one, and subject to interference in certain circumstances where 'necessary in a democratic society', the Article probably provides broader privacy rights than the United States Constitution. Under the Convention, restrictions must be justified by 'compelling social need'.[64] The most common kind of strict

---

*State* v. *Holmberg* 527 NW 2d 100, 104–5 (Minn. Ct. App. 1995) (upholding strict liability with regard to 'permitting' prohibited acts, on the ground that running a business provides sufficient *mens rea*). This last case was probably wrongly decided, because the only intentional conduct covered by the statute, operating a business, would not withstand constitutional scrutiny under the rational basis test.

[61] Michaels, 'Innocence', 896 n. 349. See also *City of Chicago* v. *Morales*, 527 US 41 (1999) (splintered court struck down loitering statute that defined loitering as 'remaining in any one place with no apparent purpose'). See generally John Calvin Jeffries, Jr., 'Legality, Vagueness, and the Construction of Penal Statutes' (1985) 71 *Virginia LR* 189, at 212–19; Dressler, *Understanding Criminal Law*, 43, 45–7.  [62] See discussion of Article 1, below in this section.
   [63] See discussion of Article 8, below in this section.
   [64] See Emmerson and Ashworth, *Human Rights and Criminal Justice*, 224 nn. 11–16 and accompanying text.

liability issues arising in the United States that this provision would implicate are probably those imposing strict liability with regard to circumstances that allow states to prohibit or restrict abortions[65] and laws that impose strict liability with regard to the age of consent in statutory rape. The latter context, in particular, is relevant also to English law.[66]

Under English law, it is a crime to engage in sexual intercourse with a girl under the age of 16. Until very recently, with the exception of offenders under the age of 24, the crime required no fault element with respect to the girl's age.[67] With the strict liability element removed, however, this crime becomes intentionally engaging in sexual intercourse with a non-spouse. While such a 'fornication' statute might or might not pass constitutional muster in the United States,[68] it seems almost certain that it would have run afoul of Article 8. Given twenty-first century reality, it is hard to imagine the 'particularly serious reasons' that would justify a ban on all sexual intercourse outside marriage. If this is right, then the principle of constitutional innocence would require a reinterpretation of such a provision to avoid incompatibility with the Convention. Such an approach eliminates the last vestige of the famous *Prince* case.[69]

[65] Under the United States Constitution, the legislature can ban abortions, where the foetus is viable (barring medical necessity), where parental notice provisions have not been complied with, and where the pregnant woman has not been informed of certain facts under so-called 'informed consent' laws. United States courts have struck down statutes that use strict liability with regard to these elements in criminalizing abortion. See e.g. *Women's Med. Prof'l Corp.* v. *Voinovich*, 130 F 3d 187, at 203–6 (6th Cir. 1997); *Planned Parenthood* v. *Miller*, 63 F 3d 1452 (8th Cir. 1995); *Schulte* v. *Douglas*, 567 F Supp. 522, at 527–8 (D. Neb. 1981), aff'd *sub nom. Women's Services, P. C.* v. *Douglas*, 710 F 2d 465 (8th Cir. 1983) (*per curiam*).

[66] The American constitutional protection of abortion rights 'has its analogue in England in the Abortion Act 1967'. Stephen Shute, 'With and Without Constitutional Restraints: A Comparison Between the Criminal Law of England and America' (1998) 1 *Buffalo Criminal LR* 329, at 338. While the 1967 Act does contain provisions that appear more restrictive than American law with regard to first trimester abortions (principally, the requirement of medical grounds for the abortion, see Abortion Act 1967 s. 1(1)), in fact these differences do not present 'any real obstacle'. Andrew Grubb, 'Abortion Law in England: The Medicalization of a Crime' (1990) 18 *Law, Medicine and Health Care* 146, at 154. In any event, the principle circumstances authorizing abortion under the 1967 Act are judged by the 'good faith' of the doctor, rather than by strict liability, Abortion Act 1967 s. 1(1), and courts have not found the statute to impose strict liability. Moreover, even if English law did impose strict liability in the abortion context (e.g. regarding the viability of the foetus), the 'constitutional' protection the European Convention of Human Rights affords abortion rights, if any, might be so limited as to provide no barrier to such a use of strict liability. See *Brüggemann and Scheuten* v. *Federal Republic of Germany* [1977] 3 EHRR 244 (doubting whether the parties to the Convention wished to bind themselves to a particular resolution of the abortion issue).

[67] Sexual Offences Act 1956 s 6. The offence has now been replaced by the Sexual Offences Act 2003, s. 9, which imposes a *mens rea* standard of negligence regarding the victim's age, unless the victim is less than 13 years of age, in which case liability is strict.

[68] See Michaels, 'Innocence', 894 n. 342. In fact, as of 1991, thirteen states and the District of Columbia still made fornication a crime. See Note, 'Constitutional Barriers to Civil and Criminal Restrictions on Pre- and Extramarital Sex' (1991) 104 *Harvard LR* 1660, at 1661 n. 9 (collecting statutes).

[69] English courts had already undermined *Prince* by holding that mistake of age can be a defence to a charge of inciting indecency under the Indecency with Children Act 1960, and to a charge of indecent assault under the Sexual Offences Act 1956. See *B* v. *DPP* [2000] 2 AC 428; *R.* v. *K* [2002] 1 AC 462. See generally A. P. Simester and G. R. Sullivan, *Criminal Law: Theory and Doctrine*

Section 444(1) of the Education Act 1996 is another English law that might run afoul of Article 8 under the constitutional innocence principle. Section 444(1) provides that 'If a child of compulsory school age who is a registered pupil at a school fails to attend regularly at the school, his parent is guilty of an offence.' English courts have consistently held that this section and its predecessors impose strict liability.[70] (This sort of strict liability prosecution is not frequently seen in the United States.)

If we assume that the vicarious liability aspects of the statute do not affect the analysis, the statute could be understood to create a crime with three elements: (1) having a child; (2) between the ages of 5 and 16; (3) who fails regularly to attend school, and to impose strict liability with regard to the third element. If, as seems likely, a statute that prohibited intentionally having a child between the ages of 5 and 16 would be incompatible with Article 8, then, under the constitutional innocence principle, a statute that imposed strict liability with regard to the non-attendance would also be incompatible. (Such a statute might also be incompatible with Article 12, which offers qualified protection to the right to 'found a family'.)

It is possible, however, that section 444 could survive for other reasons. First, it must be noted that a Human Rights challenge to the section has recently been rejected,[71] although that challenge was based on Article 6(2) (regarding the presumption of innocence) rather than on Article 8 and the principles of constitutional innocence. More importantly, there is in fact another element of the offence under section 444—that the absence from school not have been for 'any unavoidable cause'. This provision might effectively mandate proof of some sufficient culpability with regard to the non-attendance. Furthermore, because the maximum punishment is 'a limited fine',[72] the offence may not be sufficiently serious to be properly labelled 'criminal' for these purposes.[73]

## Article 10

Article 10's analogue under the United States Constitution, the First Amendment's guarantees of freedom of speech and freedom of the press, is probably the single most frequent context in which the constitutional innocence principle blocks strict liability in the United States. Certain kinds of expression that are not protected by the First Amendment—obscenity, child pornography, and false

---

(2nd edn., Oxford 2003), nn. 30–1 and accompanying text. Both those offences have now, moreover, been replaced by the Sexual Offences Act 2003, which largely restricts the role of strict liability to situations in which the victim is less than 13 years old. The principle of constitutional innocence should have the same effect, however, on this narrower provision.

[70] See *Barnfather* v. *London Borough of Islington Education Authority* [2003] EWHC 418 at para. 7. See also Jeremy Horder, 'Whose Values Should Determine When Liability is Strict?', this volume, Ch. 5.    [71] See *Barnfather* v. *London Borough of Islington Education Authority*.
[72] Ibid. at para. 31.    [73] See Michaels, 'Innocence', at 879 n. 20.

statements in certain contexts (e.g. in speaking to the police and in attorney advertising)—are frequently targeted for criminal sanction, sometimes using strict liability with regard to the element of the expression that takes it out of the protection of the First Amendment. These statutes run afoul of the constitutional innocence principle.

It appears that Article 10 of the Convention provides a similar level of protection to freedom of expression.[74] If English law employed strict liability for the elements of crimes necessary to make them compatible with Article 10, then those laws would also violate the constitutional innocence principle. Possible examples of such crimes in English law include: contempt of court (criminalizing 'publication' of inaccurate reports of trial evidence that might influence a jury decision and imposing strict liability with regard to the element of the report's inaccuracy),[75] blasphemy (a common law crime that requires publishing material that has a tendency to shock and outrage Christians but, arguably, imposes strict liability with regard to the element of having a tendency to shock and outrage),[76] and outraging public decency (a common law crime that arguably imposes strict liability regarding the effect of the act on public decency).[77] Each of these crimes, with the strict liability element excluded, would place restrictions on free expression that might run afoul of Article 10 and for this reason, were the constitutional innocence principle followed, would not be compatible with the Convention.

## Article 11

In the United States, the First Amendment guarantees freedom of association. As noted earlier, the Supreme Court has struck down statutes that imposed strict liability with regard to the element of an offence that took it out of that provision's protection (such as the illegal objective of an organization). In recent decades, however, such statutes have not been common. Once again, if English law employed strict liability for the elements of crimes necessary to make them compatible with Article 11, then those laws would also run afoul of the constitutional innocence principle.

A possible example of such a law may be found in section 11 of the Terrorism Act 2000.[78] Under the Act, a person 'commits an offence if he belongs or professes

---

[74] Indeed, Article 10 seems to provide even greater protection with regard to obscenity, which falls completely outside of the First Amendment's purview, but is within the scope of Article 10, albeit subject to significant limitations. See Emmerson and Ashworth, *Human Rights and Criminal Justice*, 231–4.

[75] Sir John Smith, *Smith and Hogan's Criminal Law* (9th edn., London 1999), 98–9; Contempt of Court Act (1981).

[76] See *Whitehouse* v. *Gay News and Lemon* [1979] AC 617; Sir John Smith, *Smith and Hogan's Criminal Law* (9th edn., London 1999), at 99 (discussing *Lemon* and noting controversy over whether it imposes strict liability).

[77] See *Gibson* [1991] 1 All ER 439; Sir John Smith, *Smith and Hogan's Criminal Law* (9th edn., London 1999), 739.

[78] I am grateful to Andrew Simester for bringing this statute to my attention.

to belong to a proscribed organization'.[79] It appears that strict liability could apply to the nature of the organization—that a person could be guilty if he belonged to a 'proscribed organization' even if he reasonably believed it was *not* a 'proscribed organization'. The language of the section suggests that result, the section expressly lists defences but not a defence of ignorance of the nature of the organization,[80] and section 12 (which covers supporting proscribed organizations) expressly includes mental elements of knowledge[81] and 'reasonable cause to believe',[82] suggesting that the absence of such language in section 11 was not accidental. Moreover, while there do not appear to be any decided cases discussing the strict liability issue, it has been held that the 'ingredients of the offence contrary to section 11(1) are set out fully in section 11(1)'.[83]

If strict liability did apply to the proscribed nature of the organization, then, under the constitutional innocence principle, the question would become whether Article 11 would prohibit the version of the crime with that element deleted, in other words, a crime of 'belonging to or professing to belong to an organization'. Such a statute would surely run afoul of Article 11's statement of a right to 'freedom of association with others' and would be too broad to come within the exception allowed for restrictions 'necessary in a democratic society in the interests of national security or public safety'.[84] Therefore, to avoid incompatibility, section 11 of the Terrorism Act 2000 would have to be interpreted not to be a strict liability offence.

## Article 1 of the First Protocol

Last, but certainly not least, is Article 1 of the First Protocol. Article 1 has no direct analogue under the United States Constitution,[85] but it would be relevant to a variety of strict liability crimes that one sees in the United States. Although the Protocol's protection of the right 'to the peaceful enjoyment of [one's] possessions' is 'highly qualified',[86] it seems likely that it would make incompatible a statute that criminalized 'possessing anything', or 'controlling premises'. Under the principle of constitutional innocence, statutes that add an additional element—for example, that the thing possessed is a weapon, or that a crime occurs on the premises—are unconstitutional if they provide for strict liability with regard to that additional element. Such statutes are sometimes found in the

---

[79] Terrorism Act 2000 s. 11.
[80] Terrorism Act 2000 s. 11(2) (providing defence that organization was not proscribed at the time the person joined and engaged in activities).      [81] Terrorism Act 2000 s. 12(2).
[82] Terrorism Act 2000 s. 12(4).
[83] *Attorney General's Reference (No 4 of 2002)* [2003] EWCA Crim. 762, [2003] WLR 1153.
[84] Convention for the Protection of Human Rights and Fundamental Freedoms, Art. 11 s. 2.
[85] The closest provision would be the prohibition under the Fifth and Fourteenth Amendments of deprivation of property without due process of law.
[86] Paul Ashcroft and Bryan Gibson, *Human Rights and the Courts: Bringing Justice Home* (Winchester 1999), 49.

United States,[87] and they have been found in English law as well. A number of English cases interpreted drug laws in this way,[88] prior to the enactment of the Misuse of Drugs Act 1971[89] and the decision in *Sweet* v. *Parsley*, discussed earlier, in which the court read in a *mens rea* requirement. The principle of constitutional innocence would force English courts faced with any such statutes to follow the example of *Sweet* v. *Parsley* and impose some requirement of culpability in order to avoid incompatibility.[90]

## 7. Conclusion

Decisions regarding the constitutionality of strict liability in the United States fit with a principle of 'constitutional innocence'. Under that principle, strict liability crimes are constitutional when, but only when, the other elements of the offence, with the strict liability element excluded, would themselves be constitutional. With adoption of the Human Rights Act 1998, strict liability in England could be subjected to analogous limitations under the same principle, with the European Convention on Human Rights playing the role of the United States Constitution. A survey of the Convention and English law indicates that application of the principle would be likely to have a restricting effect on strict liability in England.

---

[87] See Michaels, 'Innocence', 896–8.

[88] See *Lockyer* v. *Gibb* [1967] 2 QB 243; *Yeandel* v. *Fisher* [1966] 1 QB 440.

[89] See Misuse of Drug Act 1971 s. 28 (providing a defence of having no reason to believe the thing possessed was a controlled substance).

[90] Cf. Jeremy Horder, 'Strict Liability, Statutory Construction and the Spirit of Liberty' (2002) *The Law Quarterly Review* 458, at 460 (arguing that certain strict liability crimes wrongly restrict personal autonomy by threatening individuals engaging 'in activities of intrinsic worth to their pursuit of an autonomous life').

# 10

# Approaches to Strict and Constructive Liability in Continental Criminal Law

*John R. Spencer and Antje Pedain*

At first blush, any form of strict or constructive liability for criminal offences is anathema to the Continental criminal lawyer. In the doctrinal context in which he operates, the requirement that fault be established in relation to every element of the *actus reus* flows straightforwardly from the fundamental principle that criminal responsibility be based on culpability. Any suggestion that one might *nolens volens* interpret a criminal offence so as *not* to require a form of *mens rea* to pertain to any or every element of its *actus reus* raises the ugly spectre of criminal liability with insufficient proof of fault. What is accepted in the English legal tradition as a widespread, if somewhat problematic feature of the criminal law as it stands constitutes the unthinkable for lawyers who, from their first days at university, ingest the correspondence principle[1] as a cornerstone of the statutory interpretation of criminal offences, required by the need to establish the defendant's guilt. There is simply no place for strict or constructive criminal liability in the Continental lawyer's theoretical universe.

But the reality is more complicated than that. A dispassionate analysis of how Continental legal systems react to fact patterns that constitute paradigmatic instances of strict or constructive liability in English law reveals similarities as well as discrepancies of approach. While the theoretical underpinnings are different, the practical consequences of the different positions—particularly when one takes into account the conceptions of fault adopted by these systems, and the comparable ease with which fault will be established in a Continental criminal trial—are less widely apart. That said, and notwithstanding differences between particular Continental jurisdictions, in many cases where strict or constructive liability is accepted as legitimate law in the UK, the Continental systems analysed in this chapter would not just reject it on principle, but also do without any practical equivalent.

---

[1] The correspondence principle demands that the *mens rea* requirement for an offence corresponds to every element of its *actus reus*, not just the conduct element. For definition and discussion, see Jeremy Horder, 'A Critique of the Correspondence Principle' [1995] *Criminal LR* 759.

This chapter aims to explore the Continental position with a view to explaining the differences and similarities identified. Focusing on the French and German systems, the first part describes the doctrinal positions in each of these jurisdictions and illustrates their practical operation in reaction to situations in which strict or constructive liability arises under English criminal law. The second part comments on the findings: to what extent are the Continental approaches really different? What has historically driven these systems to move away from strict and constructive liability? Can its remnants be reconciled with the rationales offered for avoiding it? And to the extent that Continental criminal law does without crimes of strict or constructive liability, how does this affect the law's capacity to meet its preventative and desert-oriented objectives? The chapter concludes with some observations on the merits and limitations of the Continental approach.

Throughout this chapter, strict liability is understood as the absence of any fault requirement in relation to *every* element of the *actus reus* of a criminal offence. The expression 'constructive liability' is used whenever a criminal offence requires fault in relation to *some* element or elements of the *actus reus* (usually, its conduct element), but does not require fault in relation to one or more of the others (usually, a circumstantial or consequential element). The elements of a constructive crime in relation to which no fault is required are referred to as the 'strict liability elements' of this constructive offence.

This use differs somewhat from that of several authors in this collection. Duff, like many other writers, speaks of 'constructive liability' also where a lesser—as opposed to no—fault element suffices with regard to some element of the *actus reus*, when intention is the fault element required for others (e.g. murder committed with intention to cause grievous bodily harm).[2] We treat this as an instance where liability is based on fault and hence liability is prima facie compatible with the culpability principle, though such crimes might raise an issue of fair labelling and of proportionality of punishment. Nevertheless, we make such crimes part of our analysis of the Continental systems under review.

Any comparison of the position on strict and constructive liability in the UK and in Continental Europe has to grapple with a number of initial difficulties: the doctrinal constructions of Continental criminal law and the terminology in which they are expressed have few, if any, equivalents in the English debate. One frequently needs to look at the application of the law in order to understand the implications of the theoretical position. This is particularly so because of the interconnectedness of the issue of strict liability with the somewhat different

---

[2] See the definitions given in the first section of R. A. Duff, 'Strict Liability, Legal Presumptions, and the Presumption of Innocence' (in this volume, Ch. 6). Duff initially classifies murder committed with an intention to cause grievous bodily harm as a case of 'constructive liability' because (*in abstracto*) liability is legally strict as to the victim's death, but later justifies this instance of constructive liability by pointing to the obvious risk, present in any violent attack, of causing injuries that are more serious than those intended. In other words, he bases his justification of strict liability on the argument that liability is not (as he terms it) morally strict, but founded on negligence as to the causation of the more serious consequence.

conceptions of fault that have been developed by these systems. In some instances, they may construe as evidence of fault what in English criminal law counts as the absence of it. And the impact of any principle of substantive criminal law—such as a fault requirement—can in any case only be fully appreciated when seen in its procedural context. Furthermore, Continental systems may draw the very borders of the criminal law differently compared to the UK: on the Continent, certain responses to dangerous or harmful conduct may be thought of as purely preventative administrative reactions aimed at ensuring future compliance, and thus not be seen as raising any issue of incompatibility with principles of criminal law, when the parallel response under UK law would amount to a criminal conviction.

Finally, whether we classify something as an instance of constructive liability at all may depend on whether the strict liability element bears on the classification of an offence—its 'label'—or whether it merely identifies a serious instance of the basic, *mens rea*-sensitive, offence, to which a higher maximum penalty applies. This often seems to be an accident of legislative drafting, rather than a matter of deliberate policy. But whether we class this 'raised penalty' situation as a type of constructive liability or not, its practical effect is similar. And this should remind us that any discussion of questions of strict and constructive liability is, properly understood, an exploration of the foundations and limits of the culpability principle.

## 1. The Continental Position Presented

### German Criminal Law

German criminal law recognizes two basic categories of criminal offence, *Verbrechen* and *Vergehen* (§ 12 StGB[3]). *Verbrechen* are crimes that are punishable with no less than one year of imprisonment, while *Vergehen* are offences with a lower minimum penalty for the basic offence (i.e. discounting legislative qualifications of less or more serious cases which attract a lesser or higher sentencing scale).[4] For both types of offence, intention (*Vorsatz*) is the required

---

[3] *Strafgesetzbuch* (German Criminal Code) of 15 May 1871 (*Reichsgesetzblatt* (RGBl) for 1871, 127), republished 13 November 1998 (*Bundesgesetzblatt* (BGBl) I, 3322) and most recently amended by the 36th *Strafrechtsänderungsgesetz* (Criminal Law Amendment Act) of 30 July 2004, *Bundesgesetzblatt* (BGBl) I, 2012. It contains a general part, with general provisions on criminal liability and sentencing, and a special part that sets out the different offences. Provisions of the StGB will subsequently be cited in the usual form for German criminal law, as '§', and the German term for the offence will be given. Unless otherwise indicated, German legislation is cited as valid on 1 August 2004. The *Strafgesetzbuch* and all other German legislation subsequently referred to can be found in one of the two major collections of German legislation, the *Schönfelder* and the *Sartorius* (Munich: Beck Verlag; most recent editions), both of which are continually updated. Some English translations (not necessarily of the up-to-date version) are available on the homepage of the German Federal Ministry of Justice, <http://www.bmj.de>, accessed 25 Sept. 2004.

[4] Thus, all offences that are punishable with either a fine or imprisonment count as *Vergehen* only.

form of *mens rea* unless the law specifically states that recklessness (*Fahrlässigkeit*) suffices (§ 15 StGB). Pure offences of recklessness are in fact rare, with reckless homicide (*Fahrlässige Tötung*, § 222 StGB) and reckless bodily injury (*Fahrlässige Körperverletzung*, § 229 StGB) being in practice the most significant. The overwhelming majority of offences contained in the criminal code require intention.[5]

The principle that recklessness only suffices where this is expressly stipulated in the definition of the offence applies to all criminal offences, whether they are contained in the main Criminal Code (the *Strafgesetzbuch*) or in other codes regulating specific areas of law (for instance, the *Waffengesetz*[6] or the *Betäubungsmittelgesetz*[7]). It also applies to regulatory offences, so-called *Ordnungswidrigkeiten*, whose commission carries no social stigma comparable to a conviction for a criminal offence (§ 10 OwiG).[8] By contrast, the disciplinary offences contained in various codes that regulate the conduct of public officials and members of certain self-regulated professions (lawyers and physicians, for instance) are based on the concept of a 'culpable violation of duty', for which a finding of simple recklessness is enough.[9]

There is thus no general rule that the fault requirement is less for non-stigmatic as opposed to stigmatic offences. Rather, the position is that any penal (as opposed to a purely preventative, regulatory, or compensatory) response by the state to individual conduct requires proof of fault, and that the degree of fault necessary is intention unless otherwise specified.

However, this does not restrict the scope of criminal liability as much as an English criminal lawyer might suppose. The German concept of intention (*Vorsatz*) encompasses not only direct intention (where the agent wants to perform an act and/or to achieve an outcome; referred to as *Absicht* or as '*dolus directus* of the first type') and intention in the 'secondary' sense (where the agent

---

[5] A count was done by F.-Ch. Schröder (for the StGB as it stood on 1 April 1994) and resulted in 30 offences of pure recklessness, 245 offences of pure intention, and 39 intention-recklessness combinations (discussed in the following subsection on result-qualified offences). See F.-Ch. Schröder, Commentary of § 15, annotation 5, in Burkhard Jähnke, Heinrich Wilhelm Laufhütte, and Walter Odersky (eds.), *Strafgesetzbuch: Leipziger Kommentar*, i. *Einleitung; §§ 1 bis 31* (11th edn., Berlin 2003), hereafter *LK*, followed by the name of the commentator, §, and annotation.

[6] *Waffengesetz* (WaffG) of 11 October 2002 (BGBl I, 3970; III, 7133-4/1). The law regulates the possession and use of firearms and other weapons.

[7] *Gesetz über den Verkehr mit Betäubungsmitteln* (BtMG) of 1 March 1994 (BGBl I, 358; III, 2121-6-24). The law regulates the possession, use, and trade in controlled drugs.

[8] *Gesetz über Ordnungswidrigkeiten* (OwiG) of 19 February 1987 (BGBl I, 602; III 454-1). *Ordnungswidrigkeiten* are not offences in the formal sense. But they share all the material features of a criminal offence in that they consist of blameworthy violations of the law for which the state imposes a sanction in the form of a special type of administrative fine called a *Geldbuße* (§ 1 OwiG). Conviction for an *Ordnungswidrigkeit* does not create a criminal record. The difference between *Ordnungswidrigkeiten* (regulatory offences) and *Straftaten* (crimes) is thus merely technical: wherever the legislature chooses to impose an administrative fine for a violation of the law, the offence created is merely a regulatory one; where it imposes a criminal sanction, the offence created is a crime properly so speaking. See Hans Heinrich Jescheck and Thomas Weigend, *Lehrbuch des Strafrechts. Allgemeiner Teil* (5th edn., Berlin 1996), 56–60.

[9] See §§ 113, 43 *Bundesrechtsanwaltsordnung* (BRAO) for lawyers.

foresees an outcome as a certain consequence of his actions, although he does not desire to bring it about; referred to as '*dolus directus* of the second type'). It also includes *dolus eventualis*, where the agent foresees an outcome as a possible consequence of his actions, and is reconciled to the possibility of bringing it about (rather than dismissing the risk). Consequently, a wide range of cases that in many other legal systems, including the English one, would be treated as instances of 'advertent recklessness' are classified as intentional wrongs under German criminal law.

Recklessness (*Fahrlässigkeit*), in turn, is not restricted to 'advertent' or *Cunningham*[10] recklessness, where the agent is aware of a risk, which he does not take seriously enough to desist from acting. 'Inadvertent recklessness' also counts as a form of *mens rea*, covering situations where the agent failed to address his mind to the possibility of risk, but would have appreciated its existence had he thought about it in advance. This means that it is sufficient to show that the defendant 'would have foreseen' the risk, not that he did foresee it. In practical terms, the question the court is concerned with is whether the risk would have been obvious to the defendant, given his intellectual capacities and knowledge at the time. If the court is convinced that the defendant was able to recognize the risk in question, it finds that he 'would have done so, had he addressed his mind to it', and hence that he acted recklessly in taking the risk—albeit inadvertently. In effect, the defendant is held to the standard of a reasonable person of his age and intelligence, given the knowledge he had at the time.

By accepting inadvertent recklessness as a type of *mens rea*, the scope of criminal liability for recklessness is wider under German than under English law and extends to what English lawyers would usually classify as negligence, which under English law, except in rare constellations, is insufficient for a finding of criminal fault.[11] Furthermore, the evidential challenge faced by the prosecution is much easier to meet under German law, since even credible claims of distraction and the like cannot thwart a finding of recklessness. Thus in the comparatively rare instances where reckless conduct, reckless risk-creation, or reckless causation of harm are criminalized, German law treats as a form of criminal *mens rea* something that would not generally be regarded as such by English legal practitioners. But we should not forget that negligence, or inadvertent recklessness, *is* a form of subjective fault—a possibility that many legal philosophers in the English tradition, most notably H. L. A. Hart, have defended,[12] although their arguments only rarely have an impact on the reasoning of the courts.

---

[10] [1957] 2 QB 396.

[11] Negligence (or objective recklessness, as it is often called) used to suffice for a conviction for criminal damage (*Caldwell* [1982] AC 341, now overruled in *R. v. G* [2003] 3 WLR 1060; [2003] UKHL 50). A negligent violation of duty appears to be sufficient in cases of manslaughter by breach of duty (*Adomako* [1995] 1 AC 171).

[12] H. L. A. Hart, 'Negligence, *Mens Rea*, and Criminal Responsibility', in H. L. A. Hart, *Punishment and Responsibility* (Oxford 1968), 136.

## Result-Qualified Offences ('Erfolgsqualifizierte Delikte')

In addition to 'pure' offences of intention and 'pure' offences of recklessness, the German Criminal Code also contains a number of offences where the *mens rea* element combines intention as to the performance of the conduct element with recklessness as to the causation of a specified serious consequence. These offences, so-called intention-recklessness combinations, are effectively aggravated versions of basic, intentionally committed, conduct-related offences. By virtue of the particularly serious result, the defendant's conduct 'qualifies' not just for the basic, but also for the more serious, 'result-qualified' offence. While comparable offences in English criminal law often contain strict liability elements, § 18 StGB stipulates that 'Where the law imposes a heavier punishment with a view to a particular consequence of the criminal act, the defendant will only be liable for the heavier punishment if he was at least reckless with regard to the consequence in question.'[13] This provision applies to numerous offences of the special part where the defendant's conduct, performed with intent, already amounts to a criminal offence irrespective of the consequence in issue, and where the defendant also commits the more serious, result-qualified offence by reason of a particularly grave consequence he recklessly brought about through the commission of the basic offence.[14] The classic example for an offence of this type is aggravated bodily injury (*Schwere Körperverletzung*, § 226 StGB), where the basic offence of causing bodily injury (*Körperverletzung*, § 223 StGB) requires the intentional physical abuse or injury to health of another person, whereas the qualifying consequences, which the defendant must have caused at least recklessly and any one of which suffices, are defined in § 226 StGB as 'loss of eyesight in one or both eyes, loss of hearing, loss of capacity to procreate, loss or permanent loss of use of an important part of the body, significant disfigurement, lasting illness, paralysis, mental disorder or disability'. Many of the substantive provisions of the special part which conform to this basic pattern specify a higher degree of recklessness, gross recklessness (*Leichtfertigkeit*), as the degree of fault that the defendant's attitude to the consequence must manifest.

## Objective Conditions of Liability ('Objektive Bedingungen der Strafbarkeit')

That said, even in German criminal law there are some cases where liability depends on an external factor, other than a procedural requirement, to which no fault requirement pertains. These exceptional factors are summarily referred to as

[13] § 18 StGB *(Schwere Strafe bei besonderen Tatfolgen):* Knüpft das Gesetz an eine besondere Folge der Tat eine schwerere Strafe, so trifft diese den Täter oder Teilnehmer nur, wenn ihm hinsichtlich dieser Folge wenigstens Fahrlässigkeit zur Last fällt.

[14] Less importantly, § 18 also covers some instances where the aggravating consequence follows upon a recklessly committed basic offence, and it applies in some cases where the serious consequence is brought about intentionally, but where the intentional causation of the serious consequence has not been independently criminalized. A list can be found in *LK*-Schröder, § 18 annotations 25 and 31.

'objective conditions of liability' (*objektive Bedingungen der Strafbarkeit*). Offences that contain them are rare, and it is disputed among writers whether the absence of a fault requirement with regard to these factors can be brought under a common rationale and/or justification.

The main examples of offences containing an objective condition of liability are the bankruptcy-related offences (§ 283 StGB), offences directed at foreign governments and their representatives (§§ 102–104 StGB), criminal libel (§ 186 StGB), dangerous drunkenness (§ 323a StGB), and involvement in a brawl where one of the affected persons suffers serious injuries or death (§ 231 StGB).

Section 283 StGB penalizes various offences of defrauding creditors: deliberately failing to keep proper accounts, intentionally disposing of assets in anticipation of future bankruptcy, and intentionally incurring credit, when any of this is done with recklessness (or worse) as to the risk of eventual insolvency. The objective condition of liability in respect of these offences is the institution of bankruptcy proceedings. This key event is something in respect of which the defendant need not have been intentional, or even reckless: indeed, all the dubious steps he took before it happened, which now amount to criminal offences, may well have been calculated to prevent it happening.[15]

For the group of offences contained in Chapter 3 of the Special Part of the German Criminal Code (§§ 102–104a), which criminalize certain acts directed at foreign governments and their representatives, the objective condition of the defendant's liability under these norms is the 'reciprocity of protection' for the German state and its organs by the law of the country of origin of the victim of any of the offences.

The objective condition of liability of the offence of criminal libel (§ 186 StGB) is the incorrectness of the alleged defamatory fact. It is an 'objective condition of liability' in the sense that the defendant's *mens rea* need not extend to the objective incorrectness of his allegation; hence an honest but mistaken belief in its correctness does not negate liability.[16] Some writers have sought to explain it as a mere evidential rule (the statement will be presumed to be untrue unless the defendant proves, on a balance of probabilities, that it is true), but this explanation does not account for the fact that the defendant cannot deny *mens rea* with a view to an honest belief in the truth of his allegations. Hence, it is better to think of the incorrectness of the potentially defamatory allegation as a hybrid between a

---

[15] A point already made by Franz von Liszt, *Lehrbuch des deutschen Strafrechts* (multiple edns. until 1927; here cited after the 6th edn., Berlin/Leipzig 1894), 432 at n. 2, and is now universally accepted by academic commentators and the courts. See Adolf Schönke and Horst Schröder, *Strafgesetzbuch: Kommentar* (26th edn., Munich 2001), § 283 annotation 59 (hereafter 'Schönke-Schröder', § and annotation); RGSt 45, 88; BGHSt 1, 191. 'RGSt' indicates a decision made by the *Reichsgericht* in a criminal case; 'BGHSt' indicates a decision made by the *Bundesgerichtshof* in a criminal case. The numbers refer to volume and page number of the official collection of the decisions of the respective courts.

[16] RGSt 69, 81; BGHSt 11, 274. For the discussion about the nature of this condition of liability see Schönke-Schröder, § 186 annotation 13.

strict liability element and a shifting of the burden of proof: a strict liability element which, if 'objectively disproven' by the defendant, gives him a defence.

Section 231 StGB[17] criminalizes participation in a brawl or fistfight, where death or serious injury to another human being (whether participant or bystander) results. Only intentional participation in the fight, and neither intention nor actual or potential foresight with regard to the serious consequence, needs to be established against the defendant to found a conviction under this offence.[18] This provision provides a clear parallel for the constructive liability for unintended and unforeseen outcomes that offences such as constructive manslaughter, and some applications of sect. 20 OAPA, impose on defendants under English criminal law.

The—in practical terms—most significant example of an objective condition of liability, however, is the offence of 'dangerous intoxication' (*Vollrausch*, § 323a StGB). This makes a person punishable with a fine or with imprisonment of up to five years who, intentionally or recklessly, gets mindlessly intoxicated on drink or drugs, and in this state commits another criminal offence for which he cannot be held responsible due to a proven or possible lack of capacity at the time of the commission of the offence.[19] The commission of the 'other offence' is the condition in question: it is (as an English criminal lawyer would describe it) an element of the *actus reus* of the *Vollrausch*-offence to which the intention or recklessness of the defendant's state of mind need not relate. For instance, a defendant who forces a non-consenting woman to have sexual intercourse with him, while too intoxicated to be able to control his behaviour (someone who, as § 20 StGB puts it, lacks responsibility 'due to a severe mental disturbance at the time of the deed which makes him unable to realise the wrongness of his actions or to act in accordance with this realisation'), would be convicted under § 323a StGB, provided that he intentionally or recklessly got himself into that state of mindless intoxication.

For an English criminal lawyer, used to treating voluntary intoxication as a form of reckless conduct, proof of which is sufficient to constitute *mens rea* for a crime of basic intent,[20] the provision must appear both peculiar and superfluous. But in German criminal law, where extreme intoxication (even if voluntary) is regularly accepted as a state of mind which may exclude responsibility under § 20 StGB, it plugs an important liability gap. Without § 323a StGB, the defendant

---

[17] The provision in question used to be § 227. It was renumbered and redrafted in 1998 (6th *Strafrechtsänderungsgesetz* (Criminal Law Amendment Act) 1998 of 26 January 1998, *Bundesgesetzblatt* (BGBl) I 164).

[18] BGHSt 33, 103; Karl Lackner and Kristian Kühl, *Strafgesetzbuch mit Erläuterungen* (24th edn., Munich 2001), § 231 annotation 5 (hereafter 'Lackner/Kühl', § and annotation); Herbert Tröndle and Thomas Fischer, *Strafgesetzbuch und Nebengesetze: Kommentar* (51th edn., Munich 2003), § 231 annotation 5 (hereafter 'Tröndle/Fischer', § and annotation).

[19] Lackner/Kühl, § 323a annotation 1.

[20] *Majewski* [1977] AC 443. German criminal law, however, does recognize the doctrine of the 'actio libera in causa'. This means that a defendant will be convicted not for his 'dangerous intoxication', but for the offence he committed while intoxicated to a degree which would normally exclude capacity and hence criminal liability, if he formed the intention to commit the offence in question before he got intoxicated (see *LK*-Jähnke, § 20 annotation 76 ff.).

would simply be acquitted of the 'other offence' by virtue of his intoxicated state. By creating a separate offence of committing an offence while culpably mindlessly intoxicated in § 323a StGB, in which the 'other offence' appears as a strict liability element with regard to which culpability need not be shown, the defendant can at least be convicted—albeit still not for the 'other offence' as such.

Can these objective conditions of liability be squared with the culpability principle? The justification usually offered for them is that they are 'morally neutral' elements of the offence, 'external' to the wrong constituted by the defendant's act.[21] The wrongness of the defendant's conduct is established by those elements of the *actus reus* to which *mens rea* extends. As many German writers have recognized, this argument works for some of these cases, but is unconvincing in regard to others.[22] Quite clearly, it works for those provisions which criminalize conduct directed at foreign governments and their representatives. That such conduct is inherently wrong, irrespective of whether the German state and its officials receive equivalent protection by the laws of the victim state, is powerfully illustrated by the fact that (when it comes to acts such as criminal damage, and insults and assaults against the representatives of foreign states) they are in any case criminal under the general provisions of the criminal law. The argument also (by and large) works for the start of bankruptcy proceedings in the context of the bankruptcy offences. Improper bookkeeping, ordering goods one cannot pay for, and the like are questionable business practices at the best of times. In cases where bankruptcy is averted, considerations outside the criminal law determine the legislator's choice not to punish such inherently dishonest and wrongful ways of behaving. In these instances, dishonest conduct has created a risk of harm, but no harm has occurred. A criminal investigation and trial may well ruin the defendant's business altogether and cause the harm to his creditors that the law strives to avoid. This does not detract from the fact that the defendant's business ought to be run on more honest principles, and that a case could be made to bring the pressures of the criminal law to bear upon him. It is because of economic considerations that

---

[21] This rationalization of the objective conditions of liability was already put forward by von Liszt, *Lehrbuch*, 168: objective conditions of liability are circumstances which 'are not constitutive elements of the criminal act' (*'nicht konstitutive Merkmale der verbrecherischen Tätigkeit'*). Karl Binding defined them as 'elements of the crime which are not part of the norm it sets for human conduct', i.e. the standard it sets for the wrongfulness of the act (*'normfremde Bestandteile des gesetzlichen Tatbestandes'*) (in: *Die Normen und ihre Übertretung. Eine Untersuchung über die rechtmässige Handlung und die Arten des Delikts*, i. sect. 1: *Normen und Strafgesetze* (1st edn. Leipzig 1872) at 507), and already recognized that, given this explanation, certain of the existing objective conditions of liability, for instance the incorrectness of the allegation in the case of criminal libel, are unjustifiable (at 611). A good account of the historical debates surrounding the concept of objective conditions of liability is provided by Gerhard Haß, 'Zu Wesen und Funktion der objektiven Strafbarkeitsbedingung. Bemerkungen zur Entstehungsgeschichte des Begriffs' in: (1972) *Rechtstheorie* 23–33.
[22] An overview of the arguments is given by Claus Roxin, *Strafrecht: Allgemeiner Teil*, i. *Grundlagen, Aufbau der Verbrechenslehre* (3rd edn., Munich 1997) at 894–913. For a more comprehensive discussion see Claudius Geisler, *Zur Vereinbarkeit objektiver Strafbarkeitsbedingungen mit dem Schuldprinzip. Zugleich ein Beitrag zum Freiheitsbegriff des modernen Strafrechts* (Berlin 1998).

provide a counter-weight to an otherwise sound case for criminalization that the law takes a step backwards where the defendant ultimately is able to meet his financial obligations.

But it is much harder to argue that communicating a potentially defamatory fact about another person is inherently wrong even if one, with good reason, believes it to be true;[23] or that in a society where the consumption of alcohol is not prohibited and where it serves as the main recreational drug, it is inherently wrong to get even mindlessly drunk, as long as one does not have reason to believe that, once drunk to a degree excluding culpable conduct one might behave in ways that constitute criminal offences.[24] And mere participation in a fight in ways that are neither intended nor likely to cause serious injury to anyone seems too minor a wrong to justify criminalization, let alone punishment with up to three years' imprisonment.

In these cases, the so-called 'objective conditions of liability' are quite clearly part of what determines the harmfulness, and indeed the wrongfulness, of the deed in question. Since they are intrinsically connected to the *actus reus*, treating them as falling outside its scope seems like a manipulative labelling exercise, designed simply to facilitate conviction.[25] If they were treated as forming part of the *actus reus* of the respective offence, the defendant's actual, or even potential, awareness of their existence, and building upon that an attitude that manifests either intention or recklessness, would be hard if not impossible to prove. Since doing away with them altogether would not leave a nucleus of wrongful conduct sufficiently blameworthy to justify criminalization, the preferred solution by many writers is to reinterpret the 'objective conditions of liability' in the problematic cases as elements of the *actus reus* with regard to which the defendant must have been at least negligent. Thus, it must have been foreseeable for him when joining a fight that someone might get seriously injured,[26] an honest and not

[23] As for the practical conclusions drawn by writers, Hans Welzel demands that the defendant has to intend the statement to be untrue (*Das deutsche Strafrecht* (11th edn., Berlin 1969), 313); while Hans-Joachim Hirsch finds it sufficient that the defendant is reckless as to whether the allegation he makes is true or not (*Ehre und Beleidigung* (Karlsruhe 1967)).

[24] This line of reasoning is less convincing in cases where the mindlessly intoxicated state results from the consumption of illegal drugs. But even in these situations, one can argue that the risk of committing an offence of a particular type should at least be foreseeable, and hence exclude liability for the *Vollrausch*-offence in cases where the commission of the subsequent offence does not result from the foreseeable effects of disinhibition, but from an unusual chain of events that took even the defendant by surprise. Thus, many German lawyers would argue that someone like the defendant in *Lipman* [1970] 1 QB 152, who, while high on LSD strangled his girlfriend believing her to be a snake, should not be convicted for any criminal offence—certainly not for manslaughter, but also not for the *Vollrausch*-offence for which he would formally qualify.

[25] This tendency is particularly evident in the early writings on these conditions, when they were still more widespread and covered most instances of sentence-aggravating consequences as well. Ernst Beling, for instance, reasoned that the main function of these objective conditions of liability is to place the element in question outside the scope of the provisions which allow a defendant to deny *mens rea* because of a mistake of fact (*Die Lehre vom Verbrechen* (Tübingen 1906), 51 ff. and 201 ff.).

[26] Roxin, *Strafrecht*, 898. Hirsch (in Hans Heinrich Jescheck, Wolfgang Rick, and Günter Willms (eds.), *Strafgesetzbuch: Leipziger Kommentar*, v. §§ 185 bis 262 (10th edn. Berlin 1989), § 227 annotations 1, 13, and 15) wants to apply § 18 StGB.

unreasonable belief in the truth of a defamatory statement would be a defence,[27] and when getting mindlessly drunk the defendant must have been able to anticipate that once in that state he might commit other offences of the relevant type.[28] Increasingly embattled by academic criticism, it is probably only a matter of time before the German courts accept these arguments.

## Fault Requirements and Sentencing Considerations

Interestingly, German criminal law requires fault not only with regard to elements of the offence that are part of the *actus reus* properly so speaking, but also with regard to aspects of the defendant's deed that invoke aggravated sentencing scales for the offence. Many such sentencing-scale adjusting provisions are included in the special part of the Criminal Code, where the offence-defining provision might set out further aggravated versions of the offence, or stipulate higher sentencing scales for so-called 'typical' aggravated cases (so-called *Regelbeispielstechnik*), which may be disapplied when the court takes the view that despite the presence of features that would typically indicate a serious instance of the commission of the offence in question, the case at hand is not particularly grave.[29] An example of the latter technique is provided by § 243 (1) StGB for serious cases of theft, while § 176a StGB on serious cases of sexual abuse of children opts for the former technique.[30]

Again, the degree of fault required is intention unless the sentencing consideration relates to the causing of a particularly grave consequence. Where this is the case, the fault requirement is—by way of analogy—taken from § 18 StGB[31] and thereby brought down to recklessness.[32] The law of sexual offences provides numerous examples for both alternatives. By way of illustration, one can point to § 176a (4) No 1 StGB ('If the perpetrator seriously physically assaults the child in connection with his deed [of sexual abuse of a child as defined in § 176 StGB], he shall be punished with imprisonment of no less than 5 years'). This provision requires intention as to the serious physical abuse of the child.[33] By contrast, § 176a (3) No 3, which raises the punishment for cases where the perpetrator by his deed of sexual abuse of a child as defined in § 176 StGB creates an actual risk of serious damage to the child's health or of a serious impediment for its physical or

---

[27] Roxin, *Strafrecht*, 901; Hirsch, *Ehre und Beleidigung*.

[28] Roxin, *Strafrecht*, 898. Foresight of one's own dangerousness once drunk is demanded by Schönke-Schröder, § 323a annotation 1.

[29] Most recent legislative changes have resulted in the inclusion of aggravated sentencing scales for defined 'grave cases' in the provisions of the special part of the Criminal Code.

[30] The only practical difference between the two techniques is the greater flexibility at the sentencing stage where the law defines aggravated cases only for 'typical', as opposed to all cases where the preconditions for the application of the aggravated sentencing scale obtain.

[31] For text and translation of § 18 StGB, see n. 13 and accompanying text above.

[32] See Schönke-Schröder, § 46 annotation 26, and *LK*-Schröder, § 18 annotations 7 and 8. For *Regelbeispiele*, see Lackner/Kühl, § 46 annotation 12.

[33] Schönke-Schröder, § 176a annotation 9.

mental development, arguably merely requires recklessness as to the creation of this kind of risk for the child.[34]

Fault requirements for the application of sentencing considerations that are linked to aspects of the defendant's deed also pertain to the application of § 46 StGB, the provision of the general part of the Criminal Code that sets out sentencing rules for all offences. This is self-evident for considerations which are in any case based on the defendant's state of mind, his inner relation to his crime, such as 'his motives and objectives', 'the attitude which is expressed by the deed', and 'the degree of determination required to carry out the deed'.[35] But it is also true for such criteria as 'the degree of carelessness in violation of duty' and 'the method of execution of the deed'. The defendant must have been aware of the facts on which the judgment of the particular reprehensibility of his conduct is based, and must have chosen to act in this way. In application of the general principle that the required degree of fault is intention unless otherwise stipulated (§ 15 StGB), the fault element required in these cases is *Vorsatz*.[36]

With regard to the final deed-related criterion of the catalogue of sentencing considerations, the 'further consequences of the deed' which are not already part of the *actus reus* requirement of the offence,[37] § 46 StGB expressly stipulates that they only count against the defendant when he brought them about culpably. In this regard, however, the defendant's responsibility is not restricted to consequences that he intentionally brought about. The principle that recklessness is sufficient to make the defendant responsible for a serious outcome (§ 18 StGB) is taken to apply in this context; hence, mere recklessness suffices.[38]

The culpability principle, thus, does not merely govern the defendant's criminal liability. It also affects the sentence that the state is justified in imposing upon him. The punishment of the offender is based on the seriousness of the offence and on the culpability of the offender. German law clearly takes the view that, in so far as the seriousness of the offence is affected by the manner of its execution, its consequences for the victim or other innocent third parties, and the like, these can

[34] Eckhard Horn, commentary of § 179 annotation 31, in Hans-Joachim Rudolphi, Eckhard Horn, Erich Samson, Hand-Ludwig Günther, and Andreas Hoyer, *Systematischer Kommentar zum Strafgesetzbuch* (6th edn., Neuwied 2000), ii. There is some debate about whether an actual risk of harm (rather than harm itself) can be understood as a serious consequence within the meaning of § 18 StGB. Other commentators suggest that intention is required. The practice of the courts differs for different provisions where a risk of harm matters, and the interpretation will depend on other factors as well, not least the severity of the threatened sanction. See generally Tröndle/Fischer, § 18 annotation 2a.

[35] The quoted criteria form the first group of sentencing considerations listed in § 46 (2) StGB.

[36] Intention, which in German law also includes knowledge (see subsection on German criminal law above).

[37] Section 46 (2), read in conjunction with § 46 (3) StGB. The other sentencing considerations listed in § 46 (2) StGB refer to the conduct of the defendant beyond the immediate context of his crime: his past behaviour, his personal and economic circumstances, and his conduct after the deed (in particular, whether he made any efforts to undo the damage and/or to reconcile with the victim).

[38] Lackner/Kühl, § 46 annotation 34; critical Schönke-Schröder, § 46 annotation 26 (§ 15 ought to be applied).

only count as aggravating factors (which justify the imposition of a sentence near the upper margin of the punishment scale) if the defendant is 'responsible' for them. This is unsurprising where certain external factors have been made part of 'typified' adjustments of the sentencing scale in the relevant provisions of the special part of the German Criminal Code. But the position is no different when these factors merely stand to be considered in the sentencing decision of the judge.

In this way, German criminal law avoids holding defendants responsible for unintended and unforeseeable outcomes, be it as part of the determination of criminal liability, or in connection with the imposition of the sentence.

## Doctrinal Foundations

This pattern reflects the German criminal law's uncompromising commitment to the culpability principle (*Schuldprinzip*), which constitutes the doctrinal foundation for all its practical arrangements. In German criminal law doctrine, the culpability principle means that criminal liability requires blameworthiness, and that the reaction of the law must be commensurate with the measure of blame that attaches to the defendant's conduct. According to the German Constitutional Court, which has ascribed constitutional rank to the culpability principle,[39] the principle is intrinsically connected to the substantive dimension of the rule of law ('*Rechtsstaatsprinzip*') and 'rooted in human dignity and in a recognition of the human being's capacity for responsible agency, [principles] which the Constitution presupposes and protects in Articles 1 (1) and 2 (1), and which the legislature has to acknowledge and respect in the formulation of its criminal laws'.[40] While the culpability principle has a strong doctrinal basis, the correspondence principle (the principle that in practice prevents the German courts from interpreting criminal law provisions as containing strict liability elements) is taken to be a simple rule of statutory interpretation, which emanates from the culpability principle as a matter of course.[41] If pressed to explain the position, the German criminal lawyer is likely to reply that all the elements of the *actus reus*, not just the conduct element itself, combine to make up the 'wrongness' of the act, and thus the defendant is held responsible only to the extent that he is at fault (which is what the culpability principle requires) if he is at fault in regard to every aspect that defines the wrongness of his act, in other words: in regard to every material element of the *actus reus*. For this reason, it would simply not occur to a German criminal lawyer to question the need for a fault element with respect to the age of the victim of an offence of sex with minors,[42] the capacity of a statement that

---

[39] BVerfGE 80, 244 (255). 'BVerfGE' refers to the official collection of the judgments of the German Constitutional Court. The subsequent numbers indicate the volume and starting page of the decision, with the exact page reference for the quote in brackets.    [40] BVerfGE 25, 269 (285).
[41] See e.g. Lackner/Kühl, § 15 annotation 4. Critical of the correspondence principle is Wolfgang Frisch, *Vorsatz und Risiko. Grundfragen des tatbestandsmäßigen Verhaltens und des Vorsatzes. Zugleich ein Beitrag zur Behandlung außertatbestandlicher Möglichkeitsvorstellungen* (Cologne/Berlin/Bonn/Munich 1983), 118: *Vorsatz* extends only to the conduct element of the offence.
[42] BGHSt 42, 51; Lackner/Kühl, § 176 annotation 7 and § 174 annotation 15.

discriminates against minorities or denies the Holocaust to 'disturb public peace' (§ 130 StGB),[43] or the nature of an item that the defendant has in his possession, whether drugs or firearms.[44]

The recognition of the culpability principle is, however, much older than the present German Constitution, the *Grundgesetz*. Its first stirrings can be traced as far back as the late Middle Ages, when the administration of criminal justice in the provinces of the German *Reich* was in such a dire state that the reconstituted *Reichskammergericht*,[45] the highest court of the land, eventually called the attention of the ruling kings' assembly (the *Reichsversammlung* [46]) to the numerous complaints it had received about 'people being sentenced and put to death without reason or justice'.[47] This triggered conscious efforts of reform. Many of these were inspired by the criminal laws of the northern Italian city-states, where generations of Italian scholars had developed and rationalized the concepts of responsibility and fault contained in Roman criminal law.[48]

The most impressive of the resulting codes was the *Constitutio Criminalis Carolina* (Carolina)[49] of the Emperor Charles V. in 1532, based to a large extent on the earlier *Constitutio Criminalis Bambergensis* (1507) of one of the German provincial states. The *Constitutio Criminalis Bambergensis* was drafted by Freiherr Johann von Schwarzenberg und Hohenlandsberg, judge at the Highest Court in the Southern German town of Bamberg. Schwarzenberg felt strongly that the administration of criminal law must be based on justice if it was to be efficient. Writing *ex officio*, he declared that 'No one should be foolish enough to think that anything good or useful can come of a measure that is not just.'[50] In requiring 'that the punishment not be greater than the fault',[51] he promoted a criminal law that does not, like its medieval predecessors, penalize the accidental causation of harm or react with capital punishment to unintentional, albeit culpable, killings. In effect, what we see here is an early call for proportionality of punishment, for a judicial evaluation of the crime no longer blinded by anger at the occurrence of a harmful outcome, ready to appreciate the impulse and actor behind the deed. Article 179 of the Carolina instructs the judge to consult with legal experts when

---

[43] Lackner/Kühl, § 130 annotation 12; Schönke-Schröder, § 130 annotation 24.

[44] Lackner/Kühl, § 15 annotation 4.

[45] A brief account of the origins and history of the *Reichskammergericht* is given by Hinrich Rüping, *Grundriß der Strafrechtsgeschichte* (Munich 1981), 32–5. As a result of the comparable powerlessness of the emperor *vis-à-vis* the regional rulers, the *Reichskammergericht* was notorious for being understaffed and inefficient and in later years became the object of much ridicule. Its functions as an appellate court were more and more taken over by regional appellate courts adjudicating under the authority of the regional rulers.

[46] Assembly of the regional rulers (*Fürsten*) and the Emperor (*Kaiser*).

[47] Cited after Eberhard Schmidt, *Einführung in die Geschichte der deutschen Strafrechtspflege* (2nd repr. of 3rd edn., Göttingen 1995), 107.            [48] Ibid. 107–8.

[49] For an English edn., see John H. Langbein, *Prosecuting Crime in the Renaissance: England, Germany and France* (Cambridge, Mass. 1974).

[50] See Schwarzenberg's translation of Cicero's *De officiis*, published in 1531, cited after Schmidt, *Einführung*, 113.            [51] Ibid. 114.

it appears that the defendant 'may not have been in possession of his senses because of his youth or for other reasons', and is careful to spell out (albeit in an unsystematic fashion) the *mens rea* required by each of the capital crimes.[52]

But it was left to the writers of the Enlightenment to inspire a deepened understanding and working through of the implications of the culpability principle. In its present-day form, the culpability principle is a reflection of the German criminal law theorists' confrontation, and engagement, with Kantian, Hegelian, and Schopenhauerian philosophical ideas regarding the nature of human responsibility and the basis for blame. By 1872, Karl Binding[53] in his influential treatise on 'Norms and their Violations'[54] grounds his views on the proper basis of criminal liability firmly on a philosophy of action that defines human conduct—that which we are prima facie responsible for—as 'a realization of an impulse of the will', or a 'willed act'. Human deeds are consequently conceptualized as realizations of an impulse of the will. ('Impulse of the will' in this context means 'decision to act'; the 'realization' of this decision to act is the act itself, including its consequences.) The potential scope of our legal responsibility thus depends, first, on our pre-legal, moral, understanding of what counts as 'willed', and, secondly, on our pre-legal, moral, understanding of the concept of the deed. Binding writes:

A legally relevant act is constituted by three criteria: some change must have occurred in the outside world to which the law potentially ascribes significance. This change must be related to an act of will of a human being in the sense that this particular human being set out to bring about this precise change. . . .[55] And finally the cleft between will and deed must be bridged by a finding that this act of will brought about this deed. This finding is called imputation.[56]

It is this understanding that criminal deeds are expressions of human freedom, and also of an act of choice against the law, that leads these late nineteenth-century German writers to develop a sophisticated concept of culpability that operates both as the logical basis for an ascription of responsibility and as a justification for, and limitation of, the criminal sanction.

---

[52]  Ibid. 116–17.

[53]  Karl Binding (1841–1920) was a highly-respected theorist whose extensive writings on criminal law are still influential. Regrettably, he is better known outside Germany as the joint author with the psychiatrist Dr Alfred Hoche of a pamphlet written in the last year of his life, and published posthumously, entitled *Die Freigabe der Vernichtung lebensunwerten Lebens* ('Permission for the extermination of lives not worth living'), which argued the case for the humane killing of the mentally handicapped and terminally ill, and so provided part of the intellectual justification for the Nazi programme of exterminating the inmates of mental hospitals.          [54]  *Normen*.

[55]  This does not mean that agents can only be responsible for anticipated outcomes. Binding later argues that we need to differentiate between what we wish for and what we 'will' to occur; certain unanticipated outcomes can be part and parcel of our deed and hence our criminal responsibility can extend to them (*Normen*, 75, 104–12): 'Wir wollen vielmehr mit den Ursachen unbesehen alle ihre Folgen, weil wir überhaupt nicht anders wollen können, als dass wir die Folgen mit in Kauf nehmen. . . . Wenn sich der Wille in den Strom der Geschichte stürzt, so kann er das Ufer nicht immer gerade in dem Augenblick wiedergewinnen, in dem er dies wünscht.'          [56]  Ibid. 41.

Only the free impulse of the will and the free act are truly the deed of the human agent. Only these can count as expressions of who he is, only these are what he can be held responsible for. It is for this reason that the evaluation of such a free act throws its light and its shadow on the character of the agent as a whole.[57]

Culpable conduct is wrongful conduct resulting from a blameworthy exercise of the will. This may sound straightforward, yet Binding advances this proposition only after he has given a careful and elaborate account of 'rightful' conduct (in the sense that no legal liability will attach to the consequences of it). 'Rightful' conduct is also human action properly so speaking: it is the kind of conduct which we can be held responsible for. It requires that we can understand what is expected of us: we must be aware, or at least able to make ourselves aware, of the standards of behaviour that apply to us. Thus, we have to be conscious, we must pass a threshold of rationality, and we must know that there are norms out there that apply to our conduct and that, if we are not yet aware of their precise contents, we ought to make ourselves aware of them before we act. Our decision to act must be directed towards the realization of a lawful objective by lawful means, neither of which we expect to result in further unwanted harm. In the most praiseworthy situation, we are acutely aware that these conditions obtain; but rightful conduct also exists where our unreflected acts happen to be directed to the achievement of some lawful end by lawful means.[58] Culpable conduct mirrors this pattern in that it is either consciously, or through carelessness unconsciously, directed towards unlawful ends, and/or employing unlawful means, and/or involving further unlawful consequences.[59]

The culpability principle thus links questions of capacity and fault: both are prerequisites of responsibility. The definitive formulation of the culpability principle was offered by Reinhard Frank in 1907. According to Frank, the culpability of an agent comprises three 'elements': (1) the normal psychological make-up of the actor, (2) an actual or at least 'actualizable' connection between the actor's state of mind and his deed (intention or recklessness), and (3) the absence of unusual circumstances that affect the moral quality of the actor's conduct, or the expectations society can legitimately have of him (i.e. the absence of exculpatory circumstances). What holds these three elements together is the dimension of blameworthiness: 'Someone can be held criminally responsible for a prohibited act when he can be blamed for having engaged in this behaviour.'[60]

---

[57] Ibid. 9: 'Nur der freie Entschluss und die freie Handlung sind das eigenste Werk des tätig gewordenen Menschen. Ihnen allein hat er seinen Stempel aufgedrückt, deshalb braucht er allein sie zu verantworten. Deshalb wirft aber jede Beurteilung einer solchen freien Handlung ihr Licht und ihren Schatten auf die ganze Persönlichkeit des Täters zurück.' [58] Ibid. 101–2.
[59] Ibid. 102 ff.
[60] 'Über den Aufbau des Schuldbegriffs', in Reinhard Frank (ed.), *Festschrift für die juristische Fakultät Giessen zum Universitäts-Jubiläum* (Giessen 1907), 3.

## *The Move Away from Direct and Indirect Outcome Liability Without Fault*

There is one area of the criminal law in particular where the implications of the culpability principle were long shrouded in uncertainty, and where positions on the true requirements of the culpability principle changed significantly over time: the liability of the defendant for any unanticipated and undesired harmful outcomes of his unlawful act.[61]

Of course, there never was a time when the law did not differentiate between what in modern terms are intentional and non-intentional crimes. Early and medieval law punished much more heavily the person who performed a premeditated killing than the person who acted violently in hot blood. The first was a murderer who had to be killed, the second was guilty only of manslaughter and thus theoretically and practically able to clean himself of the deed by paying a huge compensatory fine. But so long as the harmful outcome formed the basis for any criminal liability, the legal system's grasp of why these distinctions should be drawn could only be confused: because the causation of harm remained the starting point for the attribution of responsibility and blame, medieval justice could not move towards building its differentiations consciously and coherently around the offender's state of mind. Hence, medieval law was incapable of differentiating between the agent who, intending to cause mere injury, caused death, and the agent who, intending to cause death in an open attack on the victim, succeeded in doing so. Both were manslaughterers alike.[62] The law also equated agents who caused injury, intending to cause injury, with those who caused injury, intending to cause death. And in the absence of any concept of criminal attempts, it often left unpunished those who, intending to cause a prohibited harm of some kind, failed to cause any.[63]

When medieval law first moved away from pure outcome liability (liability for the so-called *Ungefährwerke*, which we would today describe as cases of mere accidental causation of harm), it thereby merely recognized the principle that, in the absence of carelessness, no liability can result for the accidental harmful outcomes of one's lawful acts. By contrast, the legal order still accepted as a matter of course liability for outcomes caused while engaged in unlawful acts. It saw no conflict

---

[61] See in particular Hans Achenbach, *Historische und dogmatische Grundlagen der strafrechtssystematischen Schuldlehre* (Berlin 1974), and Ingeborg Puppe, *Die Erfolgszurechnung im Strafrecht*, i. *Die objektive Zurechnung* (Baden-Baden 2000).

[62] During this period, liability for murder was—as in England—restricted to 'sly' killings where the victim had been unable to anticipate and respond to the attack; hence, any death which resulted from an open fight was merely manslaughter. Modern commentators have seen in this rule another rudimentary and unreflected step towards drawing a distinction based on *mens rea*, not outcome. See Rüping, *Grundriß*, 4, 14.

[63] Ibid. 3–5, 12–14. The crime of assault provides an interesting example for how early criminal law got by without attempted crimes: by criminalizing the person who causes another to apprehend immediate violence, it contrived to catch those who attempt to inflict such violence, but are stopped before they can.

between the new focus on the mental state of the offender as the basis for blame and the continuing existence of criminal liability for unanticipated and unintended outcomes of any intentional or reckless violation of the law.

This acceptance arose mainly from the doctrine that initially led legal systems to reject pure outcome liability for merely accidentally caused harm: the distinction between *versari in re licita* and *versari in re illicita* first formulated in canonical law (which, unsurprisingly given its biblical roots and points of reference, naturally focuses more on the mindset of the offender).[64] According to this distinction, our liability for unintended and unanticipated outcomes depends entirely on the nature and quality of our antecedent causal acts. If we were engaged in activities that were good and lawful, and were reasonably careful while performing them, we can deny responsibility for the harm that nevertheless results. But when our conduct is inherently wrong and prohibited, how can we even begin to deny our responsibility for its consequences? We chose to do wrong and, 'indirectly', we chose to bring about the results of our actions.

The late medieval Continental common law (the *Gemeine Recht*) thus continued to hold people liable for any natural (and not necessarily probable) consequence of their unlawful acts, whether or not they did or could have foreseen them, and justified this position by a combination of the old reasoning that 'everybody is always responsible for the consequences of their violations of the law', and the recognition of 'dolus indirectus' ('everybody always intends the foreseeable consequences of their actions') as a type of *mens rea*.[65]

Both these doctrines, which served as justifications for the continuing extent of outcome liability in the criminal law, were later rejected as incompatible with natural justice. But as late as 1884, Franz von Liszt was happy to describe offence-aggravating harmful outcomes as 'objective conditions of liability', thereby indicating that he viewed them as criteria to which the defendant's *mens rea* need not extend.[66] While the remnants of pure outcome liability were more frequently criticized by writers in subsequent decades,[67] it was only in 1953 that legislative closure of the issue was achieved through the adoption of § 18 StGB,[68] which restricted the defendant's liability for the serious consequences of his unlawful acts to those that he brought about 'at least recklessly'.

---

[64] Ibid. 28.

[65] Ibid. 28, 43–4. The development is traced in greater detail by Friedrich Schaffstein, *Die allgemeinen Lehren vom Verbrechen in ihrer Entwicklung durch die Wissenschaft des allgemeinen Strafrechts* (Berlin 1930).

[66] *Lehrbuch*, 169. By contrast, Ludwig von Bar already deplores the 'unfairness' of this 'pure outcome or accident liability' and demands that recklessness in relation to the serious consequence should be required (*Gesetz und Schuld im Strafrecht. Fragen des geltenden deutschen Strafrechts und seiner Reform*, ii. *Die Schuld nach dem Strafgesetze* (Berlin 1907), 471–2).

[67] Wilhelm Sauer, *Grundlagen des Strafrechts nebst Umriß einer Rechts- und Sozialphilosophie* (Berlin/Leipzig 1921), at 366.

[68] Through the 3rd *Strafrechtsänderungsgesetz* (Criminal Law Amendment Act) of 4 March 1953, *Bundesgesetzblatt* (BGBl.) I at 753.

One might assume that the position is now stable, the legal development at its logical end. But there are writers who challenge even the limited weight that is given to recklessly caused outcomes under the present law. Like Simester in this volume, they recognize that liability for reckless crimes is liability incurred ultimately for the harmful consequences of our risky actions; hence, whether or not we become criminally liable for our reckless conduct is essentially a matter of luck. But the conclusion they draw from this is the exact opposite of the one defended by Simester.[69] They think that it is a hidden case of outcome responsibility that does raise an issue with regard to the culpability principle—a point made powerfully by Ludwig von Bar in his fundamental work on *Gesetz und Schuld im Strafrecht*[70] in 1907, when he observed that 'Liability for reckless conduct hinges in many instances purely on coincidence, since luckily many even very risky acts remain without harmful consequences,'[71] and argued that

in cases of recklessness, the punishment—provided that one does not want to criminalise the creation of a risk to life or limb more generally, a legislative measure which, except in cases of uncontrolled mass endangerment, must be advised against—always contains an element of injustice, provided that the recklessness was not extreme. In cases of simple recklessness one often punishes in a certain sense an accident, which even in the absence of any sanction weighs heavily on the person responsible for it.[72]

While modern writers are less inclined to challenge the legitimacy of offences that criminalize the reckless causation of prohibited outcomes, rather than reckless and risk-creating conduct as such, there are still those who think that the operation of § 18 StGB is too severe and leads to the imposition of disproportionate punishments. According to these writers, intent-recklessness combinations that impose a heavier penalty on an offender than he would receive if convicted under the intent-based offence and a separate outcome-related recklessness-offence, effectively impose a form of outcome liability on defendants that goes beyond what is justified by their moral blameworthiness.[73] The present position, which represents the culmination of more than two centuries of academic debate, may yet be subject to further changes.

## French Criminal Law

In France, the fundamental rules of criminal law and the main criminal offences are contained in what is still usually called the 'new' *Code pénal* (*CP*).[74] This was

---

[69] Andrew Simester, 'Is Strict Liability Always Wrong?', Ch. 2 in this volume, particularly his discussion in the text at nn. 65–70 and 76–80.     [70] von Bar, *Schuld*.

[71] Ibid. 473.     [72] Ibid. 475.

[73] See Tröndle/Fischer, § 18 annotation 2, and Christof W. Miseré, *Die Grundprobleme der Delikte mit strafbegründender besonderer Folge* (Berlin 1997).

[74] Published annually, with annotations, by Dalloz. The 2004 volume is edited by Yves Mayaud (and is cited hereafter as Dalloz, *CP* 2004). The text is also available on the French government's 'Légifrance' website, <http://www.legifrance.gouv.fr/>, accessed 25 Sept. 2004. This site also carries an English translation (but this is not always up to date).

enacted after many years of debate and discussion in 1992, and replaced Napoleon's Code of 1810 with effect from 1 March 1994.[75] The new Code, like its predecessor, begins by dividing offences into three categories: *crimes, délits*, and *contraventions*.[76] These categories are based on the maximum penalty applicable, and determine how they are processed by the legal system. *Crimes* are serious offences, such as murder, torture, rape, and terrorism, which carry a maximum penalty of *réclusion criminelle*[77] for ten years or more. They are tried with great formality[78] in the *Cour d'assises* by three professional judges sitting with nine jurors. *Délits* are middle-range offences; they are punishable in various ways, but never carry a maximum penalty in excess of ten years' imprisonment. A great many offences fall into this category, including theft, fraud, the less serious offences against the person (including sex with minors), and a wide range of offences against public order. They are tried, with less formality, in the *tribunal correctionnel* before a panel of professional judges. The third category, *contraventions*, consists of minor offences, for which the most severe penalty that may be imposed is a relatively small fine. These are tried by a single judge, under a summary form of procedure, in the *tribunal de police*. Although *contraventions* are in some ways like summary offences in England, as a category they are much less serious. Whereas in England summary offences often carry fines of up to £5,000 and sometimes even custodial sentences,[79] the heaviest penalty that may normally be imposed in France for a *contravention* is a fine of €1,500 (about £1,000). In certain cases the maximum is €3,000 and additional penalties may be imposed, one of which is community service: but not imprisonment. Thus a great many English summary offences would be *délits* in France, and handled by the *tribunal correctionnel*.

In principle, the French rules on the fault element in crime are clear: a *crime* requires intention, a *délit* normally requires intention but may be committed with a lesser degree of fault if the statute creating it expressly says so, and the only offences to which strict liability potentially applies are *contraventions*. This is expressly laid down by Article 121-3 *CP*[80]—an article that reflects the earlier law,

---

[75] Jean Pradel, *Manuel de droit pénal général* (14th edn., Paris 2002) (hereafter Pradel, *DPG*), § 122 *et seq.*        [76] Which, under the system of numbering adopted, appears as Art. 111-1.

[77] For *crimes*, the main punishment is called *réclusion criminelle*. The name suggests a particularly severe form of imprisonment, but in practice it is not more severe than the imprisonment imposed for *délits*.        [78] And invariably after a preliminary investigation by a *juge d'instruction*.

[79] The Criminal Justice Act 2003, Schedule 26, raises the penalty for no less than 118 summary offences from three months' imprisonment to 51 weeks (11 months and three weeks).

[80] The French text is: [1] Il n'y a point de crime ou de délit sans intention de le commettre. [2] Toutefois, lorsque la loi le prévoit, il y a délit en cas de mise en danger délibérée de la personne d'autrui. [3] Il y a également délit, lorsque la loi le prévoit, en cas de faute d'imprudence, de négligence ou de manquement à une obligation de prudence ou de sécurité prévue par la loi ou le règlement, s'il est établi que l'auteur des faits n'a pas accompli les diligences normales compte tenu, le cas échéant, de la nature de ses missions ou de ses fonctions, de ses compétences ainsi que du pouvoir et des moyens dont il disposait. [4] Dans le cas prévu par l'alinéa qui précède, les personnes physiques qui n'ont pas causé directement le dommage, mais qui ont créé ou contribué à créer la situation qui a permis la réalisation du dommage ou qui n'ont pas pris les mesures permettant de l'éviter, sont responsables pénalement s'il est établi qu'elles ont, soit violé de façon manifestement

but makes the fault requirement rather tighter. By a combination of statute and case-law, French law had previously acquired a small group of non-intentional *crimes* (mainly in the area of state security), and a larger number of *délits*, for which *faute contraventionnelle* was sufficient. In other words, these *crimes* and *délits* were, like *contraventions*, offences of strict liability, where the only defence was *force majeure*. In response to repeated criticism from legal writers, both categories ceased to exist under the new Code in 1994.[81]

## Intention

The rule that intention must be shown for *crimes* and normally for *délits* is contained in paragraph (1)[82] of Article 121–3, which provides that 'There is no *crime* or *délit* in the absence of intention to commit it.' Neither statute nor French case-law provides any general definition of intention, and for a discussion of its meaning it is necessary to look at *la doctrine*. By French writers, intention is usually described by the synonym *dol* (from the Latin *dolus*). Of *dol* there are two accepted forms, either of which will satisfy the requirement of the Code for intention: *dol direct*, where the forbidden action or the prohibited consequence is desired, and *dol indirect*, where 'the agent knows that his voluntary act will cause (certainly or almost certainly) a consequence that is not truly desired'.[83] Thus in broad terms, intention in French law bears much the same meaning as intention in the current English case-law on murder.[84] French writers also describe a related concept called *dol éventuel*[85] (from the Latin *dolus eventualis*), which is where the agent merely foresees the possibility of the result—which English lawyers would call subjective recklessness. But in French law this is not treated as a form of intention—nor is it generally paired up, as it is in England, with intention to form a composite type of *mens rea* normally sufficient to make the defendant liable for a serious offence. In France, *dol eventuel* is treated as a severe form of *faute non intentionnelle*. Thus it is never sufficient to found liability for a *crime* and only suffices for a *délit* where the statute that creates the *délit* expressly says so.

When discussing intention, French writers, like English writers many years ago,[86] tend to ignore the problem of the defendant who was unaware of prohibited circumstances, and treat this under a separate heading called 'the effect of

---

délibérée une obligation particulière de prudence ou de sécurité prévue par la loi ou le règlement, soit commis une faute caractérisée et qui exposait autrui à un risque d'une particulière gravité qu'elles ne pouvaient ignorer. [5] Il n'y a point de contravention en cas de force majeure.

[81] This provision of the *CP* was extended to *délits* created by other legislation by Art. 339 of the Law of 16 December 1992.

[82] In the *Code pénal* the paragraphs (*alinéas*) are printed without numbers. We have added numbers to make the text more accessible to readers used to British legal conventions.

[83] Pradel *DPG* § 502.     [84] *Woollin* [1999] 1 AC 82.

[85] The concept is somewhat different from the modern German notion of *dolus eventualis*, which was described in the section on German law above.

[86] e.g. *Kenny's Outlines of Criminal Law*, revised by G. G. Phillips (14th edn., Cambridge 1933), 67–8.

mistake'. From this, some French writers (like the older English writers) go on to say that a mistake of fact is a defence provided it was reasonable (or at any rate, provided it was not excessively unreasonable[87]). But others take the line that a defendant is not to be treated as committing a crime of intention where he made a mistake of fact that was honest, whether it was reasonable or not—and interpret the fact that the new *Code pénal* proclaims the basic rule that intention is essential in both *crimes* and *délits* as confirming this solution.[88] The case-law on the subject is ambiguous. Some cases treat a mistake of material fact as excluding liability without addressing the question of reasonableness.[89] But others—particularly those involving offences against minors—rule that a person is not entitled to rely on a mistake if he was at fault for making it. So for example when a brothel-keeper in Nîmes was prosecuted for 'inciting minors to debauchery' by admitting under-age clients, her defence that she thought they were over age failed because she was at fault for not checking before she admitted them.[90]

In French, unlike English, criminal law, it is crimes of intention that dominate the scene. 'From a statistical point of view they are the most common, since they constitute 93% of the offences covered by books II to VI of the new *Code pénal*: 100% of *crimes*, 90% of *délits*, and 20% of *contraventions*.'[91] In the light of this, it is not surprising to find that French law has found ways of lightening the rather severe task that the narrow French definition of intention would otherwise load upon the shoulders of the police and the public prosecutor.

In the first place, the French courts (like courts elsewhere) accept that intention may be inferred from the circumstances. From this the theory has developed that, where the defendant has done something that looks as if it was intentional, or the consequence of which was obvious, he is presumed to have acted intentionally—and it is up to him to convince the court that he was not.[92] Secondly, in at least one particular situation the French courts have stretched the concept of intention to cover something that English lawyers would probably class as recklessness. Where a person could have checked, and deliberately failed to do so, he is sometimes treated as acting intentionally with regard to the facts that would have been discovered. 'In the matter of frauds, case-law lays down a sort of presumption of bad faith against the professional or the importer who, being required to guarantee the quality of the goods he sells or imports, can hardly defend himself by claiming to be ignorant of their defects.'[93] Thirdly, French law sometimes relieves

---

[87] Pradel *DPG* § 492.

[88] Roger Merle and André Vitu, *Traité de droit criminel, Droit pénal général* (7th edn., Paris 1997), § 581; (hereafter cited as Merle and Vitu, *DPG*).

[89] e.g. *Cour de cassation, Chambre criminelle* (hereafter '*Cass. crim.*') 19 November 1926, *Gazette du Palais* 1927 I, 239: farmer acquitted of an offence of shooting a homing pigeon, because he had mistaken it for a wild one.

[90] *Cass. crim.* 4 January 1902, *Recueil Dalloz* (hereafter *D*) 1902 1 528; cf. the case mentioned in n. 112 below.

[91] Frédéric Desportes and Francis Le Gunehec, *Droit Penal General* (10th edn., Paris 2003), § 470 (hereafter Desportes and Le Gunehec *DPG*).          [92] Pradel *DPG* § 511.

[93] Desportes and Le Gunehec *DPG* § 472.

the prosecutor of the need to prove intention as to legally relevant consequences by accepting what English lawyers would call constructive crimes—as we explain below.

## Criminal Liability for Negligence: 'Faute non intentionnelle'

The rules about the fault element in *délits* for which intention is not required are contained in paragraphs (2), (3), and (4) of Article 121-3. These provisions replace the original and much simpler ones—which were found to be too severe and were altered in two stages, first in 1996 and again in 2000.[94]

In its original 1994 form, the part of Article 121-3 that dealt with non-intentional fault consisted of a single sentence qualifying the general requirement of intention as follows: 'However, where statute so provides, there is a *délit* in the case of carelessness or negligence, or where another person is deliberately put in danger.'

This led to serious difficulties because of the breadth of the French concept of 'carelessness or negligence' (*imprudence ou négligence*). In French penal theory, these terms do not mean a blameworthy failure to foresee a particular consequence that the law requires to be avoided, but are interpreted more simply as any failure to conform to accepted standards of behaviour. Thus, as French writers usually explain, 'carelessness or negligence' is established where two conditions are simultaneously present: (1) harm is caused unintentionally and (2) this results from the breach of some accepted standard of behaviour. This breach of accepted standards may consist either of a failure to behave as a reasonably careful person, or the breach of some legal rule that was binding on the actor (e.g. failure to conform to some minor regulation, breach of which is a *contravention*, normally punishable with nothing more than a small fine).

In the years immediately after the new Code came into force, the definition of 'carelessness or negligence' was thought to produce results that were over-severe in two respects. The first was that the standard of the 'reasonably careful person' was a strictly objective one; not only did the standard fail to allow for the personal abilities (or lack of them) of the particular defendant, but—more surprisingly—it also failed to make allowances for the means that the particular defendant had at his disposal. Secondly, the rule that the infringement of any legal rule automatically counted as 'carelessness or negligence' meant that a person who committed a very minor criminal offence might easily find himself guilty of a *délit* punishable with imprisonment because of the ill-chance that injury or death resulted from it. So when viewed through the eyes of the common lawyer, French law contained a large body of constructive crimes—but unlike those known to English law, they were based not on offences of *mens rea*, but on trivial offences, and sometimes even ones to which strict liability applied.

[94] Prompting the wry comment from authors of the leading textbook that four-year intervals may be appropriate for the European Cup, but are rather too frequent for rewriting the basic rules of criminal responsibility; Desportes and Le Gunehec, *DPG*, 461.

The severity of this was sharply increased by the fact that French criminal law traditionally takes a very ample view of causation. Although different theories of causation have been put forward, the dominant one is *l'équivalence des causes*: the theory that all factual causes, however small, are legally significant.[95] Thus the defendant is taken as having caused a consequence if his behaviour contributed towards it, even minimally—and it certainly need not have been the direct and immediate cause. If this is similar in principle to the rule that English criminal law applies, what is different is that French law is less willing than English law to accept the limitation that the chain of causation is broken by another person's voluntary act.[96] The consequence here was that the defendant's negligence, or breach of a minor regulation, could easily land him with a conviction for negligent homicide or negligent injury, even where the more obvious and immediate cause of the harm was the more blameworthy behaviour of another. All this bore heavily on employers, and also upon the holders of public offices. In one case, for example, a child of 7 who was bathing at the municipal bathing-area in the care of a child-minder wandered off while the minder was busy chatting to a friend, and drowned. Not only was the negligent child-minder convicted of *homicide involontaire*—a *délit* of causing death by negligence—but so was the mayor, because he was legally responsible for the fact that the bathing-area did not conform to national regulations for the safety of bathing-places.[97] Similarly, another mayor was convicted of *homicide involontaire* when an old people's home burnt down, with fatal consequences: the mayor, it was held, had caused the deaths by 'carelessness or negligence' because he was responsible for the failure of the commune to enforce fire safety regulations.[98] In France the risk of prosecution in such cases is a real one, because in French law the victim (or his family) have the right to institute a prosecution as a *partie civile* with a view to claiming damages—for which legal aid is readily available.

In the 1990s this state of affairs was increasingly criticized. Writers pointed out that the new Code, while ceremonially abolishing *délits* of strict liability, had taken back with one hand what was given with the other. And mayors—a body with political influence—complained that it made criminals out of them unfairly, and without regard to the practical difficulties that they faced in carrying out their public duties. In the debate that followed, one option canvassed was to limit liability for non-intentional *délits* to cases of deliberate endangerment: but the result was a more limited reform, which retains the principle of *délits* based on negligence, whilst raising the standard of behaviour below which the defendant

[95]  Desportes and Le Gunehec, *DPG*, § 446–§ 448-1.

[96]  Thus a court in Limoges decided that the drug-dealer who supplies heroin to an addict is guilty of *homicide involontaire* when the customer takes an overdose: see Dalloz, *CP* (2004) 263; the case is noted in the *Revue des Sciences Criminelles* (hereafter *RSC*) 1998, 549.

[97]  *Cour d'appel*, Grenoble, 23 May 1996; *Juris-classeur périodique* (alias *La Semaine Juridique*, and hereafter *JCP*) 1996 IV 2228; Dalloz, *CP* (2004) 283.

[98]  *Cour de Cassation, Chambre criminelle*, 9 Nov. 1999; *Bulletin des arrêts de la chambre criminelle* (hereafter *Bull. Crim.*) No 250; *RSC* 2000 389; Dalloz, *CP* (2004) 284.

must fall in order to commit them. The resulting compromise is contained in paragraphs (2), (3), and (4) of Article 121-3.

Paragraph (2) provides that 'where statute so provides, there is a *délit* where another person is deliberately put in danger'. On this basis, the *Code pénal* contains various *délits* of causing bodily harm where the fault element is what English lawyers would call subjective recklessness—plus a *délit* of recklessly exposing other persons to a risk of death or serious bodily harm, whether or not this actually occurs.[99] Paragraphs (3) and (4), which are rather complicated, then set out the compromise basis for criminal liability for inadvertent negligence:

> (3) There may also be a *délit*, where statute so provides, in cases of carelessness, negligence, or failure to observe an obligation of due care or precaution imposed by any statute or regulation, if it is established that the offender failed to show normal diligence, taking into consideration where appropriate the nature of his role or functions, of his capacities and powers and of the means then available to him.

> (4) In the situation covered by the preceding paragraph, natural persons who have not directly contributed to causing the damage, but who have created or contributed to create the situation which allowed the damage to happen or who failed to take steps enabling it to be avoided, are criminally liable where it is shown that they have broken a duty of care or precaution laid down by statute or regulation in a manifestly deliberate manner, or have committed a specified piece of misconduct which exposed another person to a particularly serious risk of which they must have been aware.

The first feature of the compromise is that the standard of care is now a subjective one, in the sense that the courts must take account of the practical situation in which the defendant in question found himself. The second is that a person whose carelessness or breach of regulation stands at one remove from the damage (e.g. the mayor who gives permission for something to be done which should have been forbidden, or who fails to enforce a safety regulation) is only liable where his negligence was particularly grave. In other words, the traditional broad theory of causation is restricted to cases where the defendant's fault was grave, and a tighter rule of causation now applies to simple negligence. And the third is that the breach of an official regulation, however trivial, no longer automatically constitutes negligence; the breach must have been one that a reasonable person in the position of the defendant would have avoided.[100]

There is, however, one possible exception to the rule that all *délits* require proof of fault. This is in relation to the offence of defamation. In French law, criminal liability for defamation is very much alive. Truth, as in English law, is a defence—but as in English law the defendant has to prove it, and it is no defence for him to show that he reasonably believed what he said to be true. For this reason, the offence is said to carry *une présomption de mauvaise foi*. By

---

[99] *CP* Art. 223-1.
[100] Dalloz *CP* (2004) 254, § 11; citing the decision of the *Tribunal correctionnel*, Toulouse, 19 February 1997, Gaz. Pal. 1997 396, at 399.

statute, it also carries strict liability for the proprietor of the publication in which the text appeared—but unlike in English law,[101] he does not have the benefit of a 'due care' defence. Thus, here, French law is more rigorous against defendants than is the law in England. At the same time, this part of French law is less fierce than its English equivalent, because in French law the only penalties that may normally be imposed for criminal defamation are fines.[102] Under English law, criminal libel is punishable with imprisonment. In a related context, the registered publisher of a newspaper is criminally liable for a range of *délits de presse*, even where he was not personally responsible.[103] This is best understood as a case of vicarious liability, of which there are other (rare) instances in French law.

## Strict Liability: 'Contraventions'

Article 121-3 does not expressly provide that *contraventions* may be offences of strict liability. Paragraph (5) merely provides that 'there is no *contravention* in the event of *force majeure*.' But this is taken to imply that, in the absence of *force majeure*, a *contravention* is committed by the simple act of doing what the law forbids, or failing to do what the law requires—and this is how the French courts interpret *contraventions* unless the text creating them expressly provides for some element of fault (as it quite often does). In the absence of such wording, it is useless for the defendant to argue that he took all due care to comply with the regulation, much less that it was reasonable for him to disregard it.[104] French writers regard strict liability for *contraventions* as justified because of the subject-matter that they deal with. Although they are breaches of rules that are necessary for collective life, they are not rules the breach of which involves direct injury to others, or threatens fundamental values in society, and hence their commission does not involve moral blame.[105] Not only do *contraventions* usually carry strict liability, but the simplified rules of criminal procedure that apply in the *tribunal de police* ensure that they also carry something like a reverse burden of proof. Article 537(2) of the Code of Criminal Procedure provides that, for the purpose of establishing *contraventions*, official written reports from competent officials are taken to be true unless the contrary is proved.

---

[101] Law of Libel (Amendment) Act 1843, s. 7.

[102] A prison sentence is possible where racism is involved; Law of 29 July 1888, Art. 32 (as amended). [103] Law of 29 July 1881, Art. 42.

[104] Although if the reason his non-compliance was reasonable was that he was following misleading official advice about what the law required, this may give rise to the defence of unavoidable mistake of law; Art. 122-3: 'A person is not criminally liable who establishes that he believed he could legitimately perform the action because of a mistake of law that he was not in a position to avoid.'

[105] Desportes and Le Gunehec, *DPG*, 466. Compare the arguments traditionally used in England; Jeremy Horder, 'Strict Liability, Statutory Construction and the Spirit of Liberty' (2002) 118 *Law Quarterly Review* 458, at 466.

## *Qualifications to the Fault Requirement: Strict Liability Elements and Constructive Crimes*

Many offences that contain strict liability elements as to a circumstance in English law have only fault-based equivalents in French law. In so far as French law criminalizes the illegal possession of weapons[106] and controlled drugs[107] and imposes penalties that move these offences beyond the scope of mere *contraventions*, *mens rea* is required with regard to the nature of the item in question. At one time, the French courts dabbled with the idea of imposing strict liability for *délits* in this area. They did so, in particular, for the *délit* under the Customs Code of smuggling drugs, which they turned into a *délit materiel* as part of the national attempt to fight 'this plague, which particularly afflicts the young'.[108] It was a prosecution for this offence that eventually led to the *Salabiaku* case[109]—one of the few pronouncements on this area of law from Strasbourg. With the new Criminal Code in 1994, *délits materiels* were abolished—and the abolition extended beyond the new Code to cover *délits* that existed under separate legislation. So today, the only possession offences that carry strict liability are *contraventions*. The defendant in Salabiaku's case, for example, would now be guilty only on proof that he knew the contents of the trunk in his possession were prohibited drugs: and the same is true for a defendant prosecuted for any of the more serious offences concerning weapons.

French law also contains specific offences of sex with minors—although they are less wide-ranging in scope, and not so heavily punishable.[110] The age of consent in France is 15, not 16, and the offence is limited to defendants who are aged 18 or over. The offence is a *délit*, and in the absence of any special provision as to the mental element involved this means that in principle the defendant is liable only where he acted intentionally. Logically, it would seem to follow from this that a defendant is guilty of the offence only where he was actually aware that the victim was under age: if he thought that the victim was over age he is entitled to an acquittal.[111] However, in the leading case (which was decided under the provisions of the previous Code) the *Cour de cassation* ruled that when convicting

---

[106] The *Décret-loi du 18 avril* 1939 creates a list of serious offences concerning 'prohibited weapons' (art. 24 *et seq.*). Art. 431-3 of the *CP* creates an offence of *attroupement*, which means being part of a disorderly gang; by Art. 431-5, it is punishable with 3 years and €45,000 to be part of an *attroupement* when carrying a weapon.

[107] These are contained in the *Code de santé publique*: Art. L.3421-1 (illegal use), punishable by a fine of €3750; Art. 3421-4: incitement to illegal use: 5 years and a fine; Arts. L.5132-8 and 5432-1 prohibit producing, transporting, importing, possessing, and transferring prohibited drugs on pain of two years and a fine.

[108] Cour d'appel de Paris, 10 March 1986. Gaz. Pal. 1988, *Jurisprudence*, 442–4.

[109] The case is discussed in more detail in the section on Doctrinal Foundations of French criminal law below.

[110] *CP* Art. 227-25; the offence is punishable with up to 5 years' imprisonment and/or a fine of €75,000—by Art. 227-26, rising to 10 years and €150,000 if various aggravating factors are present.

[111] Desportes and Le Gunehec, *DPG*, § 472.

of the offence a court is not obliged to make an express finding that the defendant knew that the victim was a minor—and that although the defendant was entitled to an acquittal if he could show that he was mistaken, 'he may only justify his conduct by a mistake for which he was not to blame'.[112] Transposed into English law terms, this appears to mean that the defendant in such a case is liable for negligence, and bears the burden of proving that he took due care.

If French criminal law is reluctant to accept strict liability, by contrast it has no qualms at all about constructive crimes.

The offence of *homicide involontaire*[113] is an offence for which the fault-element is *faute non-intentionnelle*, one form of which is the commission of another offence, including a contravention. This means, in effect, that French law has an offence of constructive manslaughter that is far more severe than its equivalent in English law, because the commission of any offence (however trivial) with fatal consequences will potentially give rise to it. But the consequences for the defendant are less severe than those that could theoretically follow under English law, because whereas manslaughter potentially carries life imprisonment, the maximum penalty for *homicide involontaire* in France is three years' imprisonment and a fine of €40,000, or 5 years and €75,000, depending on the degree of fault involved.

A recurrent pattern in the *CP* is a basic offence with a relatively modest maximum penalty—which is supplemented by one or more aggravated offences carrying higher penalties, the aggravating circumstance usually being that someone suffered serious harm as a result.

French law, for instance, raises the maximum penalty for the offence of bodily violence where (*inter alia*) death is the unintentional result.[114] Where the bodily harm was extreme, the defendant might be prosecuted for the more serious offence of 'torture or acts of barbarity'—an offence for which the normal maximum penalty (15 years) is raised to life imprisonment where the death of the victim is the result.[115] Similarly, where the victim dies the maximum penalty for rape, which is normally 15 years, is raised to 30.[116] The French Criminal Code also contains an offence of intentional bodily violence, for which the maximum penalty varies according to the degree of injury caused.[117] To incur liability for one of the serious forms of an offence, it is enough that the defendant intended to inflict some degree of bodily violence;[118] it is certainly not necessary that the degree of harm caused should have been foreseen.[119]

As we saw earlier, German law carries the culpability principle over into the area of constructive crimes (and sentencing more generally) by recognizing a general

---

[112] *Cour de Cassation, Chambre criminelle*, 7 February 1957; *Bull. crim.* No 126; noted by Hugueney, 1957 RSC 638. And see Desportes and Le Gunehec, ibid.        [113] Art. 221-6.
[114] Art. 222-7; 15 years' imprisonment, rising to 30 years if the offence was committed on one of a specified range of victims.        [115] Art. 222-6.
[116] Art. 222-25.      [117] Art. 222-9 *CP* onwards.
[118] French criminal law, unlike English criminal law, also contains an offence of inflicting bodily harm negligently: *CP* Art. 222-19 *et seq.*        [119] Desportes and Le Gunehec, *DPG*, § 480 *et seq.*

principle that a person is not liable to incur a higher penalty because of the harmful consequence of his act unless in respect of that consequence he was at least reckless (*fahrlässig*). In French law the position on this question is less clear.

French legal writers usually say that, in principle, the defendant should be punished more severely only in respect of consequences that he ought to have foreseen.[120] In taking this position the modern writers follow Donnedieu de Vabres, the great French *pénaliste* of the mid-twentieth century, who adopted it with approval from German law in his *Traité de droit criminel et de législation pénale comparée* in 1947.[121] Most French writers take the position that a defendant ought not to be punished for a wrong that goes beyond the scope of his fault: a wrong that French lawyers describe as *un délit praeterintentionnel*. On the other hand, 'it is accepted that the agent is responsible for all the effects which occur in the ordinary course of events, and which he ought reasonably to envisage as being possible'.[122]

Where offences of assault and wounding are concerned, French lawyers see their rules about constructive liability as conforming to this general principle. It is proper, they say, that the defendant who physically attacked another should incur a heavier penalty where an injury results that he neither intended nor foresaw. Such a defendant acts with *dol indéterminé*—which means approximately 'indeterminate malice'—and this justifies his conviction and punishment for the aggravated version of the offence, irrespective of what he actually intended: in the mouth of someone who intended to cause bodily injury, it lies ill to say that he meant to do less harm than he did:

> The person who voluntarily strikes another with anything short of an intention of killing him has the intention to make his victim suffer. But he does not know for certain the sort of harm that he or she will suffer: a simple painful sensation, bruises or swelling, slight wounds, serious wounds, or death? He knows, however, because it is a matter of common knowledge, that the germ of the whole range of these uncertain consequences is present in the blows that he inflicts. Knowing this, and foreseeing it or being able to foresee it, he should be convicted as if he had intended the precise result that he produced: *dolus indeterminatus determinatur eventu*.[123]

But the writers recognize that the general principle of which they approve is difficult to square with a number of the other constructive offences with which the French *CP*—like its Napoleonic predecessor—is replete.

The Criminal Code of 1810 punished *délit praeterintentionnel* without any qualm or inhibition. A particularly strong example was the offence that it

---

[120] Merle and Vitu, *DPG*, § 599; Pradel, *DPG*, § 510; Desportes and Le Gunehec, *DPG*, § 482.
[121] *Traité de droit criminel et de législation pénale comparée* (3rd edn., Paris 1947), § 138.
[122] Ibid.
[123] Merle and Vitu, *DPG*, § 599. (But this reasoning is not taken to the limit. It applies, in essence, to the situation where there is a basic offence of doing X to someone, with aggravated versions when X produces consequences Y or Z. It does not apply where the occurrence of the consequence means the defendant is guilty of a new and separate offence. Thus in French law, a person who kills is not guilty of the offence of murder unless he actually intended to kill.)

contained of arson. In a series of paragraphs, Article 434 set out a list of punishments for this offence, ranging from burning inhabited buildings (death) through burning uninhabited buildings (life imprisonment) to burning ricks, piles of timber, and merchandise 'in wagons not forming part of a convoy containing persons' (twenty years); then, in a final clause, it provided that if arson of *any* property within *any* of these categories resulted in death or serious injury, the death penalty applied. The new Criminal Code contains nothing quite as savage. But it still contains a number of offences, other than those directly concerning bodily injury, where a death resulting from the *actus reus* raises the maximum penalty to life imprisonment, which is the same as the penalty French law applies to murder: for example, hijacking (Article 224-7). Neither here, nor in any of the other cases where the Criminal Code provides a higher penalty where a particular consequence occurs, is it explicitly provided that the consequence must have been foreseeable or foreseen: nor does the French Code lay down such a rule by means of a general provision, as does § 18 StGB in Germany.

In theory, it might be open to the French courts to interpret these statutory provisions by implying into them a qualification that they only operate in respect of consequences that were reasonably foreseeable. They have not done so, however, and show little sign of doing so. French case-law justifies defendants' convictions under these provisions by merely stating that 'l'auteur est responsable non seulement des conséquences qu'il avait prévues et voulues, mais aussi de toutes celles qui ont pu se produire', and without reference to whether the consequence in question was foreseeable.[124] In a leading case, a worker with a taste for practical jokes put a compressed air hose against his workmate's trouser-clad buttocks and turned it on, to make him jump. The jet of air ruptured his colon, putting him off work for many months. For this, the prankster was convicted not of the offence of negligent injury, but the more serious crime of 'coups et blessures volontaires ayant entraîné une incapacité de travail de plus de huit jours':[125] which is roughly equivalent to the English offence of assault occasioning actual bodily harm. It was irrelevant, said the *Cour de cassation*, that the defendant had not intended to cause the harm; it was enough that he had caused it by a voluntary act against the victim.[126] Some years later, the *Tribunal de grande instance* (first instance court) at Pontoise refused to follow the decision when seized with an identical case.[127] But it did so on the basis that the offence of *coups et blessures* presupposes something in the nature of a hostile act: not that the consequences must have been foreseen or foreseeable.

---

[124] *Cour de Cassation, Chambre civile*, 15 December 1995; D 1966 356: a case in which a defendant was convicted of wounding a bystander—who got hurt when the defendant threw a stone at someone else, missed, and broke a nearby window, a piece of broken glass from which put out the bystander's eye.　　　　[125] Contrary to the 1810 Code, Art. 309.

[126] *Cour de Cassation, Chambre criminelle*, 7 June 1961, *Bull. crim.* No 290.

[127] Gaz. Pal. 1985, 1 Somm. 88; Dalloz *CP* (2004), 315. This particular prank appears to be international in character: see *Smith* v. *Crossley Bros. Ltd.* (1951) 95 *Solicitors' Journal* 655.

## Doctrinal Foundations

One reason that French law makes so little use of strict liability is probably hostility from *la doctrine*.

Although the culpability principle was present in the Napoleonic Code of 1810 only in embryonic form,[128] by the end of the nineteenth century French criminal law had come to embrace it—at least for serious offences. So in modern times French legal writers, like those in the common law world, have been broadly hostile to strict liability. By an interesting reversal of what has happened recently in England, their views on strict liability made little impact on the courts; but the concerns that they expressed were taken seriously by the legislator when the new Criminal Code was enacted.

Traditionally, French writers have taken the position that strict liability can be justified on utilitarian grounds in *contraventions*. These have usually been described as offences with little moral content, not designed to punish invasions of the rights of others, but existing simply to ensure, through minor punishments, 'that order is maintained in the day-to-day use of the services that the state provides'.[129] These characteristics are said to make it acceptable for them to stand outside the normal rules of criminal law. But to French writers, these arguments do not justify the imposition of strict liability higher up the scale. When the French courts, from the late nineteenth century onwards, began to extend strict liability into the area of *délits*, writers were uneasy. One objection to the creation of these *délits matériels* was the 'slippery slope' argument: the case-law drew no intelligible lines, and once it was accepted that strict liability could apply to *délits* it was unclear where the development would stop.[130]

The main objection, however, was that the *délits*, unlike *contraventions*, are stigmatic and carry the risk of serious penalties, which makes the imposition of strict liability in such cases fundamentally unjust. Matters came to a head in 1978 when the *Cour de cassation*, apparently influenced by public concerns about environmental pollution, decided that the *délit* of polluting rivers carried strict liability—and in so doing, imposed criminal liability on a person who, on the facts, had clearly taken all due care.[131] This decision was heavily criticized by a series of writers who noted the case for the French legal press. André Vitu, who was more or less sympathetic to strict liability, questioned its application to *délits* because of the severity of the penalties involved.[132] Marie-Laure Rassat denounced the general slide towards strict liability as unfair and unjust, and said that by extending the

---

[128] The 1810 Code, unlike the current Code, contained no general pronouncements about the place of intention, or other forms of fault: see generally Lebret J, 'Essai sur la notion de l'intention criminelle', *RSC* 1938 438, 441–2.

[129] Merle and Vitu, *DPG*, § 594, quoting J.-L.-E. Ortolan, *Eléments de droit pénal* (1859).

[130] Marty J-P, 'Les délits matériels', *RSC* 1982 41.

[131] *Cour de Cassation, Chambre criminelle*, 28 April 1977, *Bull. crim.* No 148.

[132] A. Vitu, *RSC* 1978 335–9.

reach of strict liability the *Cour de cassation* risked 'opening the doors of the Gulag'.[133] In more measured terms, Mireille Delmas-Marty said:

Perhaps French lawyers should follow the example of Germany. The German courts have decided that any criminal sanction presupposes at least a fault-element of negligence . . . a solution confirmed by the legislator and incorporated in the criminal code. We need to take care lest, by making excessive efforts to reinforce repression, we undermine it. Criminal law can only fulfil its civic role of influencing human choice[134] provided that, for true *délits*, some wrongful state of volition—intention, recklessness or negligence—continues to be the reason for which punishment is inflicted.[135]

Another strand in the academic debate in France was the issue of mistake of law—which was also influenced by developments in Germany. Traditionally, French law (like English law today) refused to accept ignorance of law as a defence. In German law a limited defence of mistake of law exists (full exculpation from criminal liability where the mistake of law was 'unavoidable', and a discretionary reduction in sentence where the mistake was avoidable; § 17 StGB). Influenced by this, French legal opinion eventually underwent a change of mind—the direct effect of which was the recognition of a defence of 'inevitable mistake of law' in the new Criminal Code of 1994.[136] This development had obvious repercussions in the debate about strict liability. If it was accepted that it was unjust to punish people who had acted in good faith under a mistake of law that a reasonable person could have made, how could it be fair to punish those who had acted in good faith under the influence of a reasonable mistake of fact?[137]

French *doctrine* in relation to strict liability was also influenced by the decision of the European Court of Human Rights in *Salabiaku* v. *France*.[138] This was the well-known case in which a defendant was convicted of offences of smuggling under the French Customs Code, which—as the law was then interpreted by the French courts—made a person caught in possession of contraband guilty unless he could prove the existence of *force majeure* or 'unavoidable mistake'. Before the Strasbourg Court he argued that his conviction infringed his rights under Article 6(2) of the European Convention on Human Rights, which provides that 'Everyone charged with a criminal offence shall be presumed innocent until proved guilty according to law.' In rejecting his complaint, the Strasbourg Court ruled that reversals of the burden of proof are acceptable in the context of minor regulatory offences, such as those in question here: but are not acceptable in the context of those that are severely punishable. In England, this decision has been

---

[133]  M.-L. Rassat, D 1978, *Jurisprudence*, 148–52.

[134]  This is a free translation of the French expression 'conversion de vouloir' in the phrase 'Le droit pénal ne peut remplir son rôle étatique de "conversion de vouloir" qu'à condidition . . .' A literal translation of the phrase would be 'bending of the will' or 'will conversion'.

[135]  M. Delmas-Marty (1978) II JCP 18931.

[136]  Art. 122-3: 'A person is not criminally liable who establishes that he believed he could legitimately perform the action because of a mistake of law that he was not in a position to avoid.'

[137]  Marty, 'Les délits materiels'.          [138]  (1988) 13 EHRR 379.

interpreted as dealing with procedural fairness, not fairness in substantive law. The English view is that Article 6 lays down the requirements for a fair trial, for whatever the legislature chooses (however unfairly) to decree to be a criminal offence. Thus it prevents (within limits) contracting states from creating offences the elements of which the defendant is required to disprove: but it does not impose any minimum requirements as to what those elements should be. Article 6, in other words, is about 'fair trials', not 'fair laws'.[139]

In France, however, the *Salabiaku* decision was widely interpreted as limiting the scope of strict liability as well.[140] This may at first seem surprising; but on reflection it is not so, given the way that French writers customarily arrange strict liability within a general scheme of liability for fault. Adopting an arrangement similar to one that was once popular among English writers too,[141] French writers are inclined to present liability for fault according to a tripartite scheme: (1) liability where the fault element is intention, (2) liability where the fault element is negligence, and (3) liability based on 'presumed fault': where 'the defendant is considered to be liable on the basis of his having simply committed the forbidden act, and he can only extract himself from liability by proving duress or insanity'.[142] The third category, of course, comprises what English law would categorize as offences of strict liability. So viewed, it is not illogical to take the view that Article 6 (2) of the Convention applies to strict liability. (And when we look at the offence in issue in the *Salabiaku* case[143] it appears as if it was not really a 'reverse burden' offence at all, but a straightforward crime of strict liability: the discussion of reverse burdens of proof arose not from any specific wording of the statute, but from the general rule that where French law creates a strict liability offence, the defendant, though in principle liable without fault, can still escape if he can establish *force majeure*.)

## 2. The Continental Position Analysed

### The Impact of Procedural and Evidential Rules

A major reason why the French and German criminal laws have been able to dispense with strict liability, either partially or wholly, is almost certainly the fact that the rules of criminal procedure and evidence in those countries make it relatively easy for the defendant's fault to be established. By contrast, a number of the hallowed rules of English law (and the common law in general) have the incidental effect of making this task a great deal harder.

---

[139] *Barnfather* v. *Islington Education Authority* [2003] EWHC 418 (Admin.), [2003] 1 WLR 2318. [140] Jean Pradel, *Le nouveau code pénal*, Dalloz 1995, 100–1.
[141] Blackstone, *Commentaries*, iv (1769), Ch. 2; a similar scheme was adopted by *Kenny's Outlines of Criminal Law*, Ch. 4. [142] Pradel, *DPG*, § 525.
[143] *Code des douanes*, Arts. 414 and 392(1).

In the first place, the deferential respect that English law has traditionally paid to the right of silence often makes it difficult for the courts to receive reliable, first-hand information about what the defendant intended or what facts he knew. In the pre-trial phase the defendant is legally entitled to refuse to explain himself to the police. And at trial, if the defendant pleads 'not guilty', he is not questioned until after the prosecution evidence has been heard—and even then, he has the right to refuse to give evidence. In France and Germany, as in England, the suspect is also entitled to refuse to talk to the police, and sometimes does so. But in sharp contrast to what happens in England, in France and Germany the formal proceedings that correspond to the trial[144] begin with the presiding judge asking the defendant questions. These questions he is not, in theory, required to answer: but in practice he almost invariably does so, because he knows that, irrespective of the theoretical status of his suspicious silence as a piece of circumstantial evidence, in practice the court is likely to take a dim view of it.[145] And when responding to the presiding judge's questions, he must answer them himself: his defending lawyer may object to them, but there is no question of his acting as a shield or intermediary. In a case in which the defendant's knowledge or intention is likely to be crucial, the judge at this stage will ask him pointed questions about it. If a defendant is prosecuted for an offence of sex with a minor, for example, the judge would certainly ask him if he was aware of her age—and if he denied it, he could expect further questions to test him out: 'So what did you talk about?' 'She told you she went to school: what class did she say she was in?' And so forth.[146]

This initial judicial questioning makes a French or German trial radically different from an English one, and the instant reaction of many common lawyers, if they saw it, would probably be to say that it is an oppressive and unacceptable invasion of the defendant's right of silence. This is true in the sense that, for the individual defendant who is guilty, and who has something he would rather hide, it is very uncomfortable. But in a wider context, it is not necessarily oppressive to defendants in general. If it enables the courts in France and Germany to find fault where it exists, and so enables them to do justice without extending the limits of strict liability, it is obviously beneficial to those who have acted without fault.[147]

---

[144] '*Audience de jugement*' in France; '*Hauptverhandlung*' in Germany.

[145] Roger Merle and André Vitu, *Traité de droit criminel, Procédure pénale* (4th edn., Paris 1989), § 150: 'Finally, the defendant may always refuse to reply if he thinks this attitude best suited to the interests of the defence and subject to the qualification, for the judges and jurors, of the right to draw from this attitude any consequence useful to the formation of their conviction.' In Germany, the courts are barred from drawing negative evidential inferences from the defendant's silence at the trial, provided his silence is complete. Where the silence is only partial (the defendant has answered some questions materially concerning the charge, but not others), inferences may be drawn. Thus, the pressure on the accused to answer questions put to him is merely psychological. See Lutz Meyer-Goßner, *Strafprozessordnung: Kommentar* (46th edn., Munich 2003; hereafter Meyer-Goßner, *Kommentar*, § and annotation), § 261 annotations 16–18; BVerfG NStZ 95, 555; BGH St 25, 365, 368.

[146] A practical example we owe to the German judge Günter Müller.

[147] Because a criminal justice system has to achieve a certain level of repression if it is to retain public confidence, protections for defendants tend to be subverted if they are seen to make the

Secondly, whereas the rules of English criminal procedure traditionally[148] prevent the fact-finder in a contested case from knowing that the defendant has previous convictions, or is of bad character, this information will certainly be known to a court in France or Germany (or indeed anywhere else in Continental Europe). In Germany, the defendant's criminal record is read out during the fact-finding stage of the trial,[149] and excerpts from prior decisions concerning him may be read out as well.[150] The only prior convictions that are not formally established at the trial are those which by virtue of § 51 BZRG[151] count as 'spent'; these the court is barred from taking into consideration when arriving at its decision.[152]

In theory, a French or German court hears this type of evidence not because it considers it to be particularly relevant to guilt or innocence, but because (as in England) it is thought to be highly relevant to sentence.[153] However, in French and German criminal procedure, there is no clear distinction—as there is in England—between the part of the trial at which the issue of guilt is decided, and that part where the sentence is determined. Therefore, there is an ever-present factual possibility that the tribunal of fact may take it into account when deciding the question of guilt.

Whether the court is entitled to do so is a question that is more difficult to answer. In France, the theoretical status of evidence of prior convictions in relation to the determination of the defendant's guilt is little debated in the legal literature—which is probably explained by the fact that the rules of French criminal procedure avoid any need for the question to be explicitly addressed. In a French jury trial there is no equivalent to the judge's direction in a jury trial in England; and when the undirected jury produces its verdict, it does so without giving reasons. So in France there is no means of determining either how far a jury should be influenced by the defendant's bad character, or how far in practice it

---

process of convicting the guilty unreasonably difficult; and the device by which they are subverted can make the position of defendants worse than it would have been without the protection. The classic example is torture in Continental medieval criminal procedure: introduced (at least in part) to circumvent the rule that required, for a conviction, either two eyewitnesses to the crime, or a confession. John Langbein has drawn a provocative parallel between this unhappy incident in legal history and plea-bargaining in the USA, introduced to circumvent the difficulties of proving guilt under a system of procedure and evidence perceived to be unduly favourable to the defence: 'Torture and plea-bargaining' (1978) 46 *University of Chicago Law Review* 3.

[148] For England, major changes are contained in Part 11 of the Criminal Justice Act 2003.

[149] §§ 41, 61 *Bundeszentralregistergesetz* (BZRG); see also Meyer-Goßner, *Kommentar*, § 249 annotation 10.

[150] § 249 I 2 StPO. The *Strafprozessordnung* (StPO) is the German code of criminal procedure.

[151] *Bundeszentralregistergesetz* (Law concerning the Central Federal Record of Prior Convictions).

[152] Meyer-Goßner, *Kommentar*, § 261 annotation 14 with reference to §§ 51, 66 BZRG.

[153] Prior convictions for like offences suggest that prior punishments have been ineffective in discouraging the defendant from future reoffending. Courts often take this to indicate that a more severe punishment is necessary to bring about a behavioural change in this particular offender. In practice, this often means the difference between a fine and a custodial sentence. In Germany, the sentence imposed for petty theft will usually be a fine. But if it is the defendant's third or fourth conviction for a petty theft offence, the court may well impose a sentence of imprisonment (though usually as a suspended sentence).

actually is. Where (as is more common) the trial takes place before a court composed of professional judges,[154] the court is required to support its decision to convict or acquit by a reasoned judgment.[155] But although this will contain a brief account of the evidence, it will be limited to the evidence that bears directly on the facts, and is unlikely to include at this point any mention of the defendant's previous convictions; and since a French court does not explain the thought-processes which led it from the evidence to a finding of guilt,[156] the defendant's bad character will not surface as a matter that affected its assessment of the evidence either. But informal discussions with French lawyers suggest that, in practice, the court's assessment of the evidence is likely to be influenced by a criminal record, at least to some extent.

In Germany, the courts are free to consider any admissible[157] evidence of prior convictions and of the content of prior judgments also when deciding the question of guilt and will consider it to the extent that in their view it has any useful evidential value. The mere existence of a prior conviction is not thought to carry any weight with regard to the issue of guilt: it establishes nothing beyond the fact that another tribunal concluded that the defendant was guilty of another offence of a particular kind at another time. But where a previous conviction provides evidence of facts that may be relevant to the evaluation of the charge in present proceedings—for instance, that a particular person, or a particular area, is known to the defendant, or that he possesses certain skills, items, or knowledge—the trial court can base its findings on facts recorded in previous judgments, while it remains open to the defendant to challenge the correctness of the previous court's finding of fact.[158] German legal doctrine has no principled objection to such evidence being used when it comes to the determination of the defendant's guilt.[159] With a view to the risk of prejudice against the defendant, the only concern relates to evidence about prior investigations of other matters in which the defendant was a suspect, but which did not lead to him being charged or prosecuted. Such evidence is felt to be unusable.[160]

It may well be that the court's routine knowledge of the defendant's record, if he has one, is a factor that makes it easier for the French and German courts to

[154] See n. 167 and accompanying text below.
[155] *Code de procédure pénale*, Arts. 485 and 543.
[156] Gaston Stefani, Georges Levasseur, and Bernard Bouloc, *Procédure pénale* (17th edn., Paris 2000), §§ 150–1; the authors complain that this potentially makes reason-giving by the courts an empty formality.
[157] As explained in the previous paragraph, admissibility may be banned on grounds of the length of time that has passed since the prior judgment.
[158] BGH St 31, 323, 332, BGH St 43, 106; RG 60, 267, Düsseldorf StV 82, 512, Köln StV 90, 488, Zweibrücken StV 92, 565.        [159] Meyer-Goßner, *Kommentar*, § 249 annotation 9.
[160] This information has been gleaned from conversations with judges and prosecutors. In practice, it seems likely that in Germany, as in France, knowledge of the defendant's criminal record may in any case exercise an unspoken influence on the court in the assessment of the other evidence, at least occasionally. Hence the subversive joke that is popular among German lawyers: 'In this country the courts have three sets of reasons: the oral reasons, the written reasons, and *the real reasons*.'

manage without strict liability. As we have seen, some of the most striking cases of strict liability in English law are the offences of possessing firearms. The English courts have interpreted these as carrying strict liability in a series of appeals involving defendants who—improbably—claimed they did not know the object in their possession was a gun. In many of these cases, it seems likely that the defendant was in reality a professional criminal, although this was not something the tribunal of fact was allowed to know. When a defendant caught with a gas-pistol in the street later claims that he thought it was a hair-dryer, the court is unlikely to believe him if it knows that he has a criminal record for armed robbery.[161] And a legal system that knows a habitual robber who tells a tale like this will never be believed is unlikely to short-circuit the discussion by ruling that the offence carries strict liability.[162]

This leads to a third and related matter: those who are responsible for making and interpreting the law in France and Germany are almost certainly more inclined to trust the fact-finders than their counterparts in the world of the common law.

In a serious case in England (or elsewhere in the common law world) the tribunal of fact is, of course, a jury of twelve lay people, untrained and randomly selected—and this body reaches its decision on the facts in deliberation from which the judge is rigidly excluded. This traditional version of the jury is widely supposed to have a tendency to fall for a tall story. Whether this stereotype is valid is much disputed: but true or false, it is often believed to be true. Defence lawyers apparently believe it, because they routinely object to proposals to cut down the right to jury trial on the ground that juries are less likely than magistrates to convict. Many barristers and judges believe it: the after-dinner repertoire of any self-respecting criminal advocate or judge always includes hilarious anecdotes about credulous juries that, in the teeth of overwhelming prosecution evidence, acquitted defendants whose stories were utterly implausible. It seems very likely that a distrust of juries is an unspoken element that lies behind a range of judicial decisions that, over the years, have made inroads on the culpability principle: by trying to introduce an 'objective' notion of intention,[163] by substituting 'objective' for 'subjective' recklessness,[164] and, almost certainly, some of the more extraordinary decisions imposing strict liability.[165] It was only in the belief that 'One can trust the realism of trial judges, who direct juries, to guide juries to sensible verdicts and juries can in turn be relied on to apply robust common sense to the evaluation of ridiculous defences' that the House of Lords felt confident to substitute subjective for objective recklessness as the *mens rea* required for criminal damage in *R. v. G.*[166]

---

[161] Cf. *Pierre* [1963] Crim. LR 513 (and accompanying commentary).

[162] Part 11 of the Criminal Justice Act will make evidence of the defendant's criminal record admissible in a wider range of cases. It is conceivable that this change will eventually make the English courts less inclined to favour strict liability.                    [163] *DPP* v. *Smith* [1961] AC 290.

[164] *Caldwell* [1982] AC 242.

[165] e.g. *Warner* v. *Metropolitan Police Commissioner* [1969] 2 AC 256.

[166] [2003] 3 WLR 1060, 1087; [2003] UKHL 50, para. 58 (*per* Lord Steyn).

In France and Germany the tribunal of fact is very differently composed. Minor cases in Germany are tried by a single professional judge who sits alone, and graver cases by a court composed of one or more professional judges sitting with a panel of selected lay persons (*Schöffen*).[167] Unlike English jurors, *Schöffen* are not selected at random from the population at large but are preselected by the city council, and they serve as 'repeat players' for a fixed period of four years.[168] And unlike an English court sitting with a judge and jury, in a German court composed in part of *Schöffen* the lay members and the professional judges sit and deliberate together.[169]

In France, the tendency towards professional control of fact-finding is even more pronounced. In most criminal cases, the tribunal of fact is composed entirely of professional judges. The *tribunal de police*, which handles *contraventions*, consists of a single professional judge. The *tribunal correctionnel*, which handles *délits*, consists of a single professional judge, or a panel of three professional judges, depending on the gravity of the case. In the *Cour d'assises*, which tries *crimes*, the tribunal of fact is a panel of three professional judges, sitting with a 'jury' of nine randomly selected lay people. At one time, as in the common law world, the French jury deliberated separately, but since 1941 the judges and the jurors sit and deliberate together: a change that was introduced in response to distrust of unsupervised juries, and the immediate result of which was a drop in the acquittal rate from 25 to 8 per cent![170] A system that really trusts its fact-finders is naturally inclined to leave them all the relevant facts to find.

On a practical level, it is therefore easy to see why the need to prove fault at the trial puts much less of a strain on the operation of the institutions of criminal justice on the Continent than comparable requirements do in England. Hence the often-cited instrumental reasons in favour of strict and constructive liability in

---

[167] The composition and jurisdiction of the courts is regulated by the *Gerichtsverfassungsgesetz* (GVG). Less serious criminal cases come before the Magistrates' Courts ('Amtsgerichte'; § 24 GVG), and will be heard either by a single professional judge ('Strafrichter', § 25 GVG) or by a collegiate court composed of one professional judge as a presiding judge, and two *Schöffen* ('Schöffengericht'; § 29 GVG). The single judge can only hear cases involving *Vergehen* and impose sentences no higher than two years' imprisonment (see § 25 StGB). All other criminal matters within the jurisdiction of the Magistrates' Courts (including some serious offences (*Verbrechen*) which are punishable with no less than one year's imprisonment) will be brought before the *Schöffengericht*, which can impose a sentence of up to four years' imprisonment (§ 24 GVG, read in conjunction with § 28 GVG). Some serious crimes (such as murder and certain other serious offences against the person, particularly intentional crimes which led to the victim's death) will be heard by a chamber of the District Court ('Landgericht'; see §§ 74, 74a, 74b and 74c GVG). As a first-instance tribunal of fact, the District Court sits as 'Große Strafkammer' with three professional and two lay judges (§ 76 I GVG). In many instances, it can decide to sit with two professional judges and with two lay judges instead (§ 76 II GVG). In exceptional cases (mainly concerning crimes against the state, the peace and international law; see § 120 GVG), the tribunal of fact is a panel of the Court of Appeal ('Oberlandesgericht'). As a first-instance tribunal of fact, it will sit with either three or five professional judges (§ 122 GVG).

[168] See §§ 31–43 GVG.

[169] The votes of lay and professional judges carry equal weight (§§ 30 I, 77 I GVG). Any material decision concerning the defendant's guilt or sentence requires a two-thirds majority (§ 263 StPO).

[170] Merle and Vitu, *Traité de droit criminel, Procédure pénale*, § 523.

the criminal law—the increased speed and reduced cost of a trial in which fewer facts need to be established; the concern that, if *mens rea* needs to be proven beyond reasonable doubt, too many of the guilty may slip through the net—are unlikely to carry enough weight to generate the kind of legislative backlash against the culpability principle that the English Parliament has recently exhibited.[171] But procedural considerations do not provide, in and of themselves, an explanation of why the culpability principle was accepted by these systems. The impetus for the reform of the substantive law was philosophical and theoretical. It stemmed from the conviction that 'criminal liability without fault' (whatever that means) is unfair and oppressive. The driving force of legal reform was a principled, considered, and unreserved commitment to avoid liability without fault in the criminal law.

Since that force could spend itself relatively unobstructed by countervailing practical pressures and needs, it is particularly interesting to observe that, while it led to broadly similar changes and reforms of the criminal law in Germany and in France, it did not result in identical legal arrangements. The areas where differences between the French and the German position persist and where traces of strict and constructive liability prevail in either or both of these systems deserve our attention because they are instructive, from a UK perspective, not just of the presence and limitations of workable alternatives to strict or constructive liability in the criminal law, but also of different legitimate understandings of what the culpability principle requires. The final section of our analysis will highlight these differences and consider their implications for future theoretical reflection on the culpability principle.

## Contemporary Continental Legal Theory and the Limits of the Culpability Principle: Appreciating the Differences

The most obvious difference—though perhaps also the least interesting one—between the German and the French approach to strict liability in the criminal law is French law's acceptance of strict liability for *contraventions*, which contrasts starkly with the German law's insistence on proof of fault even for minor, non-stigmatic, regulatory offences. French writers accept that non-stigmatic offences, for which only relatively small fines will be imposed, can carry strict liability, for much the same pragmatic instrumental reasons that are used by Anglo-American writers to defend strict liability in this area of law. By contrast, German writers—while recognizing the potential practical advantages of such an arrangement, and the fact that an injustice is easier to bear, and has less socially harmful consequences, when it consists of having to pay a small amount of money, as opposed to serving years in prison—have not been able to bring themselves to say that the relatively low weight

---

[171]   In the Sexual Offences Act 2003, several offences carry strict liability as to the victim's age; moreover, the definition of rape requires a reasonable belief by the defendant that his sexual partner consents to the intercourse, which puts on a par intentional and negligent rape.

of the sanction, combined with the advantages of raising pocket money for the state through the accumulated income from small, but numerous and easily enforced fines, justifies making an exception from the principle that any punitive response to a citizen's conduct by the state requires proof of fault. In both systems, therefore, the starting point is the recognition that even in the area of non-stigmatic offences carrying petty fines as penalties, a moral case can be made for avoiding liability without fault. For academic commentators, the question is not about whether the culpability principle has relevance for this area of law, but whether non-stigmatic offences are special, or 'unimportant' enough to justify a pragmatic exception to the rule that punitive responses by the state require proof of fault. While the answers to this question, and consequently the legal rules concerning the fault requirement for minor regulatory offences in both systems, differ, the sources also highlight the underlying consensus that the culpability principle matters even in the area of non-stigmatic controlling responses by the state to undesirable behaviour.

Outside the field of non-stigmatic offences which carry minor penalties only, most of the existing offences of constructive liability in English law—and many of the remaining traces of it on the Continent—involve holding a defendant criminally liable for the unintended and unanticipated outcomes of his unlawful acts. This is an area of the criminal law where 'outcome liability' still survives with regard to crimes of violence under the French Criminal Code, and where it took German law the longest to settle on an unconditional fault requirement for the relation between the defendant's state of mind and the results of his acts. It is also an area where in other legal contexts—in particular, the law of torts—the legal system is willing to hold an agent responsible and civilly liable under much wider criteria of imputation ('adequate causation'); and virtually no challenge is being made to the fairness of this arrangement even in such systems as the German one which, throughout its criminal law, has opted for purely fault-based outcome liability.

In historical terms, one way of looking at the present situation is to view the English, French, and German criminal justice systems respectively as being at different stages of a process of development that moves towards an ever greater degree of realization of, and compliance with, the requirements of the culpability principle. From this perspective, German law seems to have come furthest in reshaping its laws to ensure that all criminal liability is based on fault, appearing to be the only one of the three legal systems to have fully appreciated the implications of the culpability principle for an agent's responsibility for serious consequences, whether in the context of convicting him for an aggravated version of an offence, or in passing sentence. In contrast, English law appears least advanced, closest to unsophisticated pre-Enlightenment notions of criminal responsibility.[172] Its courts

---

[172] Paradoxically, there was a strong move against strict liability in the English law of tort in the first part of the twentieth century—led by the legal theorist Sir John Salmond, who vigorously attacked it in the early editions of his classic textbook on torts. The campaign was successful and influenced the courts to turn their back on strict liability in tort in various ways. See J. R. Spencer, 'Motor-Cars and the Rule in *Rylands* v. *Fletcher*' [1983] *Cambridge LJ* 65, at 74.

have stuck with pre-modern concepts of *mens rea* as if caught in a time-warp of medieval thinking—which may be an unfortunate side-effect of the common law method, with its predilection for unsystematic reasoning and deference to the pronouncements of lawyers from ages past. As late as 1961, British judges drew on the age-old formula that takes a person to have intended 'the natural and probable consequences of his acts',[173] without any apparent realization that such reasoning is grounded in a theory of responsibility that few writers on criminal law have been willing to defend in modern times, even in Britain: the old canon-law doctrine of *actio illicita in causa*, which makes moral and logical sense only in a philosophical environment that, in principle, accepts pure outcome liability (i.e. having been the cause of harm, for whatever reasons—except *force majeure*—and with whatever state of mind) as a legitimate starting point for the attribution of responsibility. Where modern concepts of culpability have been endorsed—as, for instance, in the recent House of Lords judgments in *DPP* v. *B*,[174] *R.* v. *K*,[175] and *R.* v. *G*[176]—contradictions between the older and the newer strands of thinking about criminal responsibility have sometimes passed unnoticed.[177]

Seen through the lenses of 'historical progression', French law appears to occupy an intermediate position between the English and the German ends of the scale. This invites the question whether this position is stable, in the sense that it can be justified through a set of coherent and morally sound principles, or whether it merely constitutes a stop-gap on the long road to a fuller recognition of the implications of the culpability principle, in which the uneasy tensions and internal contradictions of a half-way point are manifest. Certainly, in historical terms, the present-day French position was one that was much discussed, and supported by some writers,[178] in Germany at the turn of the twentieth century, where it was subsequently rejected as incompatible with the culpability principle.[179]

However, while it is tempting to analyse the present state of the law in these terms, they are unlikely to do justice to the merits and flaws of each of the respective legal arrangements. Another way of looking at the different positions concerning an agent's criminal responsibility for the unintended and unanticipated outcomes of his unlawful acts is to see them as resting on legitimate disagreements about what exactly the requirements of the culpability principle are; about *when* it is just and fair to punish someone for the harm he caused, and would not have caused had he stayed within the law. Even today, writers such as Horder argue that: 'By

---

[173] *DPP* v. *Smith* [1961] AC 290. In this area, recent judgments have given the law a more subjectivist turn; the present position is exemplified in *Woollin* [1999] 1 AC 82.
[174] *B (a minor)* v. *DPP* [2000] 2 AC 428.    [175] [2002] 1 AC 462.
[176] [2003] 3 WLR 1060.
[177] Symptomatic for this kind of 'unhistorical historicism' is Lord Hailsham's speech in *Hyam* [1975] AC 55, which—notwithstanding the morally sound outcome—draws concurrently on cases whose underlying assumptions about the basis of criminal responsibility conflict. See also Jeremy Horder, 'Two Histories and Four Hidden Principles of Mens Rea' (1997) 113 *Law Quarterly Review* 95.
[178] Karl Klee, *Der dolus indirectus als Grundform der vorsätzlichen Schuld* (Berlin 1906).
[179] See von Bar, *Schuld*, 280 ff. and 470–1.

doing something intended to harm V, D changes her own normative position, making the bad luck of V's serious injury her (D's) own. . . . [T]he fact that I *deliberately* wrong V . . . changes my relationship with the risk of adverse consequences stemming therefrom, for which I may now be blamed and held criminally responsible, irrespective of their reasonable foreseeability'.[180]

Likewise, there are academics who argue that 'punishment-enhancing' strict liability elements, as opposed to those that have a bearing on the type of offence committed, do not raise any conceptual issue of relevance to the substantive criminal law.[181] While this view is open to challenge, one cannot simply dismiss it out of hand as primitive or obviously mistaken. When it comes to liability for outcomes of unlawful acts, a moral case can be made for each one of the different solutions represented by the legal systems under review—as other essays in this collection clearly show. If the position they have reached appears to be unstable, this could be because convincing moral arguments can be presented for the alternatives, rather than because the position is morally flawed.

From this vantage point, the tenacity with which UK law clings to criminal liability for the unintended and unanticipated outcomes of unlawful actions appears not so much a historical accident as a reflection of the moral attractiveness of this model of liability, even in the criminal law. After all, there can be little doubt that it does come naturally to us to blame the disobedient boy who climbs upon a chair to reach the top shelf where his mother placed the tin of biscuits out of reach, not just for the taking of the tin but also for overturning the chair on which he stands in the process, pulling off the curtain in a desperate effort to stabilize his fall, and, for good measure, for breaking his own leg as a result! 'It serves him right', 'he had it coming to him', would be many a person's instinctive reaction. And if, instead of breaking his own leg, he broke a valuable Ming vase which was standing on the floor, we would be more inclined to view it as a serious incident of disobedience, rather than a minor prank. And it is at least open to doubt whether our blaming reaction is because the overturning of the chair was at least a generally foreseeable consequence of (mis-)using it as a ladder (indicating recklessness or at least negligence as to the resulting damage); or because the risk of falling off it was intrinsic to climbing on it and part of the reason why one should not climb on chairs to reach items that otherwise would be out of one's reach in the first place; or simply because he did climb it, knowing full well that he should not, and did fall off, causing unanticipated damage. The German position might then be taken to reflect only one possible solution among others, putting the focus firmly on conscious agency, making a choice against the law, and being quite tolerant of the small ways in which we all take risks the magnitude of which we do not appreciate, and consequently end up harming others. And the legal arrangements in French

[180] Horder, 'A Critique of the Correspondence Principle', 764.
[181] Larry Alexander, 'Reconsidering the Relationship among Voluntary Acts, Strict Liability, and Negligence in Criminal Law', in Ellen Frankel Paul, Fred D. Miller, and Jeffrey Paul (eds.), *Crime, Culpability, and Remedy* (Cambridge, Mass. 1990), 87.

criminal law seem defensible precisely because of their similarity to liability in tort law: that some are 'morally lucky' does not constitute a reason for letting the morally unlucky go scot-free, provided that a sufficient degree of culpability, and general predictability of a harmful outcome, pertains to the initial wrongful act.

With an eye to the possible usefulness of the comparative analysis, it is interesting to observe that much of the debate about 'objective conditions of liability' in German law mirrors the discussion of strict liability in the Anglo-American tradition. In particular, German lawyers explored the possibility that 'objective conditions of liability' were somehow 'external' to the wrong constituted by the offence, and discovered that once this line of thought was taken seriously, many of the existing conditions of liability were unjustifiable in principle and would have to be reinterpreted as *mens rea*-sensitive elements of the *actus reus*.[182] The similarity with Duff's analysis and justification of some instances of constructive liability in UK law is striking. German writers on criminal law also must be credited with being the first to see clearly that the culpability principle requires more than merely a commitment to having some *mens rea* element as part of every criminal offence; that it has repercussions for statutory interpretation, sentencing decisions and—most recently—for issues of criminalization (i.e. for the problem of what Duff has called morally strict liability).

This last point deserves our particular attention. The connection between the culpability principle and the discussion of the limits of criminalization has received much attention by German academic commentators in recent years. Increasingly, the problem of 'morally strict liability' is recognized by German academic writers as a problem of constitutional law. Criminalization and punishment of conduct which, when viewed in isolation, does not amount to a moral wrong in and of itself, not only restrains the prospective offender's freedom of action; it also offends against the prospective offender's right to have his personal integrity and character respected by the state (*allgemeines Persönlichkeitsrecht*),[183] since each criminal conviction stamps the convicted person officially as someone who has engaged in wrongful, antisocial behaviour, for which he deserves both moral and legal censure.[184]

It is in this context, then, that problems like the 'objective conditions of criminal liability' and the criminalization of innocuous conduct which might lead

---

[182] See text and references at nn. 26–8 and n. 66 above.

[183] The *allgemeines Persönlichkeitsrecht* is a fundamental right that is recognized by the German Constitutional Court through a combined reading of the commitment to human dignity (Art. 1 *Grundgesetz*) and the fundamental right that specifically protects freedom of action in general terms (the *Allgemeine Handlungsfreiheit* protected by Art. 2 para. 1 of the German Constitution, see BVerfGE 52, 131). It has various aspects to it; one is the protection of personal autonomy, another the respect for one's personal integrity, the third respect for privacy, especially in intimate contexts.

[184] On the impact of a criminal conviction on the *allgemeines Persönlichkeitsrecht* see Judge Graßhof's speech in BVerfGE 90, 145 at 200 (the so-called 'cannabis-decision' of the German Constitutional Court).

to harm (*Vorfeldkriminalisierung* or *Vorverlagerung der Strafbarkeit*)[185] are discussed.[186] There is a clear awareness in these debates that strict liability (and its weaker evidential cousins, the factual inference and the reverse burden of proof) are merely 'the tip of the iceberg' Many statutory offences which, in formal terms, comply fully with the correspondence principle by stipulating matching *mens rea* elements for every element of the *actus reus*, can give rise to the same concerns regarding the appropriateness of the criminal sanction as offences that openly make use of strict or constructive liability as a legislative tool. This is not just true for strategies that shift the point in issue into sentencing law or get courts to deal with it on an evidential rather than a conceptual basis. It is particularly true for the newly found panacea of creating 'fall-back offences' of morally unobjectionable conduct to be used against those against whom more serious substantive offences cannot be proved.[187] All these examples show that a useful analysis of the problems of strict and constructive liability must rest on a broader theory about the proper limits of the criminal sanction.

In this regard, it is worth noting that the recent shift in focus to constitutional law, and away from philosophical accounts of the basis of human responsibility, has not only led to a widening of the range of issues that are caught by the culpability principle, but also served to destabilize the existing consensus on points that were taken as settled. Thus, Lagodny openly suggests that if the culpability principle is grounded mainly in the constitutional commitment to the proportionality principle, it is open for discussion whether one might do away with § 17 StGB (which exempts from liability those who were labouring under an unavoidable error of law) and § 20 StGB (which exempts from liability those who were suffering from an extreme mental disturbance that made them unable to appreciate the wrongness of their actions, or to act in accordance with this realization) for certain particularly dangerous offences.[188] There is, apparently, not just 'one right answer'

---

[185] Neither term translates well. They refer to the creation of offences that criminalize conduct that typically, but not necessarily, precedes harmful conduct, and may be engaged in for perfectly innocent reasons. Examples are provided by the offences that criminalize conduct that may, or may not, be preparatory as to the commission of a real wrong (possession of a knife in a public place), and offences that penalize conduct that may, but need not, lead to the creation of any actual risk (driving a vehicle whose roadworthiness licence has expired).

[186] See, in particular, the fundamental work by Otto Lagodny, *Strafrecht vor den Schranken der Grundrechte. Die Ermächtigung zum strafechtlichen Vorwurf im Lichte der Grundrechtsdogmatik; dargestellt am Beispiel der Vorfeldkriminalisiering* (Tübingen 1996), 226 ff. and 233 ff.

[187] Such offences are often offences of possession of certain (not necessarily dangerous) items, and offences of physical presence on or near certain premises. They can also concern membership in organizations committed to the pursuit of certain dangerous objectives, which can amount to an offence even before the organization as such has engaged in any dangerous or harmful activities.

[188] Lagodny, *Strafrecht vor den Schranken der Grundrechte*, 370. The argument seems to be that once the culpability principle is grounded in the idea that punishing a person against whom fault has not been established is 'disproportionate', there may well be cases where our interest in crime control outweighs our interest in avoiding punishing the (morally) blameless, who violated the law while mistaken about its contents, or while they lacked capacity. Lagodny himself ultimately rejects this

to the question of what the culpability principle requires, but a range of answers—which seem more or less well-founded depending on the philosophical perspective from which the problem is approached.

## 3. Conclusion

The review of the position in two major Continental legal systems shows that there are many fewer instances of 'strict' or 'constructive' criminal liability to be found on the Continent than in England. Both French and German criminal law reject strict liability in principle, and insist on proof of fault for anything considered more serious than a mere regulatory offence. French law contains some residues of strict liability, mainly in its law of offences against the person, and allows it in principle with regard to mere *contraventions* (non-stigmatic offences punishable by relatively minor fines). German law has (small) pockets of it with regard to the 'objective conditions of criminal liability', and none of these are arguably morally strict (though there may be instances of moral strict liability without formal strict liability in German criminal law, for instance in the law of treason).[189]

The review of the Continental position demonstrates that there are two main strategies by which Continental systems deal with the problems posed by situations in which English criminal law imposes strict or constructive liability.

The first of these strategies is to treat the issue or element in regard to which liability in English law is strict as one that affects the question of sentence only. Thus, in France, the *Code pénal* sets out differing punishment scales for many offences, depending on which consequences resulted from them, and does not require proof of fault in relation to the consequence in order for the aggravated sentencing scale to be applied. German law in principle requires proof of fault for any serious consequence to affect either conviction or sentence, but at the same time arrives at higher penalties where a serious consequence, in regard to which the defendant was at least reckless, follows upon a crime of violence; these penalties are greater than would follow from convicting the defendant merely of the conduct-based intentional and a separate, result-oriented recklessness-based offence.

The second strategy is to treat the matter as a question of evidence. French law openly operates with a presumption of fault in certain instances: notwithstanding the presumption of innocence and the formal prohibition against making negative inferences from a defendant's choice to remain silent. German courts freely

possibility, arguing that other constitutional principles—in particular, the commitment to respect for human dignity and for treating people as rational agents—make the need to establish fault a non-negotiable border of every utilitarian balancing operation (at 415).

[189] Liability here appears to be morally strict because even where wrongful conduct of the state is exposed, the defendant is criminally liable.

draw the appropriate conclusions from 'facts which speak for themselves' in the absence of any alternative explanation. In this, the German courts are helped by a substantive definition of intention that includes *dolus eventualis*, and by a concept of recklessness which, albeit being subjectively oriented in its standard of what can reasonably be expected of a person with the individual capacities, knowledge, and experience of the defendant, includes the inadvertent as well as the advertent variety.

Despite—or perhaps because of its unswerving theoretical and practical commitment to the culpability principle, German law increasingly responds to the temptation to pave the road to conviction, not by doing away with a fault requirement, but by criminalizing conduct that is not in itself harmful, but that often leads to harm. In this way, it attempts to circumvent the burdens of proving fault in relation to the causation of a harmful outcome, while on the face of it maintaining dogmatic purity.

Thus, the comparison also underscores that the real issue underlying the debate about the implications of the culpability principle is the proper limits of the criminal sanction. Without any grounding in these substantive considerations, legislative techniques can easily undercut problems of strict liability by passing legislation that, in formal terms, complies fully with the culpability principle, but which in substance gives rise to the same concerns: whether it is morally fair, all things considered, to label the actor who violates these prohibitions as a criminal and to sanction his conduct with some form of punishment.

It is perhaps apt to give the final word to Karl Binding, who summarized the problems of what he called 'anomalies of establishing fault' in the closing sections of the first volume of *Die Normen und ihre Übertretung* in 1872. Having observed that the two main interests the state pursues with its system of criminal justice— the ideally exception-free application of the law to each and every case where a criminal offence is in fact committed, and the insistence that punishment must be just and imposed only after proof of fault—are difficult to reconcile, with the latter demanding that the state desist from punishment where an offence, which may well have been committed, cannot be proved, while the former 'pushes the state towards making the impossible proof possible, so that the law of evidence does not turn into the criminal's asylum',[190] he concluded his treatise with the following observations:

If we look at all the anomalies of establishing fault in today's federal law, they do not make a pretty picture. They owe their existence to a multitude of different reasons . . . [191] And only in one respect are all these instances alike: they are symptoms of a growing readiness of the state to impose a criminal sanction as often and as speedily as possible, even at the risk of hitting the innocent. But the rise in criminal convictions comes at a high price: Because

---

[190] Binding, *Normen*, 605.
[191] Among which Binding mentions the difficulty of identifying the person who wrote a defamatory published statement, the legitimate interest of the state to get the tax revenue due to it, but also its 'ugly appetite for the fines' of those who failed to comply with their legal duties, for instance to file a tax return, and the speed and cost of the trial.

the seeds of indifference towards drawing a distinction between guilt and innocence—even if sown only on a small patch—can only grow bad fruit. Respect for the authority of the law is endangered where such respect does not even protect one against punishment; the belief in the justice of the law is lost, when even those who were not at fault are being punished. . . . [I]n a civil case . . . the judge may have to be satisfied with a formal truth;[192] but the criminal conviction, as serious a matter for the state as for the defendant, requires a more reliable foundation.[193]

[192] A formal truth, for Binding, is a fact that a judge treats as true because it is not disputed, or not open to challenge (irrebuttable presumption), without investigating whether it is 'really true'. Binding's final remarks are aimed at the situations where the burden of proof is shifted to the defendant, and at cases where the state issues a 'suspended' criminal conviction (*Strafbefehl*) based on the prosecution's case, against which the defendant has to file objections to avoid being 'convicted'.

[193] 'Überblicken wir jetzt nochmals sämtliche Anomalien des Schuldbeweises im heutigen Reichsrecht, so bieten sie kein erfreuliches Bild. Den verschiedenartigsten Anlässen danken sie ihren Ursprung, und durchaus nicht jeder Grund rechtfertigt die Folge! . . . [N]ur in Einem gleichen sich die verschiedenen Erscheinungen: sie sind alle Symptome eine hoch gesteigerten Neigung des Staates, möglichst oft und möglichst schnell mit der Strafe bei der Hand zu sein, auf die Gefahr hin, auch den Unschuldigen zu treffen. Für seinen Mehrertrag an Strafurteilen zahlt aber der Staat einen teuren Preis. Denn die Saat der Gleichgültigkeit gegen die Scheidung von Schuld und Unschuld—wenn auch lediglich auf kleinem Felde gestreut—kann nur schlimme Früchte treiben. Die Achtung vor der Autorität des Gesetzes wird gefährdet, wenn sie nicht einmal mehr vor Strafe schützt; der Glaube an des Gesetzes Gerechtigkeit geht verloren, wo auch der Schuldlose von Rechts wegen Strafe zu leiden hat. . . . [I]m Zivilprozess . . . muss sich der Richter mit formeller Wahrheit begnügen; aber das Strafurteil, gleich belastend für den Staat wie für den Verurteilten, bedarf durchweg einer festeren Basis.'

# Index